Gradspot.com's

Guide to Life After College

D1054674

Written and Edited by
David Klein and Chris Schonberger
with Stuart Schultz and Tory Hoen

We would like to extend a very special thanks to our amazing team of writers, whose research and writing were invaluable in the process of making this book:

Julie Fishman, David Pekema, Rachel Solomon, Arielle Sachar, Karen Keller, Aryeh Cohen-Wade, Theodore Bressman, Christine Margiotta, Rebecca Shore, Jennifer Pollock, Mandy Erickson, Jenny Williams, Lauren Levinson, Josie Swindler, Julia Bonnheim, Erin Hartigan, Erin Kandel, Orli Van Mourik, Jennifer Cunningham, Jake Tuck, Sean McManus, Stephanie Berger, Molly Martin, Richard Koss, Christopher Stella, Nick Schonberger, Courtney McClellan and Tom Wiseman.

We would also like to thank the following people for their contributions and support:

Antony Clavel, Matthew Demmer, Randi Hazan, Rachel Kinrot, Chris Nakamura, Lisa Harrow, Renee Bissell, Millicent Brown, Matty Marcus, Naledge, Dr. Valerie Young, Neilesh Mutyala, Steve Rosengard, Charlie French, Alexander Arapoglou, Nate Houghteling, Kyle Berkman, Greg Konover, Seth Robinson, Ben Herzberger, Chris Catizone, Davina Pike, David Lerman, Laura Swift, Arielle Goren, Andrew Smeall, Jamie Spitzer, Charlie French, Lisa Shichijo, Elise Minter, Jay Boggis, Anna Harris, Jesse Nichols, Spencer Gellman and everyone who gave us feedback or commented on our website.

And last but not least, we'd like to thank our publisher, MG Prep Inc., and the MG Prep Inc. team (Andrew Yang, Danielle Rothman, Beretzi Garcia, Liz Krisher, Cathy Huang and Dan McNaney) for standing behind us.

ISBN-10: 1-935707-23-X

ISBN-13/EAN-13: 9-781-935707-23-3

eISBN: 9-781-935707-74-5

To order additional copies of this book, please visit: www.gradspot.com/book

Published by MG Prep Inc.

Interior design by Dan McNaney and Cathy Huang

Cover design by Karen Messing

Acknowledgements

David thanks

From pigs ears to beer to tennis to the Grateful Dead, thanks for everything Mom and Dad.

Chris thanks

Grandma and Grandad Griggs—for cups of tea, pints of bitter, and lots of love.

Tory thanks

Mum and Dad—for your support of both my education and the existential crises that ensued.

Stuart thanks

The Gradspot community for your support and letting us know what actually needs to be in this book.

Table of Contents

Start Here

Why We Wrote This Book

A few months after launching our website, Gradspot.com, we received an email from one of our users who was looking for help improving her living situation. After we pointed her to content on our site and answered some questions, she said something we haven't forgotten since: "If only you had been around when I graduated last summer, I probably wouldn't have ended up in Newark!" Now, no offense to Newark, but we fully understand her sentiment. After all, it was just a short time ago that we were leaving school and feeling completely unprepared to deal with issues like 401(k)s, sheisty landlords, and office politics.

Time and again, our peers echoed our concerns about being sent out to sea without a life vest, as have the graduating classes that followed after them. Some didn't have any clue what to expect, while those who were actually proactive enough to seek out resources found that they were either out-of-date or out-of-touch. Thus, we figured there was no better time to create a resource that could fill that void—first Gradspot.com and now this book. Ultimately, **our goal in these pages is to expose you to the issues that are most likely to arise in your first year out of school and to share the methods we and others have used to successfully navigate them.**

Consider this book a road map of sorts that will help you navigate the intimidating terrain of the "real world." You're a college grad now (really let that soak in!) and for the first time in your life, completely independent. But no worries, we're here to guide you in the right direction. You've got a lot of questions, we've got a lot of answers. Looking for a job? We'll send you down the right path. Don't know how to do your taxes? We've got you covered. Not sure where to live? We'll help get you to your ideal destination. How to buy a car? Check. Dating tips? Check. Explaining the ending to *Lost*? Sorry, we can only do so much.

On top of all of the insights we picked up from our own experiences and included in this book, we've also called upon other recent grads and college students to share their experiences. They've provided us with a wealth of "insider" tips, many of which you can only find in this book. We also reached out to a wide range of topic experts for their input; and trolled every other pertinent resource out there. We even set up a "Life After College Lab" to test out high-pressure showerheads, budgeting tools, and anything else that might make the transition a little bit easier.

Being twentysomethings ourselves, we understand what it's like to be a graduate today rather than in 1965. Times have changed, and we wrote this book to reflect the experience of a recent grad *now*. We hope that you will it indispensable and that it will ease the exciting, yet intimidating transition to life after college.

How to Use This Book

Gradspot.com's Guide to Life After College has many uses. You can prop up a wobbly chair with it, burn it for warmth when your parents kick you out the house, or "donate" it to your alma mater instead of making an actual monetary contribution.

Before you do all those things, however, we hope that you'll read it. While there is no set chronology to life after college, we've laid out the chapters in a way that approximates the general order in which you're likely to encounter different issues, from moving back home to coping with the pressures of a "one-year rut." To help you browse the book, we've created a very thorough table of contents and an easy-to-use cross-referencing system that will allow you to navigate among topics quickly. Ultimately, we hope each chapter will provide a solid foundation for overcoming a range of obstacles along the post-college road.

We've also compiled a list of links to all of the resources we mention in the book that you can find at gradspot.com/book. Many of the URLs listed in this book are obvious, but in instances where links were too long to include in the text, we've made note of it so it's clear that the actual link is available on our online resource guide.

While we can help you understand the basics, share tips and tricks about how to take the next step, and give you the tools to make informed choices, many of the decisions that need to be made are based on your unique situation and may require extra research. So even with all the acumen you'll pick up in these pages, we encourage you to be careful when dealing with major issues. Whether you're filing a tax return, choosing a dental plan, consolidating student debt, or doing anything else that we discuss in this book, always consult a professional for help if you have doubts. Remember, many of your choices now will affect you for years to come.

Visit Us at Gradspot.com!

Needless to say, no matter how long we make this book, there will always be more to discuss. If anything else comes up that you can't find in these pages, never hesitate to visit us at the online destination for life after college: Gradspot. com. There, we have additional guides, a Q&A section where anyone can post a question about life after college to experts and community members, and a community blog where users can share their own unique life-after-college experiences.

Enjoy the read, and good luck!

Start Here

Chapter I: Holy $*%#, I Just Graduated!

Holy $*%#, I Just Graduated

The last couple months of school are jam-packed with finals, parties, farewells, and finally…graduation. With so many things going on, this period can fly by in a disorienting haze of sadness and joy. But when you grab your diploma, drink your champagne, and walk out of the gates, be prepared for the heavy hand of reality to slap you right in your grinning face and for one question to arise: What now?

Up to this point, everything has been decided for you and served up on a platter—or at least force-fed. You went to high school. You did your homework (sometimes). You went to college, chose a major, and, if you were lucky, that basically accounted for all the big decisions you had to deal with for four years. But now, maybe for the first time ever, it feels like the "next step" is not completely obvious. And worst of all, you feel like you need to decide what you want to do for the rest of your life this second!

This is a pervasive fear that the vast majority of recent graduates faces. It is completely normal, but also completely irrational because now is the first time in your life when you actually have the freedom to set your own timeframes—so what's the rush?

If you feel compelled to dive head first into the "big ticket" issues, by all means skip ahead (we've more than got you covered). But a word of warning: once you start obsessing over jobs, living situations, finances, and all of the other high-stress areas of life after college, things are going to get very heavy, very quickly. That's precisely why we're starting this book out with a chapter to help you find balance: all that heavy yin needs a lighter yang. We'll cover everything from taking a year off to go traveling to food and romance, DIY education, and even grappling with the all-too-common first year rut.

This is the time when you can start anew and set the tone for your life as a college grad, so don't take that for granted. And whenever things get you down, just think about these two words: no homework!

10 Things to Do After Graduating

1) **Join a kickball league.** Already miss the college spirit? Rekindle the camaraderie from your varsity/intramural glory days while laughing at the guy in skinny jeans waddling to first.

2) **Apply to a reality TV show.** What do you have to lose (except dignity and the support of your family)?

3) **Become a bar trivia pro.** Utilize that vast wealth of knowledge you just accumulated by winning free drinks and the respect of thirtysomethings desperately trying to stay young.

4) **Travel.** The post-graduation trip is a classic move for those who can afford it, and even grads on a tight budget have plenty of options close to home. Read more on page 6.

5) **Learn to cook.** Once you're living alone sans a meal plan, the ability to whip up a fricassee will save big bucks and impress potential mates like the plumage of a peacock (or a she-cock). Read more on page 24.

6) **Spend time with your family.** Take advantage of the time you can spend with your loved ones now, because tomorrow you may be busy. Or they may be dead.

7) **Be a kid again.** Go home and rekindle all those old feelings you had as a child. Dust off your old Nintendo console. Hit a tennis ball against a wall and pretend it's Monica Seles. Whatever it takes to get that spring back in your step.

8) **Get in shape.** We're not suggesting you become the girl who's hitting the elliptical so hard that her legs are about to fly off, nor that tangerine-colored dude who exclusively does upper body and can barely run a mile. But at the very least, get rid of the lingering traces of your "freshman 15" (funny how it never quite went away) and motivate yourself to take the next step.

9) **Volunteer.** Before you become too "busy" making money for yourself, demonstrate a little of the philanthropic spirit for which you may or may not be famous. Find something that appeals to you personally and get involved.

10) **Write a book.** Or if novels aren't your thing, pursue anything that you're passionate about. Record songs, paint pictures, or write the screenplay you've been talking about for three years. Now is the time.

 Get a tattoo: My brother claims this is an awesome idea. ∎

✈ The Traveling Grad

Traveling after graduation is a time-honored tradition for many reasons, the most prominent of which is the fact that it's literally the perfect time to travel. Practically speaking, the chances of taking a two-month backpacking trip grow slimmer by the day once you're a working cog. We don't want to suggest that the clock is ticking on fun and exploration, but if you can pull it off, all of the pieces are in place for a great trip—youth, health, and a celebratory subtext. So why not get cracking on that "places to visit before I die" list?

Brainstorming Trips

The main factors that go into planning the perfect summer trip are budget, duration, and companionship. But once those are settled, the fun part can begin—what do you really want to do? There are countless places to get your post-college groove on and we have a few ideas to get you started. Needless to say, you're going to have to do some further research to figure out the ins-and-outs of traveling to these places, and you can even string together some of these destinations into a full-summer/year adventure, but we hope this section will at least help spark a wanderlust.

Note: Before you set out for a foreign country, get your passport straight (see above), and be sure to check if you need a visa or any vaccinations.

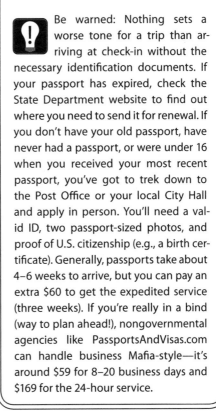

Tips & Tricks:
Passports

Be warned: Nothing sets a worse tone for a trip than arriving at check-in without the necessary identification documents. If your passport has expired, check the State Department website to find out where you need to send it for renewal. If you don't have your old passport, have never had a passport, or were under 16 when you received your most recent passport, you've got to trek down to the Post Office or your local City Hall and apply in person. You'll need a valid ID, two passport-sized photos, and proof of U.S. citizenship (e.g., a birth certificate). Generally, passports take about 4–6 weeks to arrive, but you can pay an extra $60 to get the expedited service (three weeks). If you're really in a bind (way to plan ahead!), nongovernmental agencies like PassportsAndVisas.com can handle business Mafia-style—it's around $59 for 8–20 business days and $169 for the 24-hour service.

20 Hot Post Grad Trips

So you've made the decision to head west (or east), young man (or woman). But where exactly? Zach Aarons of TravelGoat.com (a website devoted to audio tours spanning the world) offers his super-sized list of potential journeys across the globe via planes, trains and automobiles.

1) **Trans Siberian Railway:** The train is an epic journey from Beijing to Moscow. This trip passes through Mongolia, China, and myriad parts of Russia. It takes almost a month and is a perfect opportunity to meet people and unwind before starting a career.

2) **Thailand:** Spend a couple of days peeking at lady boys in Bangkok before traveling to Phuket, a gorgeous oasis of beaches and fun. Make sure to check out the enchanted isle of Koh Phi Phi, where the famous movie, *The Beach*, was filmed.

3) **New Orleans:** New Orleans is a city that has the exotic aura of foreign travel, with the expense of a quick domestic jaunt. Check out some of the best architecture in the world, eat some Po' Boys and listen to some great Dixieland jazz music.

4) **Cross Country Road Trip:** The classic post college experience. Shoot straight across the country from east to west or west to east, stopping at various cities and national parks on the way. Locations can include: Cleveland, Pittsburgh, Omaha, Chicago, Yellowstone, Yosemite, San Francisco, and others.

5) **Inca Trail:** One of the most spiritual trips in the world. Spend some time hiking through the Andes before arriving at the climax, the hidden city of Incas, Machu Picchu.

6) **California Coast:** Start in San Francisco and head down the Pacific Coast Highway, finishing up for some good drinking in Tijuana. Make sure to stop along the way at Big Sur, Santa Barbara, LA, and San Diego.

7) **Adriatic Coast:** Fly to the fantastic Medieval walled city of Dubrovnik. Spend some time island hopping to Hvar and Korcula before heading off to some of the unspoiled beaches of Montenegro.

8) **Cyclades:** The classic post graduation hedonistic retreat, island hopping in the Cyclades is glorious. Make sure to check out both Mykonos and Santorini. For a less touristy vibe, try Sifnos and Milos.

9) **White Water Rafting on the Snake River:** The Snake River in Jackson Hole, Wyoming has some of the best rapids in the world for all skill levels. It is both fun, exciting, and a great work out.

10) Nicaragua: Nicaragua is fast becoming the next Costa Rica with beautiful beaches, incredible jungles, and inexpensive prices. Make sure to check out both Managua and Morgan's Rock for an urban and oceanside experience.

11) Patagonia: The tip of the world has been luring adventurous folks for centuries. Go hiking in Torres Del Paine national park, visit the penguin colony at Seno Otway, and spend some time in Ushuaia, the southernmost city in the world.

12) Cinque Terre: These five small towns in the Liguria region of Italy are picturesque and quaint. Many tourists every year take one of the two hiking trails connecting each village. The hike can be accomplished in a day, but it is best to linger and eat some pesto pasta along the way.

13) Vietnam: Vietnam is fast becoming the destination of choice in South East Asia based on great weather, beautiful beaches, and great food. Take a motorcycle ride through Hanoi, then wade through rice paddies in Sapa. Finish on the beaches of Hoi An and get a fine tailored suit for a low price in the village.

14) South Africa: South Africa is a country on the rise, thanks to its natural beauty and great food in Cape Town, its fantastic wines in Stellenbosch, and its safaris in Kruger National Park.

15) Israel: Israel is both an educational and exciting journey. Experience the nightlife of Tel Aviv, the spirituality of Jerusalem, and the vast expanse of the Negev Desert, all a quick car ride away from each other.

16) Whistler: No matter what the season, Whistler has skiing year round. Ski both Whistler and Blackcomb mountains while stopping for some ethnic food in Vancouver.

17) Istanbul and the Turkish Coast: Once the capital of the world, Istanbul has some of the most incredible markets, mosques, and sights in the world. Follow it up with some relaxation in Bodrum on the beach, and some Greek ruins at Ephesus.

18) Goa: Even the name of this famous Indian beach town evokes a yearning for something more.

19) Buenos aires and punta del este: The city of Borges, Eva Peron, and Diego Maradona is a cultural wonderland with some of the best food in the world. After poking around the city, spend some time on the beach in Punta Del Este, Uruguay.

20) Cartagena: This Colombian colonial beach town that Garcia Marquez used as the backdrop for *Love in the Time of Cholera* has undergone a renaissance and has become a popular seaside destination. ■

Holy $*%#, I Just Graduated!

How to Travel Abroad For Free

There are plenty of ways—some common, some a little strange—to support a globetrotting lifestyle or live in a different country for an extended period of time.

When approaching the job hunt, grads with a deep-seated wanderlust should consider careers that will allow for travel—options include entering the hospitality industry, being a travel-heavy salesperson (e.g., pharmaceuticals), working for an airline (even if you aren't in the air, you usually get ace flight discounts), joining the armed forces, and many more. However, there are also some slightly more spontaneous and grad-friendly opportunities that can be leveraged for a plane ticket, room and board, and Facebook albums that will be the envy of all your friends. From NGO volunteering to life as a hostel-hopping bartender, here are some ideas to set your travel fantasies in motion.

TEACH ENGLISH. You've probably heard stories of people who teach English in Korea for $3,000 a month and free housing. These gigs really do exist, and while not all English teaching positions are so lucrative (you may live on scraps—but at least you're in Venezuela!), they all offer a great opportunity to travel. Before you can teach English abroad, you've got to get certified. There are a number of certifications—most notably, Teaching English as a Foreign Language (TEFL), Teaching English as a Second Language (TESL), Teacher of English to Speakers of Other Languages (TOSEL), and Certificate in Language Teaching to Adults (CELTA). Courses will cost around $1,000 and usually take about a month to complete (many people travel to attend a course, though you can almost always find one close to home). Some schools will offer intensive one-weekend certifications, and there are also online courses you can take remotely. But while these quick-fire and at-home options might be okay for someone who just wants to dip his or her feet into the teach-abroad waters for six months or so, people who would like to seriously consider teaching as a career should invest in a full classroom-based course—you will come out feeling a lot more confident, and you'll get to bond with other future teachers who will become your best contacts for finding gigs around the world. In addition to word-of-mouth, there are a number of good websites for finding openings, including ESLCafe.com, TEFL.com, and ESLJobs.com. Remember that each school is different, and that you'll need to make strategic decisions about which match your needs, based on location, teaching format, and pay scale.

JOIN THE PEACE CORPS. Operating in countries as far-flung as Azerbaijan and Malawi, the Peace Corps is one of the most popular options for rough-and-ready grads to really see a developing country up close and personal. (You have to commit 27 months, so this one is not for the faint of heart.) In addition to having a positive impact on a community, the Peace Corps will help you accrue some benefits that will take you to the next step, like student debt forgiveness (p. 237), credit/financial aid at many grad schools (Chapter 9), and access to government jobs (p. 62).

BECOME AN AU PAIR. Childcare is apparently something that many families the world over feel comfortable farming out to a foreigner. Visit GreatAuPair.com to find gigs, and turn to page 80 for more information on becoming a babysitter/nanny.

> **Smart Money:**
> **Hostelling**
>
> **$** Let's call a spade a spade. When it comes to post-grad travel, you're probably not going to be staying in five-star resorts. You're more likely going to find the cheapest hostel around and shack up for the night. But hey, that's great. They're twentysomething meccas and can cost as little as $2 per night…including breakfast and dinner! Hostelling International is known for some of the best hostels around, and you can also search for traveler-friendly accommodations on Hostels.com and HostelWorld.com. In certain countries, hostels are referred to as dormitories and guest houses, so don't rule those out either. Since safety is always a concern when it comes to hostels (you shouldn't be concerned but just aware), referrals are always best. Recommendations from trusted guides like *Lonely Planet* and *Let's Go* are also useful.

Holy $*%#, I Just Graduated!

FIND OTHER VOLUNTEER OPPORTUNITIES. There are countless organizations that need bright young volunteers, so don't feel bummed if the Peace Corps is not for you. Look for opportunities at WANGO.org, Idealist.org, VolunteerInternational.org, and TransitionsAbroad.com. Another site with a lot of international volunteer listings is GoAbroad.com. Note that certain organizations (e.g., some NGOs offering internships abroad) will charge you for the pleasure of building a well in a desert in the middle of nowhere. In some cases, this charge is realistic—these organizations are strapped for cash, so it's not like they can shell out to send a bunch of inexperienced workers abroad (think Habitat for Humanity). Other organizations might provide room and board but leave the rest (airfare, transportation, souvenirs) up to you—for example, Grassroots Soccer (grassrootssoccer.org) offers a 12-month internship but suggests fundraising a minimum of $10,000 to support yourself for the year.

In any case, it's important to always perform research on an organization so you don't find yourself stranded with a crappy, money-grubbing "nonprofit" in the Ecuadorian rainforest. Check out CharityNavigator.com to see if the organization has been rated, or at least search around for message board discussions or testimonials about other people's experiences. And see page 66 to learn more about finding and exploring full-time nonprofit opportunities.

JOIN THE WWOOFERS. If you've ever longed to herd sheep in New Zealand, work on a vineyard in France, or help out on a family farm in Peru, now's your chance! WWOOF (World Wide Opportunities on Organic Farms) is an organization that helps people find short-term work opportunities (usually on farms) in exchange for free room and board. Since WWOOF operates around the globe, joining up is a great way to see a new corner of the world and to engage in a real way with the local community there. But be warned: WWOOF experiences differ drastically from country to country and farm to farm. Some require some pretty serious manual labor, so make sure you understand what's expected of you before you sign on to help harvest 50 tons of rice. Check out wwoof.org to see where you can go and how to get started.

FIND A GRANT, FELLOWSHIP, OR PRIZE. Before you graduate, see what travel grants and prizes your school has to offer. Foreign Languages, History, and other departments usually have programs you can apply for with a simple application or essay. In addition, Fulbright scholarships and other travel grants are always worth pursuing, though they can be very competitive. Try to find grant or fellowship programs specific to your interests. Mira's List (miraslist.blogspot.com) tracks opportunities for artists (e.g., writers' exchange programs, photography grants), and institutions related to your field of interest may have programs, as well. There are awesomely random opportunities you can find, like the "Delaying the Real World Fellowship," which funded one twentysomething adventurer a year.

LEAD TRAVEL TRIPS FOR STUDENTS OR ADULTS. You'll likely need prior experience with a language or specific country (maybe you grew up somewhere else before going to school in the States), but leading others on an international adventure can be a great way to have an adventure of your own along the way. Check out Backroads.com, All About Visiting Earth (aave.com), or Putney Student Travel (www.goputney.com) to see if being a trip leader is right for you. If you can't get a job as a guide, you can also try joining the company in another capacity (maybe even as an intern) and working your way up to a position where you get to travel for marketing, research, or guiding purposes.

Confessions of an Adventurer: A Year *"Dans le Noir"*
by Tory Hoen

After graduating and toiling for a year and a half in New York, I was starting to feel a bit conflicted. The combination of life in a matchbox-sized studio, 12-hour workdays, and a boss who regularly told me, "You can be replaced," was starting to get me down. I often found myself staring into a spreadsheet wondering, "This is my youth?"

Before long, visions of croissants began to cloud my thoughts, and the promise of pensive strolls along the Seine and cozy afternoons spent writing in cafes lured me to Kayak.com. A voice told me, "If you book it, they will come." It turned out to be a one-way ticket to Paris on Air India…and they turned out to be a year's worth of crazy French-flavored adventures.

For the time being, I had a plane ticket, a short-term sublet, and enough savings to get me through the first few months. Beyond that, I would either A) Find a job that would sustain me, B) Find an aristocratic suitor who would sustain me, or C) Return home none the worse for having attempted an international escapade.

I ended up finding a job that was a bit—how shall I say?—dans le noir (i.e., "in the dark," also known as "under the table" or, if you insist, totally sketchy). No, I was not a prostitute, but I worked in real estate, which might be worse. Regardless, it was enough to sustain me while I pursued my real dream of writing the next great American ex-pat novel (or something like that). I found a longer-term furnished sublet, bought a pre-paid cell phone, and managed to attract some pretty cool friends. Bank account? Who needs it when you've got a perfectly good underwear drawer? Et voilà! I was off and running.

A few months into my tenure in France, I was invited to a new friend's chateau, and as I sat in the grand salon sipping '83 Château Margaux with a giant taxidermy lion's head looming above me, I thought, "Paris was a good idea."

Yes, it was a gamble, and my existence was not really sustainable in the long-run. But I love France and I wanted to live there…is that so wrong?

If you have a dream (or even a momentary impulse masquerading as a dream), I say: go with it. If you're wrong, you can always come crawling back. And if you're right, then you are in for many long wine-soaked nights of pontificating in franglais around a table of questionable French guys who self-identify as "philosophers."

Isn't this what your youth is for? ∎

$ *Smart Money:* Using Your Student ID

It may feel like the advantages of being in college (like sweatpants-all-the-time and sleep) have suddenly disappeared in a puff of smoke. But before cranking up "Glory Days" and shredding all college memorabilia in a violent fit of denial, know that there's one item not to scrap: your student ID card. You spent most of college trying to pretend you were 21; now you have to act like you're back in college to get deals on all sorts of goodies. Don't feel bad about this white lie—just claim you believe you're still a "student" in the European sense of the word (i.e., poor). Or get cracking on your own "D.I.Y. Education" (p. 14) and then you'll technically be a student in your own personal *L'école du Stuff I Want to Know.*

Note: If you're in grad school, you don't have to worry about faking the funk. And if you haven't yet left college, it's probably worth getting a new ID before you leave so you have one that doesn't look like it's been through four years of swiping already.

Tried and True

The following places are pretty lenient about offering student discounts. Remember the drill: Flash and proceed. Flash and proceed. Cool as a cucumber, you are.

MUSEUMS. Whether you're an art fiend checking out a Degas at the Getty in L.A. or an oddity fiend viewing the largest human colon at the Mutter in Philly, museums nationwide offer discounts and even free admission for students (or pretend ones).

MOVIES. If necking with the date you met at the museum isn't reason enough to go to the movies, a reduced fee should add some incentive.

PERFORMING ARTS. Ballet, opera, symphony, theater, concerts—discounted tickets are often box-office-only, but the options are limitless.

TOURIST ATTRACTIONS. View the world's largest Pez dispenser or smallest working sawmill—all at a reduced price!

LOCAL BUSINESSES. If you live near a college campus, many restaurants, bars, and bookstores offer cheaper or tax-free goods. Support their business and save enough to support that coffee habit.

Worth a Shot

Getting these deals with an expired student card might be a stretch, but this is the real world, where smoke and mirrors can be the secret to your success.

CLOTHES. Just because you're no longer a student doesn't mean you can't dress like one. Retailers like J. Crew and EMS offer reduced rates to students (until graduation). As far as your wardrobe is concerned, if you hit upon the right salesperson, graduation may never come.

VACATION DEALS. STA, Student Universe, and Travelosophy all offer student discounts on flights, hotels, packages, and tours. Consider getting an International Student Identity Card (ISIC), which offers savings everywhere from Seattle to Switzerland (and it's just $22 a year). The same company also has an International Youth Travel Card for non-students under 26. Go to Isic.org for more information.

TRAINS. Amtrak offers 15% off, but not only do you need a college ID, you must have either a Student Advantage Discount card or an International Student Identity Card. But just as two negatives multiply to produce a positive, two expired IDs can occasionally add up to one cheap train ride.

BUSES. This form of travel is generally inexpensive to start with because it is about as fun as a Brazilian wax, but Greyhound offers 15% off tickets and 50% off shipping for students. The snag? You need a Student Advantage Discount card in order to get the deal.

APPLE STORE. You need MacBooks, iPods, and iPhones like nobody's business, but fundage is limited. Luckily, Apple offers student discounts, and the word in the blogosphere is that, if you hit upon the right salespeople, they barely check to make sure your student status is legit. If at first you don't succeed, try another Apple store.

BANK ACCOUNTS. Most banks offer no-fee accounts for students. Most banks also check to see if you're really a student. The good news: if you set one up when you really were a student, you can probably coast for years to come.

Holy $*%#, I Just Graduated!

Moving and Storage. If you're moving or storing stuff, inquire about potential student discounts. If you're like many grads, moving is going to become a major theme in your life over the coming years. The fact that you're moving from college or your parents' house might be a dead giveaway, but whatevs—no harm in trying.

Cell Phones. Beware: A lot of cell phone companies claim to have student discounts when what they're really offering is just a plan geared towards college-aged kids (more text messages, free ringtones, an anti-drunk dial device, etc.).

Public Transportation. Major cities sometimes offer major reductions on subway and bus cards. Don every item of university paraphernalia available and hand the attendant the card while singing the school's fight song. If "Hail to the Victors" does not make you victorious, nothing else will. (Note: You could get fined pretty badly for this one.)

D.I.Y. Post-College Education

Unless you decide to go to grad school (Chapter 9), you may experience pangs of guilt about whether or not you fully took advantage of your college experience. "Uh oh," you might think to yourself while watching *Are You Smarter Than a 5th Grader?* "Has my window for enrichment passed me by in a haze of whippets and '80s parties?" Of course not. As Mark Twain once said, "I have never let my schooling interfere with my education." Now you have the opportunity to set a precedent for a lifetime of learning, and this time, there's no homework or tuition!

A little digging around online can reveal an endless fount of free content covering almost any topic imaginable, from the intellectual (e.g., university lectures) to the practical (e.g., how to fold a shirt like a Japanese store clerk). Even beyond your computer screen, there are plenty of ways to flex your brain muscles without paying tens of thousands of dollars for the privilege. Here are some great places to get your D.I.Y. education off the ground. **Some of the following URLs are too long to include here; to find these links and even more great resources, head to gradspot.com/book.**

College Redux

Justice (justiceharvard.org). The most popular class at Harvard is now available to everyone thanks to a partnership with Boston public television and a great website. The class broadly covers the question, "What is the right thing to do?" Through the lecture videos, you'll learn about the philosophies of such pivotal thinkers as Immanuel Kant, Aristotle, John Locke (no, not the dude from *Lost*), and John Stuart Mill, then watch as Professor Michael Sandel and a bunch of Harvard kids debate issues like affirmative action, abortion, and whether or not it's okay for Abercrombie & Fitch to hire only hot people.

Academic Earth (academicearth.org). Free video courses from leading universities, broken down by subject, university, and lecturer. Watch a Yale class on the Old Testament or find out what Guy Kawasaki has to say about entrepreneurship at Stanford.

100 Podcasts from the Best Colleges in the World. It's funny how much easier it is to listen to a lecture when you're not busy swinging crude text messages to your friend across the auditorium. Why not download an educational podcast once in a while and listen to it on the way to work or in the gym? Choose from subjects such as "The Future of the Internet," "Italian Culture," "Nintendo: A History of Innovation," and "String Theory." Or just keep listening to "Poker Face" instead. Whatever floats your boat.

Ten Places to Get Free Online Business Courses. If you listen to that guy from *Wired*, giving stuff away for free is the greatest business model of all time. So when places are giving away free lessons on everything from starting your own business to marketing, networking, and nonprofit management, we're inclined to think they probably know what they're talking about.

Ten Universities Offering Free Writing Courses Online. Some people think writing can't be taught, while others challenge that it might just be the key to unlocking the talent that's waiting to explode. Instead of investing $100K in grad school to find out, try checking out a UCLA screenwriting course or MIT's "Introduction to Fiction."

Free Berkeley Courses. The left-leaning university offers free video and MP3 lectures from a wide range of courses, including Chemistry and the Roman Empire.

The Gilder Lehrman Institute of American History (gilderlehrman.org). Fancy yourself a bit of a history buff? The Gilder Lehrman Institute was created in 1994 for the express purpose of "promoting the study and love of American history." It's not a college, but it does offer over 50 free podcasts and video lectures on the founding fathers, the Civil Rights Movement, and everything in between.

Holy $*%#, I Just Graduated!

General Education

LibraryChick.com. This utterly overwhelming page is like an all-you-can-eat buffet of self-education. Check out free textbooks, audio books, and resources from this beneficent librarian. There's even an "Online Learning" section featuring links to courses, tutorials, and more.

The 60-Second Lectures. Every fall and spring, professors at the University of Pennsylvania are asked to give one-minute lectures on any topic of their choosing. Sometimes they run a little bit over, but for bite-sized snippets of high-minded intellectualism (topics range from the human brain to JFK's sex life), this archive is a great place to waste some time.

BigThink.com. Cut through the hot air of talking heads and commentators by finding out what "ideas" politicians, thinkers, and other doers have about the topics you care about. Check out short videos on everything from John McCain's thoughts on terrorism to Moby's advice for young musicians.

TED.com. Authors, politicians, designers, and other people with "ideas worth spreading" meet at conferences in Long Beach, CA, and Oxford, England, each year to give talks lasting about ten to 20 minutes on whatever they want. They all go up on TED's fantastic website, where you can watch Al Gore talk about climate change or see "mathemagician" Benjamin Arthur race a team of calculators to solve problems.

Fora.tv. More big names talking about big ideas. As the site explains, "We gather the Web's largest collection of unmediated video drawn from live events, lectures, and debates going on all the time at the world's top universities, think tanks and conferences." Deepak Chopra on the afterlife of Michael Jackson? Yes, please.

Lifehacker.com. Leading the charge in the "efficiency movement" is Lifehacker, a site where you can procrastinate for hours learning a thousand and one ways to…stop procrastinating. Irony aside, it features tons of great tips, as well as frequent links to how-to and free education sites.

Skill-Building

Learn a language. We all know the best way to learn Spanish is to go live in Spain (or El Paso). But whether you're trying to brush up your skills or start from scratch, there are plenty of online tools to help you get the ball rolling.

Check out MyLanguageExchange.com to find native speakers who will be your email/text/video-chat pen pal. Also worth checking out is LiveMocha.com, which offers free online classes and the chance to interact with other speakers. If you're just looking for a little vocab building, Learn10.com will email you ten new words a day in whatever language you want.

Learn computer skills. Web skills are pretty bankable these days (see page 71 for more on freelance programming), and who knows—one day knowing computer languages could be just as important as knowing foreign languages. W3Schools.com has free web-programming tutorials that look pretty basic but definitely do the trick for beginners. For a monthly fee of $25/month (or $250/year), Lynda.com offers a wide variety of tutorials covering programming, design, Photoshop, Flash, digital photography, and much more. WebMonkey.com is the original free resource for web developers, offering a comprehensive list of tutorials and an easy-to-search "code library." Of course, you can always just try Googling what you want to learn along with the words "how to" or "tutorial."

Learn random skills. Want to know how to avoid wrinkles, start a fire with a battery, and fold a shirt correctly? Check out Howcast.com, Instructables.com, 5min.com, and VideoJug.com for short videos and posts on all sorts of stuff—both practical and useless.

🏃 Dating

The transition to life after college is hard enough without the added complication of figuring out how to woo potential mates. In some ways, dating will never be as easy as it was in college (although would you actually call what you did in college "dating?"). If we remember correctly, a combination of raging hormones, close quarters, and socially acceptable binge drinking meant that people were hooking up left and right. This is all well and good, but the transition to real life provides a great opportunity to meet people beyond the confines of the keg room. For some, it can be a rude awakening; for others, it's a breath of fresh air.

Beyond actually finding dates, one of the biggest challenges of post-college dating is simply making the time. Once you start working, your free time becomes more precious than ever, and it can be frustrating to waste it on one dud after another. In fact, some people become so career-oriented in their twenties that they only look for casual relationships, keeping any emotional investment that would take up too much time and energy at arm's length. Others feel like

Holy $*%#, I Just Graduated!

they need a stable relationship to counteract all the other uncertainties of life after college.

Honestly, we can't really get into all that—this isn't Dr. Phil! Relationship advice is a dish best served by friends. But before you throw on your "going-out shirt," we wanted to bring up some key aspects of post-college dating that tend to catch recent grads off guard.

Keeping an Open Mind

Many recent graduates say the hardest part about post-college dating is figuring out how, when, and where to meet people. You may find yourself wondering why dating seems to require so much effort and strategy. After all, you're young, you're cool, you're pretty good looking...what's the problem?

Often, it's a matter of expectations. It's possible that you and so-and-so will lock eyes and fall in love while reaching for the same box of Trader Joe's Os, but it's unlikely. While relationships may develop naturally for some people, others have to be a bit more creative. Picking up strangers in bars is not for everyone (nor is it as easy as it looks), and even more structured social scenarios can leave a lovelorn grad wondering how to make the first move. Without a built-in social scene at your disposal, you might have to think outside of the box when on the prowl.

The key is to stay open-minded about how and when you might meet people. In college, you may not have thought to put out the vibe until you were three drinks in on a Saturday night. In the real world, you are more likely to meet someone interesting when you least expect it: when helping a friend move into her apartment, or when your boss sends you to pick up a document from someone with a cute assistant, for example. You don't have to start dreaming about what your children will look like or whether a hottie is "open to adoption" every time you meet someone new, but keep in mind that sometimes love can bloom in the least likely (and most awkward) of situations.

Prime Prowling Grounds

If you know you're in the mood to dip into the dating pool, try attending cultural events, joining co-ed sports leagues, getting involved in your school's local alumni association, volunteering at a local nonprofit, or attending readings, screenings, performances, and lectures. Zeroing in on an activity or subject you love is a great way to connect with people who share your passion. Think about it: If you're hoping to find a girl who loves kickball as much as you do, your chances of meeting her are better if you actually join a kickball team (it can be one of those drunken-Sunday-afternoon ones, if that makes things easier). If you want a guy who appreciates art, start attending art openings and try to join a committee at a local museum or gallery. Bonus: When you're passionately pursuing your own interests, you appear that much more attractive to other people, and if no flames are lit you won't feel you wasted time doing something you didn't actually want to do. MeetUp.com is a great site for finding groups whose interests align with yours—from cyclists to classic film buffs, artisanal beer lovers to design junkies.

Online Dating

Young grads often make love connections through Facebook. If you fancy yourself a "Computer Love" aficionado, there is also the next level—online dating sites. These are a great source of contention among recent grads. To some, they are sketchy and sad—an admission that you've hit rock bottom and are ready to throw caution to the wind. To others, they make total sense. We live so much of our lives on the Web, and we're as adept as ever at making basic judgments about people from their online profiles, so why not move the awkward flirty stage of dating to the 'net to cut out a lot of hassle? The stigma is definitely fading—in 2006, a Pew Poll reported that 31% of adults in America knew someone who had used an online dating service, and the popularity of online dating continues to rise.

If this approach appeals to you, start by visiting the most popular sites like PlentyofFish.com, Match.com, eHarmony.com, and Yahoo! Personals. There are also options catering to individual preferences, such as JDate.com (for Jewish singles), Adam4Adam.com (for gay guys), and Lesbotronic.com (for gay girls). In all cases, just remember why you're using these sites: The point is to expand your potential dating pool and eventually turn some of the connections you make into *offline* dates. It's easy to get bogged down in "winks" and other silly features without ever meeting anyone in the flesh.

Another option for efficiency freaks is speed dating, which offers the ability to meet a ton of people in a very short period of time. You may not fall in love, but you'll inevitably gain some stories that you can later use to regale your chums (and their single friends). Check out 8minutedating.com and HurryDate.com for events in your area.

Holy $*%#, I Just Graduated!

Hazard:
When it just isn't meant to be

One of the things that's both difficult and liberating about post-college dating is that you may date someone who has no ties to your social network. This can feel like an adventure, but it can also lead to anxiety and confusion. Out in the wider world, it becomes easier to make out one minute and then disappear off the face of the earth when you no longer want to see the former object of your (momentary) affection. That's not meant to be a depressing revelation, but rather a caveat for those who are used to the more insular dating pool college provides. Whereas mutual friends used to ensure that you knew what your college makeout buddy was thinking and where he or she lived, those you date in the real world may be less accessible. Sometimes romantic mysteries go permanently unsolved. Luckily, there are plenty of fish in the post-college sea. Eat a tub o' Chunky Monkey and keep it moving!

Taking the Dating Plunge

Whether you're meeting a date online or in-person, it can be intimidating to put yourself out there. Keep in mind that there's a reason why half of every standup routine is devoted to relationships—dating ups and downs are something almost everyone has to encounter, and having a sense of humor and adventure will help you deal with any bumps on the road. Nothing ventured, nothing gained, right? (Of course, if you're setting up a date with someone online, use common sense and plan your first meeting in a public place with lots of other people around.)

The Anatomy of a Date

When you do score a "real world" date, there are a few basics to keep in mind. Try to choose a spot or activity that is convenient and/or appealing to both of you. If you don't know the person that well yet, veer away from stuff that's egregiously guy-centric or girlie. Also, while group dates can work if there's some mutual acquaintance or it's billed as such beforehand, don't immediately throw your new date into a pressure situation where they have to hang out with all your best friends—wait until you know if you actually like the person to save everyone the effort of being nice to a new person!

Once you're out on your date, make like a Buddhist and be in the moment. While you might think that your BlackBerry's constant vibrating is a sign of your importance (and therefore a turn-on), it's actually more likely to distract than it is to attract. Turn off your technology, and turn on the charm. When it comes time to pay the bill, proceed with caution. It often makes sense for the inviter to pay for the invitee (at least at first). It's a modern world, and we don't want to imply that the guy must pay (particularly if there are two guys on the date), but a lady does like to be treated right. On a first date, it's a nice gesture if the guy offers to pick up the tab. Ladies, beyond the first date, it's considerate if you start pulling your financial weight. On a related note, don't choose a restaurant that's way out of your league just to impress someone on a first date. Keeping up the façade will quickly drain your funds, and besides—don't you want to find someone who loves you for you?

Long-Distance Relationships

If you graduated in love or somewhere close to it, you may find yourself in the extremely difficult situation of dating long-distance. Maybe your beau has yet to graduate, or maybe you and your mate have decided to pursue opportunities in different cities. There's no magic formula for a successful "LDR," but start off by having a candid conversation about your expectations and set a realistic timeframe for how long you will remain apart. Temporary distance really can make the heart grow fonder—or it can make the heart completely forget about the other person, which also simplifies things. Another issue to discuss is whether you are going to have an open or closed relationship. If it's the former, will you be expected to disclose your extracurricular activities or keep them to yourself? Going with the "let's see what happens" approach might work for some couples, but it also breeds suspicion.

Presumably one or both of you is moving to a new place and meeting lots of new people, so long periods of "radio silence" might not go over well, especially if someone's latest Facebook album features him or her doing body shots. Realistically speaking, however, these are all just things to think about. There is no set rulebook for LDRs, so the real key is just to be honest with yourself about your motivations and feelings. If you feel dissatisfied, is it because you wish you could be with your boyfriend or girlfriend, or because you wish you could see other people? Follow your gut rather than intellectualizing the situation to death, because there are few ways to rationalize a $200 phone bill (hint: get Skype) and months of loneliness.

Holy $*%#, I Just Graduated!

Confessions:
Breaking Up in the Age of Gchat
by Mary Kathryn Burke

Two years post-college, I had my first real-adult dating experience. I was 24. It was about time. It was classically too-good-to-be-true, and I wanted to tell anyone who would listen: Doorman…drycleaner…butcher, baker, candlestick maker…you name it. He pulled out chairs and wore a suit to work and put his tasseled Cole Hahn loafers on shoe trees before flossing, perusing the WSJ one last time and going to bed at a reasonable hour. You know, a real-adult man. And with that came a subsequent, inevitable, real-adult breakup.

Well, it's been a while now and from my toils, I offer a few humble tips for a more graceful breakup in 2010 and beyond. From someone who (hopes she) learned the hard way. As my dear friend and fellow Gradspotter Christine would say, "It used to be just tearing a photo in half. Now it's much more complicated to rid ourselves of the relationship residue." These days, comrades, it's everywhere. And it's your choice to pick a place to draw the line.

1. **Texting/Calls.** Eventually the goal is to stop. But let's be honest—it's going to happen. Especially if you're not teetotalling. While weaning yourself off your cell dependency, the next best step is warning your future 4 am self not to call or text him. Change the name in your phone from "John Perfect" to something that will make you think. Something like "Doyoureallywanttodothis?" This way, at least if you slip up you will first get a little reminder that you should feel guilty about it from your formerly sober self. It's like Nicorette gum except with words and without the chewing and the drug rush.

2. **Outlook**. Dear innocent college kid on PINE, webmail, or Macmail: Someday you will sit in an office…in a cube. Like the one I am sitting in right now. And when you work in this cube you will undoubtedly email the coworkers 20 yards away from you all day in an email system known as Outlook. And Outlook, despite its many inefficiencies, is remarkably adept at remembering every damn person you ever emailed. One of those people is probably the boy you just broke up with. You may or may not have spent the better part of your days at work emailing him over Outlook at J.T. Marlin or wherever the hell he worked. Maybe you even sent him clever calendar reminders. Delete, delete, delete. Go into your address book at D-E-L-E-T-E. There is nothing worse than going to email your innocent

intern Johnny and having John E. Breakup's email address come up. It's not worth it. Delete.

3. **Blackberry Messenger.** I don't do this, but I've heard stories and it sounds like trouble. (See #1.)

4. **Gchat.** Now we're talking. Something with nuance. Gchat has a lot of options, and the best thing to do is to try what is right for you. For a while you might want to go "invisible." You might be tempted to block him, but that's too transparent. Even more transparent than "invisible" if you can believe it. Do this: Hover over his Gchat name. Choose "more" and then "never show." He can see that you're online, but you won't have to stare at his name... and picture... and cutesy away-status. Tempting you. Mocking you. Added bonus: Make sure your picture is something fabulous you did in his wake.

5. **Twitter.** Don't tweet unless you are a celebrity. If you are a celebrity, go on a date with some ladykiller your PR person calls, then have your assistant tweet Page Six and make sure your ex gets a link. If you must tweet, at least stop "following" him.

6. **Online "Date."** Or, rather, browse. You don't have to go on a date with someone from Match, JDate, or Eharmony—just look around. Get a feel. We have our entire thirties to date on these sites. But it's a better distraction than Facebook, phone, Blackberry, and iPod, tempting us to break rules 7, 1, and 3, respectively. Have a coworker sign you up for one of these things and just look. Because eventually, you will be in your apartment, tempted to break rule 4. And you have to remember that there are other guys floating around whose hearts you have yet to break.

7. **Facebook.** This is the biggie. "Hide" him in your feed. Make sure your best friend "hides" him on her feed. And if worse comes to worst, gracefully "defriend." He's not dead. You can always say hi later, a long time from now. But in the interim just get off your devices and get out of your room. You survived college, and you'll survive this.

Remember, you're an adult... sort of. ■

⬚ Cooking

One of the harshest realities of living independently is dealing with the necessity of feeding yourself. For many of us, dining hall meal plans only reinforced a lifetime of culinary ineptitude. Maybe you mixed a nice salad or figured out that making *matzo pizza* was not as disgusting as expected, but beyond these trial-by-fire experiments, most college students graduate with no basic grasp of how to buy, store, and prepare food. "Home economics" isn't at the top of the curriculum anymore and, let's face the facts: some parents are horrible in the kitchen, as well.

One thing is for sure: You watched the Food Network. And it turns out that after watching over 1,000 hours of programming, you know how to properly remove the meat from a snow crab yet you still don't know how to boil an egg. There's no real shame in that—any self-respecting person would rather watch Gordon Ramsay tell someone to go screw himself than write down a Rachael Ray recipe. That said, a rotation of simple, quick recipes is essential to any budget- and body-conscious grad. This talent, in turn, has a trickle down effect into your broader life, allowing you to impress friends, dates, and colleagues with your culinary acumen. Of course, the allure of takeout menu roulette is always tempting, but it is ultimately a far more expensive and less satisfying option than going DIY in the kitchen.

Web Links:
Finding recipes

Along with Gradspot.com's "Recipe of the Week," check out these sites for recipes, tips, and cooking inspiration:

🍽 Chowhound.com	🍽 CookThink.com
🍽 FoodNetwork.com	🍽 Recipes.com
🍽 Epicurious.com	🍽 Rouxbe.com
🍽 Cookstr.com	🍽 Mark Bittman's NYT blog

Kitchen 101

More than likely, your kitchen looks more like a small closet than the *Iron Chef* Kitchen Stadium. But that doesn't mean you can't whip up a few well-practiced dishes. Before you get started, it's important to make sure your cooking area is clean. (*Ratatouille* is a bit unrealistic—having a rat infestation is not going to make you into a master chef.) Use a disinfectant to wipe down surfaces, especially after handling raw chicken. Clean all your cookware and utensils to avoid germs and food that always tastes like the *last* thing you cooked. ("I really want stir-fry on Thursday, so let's have it on Wednesday, shall we?") As annoying as it may sound, it really is easier to give things a quick rinse and scrub immediately after using them than battling with a dried-up, filth-encrusted mound of dirty dishes at the end of each month.

All clean? Okay, let's proceed. Hopefully you have a stovetop, oven, sink, and refrigerator. If you're lucky you have a microwave and a coffeemaker, but those are luxuries. When push comes to shove, you can do most cooking with some pretty simple tools—don't be lured by the apple slicer and fresh yogurt maker when you reach the checkout at the kitchen supply store. Here are a few essentials that should serve you well. **Depending on where you shop, you should be able to outfit your whole kitchen for $150 to $200 total.** To reduce costs significantly, try to pick up as many items as you can from home (your parents or grandparents probably have stuff lying around), and try to find a local kitchen supply store for wholesale prices.

Large saucepan (3+ quarts; $14–25)	You want it to be big enough to cook a whole package of spaghetti or make a batch of sauce/soup.
Medium or small saucepan ($9–20)	For heating soups, sauces, etc.
10" frying pan ($13–15)	For cooking eggs, sautéing meats, making stir-fry, etc.
13"-by-18" metal baking sheet ($5.75–15)	For baking and toasting bread.
Roasting pan ($6.50–10)	For roasting chicken, making lasagna, etc.
Mixing bowls (set of three; $5–11)	For preparing food, serving, and storing leftovers.
Measuring cup ($6.50–7.50)	For measuring out ingredients.
Peeler ($3–6)	For peeling vegetables like carrots, potatoes, etc.
14" colander ($7–10)	For draining pasta and other food cooked in water and washing fruits and veggies.

Holy $*%#, I Just Graduated!

Wooden spoons (set of three; $3–10)	These are better than metal because they're easier on the surfaces of pots and pans.
Ladle ($2.50–3)	For serving soups, sauces, etc.
Bread knife ($3–8)	For breads, bagels, etc. Serrated edge also works well for cutting tomatoes.
Chef's knife (medium-sized; $10–13)	Good for chopping pretty much anything (including your fingers—be careful!).
Paring knife (might come with chef's knife; $3)	Useful for cutting small items and peeling.
Rubber spatula ($4.50–8)	For flipping pancakes, making scrambled eggs, sautéing, etc. Rubber is easier on surfaces than metal.
Whisk ($3–4)	For whipping up scrambled eggs and batters.
Can opener ($4–10)	That can of soup will taunt you if you can't open it.
Measuring spoons ($1–5)	For teaspoon and tablespoon measuring.
Cutting board ($6–9)	Plastic ones are a lot easier to clean (crucial when you're cutting raw chicken and other potentially dangerous foods).

Learning to Shop and Cook

Stocking "the pantry" (or the mini-fridge and cupboard, as the case may be) can be an inordinately onerous task for recent grads with no kitchen know-how. When you do a lap around the supermarket and end up with cereal straws, a steak, Kool-Aid mix, Double Stuf Oreos, Dave's Insanity hot sauce, and some Kraft Singles, you know you've got a little work to do. Putting some thought into your purchases beforehand (or even bringing—dare we say it—a *shopping list!?*) can help cut down on impulse buys and produce a more useful end result. So, what should you look for?

Beyond the obligatory salt-pepper-olive oil triumvirate, take stock of what you like to eat and build your pantry based on your preferences. Do you like hummus? You probably do. But did you realize that keeping garlic, oil, a few spices, and a can of chickpeas around will help you to make it whenever you want? The fun of learning to make your favorite foods from a few staple ingredients is threefold: 1) You save money; 2) You can experiment with a food that you already know; and 3) You can create a personalized version of a favorite dish that will wow your guests.

Rice, polenta, and oatmeal are other good stock items; they will never leave you hungry, and they are extremely versatile. Frozen chicken, pork, or sausage all serve a similar purpose in the kitchen—they provide a good base protein and can be deployed in a wide range of dishes. Pasta is also a major staple for the young adult, but unfortunately most pre-made sauces are gross. We recommend keeping a can of crushed tomatoes around at all times to make a quick sauce from scratch. Over time you will develop a "signature" sauce, and everyone will think you are either a) of Italian ancestry, b) the jam, or c) both. A basic tomato sauce is the perfect base for a variety of add-ons, and it requires only minimal cooking time. After you get a great multi-use sauce going, make a big batch and save it for pastas, pizzas, or whatever else you dream up.

Holy $*%#, I Just Graduated!

Smart Money:
The Under-$50 Pantry

You don't want to be running to the store every time you try to make a recipe that involves "salt and pepper." There are some basic items that you want to keep on hand at all times—they'll last a long time and make your cooking forays a whole lot easier. (Prices vary according to geography and store, but these prices from a Safeway in the Bernal Heights neighborhood of San Francisco shouldn't be too far off what you can find.)

Olive oil (25 fl oz, generic)	$9.99
Salt	$0.89
Pepper	$3.79
Dijon mustard	$2.99
Butter (1 stick)	$1.49
Mixed Italian seasoning	$5.49
Balsamic vinegar	$4.58
Soy sauce (10 oz)	$2.59
Red pepper flakes	$4.61
Cumin	$4.19
Chili powder	$4.69
Pam Cooking Spray	$3.99
Total	**$49.29**

Ask The Expert:
Cooking Advice From Mark Bittman

Mark Bittman is best known as a food columnist for the New York Times, a regular guest on NBC's Today Show, and the author of the classic cookbook How to Cook Everything. *He's also traveled around Spain with Gwyneth Paltrow and Mario Batali for a television series on PBS and given a TED talk entitled "What's Wrong with What We Eat." We think he's pretty much the man, and his philosophy on his craft makes him the perfect guru for post-college: he rejects the notions that tools and ingredients must be expensive, that recipes must be followed to the letter, and that cooking isn't worth the effort. We caught up with him to get his advice for twentysomethings making their first forays into the kitchen.*

How did you start cooking for yourself?

My senior year of college and my first year after college I lived alone. I cooked every day—sometimes alone, sometimes with other people—and I really taught myself how to cook. In school I wasn't an over-achiever. I was always looking for shortcuts to get the grades I needed, and I approached cooking the same way: I never followed the directions exactly. I improvised as needed, and most of the time it came out okay.

What do you actually need in your kitchen to cook?

It's not $20 worth of stuff, it's more like $150–200 worth of stuff. Get stuff from your parents, grandparents, Salvation Army. Second-hand places are a good deal; if something was able to make it to the store, it's probably in pretty good condition. Even if it's rusted, you can literally throw it in a fire and the rust will burn off. You don't need fancy stuff when you're young; [the expensive things] only help when you're in your '60s and '70s and you're less likely to want to hold heavier things.

How do you figure out what to buy for the week?

The most important thing about shopping is the pantry. If you stock a good pantry, then you don't have to shop that often, and there's no excuse to run out to buy a slice of pizza at 10 pm. If you have grains, beans, eggs and onions, spices, and herbs—a very, very basic list—then you don't have to run out shopping. It can be a $25 investment a week until you build a full pantry. And then every now and then you have to run out and buy the fresh things, milk or lettuce, and that's how you take care of the fresh items. People always say, "Ahh, but I didn't have X, Y, or Z," and it's complete nonsense. There's no excuse not to cook. I have a small kitchen, I don't have a ton of stuff. I have maybe 50 things, $200 worth of things, and I can always cook whatever I want. Shopping is never a big deal.

What are entry-level things that grads should do if they want to start cooking?

People should always invest in a cookbook. These days you don't really need one because you can go online, but it's hard to judge if it's a good recipe or not. And if you don't have any cooking experience you really can't tell. You want to invest your time in learning to cook something you want to eat. Find a recipe, find how long it's supposed to take to make, and then double that time, because you have no idea what you're doing, and then go to work. It's not going to be Michelin-quality beautiful, but it's going to be fine. You just have to go for it. When people recognize how simple and straightforward cooking is, that's when they get into it.

Why do you think people eat healthier if they cook for themselves?

Well, there are many reasons—it's portion, it's ingredients, it's many things. I don't believe you can make yourself an 1,800 calorie salad. You look at what's going in there, and you think, "I don't even want to eat all that crap!" If you go to the store, you'll buy vegetables, and then you'll come home and cook them. You'll eat only what you buy. You can't possibly eat as badly as when you're not cooking. People who don't cook eat terribly. Two-thirds of Americans are overweight or obese—those are not cooks. I doubt even 10% of those people are real cooks.

You have a daughter who's a recent college grad. What are your observations about people our age when it comes to cooking?

I'm optimistic about your generation because I feel like we've hit rock bottom. [Laughs.] I'm pessimistic about your generation because so many people of your generation grew up eating prepared food, take-outs, ordering in, and so much of this thinking is shaped when you're young. It's going to be up to you guys when you become parents to demonize over-eating. There was this ad with this kid saying to his mom, "Why are you smoking?", and the same is going to have to happen with over-eating: the kid has to be able to ask his mom, "Why are we going to McDonalds?" I think McDonald's is trying to change and I'm not saying those places are all bad. Those places are fine for a special occasion if you always eat at home, but to think of McDonald's as a staple place for eating? That's tragic. ■

Finding the Time to Cook

At the end of the day, it's important to remember that "when you're hungry" is not the only time of day to cook. Take an hour on the weekend to make a large casserole or chili that you can freeze and eat throughout the week. If you have roommates who are also interested in eating at home, set up a rotation where you cook for one another. Finally, don't be intimidated—with basic ingredients it is hard to make food that is inedible, and remember that, these days, you've always got the Internet as a resource to tell you the difference between frying and sautéing, or to provide simple recipes for almost anything. Once you nail one dish, you can build off that and mix and match with others—before you know it, you'll have a whole range of tricks up your sleeve.

Now that your kitchen is locked and loaded, it's time to actually get cookin'. Turn to the Appendix for some of our favorite recipes.

 Drinking

The "transition" may drive some recent grads to drink. But while shot-gunning Bud Lights and sake bombing were considered power moves in college, they begin to lose their cachet after graduation. Now's the time to add a touch of class to your alcoholic endeavors.

Needless to say, not drinking is also a totally reasonable lifestyle choice (especially if you've discovered Abita Root Beer, perhaps the most delicious root beer ever made). You don't have to booze to be the consummate grad. The point is that if you are going to partake, it's worth expanding your horizons beyond Carlos Rossi and red Solo cups. So fill up your glass, light a fire, and let's talk drankin'.

Wine Appreciation 101

Whether you're looking to sound savvy at a business dinner or trying to impress that hottie from next door, a little wine knowledge goes a long way. There's no need to emulate that ostentatious guy from *Sideways* with his Merlot-phobia, but being able to navigate a wine menu can add an intriguing string to your post-grad bow. The world of wine is complex; the basics are not. Let us help.

Types of Wines

The three main categories for wines are red, white, and sparkling. (Note: Rosé is also quite popular as a warm-weather drink among Euros and wannabe-Euros.)

Within the three main categories, the options are endless, but here's a quick rundown of wines you are likely to find at restaurants and bars in the United States (where wines are generally categorized by varietal).

Red

- Y **CABERNET SAUVIGNON.** Generally full-flavored with a smooth and lingering finish.
- Y **SYRAH (OR SHIRAZ).** Tastes full-bodied with flavor notes of anything from raspberry to espresso to spice.
- Y **MERLOT.** Has a medium body with hints of berry, plum, and currant, and a buttery finish.
- Y **PINOT NOIR.** A light crisp wine with an acidic finish.

Whites

- Y **CHARDONNAY.** One of the most versatile wines, it's often oaky, but it can also be soft with fruity flavors or smoky with flavors of vanilla, caramel, or butter.
- Y **SAUVIGNON BLANC.** Tastes crisp, dry, and refreshing with flavors ranging from grass to tropical fruit.
- Y **PINOT GRIGIO.** Can be good for beginners due to its sweet, light, crisp, and neutral flavors—but not all pinots are created equal.

Sparkling Wines

- Y **CHAMPAGNE.** Designation reserved for sparkling wines produced in France's champagne region (the gold standard in sparkling wines). Think Dom Perignon, Moët et Chandon, and, of course, Cristal. Always go for "Brut" (i.e. dry) champagnes unless you like your bubbly very sweet.
- Y **PROSECCO.** Italy's answer to champagne. Generally cheaper in price than actual champagne.
- Y **CAVA.** Spain's version of champagne. Also cheaper in price.
- Y **SPARKLING WINE.** The general designation for any carbonated wine.

Holy $*%#, I Just Graduated!

Lingo:
Vino Edition

There's no need to be overwhelmed when it comes to wine speak. When the waiter explains that a certain wine has notes of aged English leather and tiger lilies with a smooth, walnut-y finish, you may be tempted to opt for a mineral water instead. But don't let the pomp and circumstance deter you. Here's a list of the terminology you need to know. And even if you don't know it, you're still allowed to drink.

OLD WORLD: Generally refers to wines produced in regions with long histories of winemaking (e.g., Europe, parts of the Mediterranean basin).

NEW WORLD: Generally refers to wines produced in "newer" regions such as the United States, Australia, South America, and South Africa.

VARIETAL. A fancy word for a type of grape and a way of classifying wines. Examples of different varietals include Chardonnay, Merlot, Pinot Noir, and Riesling.

REGION: An indicator of where the wine was produced and another way of classifying wines. Examples of regions include Burgundy, Bordeaux, Chianti and Rioja. (Many European wines are classified according to region.)

FULL-BODIED VS. LIGHT. A way to describe the "weight" of wines in your mouth. Does it feel inky? Watery? The more robust the flavor, the more "full-bodied" it is.

VINTAGE. This refers to the year in which the wine was produced, and some years are better than others for specific wines depending upon the weather and other factors. That's not to say that 2005 was a great vintage for every wine, but it might have been for some. If you know the key years for specific wines, you'll be able to pick out some stellar bottles.

BLENDS & TABLE WINES: "Blends" and "table wines" are made by blending different types of grapes, which can yield delicious or disastrous results. Table wines are usually on the cheaper end of the spectrum and can be pretty tasty if you find the right one.

Holy $*%#, I Just Graduated!

EASY-DRINKING WINE. This is one of those vague phrases that wine people like to throw around, but it basically means that the wine at hand is fairly innocuous, will please a variety of palates, and can be enjoyed alone or with food. It's smart to choose an "easy-drinking wine" if you're trying to please a group whose preferences vary from one person to the next. New World wines tend to be good crowd-pleasers.

FINISH: A word used to describe the "impression" that a wine leaves as it's being swallowed. The finish is often described in terms of acidity or specific flavors (oak, fruit, spice, etc.)—or emotions if the person is a total BSer.

For more information on wine terminology, check out the helpful online encyclopedia at Wines.com.

Ask The Expert:
How to Order Wine at a Restaurant

As an aspiring writer, Gradspot.com contributor Adam White has learned a thing or two about waiting tables. And with waiting tables comes the opportunity to try wines... lots of wines. We asked Adam rules of thumb for mastering the wine list (or just faking your way through it). You probably won't be going to too many somelier-staffed parties with your friends, but you never know where your work and romantic life might take you.

1. Be confident in your knowledge level. You don't have to pretend to be a know-it-all. Even if you're telling your server, "I know very little about wine," engaging him or her on the subject will ensure that you end up with an interesting bottle.

2. Cheap is fine. Don't be intimidated by the high price tags in the Burgundy section—nobody ever orders the thousand-dollar Grand Crus (they're like the beautiful convertible in the window of a car dealership that's only there to lure prospective sedan-owners). Every wine list has hidden gems; it's your job to get the server to reveal them to you.

3. Ask for the somme. If you're at a fancier place with a sommelier, tell him or her what you're looking for (keep it simple: red or white, full-bodied or light, Old World or New World) and ask for a recommendation. Say, "I don't drink much wine, but I'm learning and I'd like to try something interesting—preferably for less than [insert budget here]." You're likely to come away with a beautiful bottle, an education, and maybe a new friend.

4. Just sniff. Until you master swirling and sipping (especially under pressure), smelling the wine will do. All you're smelling for is wet newspaper (which means the wine is corked) or an overwhelming molasses smell (it's oxidized). These are the reasons you would send it back. If you do taste, you are not tasting to see if you *like* the wine—you're tasting to make sure it's in good condition. A classic rookie move is to send it back because the taste is not what you expected.

5. Get drunk. Wine novices tend to sip slowly and tentatively. This makes no sense. Good wine is intended to be appreciated, yes, but it's also intended to make you feel good. Once you make it through the ordering, reward yourself by boozing it up. ■

Exploring the World of Beer

According to the Brewers Association, the total number of U.S. breweries on July 31, 2009, was the highest total in 100 years: 1,525. The craft beer industry has grown exponentially in the past ten years—beer bars are on the rise in every major city, more and more restaurants are offering beer pairings with their dishes, and innovative new beer styles are constantly being invented. If you're interested in drinking connoisseurship (a great pursuit to grow old with), you no longer have to feel like Joe or Jane Sixpack just because you'd rather grab a brew than a Bordeaux. Beer is *en vogue*!

Before you embark on your journey into the wide world of beer, let's get one thing straight: drinking beer should be fun, enjoyable, and never stressful. Never drink beers that you don't like, unless there are no other beers available and you just want to get drunk. Some varieties are considered "trendy" and "refined" in the same way certain wines are, but if you are ordering a Tripel to look sophisticated, you may end up regretting the decision. Your best bet is to try a bunch of beers and see what you like. Here's a very quick overview of some popular types of beers worth exploring, as well as some terminology that will help you ask for them at stores and bars.

Types of Beer

Ales and pale lagers are the most common families of beer, but there's a vast world out there to explore. Here's the tip of the iceberg.

> **LAGERS.** Lagers are the most popular beers in the world, and probably what you've been drinking most of your college career (Bud, Miller, Coors, et. al. belong to the family of pale lagers). That said, the world of lagers is extremely varied, and each beer-drinking country has its own varieties. Light lagers are generally—but not always—lower in alcohol and more carbonated than dark lagers, which get their richer flavor and color from roasted barley and hops. Another popular variety is the pilsner, a light-colored lager hailing from Europe—it is generally hoppier and more bitter than its American cousin. You might also run into German lagers of the "bock" family—you'll notice they're maltier and higher in alcohol content. Lagers are usually stored and served at cold temperatures, and in general you can expect an ABV of about 4–5.5%.

▶ **Ales.** As with lagers, the diversity of ales is astounding. However, if you need some basic ways to differentiate, here goes: Ales are less carbonated, lower in alcohol, and have a stronger taste of malty hops. There are bottled varieties, but ales are really best when cask-conditioned and served from the tap. "English Bitters" are the kings of ales, especially when served at room temperature with a nice pie. Brown ales—most famously Newcastle Brown Ale—are also popular, and they're generally distinguished by their reddish-brown coloration and a sweeter taste of fruitiness or nuttiness. Darker "porters" are heavier and have a complex, chocolaty flavor. Finally, pale ales are generally known for their balance of malt and hops.

▶ **STOUTS.** Technically, stouts are a sub-category of ales, but we think they're worth mentioning in their own right, mostly because a lovely drop of Guinness is always a great fallback. Stouts are dark, often with a creamy head and taste of roasted barley (think chocolate and coffee undertones). Oatmeal, chocolate, and oyster stouts are also interesting options.

▶ **HEFEWEIZEN.** The hefeweizen, hailing from Germany, is the most popular variety of wheat beer. Wheat beers are highly carbonated and generally have a cloudy appearance when poured. The wheat provides a crisp, refreshing taste that makes these beers popular in summertime.

▶ **BELGIAN/FRENCH/TRAPPIST.** Expect far higher alcohol content, stronger tastes, and funny glasses. Generally, these are considered "sipping" beers, so you won't find them in a standard Irish pub or late-night hot spot. True "trappist" ales are rare because they are literally brewed by or under the control of Trappist monks. Only seven of the 171 Trappist monasteries produce beer (six in Belgium, one in the Netherlands), the most famous of which are Chimay and Orval. The different strengths are generally labeled Enkel ("single"), Dubbel ("double"), and Tripel ("triple"). Belgian blonde ales, being lighter and more akin to a hefeweizen, are a good introduction to the often intimidating world of Belgian and French beers.

With the ranks of Duvel-quaffing beer geeks filling up fast (thanks hipsters!), the call has come to separate the wheat from the chaff in the beer community. No longer does "hating Coors Light" make you eligible for the club. So get out there and learn what great beer is all about!

Hazard:
Coping with the One-Year Rut

While this chapter has focused on the lighter side of graduation, we'd be remiss not to acknowledge that you'll inevitably hit some speed bumps as you transition into life beyond the dorms. So before we immerse you in the joys of the job hunt, finding an apartment, getting health care, and all that fun stuff (ie. the rest of this book), we wanted to make a quick P.S.A....

We aren't going to lie: Post-college life isn't all fun and games. No matter what stage of the post-college transition you find yourself at, it's almost inevitable for a "grass is always greener" mentality to creep into play at some point. For one thing, missing college is totally normal. Yet, there are also more complex dilemmas. The people who jump right into a job begin to feel burnt out and wonder if they should have taken time off. The ones who took time off fear that they have fallen behind. Socially, it can grow harder to stay in touch with friends, and demanding work schedules make dating and hanging out much more difficult than they were in college. To add insult to injury, in comes the myriad of new responsibilities to seize and issues to confront that, quite frankly, most grads aren't prepared to face.

We aren't telling you the above to worry you. It's quite the opposite. We're telling you to prepare you for what's going to occur. You're going to hit some ruts, but just like the millions of recent grads who came before you, you'll persevere. How do we know? Because yes, even we, the good folks at Gradspot.com, recently went through and got through it all ourselves, as did our friends. And you and your friends will too. However, as you're navigating the at times bumpy road ahead, make sure to maintain the perspective that you are not the victim of a massive anti–recent grad conspiracy—"the rut" is normal, and you're in control of your own life, so get out there and do your thing. As you keep reading, please keep this chapter in mind and continue to reference it every so often in order to take some of the attention off work, roommate problems, and anything else that's getting you down. And whenever you do confront an issue, instead of freaking out like we may have done, just turn to any page in this book and find a solution to your problem. Journey forth, young grad (and turn the page). ■

Chapter II: Career Options

Career Options

If it hasn't happened already, you will soon discover that people will be more than happy to give you all sorts of half-cooked advice about choosing your first job, ranging from the New Agey ("do what you love, dude") to the depressingly practical ("whatever pays the bills"). Somewhere between the existentialist and realist approaches, you may find something that resonates with you and sets off a light bulb. But our take is that finding "the right job" is more of an active process than a philosophical one.

The first step, as cheesy as it sounds, is simply to expand your frame of reference and realize that there are a *lot* of options out there (see page 52 to start brainstorming). But at a certain point, you've got to bite the bullet and go for something. If you like it, then you've chosen well; if not, then you've at least narrowed down the field and picked up some valuable perspective. Finding the job you love often comes down to a process of elimination.

In this chapter, we'll help you size up the job market, figure out what you might want to do, and then find the openings that interest you most. In addition, we'll highlight a few popular options like government and nonprofit work, as well as some of the ways you can avoid the rat race and take control of your career destiny. From temping to internships to finding a permanent job, we'll cover every avenue on the road to employment and make sure you head off in the right direction.

Building Your Story:
Five Things to Do Before You Get a Job

It's often said that "searching for a job is a job in itself." Like most maxims, there's some truth to that, but it would be insane not to do anything else with your time. In fact, the worst thing that you can do while job hunting is to do nothing but look for employment. The question, "What have you been up to since you graduated?" will come up many times over the course of the job hunt and a response of "I've been looking for a job" ain't gonna cut it. By doing this, you're essentially framing your story so it revolves around someone that nobody wants. But if you spend your time enhancing your story by keeping active and learning new skills, you've now presented yourself as someone who is motivated and multi-faceted, important attributes that will help you get a leg up over your competition. There are a bunch of things that you can do to improve your prospects before you even have a "job"-job, and many of them have the added benefit of keeping you sane. In fact, any of these five options is a fantastic way to begin your career story.

Five Things to Do Before You Get a Job continued...

1. Get an internship or volunteer (paid or unpaid) position. This common exchange of your time for experience and a few resume bullets not only makes you a better job candidate, but it also allows you to get your foot in the door of an organization and to build your network. (For more on internships, see page 73).

2. Build a new skill set. When you have nothing else to do, learn something! This can be anything from mastering a language that will help you secure a niche job, to developing a skill like computer programming that will allow you to freelance for money. And today, with the plethora of free tutorial websites and local meetup groups, you can easily do all this for free (see page 16). One thing is for sure: Employers dig skillz.

3. Consider graduate school. If you didn't land a job right out of college but you know you're interested in a career path that requires an advanced degree, now may be the time to get the testing and essay writing out of the way. When the time comes to actually apply and you're bogged down with work, you'll be thankful you already have this stuff done. (For more on grad school, see Chapter 9.)

4. Freelance or temp. Sometimes you just can't afford to take that unpaid internship or double-up on student debt and go to grad school. When that's the case, consider freelance (p. 69) or temp work (p. 85). Essentially, you'll be earning cash and getting your foot in the door of various companies. There are countless tales of freelance and temp gigs turning into full-time paying jobs.

5. Travel abroad. While we all have dreams of jetting around the world à la Brangelina, traveling after school doesn't always have to be expensive, nor does it need to involve the adoption of foreign orphans. You can hostel-hop or even find a money-generating gig out of the country, like teaching English as a second language. Maybe you can even find a grant from your school or a national organization. (For more on traveling on the cheap, see page 8.)

No matter which option you choose to pursue, make sure that you can leverage it to help you secure career opportunities down the road. ■

Understanding Your Ideal Job Profile: Industry, Organization, and Function

Whether you're ready to pursue a job today or are just planning ahead, it's a good idea to start looking at jobs in terms of *industry, organization*, and *function*. To do so, think about how your friends tend to talk about jobs. "I'm good with numbers—I think I'd make a fine accountant," one person might say. "Ever since I threw up on Mickey Mouse after riding the teacups at the Magic Kingdom, I've loved Disney; it's my dream to work there," says another. "Ladies," exclaims the third, "Just look at me: I mean, how could I *not* work in fashion?"

These declarations of intent may all sound similar, but there's a subtle difference between them. Check it: Fashion describes an *industry*, but it leaves a lot of questions unanswered. Does your friend want to be a model? Would she like to do public relations for an up-and-coming designer? Or how about working as a buyer at a national department store? On the other hand, Disney is an *organization*, and its size dictates a lot about it (including the fact that it's large enough to employ that creepy person in the Mickey Mouse suit). Finally, Accounting is a specific job *function*, and you can do it at many different companies across almost any industry (every business needs to keep its books in order).

Understanding these distinctions is crucial to a smart job hunt. One trap a lot of recent grads fall into is immediately obsessing over a specific position (e.g., "I want to be the editorial assistant for the music reviews section at *Rolling Stone*"). While it's great to have a particular goal, you severely limit your chances of success in the job market if you maintain such a narrow view of what your first job should look like. As headhunting pro Maxine Martens says, "Instead of looking at one job, you should be saying, 'Who needs me?' and, 'What [function] do I want to do?' When people are very focused on the specific job, it has less resonance."

By all means, apply to your dream job, but don't forget to apply to other similar jobs, as well. By looking at how job functions, organizations, and industries play into one another, you can begin to make sense of the job market and where you will eventually fit

Career Options

> **Tips & Tricks:**
> **Let your newspaper guide the way**
>
> One simple litmus test for figuring out what job you should get is suggested by Lindsey Pollak in her book *Getting from College to Career:* Start picking up the paper every morning and see what section you gravitate toward. Do you hone in on the front page or flip straight to the arts section? Are you more interested in the stock prices or the box scores? It seems kind of silly, but it makes sense. As a whole, a good newspaper provides a representative swath of what's going on in the world. Whatever you find most interesting is probably where you should focus your efforts.

into it. To help you get started, we've provided an overview of your options as they relate to these three areas.

Industry

From the advertising-obsessed *Mad Men* fanatic to the travel nut who selects hotels based on the thread count of their sheets, some people find themselves intrinsically drawn toward a specific industry. That's cool, and we say follow your instincts. But sometimes, it's worth seasoning those instincts with some reality sauce. For example, if you want to get into the newspaper industry, it's likely going to be difficult to find a good opportunity in the current climate, so maybe you can figure out how to pursue the same function—writing—in a new media environment. Alternatively, it might pay to focus on the industries with the brightest or the safest prospects (see "Which Industries Are the Safest in a Recession?" on 45).

Here's a smattering of industries to whet your appetite.

- Hospitality (e.g., hotels, restaurants, clubs, bars, resorts)

- Retail (e.g., boutiques, chain stores, department stores)

- Commercial Finance (e.g., banks, investment firms)

- Real Estate (e.g., construction, investment, management)

- Consumer Goods (e.g., household products, toy manufacturers)

- Fashion/Beauty (e.g., cosmetics companies)

- Publishing (e.g., book publishers, magazines)

- Journalism/Media (e.g., newspapers, blogs, TV, radio, online video hubs)

- Entertainment (e.g., film, music labels, talent agencies)

- Software (e.g., Oracle and Microsoft)

- Aerospace (e.g., plane manufacturers, NASA)

- Insurance (e.g., automobile insurance, home insurance)

- Health (e.g., hospitals, device manufacturers, pharmaceuticals)

- Government (e.g., political offices, various state and federal departments)

- Education (e.g., schools, administration)

- Food and Beverage (e.g., beer and wine companies, snack food companies)

Ask The Expert:
Which Industries Are the Safest in a Recession?
by Alexandra Levit

Alexandra Levit is a nationally syndicated Wall Street Journal columnist and author of such books as New Job, New You: A Guide to Reinventing Yourself in a Bright New Career *and* They Don't Teach Corporate in College. *We asked her to weigh in on a question we've been asked repeatedly by the Gradspot community.*

A lot of people ask about the best types of jobs to pursue during an economic recession. It's not surprising that when people see constant news about ailing industries like finance and print media, they wonder if all jobs are likely to disappear in the next five years. What I tell them is this: While no job in the world will ever have complete security, there are many industries that are considered more "recession-proof" than others. Here are a few of my favorites:

Health Care: While the debate about health care is divisive, you can bet there will be a lot more government spending making its way to the industry. There is already a major labor shortage in nursing, and this is only bound to increase as the boomers

Which Industries Are the Safest in a Recession? continued...

continue to age and need more services, more often. Others will continue to get sick and be treated whether they can afford care or not. In fact, according to the site WheretheJobsAre.org, there are more than 54,000 projected hires in medical and public health positions by 2012.

Education: Children in the United States are still guaranteed schooling until the 12th grade, and many states are perennially experiencing teacher shortages, especially as a large number of current teachers reach retirement age. Also, laid-off or unsatisfied adults are returning to school in record numbers, creating opportunities in adult education. (See page 349 for more on teaching degrees and careers in education.)

Accounting: Don't lump this one in with "finance." It has been hot since federal regulations forced companies to get serious about their books a few years ago, and when times are tough, more people look for accountants to help them pinch every penny they can. To become a Certified Public Accountant (CPA), you'll need to pass the Uniform CPA Exam, which requires serious studying and potential prep courses beforehand. Google "State Boards of Accountancy" to find the eligibility requirements to sit for the exam in your state.

Agriculture and Utilities: The economy may be sickly, but the first things people pay for are food to eat and gas to heat their homes. These jobs are not affected by the loss of discretionary income and will remain intact.

Local Service Sector: Every town needs at least one plumber, electrician, and hairstylist. During a recession, just make sure you live somewhere where the demand outweighs the supply.

Local, State, and Federal Government: The government keeps on chugging, even when the country's in a hole. Generally speaking, budget cuts don't tend to affect the jobs of public safety officers, court clerks, administrative service managers, and other such positions. (For more information on government jobs, see page 62.) ■

Organization

Many people will zero in on a particular organization where they want to work. But what is it about that organization that they like? Is it the actual company (e.g., they've wanted to work for F.A.O. Schwartz ever since seeing *Big*)? Or is it the "type" of organization (e.g., small, large)? These are two very important factors when considering which organization you want to work for.

If you are dead set on a specific company and want to get your foot in the door today, focus on the long-term and don't let the quality of the jobs offered today derail your pursuit. Few people would willingly choose "intern" or "administrative assistant" from a lineup of job titles at a company. But if you ask them if they want to be an "account manager" or a "vice president" at that same company, they'd probably sing a different tune. Sometimes you just have to start in the proverbial mailroom.

While we're all about your applying to your dream employer, just consider that it might not be wise to put all of your job-hunting eggs in only the basket of a single company. After all, what happens if there's a hiring freeze? According to Jason Hill, a managing partner at a staffing firm in New York, you should always pursue your dream company while also casting a wider net: "If you want to work at Goldman

---

Tips & Tricks:
Look at mid-sized and small companies

 Particularly in a competitive job market, it's key to expand your search beyond big companies. Smaller companies can have specific hiring needs at any given time, and their scale allows them to be a bit stealthier than their unwieldy competitors. To capitalize as a hunter, you too must be stealthy, because opportunities at these companies don't always show up on job boards, and it isn't even always easy to learn about smaller-sized organizations. A great first place to turn to find interesting companies is *Inc.* magazine's "Inc. 5000" (available at inc500.com). It's an annual report of the fastest-growing private companies in America, many of which have 50 employees or less. In addition, be vigilant about tracking industry news to see who the new movers and shakers are. Then cold call. If a company just received venture capital funding, launched a breakout product or service, or got acquired by a larger entity, be the first one to reach out. While you might not like prospects of cold calling, the good news is, you're a lot more likely to get through to someone in a hiring position at a smaller company than when you attempt to navigate the labyrinth of a large corporation.

Career Options

> *Tips & Tricks:*
> **Top entry-level employers**
>
> If you're not sure which organizations to target, why not start with the ones most likely to hire someone of your experience level? Seems like a smart move to us. Luckily for you, every year CollegeGrad.com compiles a list of companies that hire the greatest number of entry-level employees, which includes familiar names like Verizon Wireless, Progressive Insurance, and Boeing. But have you ever heard of BearingPoint, Epic Systems, and Schlumberger? It's definitely worth taking a browse through the list over at collegegrad.com/topemployers, which also includes a link to their top internships list as well.

Sachs, for example, you should be thinking, 'Who are Goldman's competitors?' And then you should network with people at those firms, schedule informational interviews, and research what the companies are all about." You should also be looking at companies that act as feeders into the company that is your first choice.

Whether you've chosen to pursue a specific company or not, it's important to recognize that each organization fits into a general 'type' related to its size, culture, and way of doing business. Clearly, there are organizations that buck the trend (in the same way there are Swiss people who are actually quite bellicose). But it's worth considering the most common pros and cons associated with each so that you can figure out which types fit your personality, skills, and career goals best.

Large Corporation (e.g., Target, JPMorgan, Johnson & Johnson)

Pretty much any company whose ads you've seen or products you've used would fall within this category.

Pros: Formalized training, extensive benefits, job security (sort of), room for advancement, resume-building, geographically diverse assignments (including international locations), vast resources.

Cons: Bureaucratic, potential to be pigeonholed into functional role, lack of autonomy, slow advancement, "corporate" culture off-putting to some people.

Professional Service Firm
(e.g., Skadden Arps, Deloitte, Ogilvy & Mather)

These are firms that provide financial, legal, accounting, advertising, consulting, or other services to large corporations.

Pros: Hands-on training, high-level work, very good benefits, strong network-building potential, large class of young colleagues, resume-building, great pay.

Cons: Intense work schedule, tough to maintain work/life balance (i.e., you may travel frequently or be constantly on-call for clients), lower job security (if a client leaves, firm loses staff), high turnover typical, managers inconsistently interested in junior staff, very hierarchical.

Start-Up Company

This is a growth-oriented new company that is in its early stages of development. If it's a real start-up, you probably haven't heard of it yet, unless someone you know is working there or you surf the start-up blogs. (For more on start-ups, see page 60.)

Pros: Exciting pace, quick advancement, skill-building, ability to influence decisions, relationship-building with colleagues, low bureaucracy, chance to gain equity, less "corporate" environment.

Cons: Limited resources, low job security, low success rate, potential low pay, lack of good benefits (sometimes), high commitment (expectation to "live and breathe" the company), less structured.

Small Business/Office
(e.g., doctor's office, independent store/service)

These are businesses with staffs of 100 people or less. Most businesses fall within this category.

Pros: Low bureaucracy, flexibility, skill-building/practical know-how, high client interaction (good if you're a people person).

Cons: Fewer resources, lower job security, less generous benefits, often personality-driven, less well-known/reduced resume cachet, ceiling on advancement, functionally oriented roles.

Career Options

Nonprofit and Government
(e.g., Clinton Foundation, Department of Labor)

In very simple terms, these are organizations or entities that work towards the achievement of a specific goal or that tackle/manage a set of issues (rather than seek to make a fiscal profit). Examples include all branches of federal, state, and local government, as well as NGOs, museums, universities, hospitals, and local charitable organizations. For more on government jobs, see page 62; for nonprofits, go to page 66.

Pros: Pro-social mission, job security, good work-life balance, potentially interesting work.

Cons: Bureaucratic, slow advancement, potentially low pay, frustration arising from lack of funding and/or resources.

Function

Career Options

Every grad should have a dream. But once you've finished indulging abstract fantasies like having "a career in film" or "working with animals," it's time to think about what you actually want to do on a day-to-day basis. This doesn't mean you should give up on film and/or animals (after all, the *Air Bud* director did pretty well for himself). It simply means that you should be honest with yourself about whether going on coffee runs for a director or grooming show cats will really fulfill you on a daily basis and help you meet your career goals. While a prestigious company or the allure of a certain industry may seem cool for a second, the things you actually *do* at work are what will determine whether you are happy or not and move your career forward.

If you think you know exactly what you want to do professionally, then speak to people who are doing it and figure out if you can jump in right after college or if you're going to have to take a more circuitous route from a job-function perspective (i.e., it's a great idea to work for an accountant before you decide to become one). In order to truly succeed you also need to enjoy what you're doing. So if the thought of sitting at a desk behind a computer all day (note: playing video games and surfing Perez Hilton doesn't count) scares you, you should consider a job that involves more extensive and regular face-to-face interaction, like a sales position or a job in a hospitality organization. If you like to play with spreadsheets and numbers, then maybe finance or accounting would be a good fit. And if you're not sure what you'd like to do at all, talk to people who perform different functions and ask them what their typical day looks like. They may give you the old "my job is so exciting, there is no typical day" line. Don't let them off the hook that easily; ask them what their most boring day looks like— and find out how often these days occur. Better yet, try to follow them around for a day or two.

In addition, when exploring job functions, recognize that in the working world you can often leverage your natural talents more fully than you did at school. In academia, there are few classes where being hilarious or being able to sweet-talk clients really helps you that much. But out there beyond the ivory tower, there are jobs that match all sorts of talents. Do you have a nice way with children? Do you have an extraordinarily refined palate? Can you stay up extremely late? All of these are marketable skills in the working world. The key is to determine where your talents will be valued and then figure out how to sell them effectively.

If you're still not sure what the hell we mean by "function" and are slightly scared we're talking about something to do with math, here are some examples of high-level functions to give you an idea:

Management	Design/Production
Sales	Technology
Advertising	Legal
Finance	Copywriting
Operations	IT
Accounting	Sales
Human Resources	Public Relations
Product Development	Admin

Career Options

A company of significant size will have staff in every high-level function described above. For example, at General Mills there are Managers, Marketers, Finance Staff, Operations Staff, Accounting, Human Resources, R&D, etc. They'll also have more specialized functions. And there are even more functions that don't even require the confines of a big corporate structure. To explore these, step into The Wide World of Jobs! (on the following page)

The Wide World of Jobs

Sometimes the pre-graduation job rush can make the working world feel remarkably small and generic. As so many of your classmates vie for similar jobs, it's easy to forget that in addition to traditional career paths, there are thousands of niche jobs (and just plain bizarre jobs) that might appeal to you if you keep an open mind. Take the time to consider jobs that you may have never heard of—they are often the most interesting. We don't necessarily expect you to find your calling by looking at the list below, but here are 51 not-so-average jobs to get the wheels turning...

Environmental Engineer	Internet Entrepreneur	Franchise Owner
Archaeologist	Graphic Designer	PR Executive
Nonprofit Fundraiser	Sommelier	Dog Walker
Astronaut	Advertising Salesperson	Chef
Civil Servant	Photographer	Fashion Buyer
Car Reviewer	Website Programmer	Video Game Tester
Travel Writer	College Student Advisor	Interior Designer
Tutor	Musician	Personal Assistant
Pharmacist	Social Worker	Radiologist
Alaskan Crab Fisherman	Ski/Surf Instructor	Tour Guide
Teacher/Professor	A&R Rep	Flight Attendant
Wedding Planner	Head Hunter	Blogger
Construction Manager	HR Manager	Actor
Real Estate Agent	Farmer	Financial Advisor
Paralegal	Talent Agent	Art Gallery Manager
Management Consultant	Truck Driver	Actuary
Stock Agent	Airline Pilot	Computer Systems Analyst

Changing Industries, Functions, and/or Organizations

As your career story evolves, it's likely that you will want to switch it up in terms of the function you play at work, the type of organization you work at, or the industry in which you work (or all three). There's no reason why you can't try out a number of different combinations over the course of your life, but be strategic about how you do so.

"You can change your functional area or the industry you're in, but it's tough to change both at the same time," says Michelle Kedem, a cofounder of recruitment firm On-Ramps. For example, if you do HR for a pharmaceutical company and you really want to do marketing for a book publisher, you might consider using your HR background to snag a publishing job and then change functions once you've established yourself in the company.

Another approach to making a big switcheroo is to be willing to start at the bottom, possibly even as an intern. In some cases, grad school (Chapter 9) can also provide a natural way to shift toward a new career, though you need to go into it with a clear goal. Beyond that, there's always good old-fashioned elbow grease (and luck).

Web Links:
Researching Career Options, Companies, and Industries

Whether you've decided to pursue a specific career or are just exploring your options, there are a ton of online resources that provide background information on companies and industries as a whole. These sites also provide cover letter and resume writing advice, job search tips, and useful tools. For our advice on resumes and cover letters, see page 93.

GRADSPOT.COM (listed first due to contractual obligations!). If you don't find what you're looking for in this book, check out our website for over 100 survival guides and tons of other content to help you with your job hunt (and anything else life after college throws your way).

VAULT.COM. If you haven't come across it yet, Vault is a key piece of weaponry in your job-hunting arsenal. The website offers free company rankings in many different industries that can provide a useful overview of who the players are in any given field. The most invaluable tools, however, are its industry guides ($15–$20), which provide a pretty good rundown on what employers are looking for in that industry, along with sample interview questions and other goodies. And while the job board section is kind of a dud, the comprehensive company guides ($16.65 per month) have relevant information on specific companies (though you can most likely find a lot of the same stuff with some Googling). Just make sure to check with your college career office before shelling out any cash; many colleges offer their students free access to Vault.

WETFEET.COM AND GLASSDOOR.COM. WetFeet is an extensive online "magazine" for job seekers, providing articles about the job search, as well as industry and company overviews. It's a good complement to the job-hunting tips you'll find on Gradspot. Glassdoor is like a cheat sheet for interviews: Previous candidates who interviewed at particular companies give the lowdown on the questions they were asked. It also provides company reviews and salary information.

OCCUPATIONAL OUTLOOK HANDBOOK (www.bls.gov/oco). Produced by the Bureau of Labor Statistics, this handbook provides you with important information for a ton of different jobs—including education and training requirements, earnings, working conditions, and what the role entails on a day-to-day basis. If you have some idea of what job or field you might like (i.e., "I want to be an engineer but am not sure what kinds of engineering work is out there"), this is a resource that will allow you to dig deeper.

SALARY.COM. It's basically what it says it is: information on how much you will make in certain jobs in a given geographic location. If you're thinking of moving to a new city to pursue a job, match up your expected salary with average rents to see if you'll be living large or living on the streets (p. 198).

We've just highlighted the key resources you need to research a variety of careers. However, they are by no means the final word. Some other helpful websites include QuintCareers.com, OneDayOneJob.com, and JobWeb.com. And don't forget about actual people—chatting with people you know can also help to crystallize your goals and help you figure out how to make the next step.

Ask The Expert:
Doing What You Love

After meeting at the University of Pennsylvania, emcee Naledge and producer Double-O formed the rap duo Kidz in the Hall. In 2006, they released their critically acclaimed debut School Was My Hustle on Rawkus Records. We talked to Naledge about translating an Ivy League degree into a rap career.

What other careers did you consider when you left college? I was interested in music journalism, public relations, and possibly advertising. Whatever I ended up doing was going to involve the world of media and entertainment.

How did you make the decision to pursue music full-time? I did what most of us artists call "jumping off the ledge." I just quit my job cold turkey and told myself I was going to either sink or swim. I lived for a year as a starving artist in Los Angeles. Eventually I made enough contacts and got enough people interested in my music that I knew a deal was going to come. I wouldn't have been able to survive if it wasn't for the money I saved while I worked at a public relations firm.

Did you receive any discouragement from parents, friends, or teachers? My parents supported me 100%. To most of my teachers, hip-hop music was a foreign world, so they would often stress to me that I needed to use my education as a backup plan. Most of my friends thought I was crazy to not go the conventional route and get a corporate job. Most of them didn't think that I could really get a record deal. Oddly, they are the same ones that say they believed in me all along.

Do you have any advice for recent graduates who feel pressure to get a traditional job instead of pursuing their passions? Chasing your true passion is always going to be more rewarding, but it is key to be realistic about your situation. Sometimes you will need to supplement your passion with a "9-to-5."

Are there good and bad reasons for getting involved in a creative industry? The monetary return is not always great, but you will be much more emotionally rich. ■

Career Options

Where to Actually Find a Full-Time Job

A job search is a rite of passage, and no rite of passage would be complete without a ritual. Don't worry, you don't have to shave a Labradoodle and burn its hair in a terra cotta oven—this ritual is all about making a commitment to scan job listings on a regular basis. It can become a bit of an obsession, but that's okay—you don't want to miss out on an awesome job just because you don't have your head in the game.

After browsing the major sites like Monster.com, CareerBuilder.com, Indeed.com and, yes, Craigslist, it's time to get down to the nitty-gritty. Each industry has its go-to destination for job postings, so it's important to know where to look. While you're at it, always take advantage of any job leads your school can send your way.

YOUR ALMA MATER. Recent college grads have three unique and effective resources at their fingertips, and many grads get their jobs through one of these avenues:

- *College Office of Career Services.* Not only will the office hook you up with other alums on similar career paths, but it may also furnish you with openings from companies that are specifically targeting your school, on-campus interviews, and networking sessions with companies interested in hiring.

- *Alumni networks.* For some reason, Hoyas like helping other Hoyas, Tarheels follow Tarheels, and so on and so forth. Contacting fellow alumni can put you on the receiving end of some odd reminiscences (you might not want to know about the Class of '66's penchant for streaking), but it is a must for anybody on the job hunt.

- *Professors.* Often, the people with the coolest jobs are the ones who were set up by professors that took an interest in their futures. Think about professors with whom you've developed a special rapport and talk to them. They might have some great ideas.

INVESTMENT BANKING & CONSULTING. The best time to apply for an entry-level finance or consulting position is in the late summer to early fall, a year before you'd start working. Since most major banks and consulting firms have structured programs for their entry-level employees, they hire the majority of their recent grads during this time. Your first step should be to try applying through your career office, which may have preexisting recruiting relationships with companies. However, if you've been otherwise instructed, or a specific firm that you're interested in doesn't recruit on your campus, you can apply to any of the major banks and consulting firms directly through their websites. Investment banks like Citigroup and Goldman Sachs accept online applications, as do consulting firms such as Boston Consulting Group, Bain & Company, McKinsey, Monitor, and Mercer. Note that this list doesn't even scratch the surface for potential employers in these fields. You should also check out a financial headhunter organization (e.g., glocap.com) that can find you placements at a variety of companies, though these companies will generally only work with more experienced candidates.

If you have an interest in a particular industry group (such as energy, industrials, financial institutions) contact the bank's HR rep and let him/her know. This could potentially lift you towards the top of the pile when resumes are distributed amongst particular groups.

If things don't go your way this time around and you're willing to work beyond New York, Chicago, Los Angeles, et al., try pursuing work at a small, regional firm (there are several throughout the country). This will ensure that you won't fall behind your peers and after about a year of work, you can reapply for a job with the big boys with an enhanced resume in tow.

For more information on pursuing a career in investment banking, we highly recommend procuring a copy of the Vault *Career Guide to Investment Banking*, a.k.a the bible when it comes to landing an I-banking gig. Same goes with Vault's guide to consulting.

NEW MEDIA & MARKETING/ADVERTISING. In light of the shifting forms of media consumption from traditional media to innovative online formats, marketing/advertising is an incredibly interesting field to get into right now. New media gigs are listed on PaidContent.org and MediaBistro.com, and start-ups are always on the lookout for marketing directors, researchers, and content producers (keep reading for a list of job boards for start-ups). Joining one of the major marketing/advertising companies (e.g., Grey, Ogilvy, BBDO, Digitas, Razorfish) might be a smart first step. Check with your career services office for firms that recruit at your school, and browse the career sections on the websites of any companies that pique your interest.

Career Options

> **Hazard:**
> **Don't spend money to get a job**
>
> Regardless of which career resources you end up using, check with your school's career office prior to shelling out cash for any subscription fees that might pop up. More often than not, career offices will offer free subscriptions to their students and alumni. That said, be prepared to shell out a few dollars here and there for resume photocopies at Kinko's, stamps for mailing applications, etc.

PUBLISHING & JOURNALISM. If it's a career in publishing or journalism you seek, check out Mediabistro.com, Ed2010.com, Mandy.com, journalism school listings, IWantMedia.com, and even *Variety*. For listings in the book world, BookJobs.com and PublishersMarketplace.com are good options. After surveying those resources, it often helps to go straight to the source in this industry. Track down your favorite websites and publications online, then check to see if they have a "Careers" section. Don't be dismayed if you only see internship programs—while we know you see yourself as editor-in-chief, sometimes internships are the only way to develop the contacts and clips you'll need to get there. (For more on interning, see page 73.) You should also find out who owns the magazine/newspaper/website where you want to work. For example, the Condé Nast media empire includes *Vogue*, *GQ*, *Wired*, and *The New Yorker*. Maybe you know someone at a publication that falls under the same umbrella as the one you want to work at, or maybe you can get a gig at *Teen Vogue* but not *Vanity Fair*—at least you'll gain access to the Condé Nast HR department (and what we hear is a ridiculously delicious cafeteria). That connection alone will give you a leg up on the competition when the next *Vanity Fair* position opens up.

START-UPS. Becoming CEO of a start-up company is easy—just make some business cards and announce your new position on your Facebook profile! However, another (usually better) option for getting involved with a start-up company is to join an existing one. There are thousands of new companies started each year, and there are two distinct approaches to finding the opportunities they create. The first approach is to check out niche sites that list start-up jobs. These include VentureLoop.com, Startuply.com, PartnerUp.com, HotStartupJobs.com, and StartupZone.com, as well as the job listing boards of entrepreneur-focused blogs like TechCrunch.com (which is tech-focused), PaidContent.com (publishing and media), and more. The other way to look for an opportunity is to work in reverse: First find the start-ups and then see if they're hiring (keep in mind that a successful start-up—i.e., the type you want to work for—is continuously growing and most likely looking for people). To do this, you just need to stay on top of the industries you're interested in, because people will always be talking about up-and-coming companies. Check out industry rags, read more general magazines like *Entrepreneur* and *Inc.*, and follow relevant blogs and Twitter feeds (p. 212) to stay up on the latest news.

PARALEGAL & LAB WORK. For paralegal positions, check out ParalegalJobs.com, EmploymentSpot.com, or the paralegal jobs forum at Indeed. com. Besides searching for paralegal positions, also look for "legal assistant" gigs. These terms are often used interchangeably, although there is actually a paralegal certification, which requires a bachelor's degree, some coursework, and passing an exam (many firms don't need you to be certified). Along with looking at job boards, identify large firms in your city by going to Vault.com and ILRG.com. Once you've found them, go straight to the companies' websites, which should have an employment section and information about the nature of the position and the experience requirements. If you're considering law school, being a paralegal is a great way to see up close if the lawyer life is right for you. For lab jobs, check out eLabRat.com, lab positions at Indeed.com, or postings at university medical schools.

ENTERTAINMENT. Want to be a big-time shot caller in Hollywood? Working at an agency is the traditional route for getting a foot in the door in Hollywood, and everyone has to start in the mailroom before moving up to a "desk" (basically acting as an agent's assistant). You can look for these entry-level gigs at Variety.com or go directly to the websites of agencies like United Talent Agency (UTA) and William Morris Endeavor.

If *Entourage* has turned you off to the whole agency thing, we don't blame you. However, getting a job in the biz (even getting hired as a lowly production assistant) is rougher than Zach Galifinakis' beard. For the most part, jobs are circulated by word of mouth so connections are key. If you're looking to pursue a career in television, your best bet is to find the production office phone number for every show you can think of (these can be found calling the main number of the show's network… you can easily find those via Google). Start calling around June (that's when shows usually staff) and ask if they are looking for any openings.

If motion pictures are more your bag, try your luck by calling some of the major production companies such as Sony and Warner Brothers and ask to be connected with HR. You might have better luck getting in touch with smaller companies such as Ron Howard's Imagine Entertainment (peruse imdb.com for a list of such companies). Internships (see page 73) are also a major stepping stone towards landing a full-time gig. Again, the key word is connections. Connections. Connections!

GOVERNMENT & NONPROFIT. Finding government jobs is unlike searching for any other for-profit opportunity. As a result, we've devoted the entire next section to them. We also discuss the nonprofit industry in detail starting on page 66.

"OTHER." If you don't see the industry you hope to enter here, don't despair. In fact, the best way to find a job remains your alma mater's career office, because if a company lists a position there, you know it has a vested interest in your school (and, by extension, you). Unfortunately, not even your career office will have every job you want. If it doesn't, head over to your dream employer's website and apply directly. If you know the industry that interests you but not the companies that might have openings, check out one of the job information resources we listed on page 56 to find lists of the top employers by industry. Finally, you can always cold call a company to find out what positions they have available. You've got nothing to lose, and you could end up being tipped off about a job that has not yet been publicly announced.

Ask The Expert:
How Do I Start My Own Business?

The current state of the job market is forcing more and more grads to reconsider their options for employment opportunities and think outside the box. One of the benefits of this has been a recent boom of young entrepreneurs taking matters into their own hands and forming their very own companies. Starting your own business is no easy task, but if you have a great idea and a strong game plan you can become a successful business owner in a matter of months. Natasha Case and Freya Estreller are the visionaries behind the Coolhaus ice cream sandwich company. Since officially launching their company in April of 2009 with an ice cream sandwich truck at the Coachella Valley Music Festival, their enterprise has grown to include a fleet of three trucks in Los Angeles, as well as distribution to several restaurants and shops across LA and Austin. A storefront in LA and two New York trucks are set to launch in June of 2011. Below, they offer ten tips on how to get your DIY business (in any industry) off and running.

1) Find a product or service that fills a niche and that you're passionate about. Develop your idea, do initial research online.

2) Create a business plan and financial model to understand your idea's potential/profitability. You can find templates by searching Entrepreneur.com.

3) Explain your concept to family/friends. Use them as guinea pigs and gather feedback via surveys with questions such as "Would they pay $____ for this?" "How often would they utilize the business?"

4) Bootstrap: Start producing your concept and creating the brand as cheaply as possible so that you can test the business on a larger pool but without too much initial investment.

5) Create your corporation (llc/s-corp/c-corp). Obtain necessary permits, tax id's, etc. If a lawyer is outside of your budget capabilities, check out MyCorporation.com and LegalZoom.com.

6) Bring a business plan before investors (could be family and friends if little capital is required, or an angel investor if larger capital is required).

7) Use initial capital as the operating budget to get necessary equipment/infrastructure (office, website, utilities), but remember to pay yourself! If you can't pay yourself the business model doesn't work.

8) Start hiring the right people (hire slow, fire fast). Create the organizational controls, systems and structure so the business can eventually operate without you.

9) Do PR! Get the word out as much as possible about your business; utilize any connections possible (i.e. media connections—people who work for publications, blogs, etc.) to publicize your newly launched business and bring in as many customers as possible. A launch party/event is also helpful so that there is something newsworthy to focus the new attention on your business. Utilize Twitter and Facebook to get the word out for free.

10) Keep your eye on the prize, don't give up, and stay positive. There will be a lot of bumps in the road and you have to believe in yourself, your team and your product. ■

Career Options

Government Jobs

Though Walmart is forever doing its damndest to catch up, the largest employer in the United States remains the government, so we thought it made sense to dig a little deeper into various opportunities offered by Uncle Sam.

In addition to offering an unlimited variety of positions, the government is an ideal employer for recent grads because it offers excellent job security (workers joke that only an act of Congress could threaten their job); a reasonably good salary (salaries start at $27,000, and long-term salaries can exceed $100k); and great benefits, retirement plans, and student debt forgiveness ($10,000 per year, up to $60,000 total).

If we've piqued your interest, let's consider some of the options you can pursue at the three main levels of government: federal, state, and local. Before you dive into this job pool, be sure to clean up your Facebook profile (see page 92); we hear the CIA is a stake-holder.

Federal Jobs

The federal government alone has over 1.9 million employees. That's not hard to imagine when you consider that it's composed of over 100 different agencies, from the Department of Education to the CIA. And the best part? They're all understaffed! Enter you.

Pick an Agency, Any Agency

The first step in looking for a federal job is to figure out what's important to you. A great place to start exploring opportunities is the exhibit published by the U.S. Office of Personnel Management's (OPM) that matches undergrad majors to agencies, located at http://www.usajobs.opm.gov/ei23.asp. Or, you can begin by just browsing a list of federal agencies at USA.gov. Finally, take some time to check out "The Best Places to Work in the Federal Government" (data.bestplacestowork.org)—the result of an annual employee satisfaction report—as well as "Where the Jobs Are" (data.wherethejobsare.org), a continually updated report of projected job openings at agencies. Just keep in mind that as you peruse the smorgasbord of federal agencies, some might be located in D.C., while others (85%) are scattered across the U.S., and 44,000 position are housed abroad.

Classifications of Federal Jobs

There are two different ways that federal jobs are classified: according to preferred applicant criteria and according to pay scale. When it comes to applicant criteria, Competitive Service positions are open to anyone, but Excepted Service positions favor candidates with specific credentials (e.g., veterans).

Pay is measured according to the General Schedule (GS) pay scale, which ranges from GS-1 to GS-15. As a recent college graduate, you should be looking at jobs classified between GS-5 and GS-7, which have average starting salaries of between $27,000 and $33,000, respectively. If you go to grad school first, you'll be able to enter most agencies at GS-9, with a starting salary of $44,000. (See Chapter 9 for more information on grad school.)

Where to Find Federal Openings

Once you've determined which agency might make sense for you, the best place to look for an opening is www.usajobs.gov. While a majority of federal government opportunities are listed there, some will be listed exclusively on the specific agency's website, and thus it's always worth looking at both. You can also give govcentral.monster.com a glance—it's more of a free for all, but you never know when you might find something perfect that you would have otherwise missed.

Applying to Federal Positions

When applying, attention to detail is key. Many agencies will enable you to fill out an entire application online (usually through www.usajobs.gov or through their own website), but be mindful that your resume for a government job will have to be more comprehensive than one for a private sector application (see page 94 for more on resumes). Many agencies will request a resume that lists all of your work experience, the number of hours you worked per week at each, and what you were paid. So don't be surprised if your resume goes beyond one page; this is the one time that's okay. For certain jobs, you'll also have to complete a Knowledge, Skills and Abilities (KSA) assessment. Throughout the application process, resist the temptation to lie, even about drugs. The truth will come out, whether through a polygraph (administered if you require security clearance) or extensive background checks.

Capitol Hill

While many people use the terms "Capitol Hill" and "D.C." interchangeably, Capitol Hill actually refers to a specific subset of the federal government—most notably, positions with congressmen, senators, and lobbyists. Not surprisingly, it's a breeding ground for politicians and people who want to network with decision-makers. While the pay is not great and the hours can be more grueling than other government jobs, many people think Capitol Hill is an unparalleled place to start a successful career in anything.

Tips & Tricks:
Campaign Your Way In

 Whether you volunteer for a political campaign or work as a full-time staffer, the experience you'll get in this high-stakes environment can be huge when you're applying for a government job. Look out for local election posters, browse local papers for major legislation, and stop by your city or town hall to see if there's any way you can lend a hand. Candidates and groups pushing legislation will have websites providing clear instructions on how to join the cause. And don't think this is only appropriate if you want a job on Capitol Hill. It can also help if you want to pursue opportunities in state and local government, as well. The best part is that if the campaign goes well, there might be a job waiting for you when your boss becomes mayor (or whatever he or she was running for).

Finding Capitol Hill Jobs

There are two approaches to looking for opportunities. The first is traditional networking. Try to snag a position with a representative from your state and comb your personal network to see if you have any connections. If that route doesn't have legs, you can default to job boards. RCJobs.com and OPAJobs.com offer a smattering of full-time opportunities, and HillZoo.com offers a mixture of full-time and intern work.

Working on Capitol Hill

The most common entry-level positions are Staff Assistant gigs. You'll have to answer the phones, sort through mail, receive appointments, do research, manage interns, and generally be the office factotum. Ultimately, however, your lifestyle will depend upon the representative that you work for; if he or she is a "family person" that goes home by 7pm most nights, so will you. But it could easily go the other way. In addition to Staff Assistant, you should also consider interning (interns are called "pages" on the Hill), which is a great way to test the waters and get a foot in the door.

State & Local Agencies

State and local governments employ approximately eight million Americans and are planning to hire another 1.4 million within the next ten years. When job prospects are looking rough, this is the employer to turn to.

The Difference between Federal and Local and State

Local and state governments are literally the local versions of the federal government, with some extra offices. For example, there's a Federal Department of Transportation, and there's a local and state one, as well. There's Congress, and then there's the State Assembly. Conveniently enough, local and state positions are easier to snag, and you have more geographic security because you know you'll always be working in your state. According to the Bureau of Labor Statistics, work schedules are also more lenient. On the flip side, the pay scale for local and state positions is slightly lower than federal, but it's still competitive.

Finding a Local or State Position

Locating job opportunities on the local and state level is a bit trickier than it is on the federal level. Most state agencies won't post jobs on major boards, instead keeping them on their own websites. Tracking them down requires some handy-dandy Googling and use of the admittedly shady-looking directory of local and state government job websites found on 50statejobs.com/gov.html. Govcentral.monster.com is worth a shot—when you search it, make sure to include "State of..." and "City of..." as keywords. If you're more interested in the local politician route (e.g., working for a state assemblyman or mayor), you should take a similar approach as you would for finding a Capitol Hill job (see page 64). Look for connections, browse the boards, or find issues that matter to you and then match them with politicians' causes.

Career Options

Nonprofit Jobs

Although the government is a nonprofit entity, most people associate nonprofit work with "doing something good for the world," not working for the Department of Transportation. But even this distinction is thin—there are over ten million U.S. citizens working for nongovernmental nonprofits, and you can be sure that not all of them spend their days saving Africans or dispensing aid to hurricane survivors. So before you dive into the nonprofit world head (or heart) first, let's take a moment to consider what types of jobs are available, as well as the challenges and rewards you can expect if you take the plunge.

The (Very) Wide World of Nonprofit Jobs

If you can think of a cause you care about, there's most likely a nonprofit that focuses on it. But in addition to things like "rehabilitating dogs with no legs" and "teaching inner-city kids to play badminton," you should think about the institutions and services that serve the greater good—such as public television and museums—since many of these are operated on a not-for-profit basis too. To give you a sense of how varied the nonprofit sector is, here is just a handful of organizations that fall under this umbrella: *American Cancer Society, American Red Cross, Bill & Melinda Gates Foundation, Carnegie Hall, Council of Better Business Bureaus, Inc., Ford Foundation, Habitat for Humanity and, The Metropolitan Museum of Art.*

The Importance of Funding

Unlike for-profit organizations that are capitalized by their shareholders or government organizations that are funded by taxes, nonprofits live and die by funding, which comes primarily in the form of donations from individuals and other organizations (including the government, in some cases). The result is one hell of a double-edged sword for an employee of a nonprofit. On the one hand, it's incredibly exciting to be able to focus all of your effort on a specific cause instead of worrying about financial returns or the public at large. On the other hand, depending upon the economic and political environment, funding can be tough to come by, and when the well runs dry, your hands are tied.

The funding issue also trickles down to the everyday realities of nonprofit work in two key ways. First, since resources are so limited, nonprofits can only afford to hire individuals who are able to add value starting day one, which makes it more difficult for a recent grad to snag a nonprofit gig. Second, most nonprofit organizations' employees are generally paid less than an individual fulfilling the same functional role in a for-profit job. (Presumably you're not considering nonprofit work as a get-rich quick scheme, though.)

Ultimately, funding issues may be a hard pill to swallow, but if you're the type to say, "Let's do the best we can with the resources we have," you may flourish in this line of work.

Browsing and Evaluating Nonprofits

Just because a nonprofit supports a cause you believe in doesn't necessarily make it a good organization. You need to research it as you would any other company. The first place to turn is CharityNavigator.org, which provides reviews of nonprofit organizations based on their effectiveness and funding. If you don't know which nonprofits you want to investigate in the first place, a great resource is the "Causes" application on Facebook; just browse through the hundreds of thousands of causes to find associated nonprofits. Once you're sure you believe in an organization's mission, its funding should be the second-most-important characteristic you focus on. A great place to turn to in order to gauge an organization's financial health is GuideStar.org.

If you can't find your target nonprofit in any of these places, that doesn't necessarily mean it's a money-laundering operation. Call them directly to make sure they're a registered 501(c) organization (i.e., a licensed U.S. charity); if you're interested in working there, they should be willing to answer all your questions about funding and milestones.

Applying to Nonprofit Jobs

Nonprofits in general don't plaster job postings all over newspapers, websites, and colleges like for-profit organizations might. Instead, they tend to list openings primarily on their websites or major nonprofit job boards. If you are down to wade through hundreds of openings, then the folks at Idealist.org will quickly become your best friends. (Idealist.org also publishes a free e-book about nonprofits, which you can download from its resources section.) In addition to Idealist, The Foundation Center (http://fconline.foundationcenter.org/) offers a great jobs newsletter.

Once you apply for a nonprofit job, steel yourself for a competitive process. While your passion for the cause is practically a prerequisite, it's your relevant skills and prior experience that will set you apart (they don't usually have the money or time to train you, so they'll need you to be able to hit the ground

Career Options

> ### Hazard:
> #### How to get past the resume robots
>
> Because some companies and hiring centers get such an enormous volume of applications, they actually use automated computer programs to serve as a preliminary screening mechanism for resumes. One such resume-scanning system is Resumix, which is used by government agencies. It may sound like something out of *Minority Report*, but it's the way things are, so you need to know how to sweet talk the robots (hint: they have no feelings!). The trick is to "optimize" your resume for the process of being trolled by keyword crawlers. Software like Resumix creates "skill buckets" for every job, based on keywords—if your resume does not contain the skills searched by the robot, then it's *adios, amigo*. Your best bet is to study the language used in the job posting and parrot it back in your resume. ResumeEdge.com suggests that if the posting doesn't actually mention specific skills, you should search for similar jobs and use them to create a list of the top 25 skills required for that job. (You may also be able to find relevant skills by reading profiles of professions on Vault.com.) In addition to skills, the robots will look for required years of experience (if appropriate) or any other basic qualifications, so make sure you meet these and include them in your resume.

running). Remember that nonprofits need people who can fulfill specific functional roles just like for-profit companies. Do you want to be a researcher? Do you want to be in admin (e.g., accounting, HR, fundraising)? Do you want to deliver relief services and be "on the ground?" Thinking about where you fit into an organization is crucial when you're on the job hunt.

Alternative Routes to Finding a Nonprofit Opportunity

If your heart is dead-set on a specific organization and you don't have the skills to snag a position today, look for volunteer positions or internships (p. 73) that will help you build your story, skill set, and resume prior to applying. Another approach is building skills in the for-profit sector and then using those skills to transition to a nonprofit down the line. Indeed, nonprofits often value candidates with private sector experience because many of the job functions are transferable, and they may have important connections to fundraising sources. If you do decide to take this roundabout route into the nonprofit world, just be sure to stay involved with the causes you care about through volunteering or pro bono work. Those private sector paychecks can be addictive though, so watch out!

Another way to dive right into nonprofit work that's custom-made for recent grads is through term of service opportunities. These include positions with organizations like AmeriCorps, the Peace Corps, and Teach for America, and they usually require an initial training period before you're sent off into the field. While they might not pay you a salary, they sometimes provide stipends, benefits, places to live, debt forgiveness, tuition help, and more. (Note: AmeriCorps and Peace Corps are both government agencies, but they provide work opportunities that people would associate more with "nonprofits" than traditional government work, and as a result, provide a great introduction to both the government and nonprofit sectors.)

Freelancing

Are you someone who literally can't stand the idea of working a 9-to-5? Do you want to set your own hours, name your own price, and rarely get fully dressed? If so, freelancing might be for you. It may take a while to establish yourself, but once you hit your stride as a freelancer, you can work from anywhere, determine your own schedule, accept or refuse projects as you wish, and drink on the job!

Beyond flexibility, freelancing is a great way for recent grads to explore various interests and skills without committing to a full-time position. Plus, in the age of outsourcing, it's becoming increasingly common for companies to seek outside consultants and freelancers who can work on a project-to-project basis. Freelancing is something you can do at the beginning of your career, in between jobs down the road, or even on the side if you have a full-time gig that allows you enough time to work on other projects.

> *Web Links:*
> **Resources for freelancers**
>
> No matter what your skill or service, there are many resources online where freelancers can connect with each other and potential clients. If you're tired of working alone, visit MeetUp.com or search Google for coworking organizations to find freelancer groups where you can get to know others who share your lifestyle. Post an ad on Craigslist and scan the "gigs" section. There's some weird stuff in there, but you may find legit work as well. ifreelance.com and freelanceauction.com are other sites you can browse according to skill set. Solvate is a company that contracts with freelancers and matches them up with companies who have specific project-based needs. Finally, there are tons of freelance job boards like elance.com, Amazon's Mechanical Turk, oDesk, and many more so it's worth taking a look around.

But before you tear up your resume and change into sweatpants, hear this: Getting started as a freelancer is not easy. Instead of job hunting once and then settling into a company, you must be constantly on the prowl for new projects and clients. Once you actually have those clients, it can feel like you have ten bosses instead of just one (even though none of them give you benefits— another drawback of the freelance game). And in addition to doing the actual work, you have to act as your own marketing team, building your brand and getting the word out that you're available for hire. One satisfied client should ideally lead to the next, but in the meantime, prepare to pound the pavement (or the 'net) and live on pasta and PBR. (For tips for marketing yourself, check out the "Make Some Extra Cash" template on page 84.)

What Skills Can I Sell?

Freelancing makes most sense for people who have an existing talent or skill that can be converted into freelance work (e.g., graphic design experience), but anyone can take classes and workshops to gain bankable skills (e.g., massage therapy).

Tips & Tricks:
Freelancers are citizens, too

In other words, just because you're a freelancer doesn't mean you don't have to pay taxes or go to the doctor. If you're fully self-employed you'll have to keep track of your own income and file taxes quarterly (search around online for information on how it works—freelancers love to procrastinate by sharing tips on message boards and in blog posts). If a given employer pays you $600 or more for your services in a given year, it is responsible for providing a 1099 Misc form 275. If you don't receive it by January, follow up and see what's happening. In terms of health care, there are many options for getting insurance without the aid of an employer, such as individual plans, short-term plans, and the Freelancer's Union. For more information on insurance options, go to page 311.

Don't overlook the fact that what begins as a freelance experiment could morph into a start-up and ultimately a real company. Be on the lookout for growth opportunities, if that's what you're after. Below, we'll dig into four common examples of freelance pursuits to give you a sense of what to expect and how to get started.

WRITING AND EDITING. If you're a writer or editor, you may be able to find assignments via Craigslist, Indeed.com, MyJambi.com, Sologig.com, Mandy.com, Ed2010.com, or Mediabistro.com. If you're really serious, you'll purchase a copy of the most up-to-date *Writer's Market* (or become a member of the website for $29.99), a resource for writers that has contact information for hundreds of magazines, journals, and agents you can pitch. It also provides pay ranges and guidelines for query letters (i.e., written pitches). Those pay ranges vary drastically, but you can expect anything from $5 per review on a random start-up music website to upwards of $0.50 per word at a legit publication. It's also very common to see gigs that don't pay but will offer "great exposure and resume credentials." Don't take their word for it! If you've never heard of the publication or website, do some research into circulation and web traffic (you can use Compete.com to see how many visitors a site gets), and decide whether you think an article published there will give you credibility when you pitch bigger fish. Writing stuff you don't want to write for other people is not worth it (after all, you've got your own coming-of-age novel to work on), so make sure each assignment fulfills one of three criteria: 1) It will be a great "clip" for your portfolio; 2) It will help you develop a relationship with an editor at a place you want to write more for; or 3) It pays well (or is just cool enough that you're willing to do it for free). Even after you start getting regular gigs, brace yourself for the inevitable ups and downs of the writing world.

PROGRAMMING. If you have a knack for problem solving, logic games, and cracking awesomely dorky jokes, programming might just be your calling—and a lucrative one it can be. Freelancer programmers can usually bill at $50 to $150 per hour once they've proven their mettle. You can look for gigs on Craigslist, Elance.com, Guru.com, and RentACoder.com or contact programming shops to see if they're looking for any freelance help. However, in an age where everyone and their grandma has a start-up idea, it's definitely worth mining your personal contacts and your parents' network for potential work. Perhaps most important, you should leverage the robust communities that exist in the world of programming—each programming language and platform has its own community—not surprisingly, all of the members live online and share information about gigs.

GRAPHIC DESIGN. You may consider yourself an artist, but you still have to eat. Graphic design is a great way to exercise your creativity while still making a living (not to mention that graphic designers are just plain cool). Large companies regularly farm out design gigs to freelancers, so if you have a degree in this field (or have amassed enough knowledge to know what you're doing), you should be able to break in as a freelancer without too much trouble. Knowledge of the Adobe Suite (PhotoShop, InDesign, Illustrator) is a must, and depending on what type of design work you are doing, you should research other

Career Options

software options as well. But you can figure all that out on-the-fly. According to Benny Gold, a San Francisco–based designer who has worked with companies like Burton and Nike, "The strongest skill you need for design is being able to develop concepts. Almost anyone can learn the programs, but your concept abilities will set you apart." Pay is either hourly ($25 to $200 depending on experience) or project-based ($350 is an average fee for a custom logo design). In graphic design, it is essential to have a website where potential clients can browse your portfolio and familiarize themselves with your capabilities. Your site will become synonymous with your identity as a designer, so it's important to make sure it's well-organized and aesthetically impressive. While it's smart to remain versatile as a designer, you might want to consider finding a "niche" (album covers, T-shirts, blog design, etc.) that you can market in order to distinguish yourself.

SOCIAL MEDIA GURUING. As organizations begin to realize the power of viral videos, Facebook fan pages, blogs, and all that other good "Web 2.0" stuff, they're increasingly looking for new blood to shake up their old-school marketing departments. You can actually get full-time jobs with major companies (e.g., Dominos, JetBlue) as a "social media manager" these days, but a knack for these tools can also be leveraged into freelance consulting gigs. (Word to the wise: There's a lot to know—don't assume you're an expert just because you spend four hours a day on the 'Book). To find opportunities, check out SocialMediaJobs.com (look at the "Consultants" category) and Mashable.com's job board. You can also try techie sites like Elance.com and Odesk.com to find people looking for social media experts. But if you're low on experience, start small by pitching yourself to smaller organizations that aren't necessarily looking for a social media pro until you tell them they need one (e.g., charge $500 to teach the nice silver-haired ladies at the library what Facebook is). Try approaching a local museum, a pizza parlor, or one of your parents' friends who has a small business—you might even do it for free the first time. If your strategies work, there's nothing stopping you from finding new clients and charging a lot more to build out a company's online presence, create a viral Twitter campaign for a tutoring company, or shoot promotional YouTube videos for a nearby Yoga studio.

OTHER. Below is a brief list of possible other paths to consider.

- 🐾 Teach a foreign language/translate

- ✍ Copyedit for businesses or publications

- 📖 Tutor students who want to brush up on a specific subject (p. 78)

- ♪ Give lessons (music, karate, meditation, whatever you can credibly teach)

- 🍽 Be a personal chef/cater private events

- ⅄ Teach yoga/private fitness training

- ☾ Astrology (learn to read peoples' charts)

- 🐕 Dog-walking/pet-sitting (p. 79)

- 🎥 Be a wedding or event photographer/videographer

Internships

Don't underestimate the power of a great internship as an important piece of your career story. While there are plenty of examples of people who land great jobs right out of college, more often than not, getting to the gig you really want requires a long-distance run, not a sprint. An internship is one of the best stepping-stones to full-time employment, one that allows you to test the waters of an industry/company before diving head first. In fact, the **intern pool is by far the most common source of new hires at many companies.** While you may not yet have the skill set to be a strong candidate for your dream job, as far as competition for internships goes, you're a great white shark in a pool of guppies. Your college degree makes you a superstar candidate, so leverage it to get your foot in the door of a company where you might ultimately like to work.

Once you've landed an internship, your job duties may involve a trip or two to the local latté purveyor, but don't get caught up in the details. Internships are a great place to start out—they provide a setting to learn new skills, network, bolster your resume, and dip your toe into an industry to see if you actually enjoy it. And just as important, taking an internship can help you maintain momentum in your job hunt instead of getting frustrated because nothing's opening up or a particular company is beginning to look like an impenetrable fortress. (Yes, you should absolutely continue to look for jobs *while* you're interning, and many companies will encourage you in this process.)

Career Options

How to Find Great Internships

Finding an internship is not entirely different from finding a full-time job, so be sure to check out the job listing resources section on page 56. In addition, here are some more great resources geared specifically toward internships:

YOUR ALMA MATER. Check with career services and the alumni office to research various internship options. Make sure to ask whether your school has strong relationships with any programs in particular.

THE WEBSITE OF THE COMPANY WHERE YOU WANT TO INTERN. If it has an employment section on its site (usually listed in the "Careers" or "About Us" sections), you can usually find details about the internship program there.

BOOKS. There are plenty of books with profiles of different internship programs. You don't need to buy them—just spend an afternoon at a bookstore or the library and see what you can find. *Vault Guide to Top Internships* and *The Best 109 Internships*, both by Mark Oldman, are good places to start.

LISTS OF TOP-RATED INTERNSHIPS. *BusinessWeek*, Vault, and CollegeGrad. com all publish rankings of the best internships, so track these down. The *BusinessWeek* one even includes information on pay and the percentage of interns that get full-time offers.

INTERNQUEEN.COM. Provides a decent smattering of internship opportunities, though it should be noted that the listings skew toward media-related fields.

COLD CALLS. It's easier to cold call a company and offer free labor than it is to ask for a job (however, there are fuzzy laws about unpaid internships so they may say "no" even if they want you). Find a company that interests you but doesn't have a formal internship program, and see if they'll take you on. This approach can be particularly effective at small to mid-sized companies (see "Tips & Tricks" page 47).

Do Your Homework

Not all internships are created equal. Some places take on interns without thinking too much about what they're going to do with them, whereas others have excellent programs designed for maximum immersion. To separate the wheat from the chaff, you'll have to do some research. Once you've identified a few programs that interest you, visit InternshipRatings.com to see how different companies' programs are rated. More important, track down some people who have previously interned at the companies you're interested in (try Facebook, LinkedIn, and school networks) to ask what they thought of the experience. Don't forget to see if they have any particular advice for the interview process.

For tips on how to go about preparing your application and interviewing, check out pages 102 and 117, respectively.

How to Thrive at an Internship

Once you've landed an internship, hit the ground running and make the most of the opportunity from day one. Even if you're only planning on being there for a few months, treat it as if it were a "real" job—you never know, it might become one. Here are a few tips on what you can do to stand out from the other 'terns.

DON'T ACT LIKE YOU'RE TOO GOOD TO GET COFFEE. There are three reasons people make you get coffee in an internship: 1) They want to break you down and make you aware of your inferiority (see *The Devil Wears Prada*); 2) They are too lazy (or hung over) to get it themselves; or 3) Everyone in the office goes on coffee runs and sometimes it just happens to be your turn. The second two scenarios are far more common than the first. Still, even if there is a little bit of hazing going on, having an ego won't help anything. Someday, you'll be the one in a position to tell people what to do, and then you can either exact your revenge on the world or make it a better place by being nice to your interns.

AVOID THE "NERVOUS INTERN" SYNDROME. Every office has an overly nervous intern. This intern is very sweet and well-intentioned, but ultimately a pain in the butt that no one wants to deal with. Remember: When you're an intern, no supervisor is going to put you in the room with the red button. Nothing you do is going to be do-or-die, so if you're given an assignment, don't ask a million and one questions about how to do it—at that point, the person who assigned it to you might as well have done it himself. Instead, try to get as far as you can on each project, and if problems arise, then pose a few thoughtful questions at one time.

BECOME INDISPENSABLE (AND BE PROACTIVE). Is there a task that you can do better than anyone else in the office? Then work it to the max, and the company may have no choice but to hire you. If you're not getting enough work, don't sit around IMing your friends and bemoaning the

> ### Tips & Tricks:
> ### Can I look for jobs while I'm interning?
>
> Of course! In fact, that's precisely what you should be doing. In the broad sense, "job loyalty" is not a big deal at internships because everyone's on the same page about your ultimate goal (i.e., to get a job, there or elsewhere). If people like you at your internship, they should either be looking to hire you as a full-time employee or help you move on to your next opportunity. Be respectful of your position and your duties (browsing job-hunting sites while you're at work is not a good move), but don't be shy about taking time off for interviews or networking engagements you can't reschedule. If you get a job elsewhere and have to leave your internship early, so be it. That's the whole point!

fact that you're not being given the opportunity to prove yourself. Get up and walk around the office. Introduce yourself to people who may not be in your immediate work area and see if you can help them. Anticipate ways to make your supervisor's life easier and then execute. Unfortunately, the chance to shine is not guaranteed, so do anything you can to show your supervisor what you've got before your internship is up.

MAKE CONNECTIONS. The "only speak when spoken to" approach won't get you too far at an internship, and here's why: Interns come and go, but full-time employees are set in routines that they may have fostered over the course of many years. If they're friendly human beings, they'll interact with you, but some people will just go about their business as if you don't exist. It's not necessarily that they're rude, they're just busy, and taking you under their wing is not part of their job description. For this reason, it's on you to put yourself on colleagues' radars and make them want to teach you, give you work, or mentor you in other ways. For the most part, you can easily accomplish this by introducing yourself and asking some questions. This simple act will puncture that weird workplace aloofness and put you in a position to make an impression. Sometimes the memorable intern gets the job (just make sure you're remembered for your hard work and not for always leaving your fly down).

REMEMBER WHY YOU'RE THERE. The hardest part about internships is staying motivated. Your stipend might be laughable (or even nonexistent), but don't get hung up on the details. Instead, you've got to think like a benchwarmer trying to be a starter. If you're dazed and out-of-shape when you finally get put in the game, people aren't likely to be impressed with what you can do. So stay on point, and be ready to pounce. Otherwise, why are you there? Slaving away for peanuts is a waste of your time (and the company's) if you're just going to slack your way to the finish line.

Before You Leave an Internship

Any respectable "things to do before leaving the office" checklist should include stealing a few paperclips, getting digits from any other cute interns, and coyly dropping hints that you like cupcakes as the final week approaches. More to the point, though, it's important to be strategic about your exit for the same reason we've already discussed: you're a blip on the radar for many people whose entire professional lives take place in the office, so it's up to you to ensure that you're not forgotten the moment your log-in privileges are revoked.

There are three simple steps to leaving with your head held high and your Rolodex brimming with new contacts. First, initiate a real conversation with your supervisor about prospects for the future. If there's no official evaluation process, ask for feedback—a major goal of an internship is to learn what employers see in you and how you can improve. If that supervisor seems to like you, get a reference letter, or at least ask if it would be okay to list him or her as a reference in the future (see page 104). Second, say thank you and goodbye to anyone and everyone you interacted with in the office as well as leave them with your new contact information. Finally, take away anything from the office that could be of use as you take the next step. Did you get a great handout about financing or sales techniques? Did you have a good rapport with a client whose contact information is going to be trapped in your work email if you don't get it ASAP? Think about what you've learned and whom you've met, and make sure you're not leaving anything behind that you can't get back.

$ *Smart Money:* **Plan B (How To Earn Cash Now)**

When it comes to the current job market, there's no doubt that it's hard out there for a recent grad (to put it mildly). It's hard enough to choose a particular industry in which to find employment let alone land an actual job. If you find yourself in employment limbo, don't stress: it is perfectly acceptable to find ways to make some coin without becoming a slave to the grind (at least, for now). While you continue to seek out a job and weigh your options keep in mind that there are plenty of ways to start filling your piggy bank sooner rather than later, almost all of which can be done without learning any new skills (unless you need a primer on "hustle"). The best part is that in all cases we've highlighted below, you'll be able to maintain enough autonomy and flexibility to make it through the summer—and in some cases well beyond—without sacrificing the opportunity to watch every *Hoarders* marathon that comes on. If none of them strikes your fancy, learn how to apply the approaches that work in the below examples to anything you want in the "Make Some Extra Cash" template on page 84.

Tutor

You went to college. Many parents would very much like for their kids to go to college. Ergo, if you act like you know the secrets of the SAT or admissions essays, you can convince those parents to cut you some serious checks (anywhere from $10 an hour to over $30k a year if you stick with it for a while and bag some rich kids in the right market). This gig is practically custom-made for recent grads, so take advantage of your credentials while they're still fresh.

Is it for me? If you have a geeky love of standardized tests or you like teaching but don't want to commit to it as a career, tutoring makes a lot of sense. But be warned: Being a good tutor takes a lot more than just showing up and answering a few questions. Tim Urban, the founder of Launch Education (and a former *Apprentice* contestant), says it all boils down to that moment when Little Timmy shows up and says, "I did all my homework except for this really hard one. Can you show me how?" In other words, you can't just waltz in and expect that being "smart" will suffice. Even if you did well in high school and college, you will almost certainly have to crack open a book and make sure you're able to respond to questions when you don't have an answer key. You also need to have Zen-like patience to work with some of these little rascals until they really get the concept their teachers don't have time to teach them.

How do I get started? Generally speaking, no certifications are necessary to join the tutoring circuit, but you need to have a strong grasp on the subjects you're likely to teach. Once you've narrowed those down, there are two general approaches to tutoring—find your own clients or join an existing company.

Option 1: Join a company. The advantages to joining a company like Kaplan or Princeton Review are that you can start cashing checks pretty quickly; the disadvantage is your earning potential is stifled since you only get a portion of what each student is paying. When you start out, the company provides materials and students, plus you may get some classroom experience. The pay ranges from about $12 to $20 per hour, depending upon the market and the subject. Ultimately, if you just have a short-term work gap to fill before you do something else, this route might be your best option in terms of convenience and ease. You can usually work part-time hours while pursuing other jobs or classes.

Option 2: Do it yourself. While it's certainly easier to teach classes for a big company (they provide you with materials, students, and a space), you don't have to split the money pot if you get paid directly. (The national test prep companies charge dramatic mark-ups on your time, so if you're getting paid $20 to tutor someone, the parents of your students are often paying $40 per hour or more!) Entering the tutoring market as a free agent is definitely a tougher and more long-term approach, but such is the nature of entrepreneurship—bigger risks, bigger rewards!

Pet Sitter & Dog Walker

Though tales of dog walkers making over $100k a year usually involve words such as "celebrity" and "whisperer," taking pups out for a stroll can be a fun way to make a few extra bucks, or even build a small business. And if you don't live in an urban area where people need walkers, you can always take care of their furry friends when they go on vacation.

Is it for me? Any genuine dog-lover who is in good shape and moderately personable is a prime candidate to start a walking and sitting biz. That said, it's worth taking a reality check: you may like your golden retriever back home, but are you ready to hit the streets for two or more hours a day, rain or shine, and have a dog that's not your own poop on your rug?

> ### Tips & Tricks:
> ### Cheap business cards and websites
>
> Whether you're pitching yourself as a dog-walker or a personal style guru, a business card can provide that little boost of professionalism and a way for people to remember you. For budget-friendly business cards and websites, look no further than VistaPrint.com. The site offers 250 business cards for free (though it's probably worth paying the extra $3.99 to get the ad off the back), as well as a bunch of other promotional materials for little more than the cost of shipping. The ready-made website templates aren't exactly going to win any design awards, but they'll do the trick when you're first getting started. Just create a one- to three-page site with information for your potential customers and set up a unique email address to put on those biz cards (e.g., sophie@downtowndogs.com).

How do I get started? Finding customers is the toughest part of starting your own outfit, and many full-time walkers will tell you it took them six months to a year to get a full slate of customers (that being said, it's not impossible to get a pooch or two pretty quickly, especially if you have dog-owners in your building/ neighborhood). Since people treat their pets like their children, nothing will ever beat a personal recommendation. Thus, your first step should always be to tell everyone you know about your business. When that pool is maxed out, do some local marketing (flyers!) at apartment buildings and condo blocks, dog parks, pet stores, vets' offices, and anywhere else dog owners might assemble.

In addition to pulling together some basic marketing materials like business cards and a simple website, you'll want to get insurance. Pet Sitters Associates (PetSitLLC.com) offers membership and dog-walking insurance for $164 a year. This will cover you if your dog hurts another dog or person or destroys someone's property. And, if nothing else, it will also give your potential clients peace of mind. (Let them know on your business card and website that you're insured.)

How much can I make? Google the local competition to make sure your rates are competitive. In general, hard-working sitters and walkers can rake in about $10 to $20 for each 30-minute walk (more for dog-running), and $40 to $75 for an overnight stay. Just think: $10–20 for a 30 minute walk × 9 dogs (3 groups of 3) × 5 days a week = pretty good pay for staying fit and hanging with pups! And while "cash-in-hand" may not be a phrase the IRS likes, there's certainly nothing stopping you from keeping all the pup money in a brown paper bag, far away from any stimulus packages (where was the money for dog parks, anyway?). Then again, starting your grad career off dodging the law probably isn't the best idea!

Babysitter & Nanny

If you grew up reading the *Baby-sitters Club*, you've already got your homework out of the way. Taking care of local youths when their mom and dad head off for some alone time is not only a good way to make some extra money, but in some cases it can also be your ticket to traveling abroad for free. Open up a notebook—it's time to start your very own *Nanny Diaries*.

Is it for me? The most important thing to understand is that taking care of someone's children is a *major* responsibility—CEOs lose millions of dollars all the time, but the anger of their stockholders is no match for the wrath of a parent if you lose her child. Patience, energy, and organization are as important as a genuine love for kids—even when they eat dirt and spray you with Super Soakers. A love of travel may also motivate you if you're able to snag an au pair gig abroad.

How do I get started? As with dog-walking and tutoring, you need to be deemed trustworthy, so build a pitch that emphasizes your dependability and any relevant experience, even if that's just taking care of your five younger siblings. It's also helpful if you have or can obtain CPR and First Aid training, which you can find via most health organizations, including the American Red Cross, for between $20 and $100. Word of mouth is golden for getting gigs, but there are some agencies that place sitters and au pairs. One good website to check out is GreatAuPair.com, where you can post a profile for free and search for families. You do have to pay in order to get contact info (it costs $60 for a 30-day membership), but since many families purchase a membership, it is not always needed (you can just post a profile and wait for families to contact you). If you're looking to travel abroad but don't have the money, you can try the au pair route—check out TransitionsAbroad.com for listings in different countries. Finally, Craigslist is always worth a shot—go to the "childcare" section, which is under the "community" heading.

If you find yourself having trouble finding your first client, be sure to reach out to friends and family for easier-to-find gigs. Your neighbor who has known you since you were eight might not pay the best, but any gig you can get will build references and bullets on your babysitting resume.

Total start-up costs? None, unless you pay to get certifications or sign up for employment websites.

How much can I make? That's a tough one, as there are often nonmonetary benefits to nannying or being an au pair, like room, board, and the opportunity to travel to another country. (Some nanny jobs we've seen advertised even offer health benefits and salaries above $40k!) For plain old babysitting, we've heard quotes ranging from about $12 to $20 an hour, depending on the number of children, their ages, and what tasks are expected of you.

Waiter, Waitress, Bartender and Barista

Working at a Starbucks or the local faux-French bistro may not be the same as working for yourself, but there's definitely an entrepreneurial spirit and a ton of camaraderie amongst table servers, baristas, and bar staff who battle it out for the biggest tips they can possibly muster.

Career Options

Is it for me? If you are talkative, energetic, and outgoing, any of these jobs could be a perfect way to pay the bills (or maintain flexible hours while you pursue other passions). It's very gratifying at the end of a shift to go home with a wad of hard-earned cash in your pocket. On the other hand, the job can be exhausting, and you may have to deal with the occasional overstressed manager and/or obnoxious customer.

How do I get started? Many restaurants in huge food cities (e.g., NYC, LA, Chicago, Atlanta) will not even consider you if you lack serving experience, so your first move should be to get a gig anywhere you can. A café or small chain restaurant will usually be the easiest place to get your foot in the door. You can also be a "host" at a restaurant with little to no experience. And for bartending gigs, one way to break into the biz is by attending bartending school. Classes usually run for two hours each weekday, over the course of close to a month, at which point the school should help you find a job. However, many 'tenders say it's not necessary to do a course and that experience, no matter where you get it, will be a lot more useful. So if you've got the confidence to fake the funk a little bit, try going for a dive bar or laidback restaurant bar, pick up some on-the-job training, and then go for tougher cocktail lounge or swanky bar gigs.

For all types of restaurant and bar work, Craigslist is your best friend, though coffee chains and larger restaurants/restaurant groups will generally have an employment page on their websites. Plus, you can always walk around your neighborhood of choice and ask if anyone's hiring.

How much can I make? Since tips are the name of the game, it all depends on how busy your shift is. Instead of getting too frustrated, realize that the big nights make up for the crappy ones. So if you make $300 in four hours on a Saturday night, don't be too upset when you make $40 the next morning. It's not unheard of for experienced full-time servers to make up to $50,000 a year. At a coffee shop, where tips are limited, the potential payout is going to be slimmer. Starbucks, for example, pays anywhere from around $6.75 to $10 an hour depending on where you are in the country.

Retail

Retail doesn't quite have the same cachet as some of the other examples we've discussed, but these jobs are widespread and relatively easy to land—and as an added bonus, you could get some helpful discounts on your "real world" wardrobe or a new flat-screen TV. If any fools try to give you a hard time for working alongside high-schoolers, just remind them you're following in the footsteps of greatness: Madeleine Albright started her career selling bras at a Jocelyn's Department Store in Denver.

Is it for me? Do you like interacting with people? Can you be patient with people who just can't decide on the red with sleeves or the blue with no sleeves? Are you comfortable being a salesperson and dealing with customers who are pissed that their microwave broke? Can you handle long hours on your feet? If you said "yes" to all of the above and you're knowledgeable about cell phones or shoes or anything else people buy, then retail may very well be a good money-making option for you today.

How do I get started? While some of the larger retailers maintain employment pages on their websites and throw positions up on generic online job boards (e.g., Monster, HotJobs, etc.), people tend to have the most luck by just walking into establishments at the mall or local shopping area and asking if anyone is hiring. Start by schmoozing with salespeople or managers—drop a little banter and display your knowledge of the store, *then* ask if they're hiring. Even if you're really desperate, you should try to focus on a certain type of store instead of hopping from Best Buy to J. Crew to Foot Locker, because preparation will be your greatest asset. At the very least, make sure you're familiar with the clothing lines or products being sold there.

How much can I make? Most employers are hip to the game: They know you're not going to stay forever, so they generally start out paying at minimum wage (the federal minimum is $7.25 per hour, but it varies from state to state) and then raise the rate if you stick around. Some big box retailers may pay a little more than smaller shops.

Career Options

The "Make Some Extra Cash" Template

If you look at the examples listed above, you'll notice some common themes running throughout that can be applied to any number of entrepreneurial endeavors. So if tutoring algebra or evading projectiles from insane children isn't your cup of tea, here is a rubric you can follow to turn any skill you've got (or can learn relatively quickly) into a source of income.

Choose Your Talent. What are you good at, or what would you like to be good at? Can you parlay this skill into a service people would pay for? Is there a precedent for people paying for it, or would you have to create the market?

Examples: Music instructor, personal trainer, copy editor, bespoke chocolate-maker, landscaper, dock-builder, Ikea furniture constructor, driveway installer, computer fixer, chauffeur, personal chef, party promoter.

Become an expert. Even if you have honed the skill already, become an expert (or at least a good BSer) so you can convince other people to pay you to either perform your skill or teach it to them. Troll the Web for articles; find out the best books on the subject and hit the library; take a class or online tutorial. In some cases, an investment in a workshop or certification will boost your credibility and allow you to gain clients much more quickly.

Examples: Taking a homeotherapy workshop; reading books on yoga practice; studying up on a store's merchandise to get a retail position.

Develop your pitch and sales materials. Aside from knowing your stuff, how are you going to convince real, sentient humans to knowingly part with their money? You need a pitch that establishes you as trustworthy, knowledgeable, and capable. You also need materials, such as handouts, business cards, flyers, a website, and a lesson plan. The point is, make it look like this is something you are passionate about and not just a way to make a quick buck.

Examples: Make a video showing you acing various yoga poses and upload it to YouTube; give out free samples of your mail-order sweets at a farmers market; create a flyer for your guitar lessons and bring it to a local college campus.

Find clients. Ah, the thorny issue of clientele. For gigs like waitressing and selling those weird Cutco knives door to door, this is not an issue. But for other endeavors, you'll probably have to put on your marketing cap and think to yourself, "Who is my potential client, where does my potential client go (online or off), and how can I attract his or her attention there?" If you're living at home, you can try mining your parent's network or your childhood network, especially if you're providing basic services like house painting, mowing lawns, or shoveling driveways (which can easily make you $10 to $18 an hour). For example, if you were a college-level basketball player and you think you can run a clinic or one-on-one lessons for middle school students, try going to your old school and networking with any faculty who remember you. Finally, once you snag your first client, the best way to get more is through your performance, because word-of-mouth referrals will speak louder than any marketing materials you create.

Examples: If you're selling something fitness-related, target the gym. Pet-related? The pet store and park. Sex-related? The darkest alley you can find.

Grow responsibly. Once you've got some clients, it's off to the races to see how big you can get. If you're really making money as opposed to just a little chump change for the bar tab, then you may consider (ahem) paying taxes on your business, as well as making it an official legal entity. These steps will be particularly important if you decide to hire anyone and don't want to be screwed if they get you sued somehow.

Examples: Establish a single proprietorship for your copy writing business by hiring a local attorney or using LegalZoom.com. Create an LLC for your tutoring outfit by using MyCorporation.com. ■

Temp Work

Pop culture has painted temps as gum-smacking receptionists and no-hopers dressing up in giant burrito costumes. But pop culture has led us astray before (like when it told us to listen to Fergie). So let's take a wider view. Traditionally, temping simply refers to a job placement where you work for an employer over a short period of time—on the job continuum, think of it as somewhere between an internship (but you get paid better) and a full-time job.

The cons of temp work are pretty obvious: You have little to no job security, the tasks are not always the most exciting, and there's often more pressure to not completely screw everything up than to do something outstanding. Plus, temping probably isn't what you dreamed of the day you got your diploma. But for a recent grad, it can be a great stop-gap option, especially if you are trying to get a full-time job: 90% of companies use temps, and the staffing agency Manpower reports that 40% of its placements go on to get permanent positions (just look at Ryan from *The Office*).

At very least, temp work can help you add bullets to a blank resume and build a new skill set as you begin to create your job-hunting story. In fact, many employers say they view temping as a sign of a good attitude and a strong work ethic—two great aces up the sleeve in an age when everyone thinks of our generation as entitled and high-maintenance!

Types of Temp Work

There are a few main categories of temp work you'll encounter. The most common is "temporary help," where a staffing agency hires you and then deploys you for however long you're needed. "Temp to hire," on the other hand, is basically like a tryout for the job. A third type you might see is "long-term staffing"—in these cases, staffing agencies recruit, screen, and assign workers to specific positions.

Under these umbrella categories, the temp world is as varied as the industries that hire temps, but unless you have some specific credentials (e.g., technical IT knowledge, lab experience, research or health care experience), the most general opportunities are in professional occupations (i.e., office/clerical) and industrial labor (think assembly line workers, food handlers, cleaners, etc.). For quick money, there's nothing wrong with arranging traffic cones or watching over an endless river of M&Ms looking for the overly bulbous ones. But if you also want to use your temp experience to build skills and dip your feet into career-oriented industries, you might be better served seeking temp work of the office variety.

Many of the functional office positions companies fill with temps are in billing, payroll, office support, and data entry/processing. When tax season comes around, accounting and bookkeeping gigs see a major spike. Customer support centers also use temps to provide phone or online support for their products—at least the ones that haven't been outsourced to Bangalore. The pay levels ($12 to $20+ per hour; see page 102 for more) depend on your experience, skill set, and position—you'll notice various levels for different roles, like "Admin I" (very basic reception work), "Admin 2" (involves multitasking and answering to between one and three managers), and "executive assistants" (these positions generally require experience—up to three to five years—assisting CEOs).

All of the above positions can be found via staffing agencies, which we'll get to in a second. Once you get placed, most assignments last anywhere from a few hours to three or four months, and then you can go back to your contact at the agency to find something else. On the plus side, you won't have too much time to get bored, and working in a bunch of different offices is like career speed-networking, only less superficial. By the time you're done temping, you could have potentially made friends and contacts at several good companies—in this world we call "the working world," that's nothing to scoff at! In some instances you may even stay with a single company, working on an as-needed basis, and be in a good position to get hired if a full-time position pops up.

To learn more about the range of occupations available through agencies, check out the American Staffing Association's (ASA) website, AmericanStaffing.net.

Staffing Agencies

It should be clear by now that the first port of call for any temp candidate is a staffing agency. These go by many other names—temp agencies, employment agencies, and so on—but the general idea is simple: Companies use agencies to find candidates for temporary roles, and agency recruiters work with you to match your skills with the right gig. In addition to providing access to employers, most staffing agencies also provide training to help you get work—the ASA recently reported that 90% of agencies offer some kind of free training, ranging from free tutorials on the latest versions of software applications to interview workshops.

A good place to start your search is with the big national agencies like Manpower (surprisingly not a porn site) and OfficeTeam (surprisingly not an office supplies site), which likely have locations in your area. Net-Temps.com also posts nationwide positions. However, you should also narrow your focus. Many staffing agencies specialize in a particular profession or field of business, such as general industrial labor, accounting, or secretarial work. Also, local agencies may be better suited for opportunities in your particular town or city. To find these more specialized shops, Terri Abbe, Director of Service Quality with Pace Staffing Network in the Pacific Northwest, suggests hitting up Google and the Yellow Pages (remember to try not only "staffing agencies" in your search but also "temp agencies," "recruiting," "employment agency," etc.). When you find some places, she recommends checking out their websites or calling them up to ask the following questions:

- Are there any testimonials from clients and employees? Are they reviewed on Yelp.com?

- Do they work with reputable employers, or places that seem sketchy?

How long have they been working in the area? (Longevity usually means good connections to local employers.)

Do they appear to have relevant jobs listed?

In a booming economy, signing up with one firm would be totally fine. But in darker days, Abbe recommends signing up with around three firms. You could go to even more, but play it cool—agencies may ask you who else you're working with, and if you list ten places it won't make them feel that you'll be worth their time.

The Payoff

So how much can you make? Typical hourly rates in most locations start at $12 to $15 an hour, but higher-level positions (like executive assistant or clinical trial administrator) might pay $20 an hour or more. Check out suggested hourly rates on your state's Department of Labor website and at Payscale.com. You can also check Craigslist for temp listings to get a sense of what people are paying in your area. If you're working with a staffing agency, they'll often even provide basic health benefits, as well as vacation/holiday pay and even retirement plans. Assuming you're using temping as a short-term solution, the biggie here is the health insurance, which could be a lifesaver if you need to find coverage before you have a full-time job (see Chapter 8 for more on health care).

Career Options

Chapter III: Getting Hired

Getting Hired

The job hunt can be the most trying of all post-college obstacles because it distills so many doubts and challenges into one seemingly all-important process. Once you've tackled the process of deciding what you even want to do (not always a simple task), you then have to address the thorny issue of actually landing a job. And according to outplacement firm Challenger, Gray and Christmas, the average job search lasts four months.

For most recent grads, one of the most frustrating aspects of the job market is the lack of clear-cut expectations. In college, you pretty much knew what you had to do to get a good grade, and if you messed up, your teacher told you what you did wrong. During the job hunt, you will almost never get any explanation of why you didn't get a job. In many ways, it's more like the college application process—no matter how stellar your credentials are, sometimes the other kid's grandfather donated a building.

Needless to say, inexplicable rejections, unanswered emails, and botched interviews can take the wind out of anyone's sail. But letting these setbacks fester never helped anyone. Instead, realize that while there are no "rules" to the job-hunting game, there are *plenty* of best practices (which we're about to share) that will help you stand out from the pack. Trust us: Being in the dark about why you didn't get a job feels a lot better than knowing you got cut for making a simple resume error or failing to dress appropriately for the interview.

In this chapter, we'll debunk the mysteries of the job hunt and give you the tools you need to tackle the process with confidence. Just remember that the job hunt is a rite of passage, and like all rites of passage, it will probably be sort of uncomfortable and humiliating, but one day you'll either romanticize it into a great yarn or block it from your memory entirely.

 ## *Major Hazard:* Cleaning Up Your Online Identity

First things first: Before you begin networking and applying for jobs, make sure your online persona is up to snuff. This doesn't mean your past has to be picture-perfect. Everyone knows you went to college and probably got caught on camera acting a fool. The point of cleaning up your online identity is simply to ensure you are putting your best foot forward and avoiding giving a potential employer an excuse to reject you—using a profile picture of you rocking a keg stand in your underwear or picking up M&Ms with your feet at a sorority pledge event is not a good move. You don't have to censor all personality out of your online game; just use some common sense and avoid shooting yourself in the foot for no reason at all.

Facing Facebook

For most recent grads, protecting your rep online is mostly about rethinking your Facebook profile, which basically boils down to two words: **privacy settings**. (A similar process can be iterated across other networks like MySpace, FourSquare, Twitter, etc.)

Regardless of who is able to access your page, pay close attention to the four basic types of content that could get you in trouble: your personal profile, photos/videos (not only yours, but also friends who tagged you in theirs), status updates, and wall posts. In other words, the places where you're most likely to crack a risqué joke or "reveal too much."

It is important to realize that even if you make your page available only to a select group of people, your data will probably still get out (we've heard stories of sneaky employers finding people with connections to their potential hires in order to be able to see what they marked as private—hopefully you don't know any snitches). Of course, employers aren't out to get you, but if you're really paranoid (or some people might say smart) you should consider making everything except your most basic information private during the course of the job hunt.

It's really up to you to decide how private you need (or want) to be. If you're angling for a government job or for one in a very conservative company, you may have greater concerns than others about potential employers viewing your profile and pictures. Moreover, job hunt aside, some people just don't

> ### Tips & Tricks:
> #### Change your voicemail recording
>
> It's a huge turn-off for a potential employer to call your cell phone and be redirected to an absurd voicemail recording. ("Hey, this is Dylan. You know the drill," may have worked on *90210*, but it won't work now. Trust us.) Be brief and professional. Go with something along the lines of, "Hi, you've reached Megan Werner. I'm unable to answer the phone right now, but if you leave your name and number I will get back to you as soon as possible." You'll sound like a dingus to your friends, but it's a small price to pay for a sweet job.

feel comfortable being easily stalkable, while others derive great pleasure from online exhibitionism.

The Self-Google

Sure, Googling yourself sounds vain. Heck, it's often referred to as "egosurfing". But in the case of the job hunt, it just might prevent a potential employer from discovering an embarrassing incident from your past.

Google all variations of your name and nicknames (with quotation marks— "Justin Bieber"—and without—Justin Bieber) and see if you find anything you're not happy about. If there is nothing unsavory, or if your name is common enough to render you anonymous for search purposes, then you are in the clear. Otherwise, the best you can usually do is to make your Facebook and LinkedIn profiles public (assuming you've cleaned them up), and contact webmasters to request they take down anything that you'd prefer not to have on the 'net. The latter tactic may be useful when your friends tag your name and the phrase "superman that ho" on pictures they posted at Urban Dictionary. But if the *Waterloo Courier* ran a story about the time you were arrested for streaking through the mall, there's not too much you can do about it.

Compiling Your Life on Paper

Once you've cleaned up your online act, it's time to get your job-hunting ducks in order so that you'll be able to strike when the iron is hot. For most positions, you will need to present a resume and a cover letter. If you're applying for a creative position or media job, you may also be required to submit some samples of your previous work (e.g., a portfolio in creative fields, "clips" in journalism). And for some jobs, you may have to take a skills, grammar, or knowledge test. Certain jobs will also require references, and while they typically only request them once you've interviewed and are being seriously considered for the position, it's a good idea to plan ahead and line up your references before you apply (see page 104).

As you get started, remember that "attention to detail" isn't just a skill you'll need on the job— it's a skill you'll need during the job hunt as well. A sloppy resume or typo-riddled cover letter will leave you grounded before you even get a chance to take off. Put some time into nailing these

Getting Hired

items down—they will not only be crucial in helping you snag interviews, but they will also give you confidence as the search progresses and things start happening quickly. When someone calls and says, "Meet me for coffee in half an hour. Bring your resume," you don't want to be scrambling like an idiot. Preparedness is the cousin of "getting a job." And they are cousins that actually like each other.

Resume

It's often said that an employer should be able to glance at your resume for 20 seconds and have a strong impression about whether or not you're a good fit for the job. Here's how to make sure you make it past those 20 seconds.

Be Clear, Concise, and Honest. Don't get bogged down in jargon because you think it will make your duties sound more official. While it's acceptable to candy-coat tasks like coffee-making and photocopying with phrases like "performed administrative duties," there is no reason to pack your resume with white lies. Use action verbs (e.g., administered, built, reviewed) and articulate each task in one or two phrases. If anything comes up in an interview, you should be able to expound upon it without having to say, "I guess by 'managed the books' I meant that I opened the mail, and my boss often received a lot of books." Similarly, don't be dishonest about your skills and background. Even if you pull the wool over an employer's eyes by saying you are proficient with InDesign or Excel, they are not going to be too pleased when you arrive on the first day and suddenly need training. That said, you should certainly emphasize your skills when applicable and make an effort to be as precise as possible in your resume descriptions. Lastly, in today's age of Monster.com-type websites and massive HR departments, you need to make your resume highly searchable online by packing it with keywords. This technique is particularly important when applying to government agencies, many of which use a system called Resumix to automatically sort through resumes. (For tips on getting past the resume robots, see page 68.)

The Power of One. Keep it to one page. Most employers of recent grads are dealing with a high volume of resumes, so HR managers don't have time to wade through multi-page documents. But more important, the resume is the first test to see if you can present information clearly and concisely. If it takes you more than a page to outline yourself, then you are effectively outlining your professional aspirations in chalk. Ya dig?

Getting Hired

Design. Unless graphic design is essential to the job you're applying for, having a slick-looking resume is not going to help you, and it certainly won't gloss over a lack of relevant experience or skills. Avoiding a lot of white space on the page will help you fit more information, but in general, don't get hung up on aesthetics. Just make sure your resume looks neat and, if possible, spatially balanced.

To include my GPA, or not to include my GPA. In the realm of resume quandaries, this is one of the trickier situations to navigate. Everyone wants a rule of thumb, and the one that gets invoked most often is that you should include your GPA if it's over 3.0, or include only your GPA within your major if it's significantly better than the overall number. But every thumb is different, just like snowflakes. Generally, technical jobs (think engineering, Google, etc.) will definitely be interested in your GPA, and if you don't include it they will ask for it in the interview. In this case, leaving a GPA off your resume will read like an admission of guilt, so you'll have to decide whether it's really bad enough to try to keep under wraps. If it is particularly low and there is a good reason (e.g., you worked a job while going to school or held multiple leadership positions), be sure to address this in the cover letter and/or interview. Finally, specify the scale used—different schools have different ways of expressing GPAs, and 3.5 out of 4.0 is quite different from 3.5 out of 15.0. If you're lucky, you went to one of those "progressive" schools that doesn't have GPAs.

> ### Tips & Tricks:
> ### Adapt yourself for each job
>
> Different jobs (and sometimes similar jobs within different industries) expect different things from new hires. Consider reworking your resume and writing a variation of your cover letter for every position. When putting together an application, always check the original job post and the career section of the company's website to pick up keywords and figure out what the employer is looking for. Then, tailor your skills and experiences to show that you are the ideal candidate for the specific position. If your previous experiences don't specifically correlate to the type of job you're seeking, adapt (for example, use your experience as a camp counselor to highlight your leadership skills). This approach should trickle down through the entire job-seeking process—from the resume and cover letter right through to the interview. To help customize your pitch, we've polled professionals across many industries to see what traits they look for in prospective hires. For a list of skills to stress by industry, visit gradspot.com/book.

Getting Hired

Proofread. Proofread. Proofread. The administrative staffing service Office Team reports that 47% of executives said they would throw out a candidate's resume for just one typo. This statistic might seem a little harsh. Should a typo really be that big of a deal? But you've got to think about it from the perspective of the employer: HR departments have to wade through a huge amount of resumes, so separating out the typo offenders is a quick sorting device to make their job easier. Furthermore, a typo on a one-page document does not really scream "detail-oriented" or "professional," which are two qualities that you should be shouting about. In particular, make sure that you don't mention the wrong position or company in your materials—an easy mistake to make when applying to numerous jobs. Basically, don't give a potential employer an excuse not to consider you.

Read This, It'll Knock Your Socks Off. Once you feel confident about your resume, run it by as many people as possible. The extra eyes will help weed out the typos and also provide you with feedback about how well you're selling yourself. It's ideal to get some feedback from someone working in the industry you're interested in, because he or she will have a sense of what specific employers will want to see.

Laying Out Your Resume

Now that you're ready to type out your resume, you'll be breaking things down into the following sections. Use the sample resume on page 98 as a visual reference (or check out a copy online at gradspot.com/book):

Contact Info. Make sure your name is displayed prominently at the top of the page and all of your contact information is up-to-date. You want to make yourself accessible in the long run, so don't give the landline number of the apartment that you might move out of next month (in most cases, it's ideal to use a cell phone number.) Furthermore, give a professional email address (sk8Rchick86@yahoo.com won't impress anyone). Make sure it's permanent (e.g., Gmail) and will not expire when you leave school or a job.

Objectives. This section is optional, but may be useful if you need to fill up space or if you are applying for a job that doesn't obviously align with your experience. State your objectives in one or two tight sentences and make them as specific and compelling as possible. If you are applying in an industry where you have no experience, tell a story (the extreme CliffsNotes version) of why you want to go from finance to nonprofit work, for example.

Education. This is where you'll include your school info, GPA (if necessary... see above), and relevant course work. if you need to save space, consider nixing your high school—it is obvious that you went to one, and it's unlikely the employer will know the school unless it happens to be local or well-known.

> *Tips & Tricks:*
> **What did I do for the last year?**
>
> If you get to the end of an internship or leave a job and are having trouble articulating what exactly you did there, check the job posting for the position you are leaving and see what the description is. Hypothetically, it should cover what you did (or were supposed to do).

Work Experience. When choosing which jobs/internships to include, make sure to prioritize by relevance in regards to the job to which you are applying. Under each entry, the bullet points describing your duties and achievements should be prioritized as well. If you are having trouble articulating what exactly you did, check the job posting for the position you are leaving and see what the description is. Hypothetically, it should cover what you did (or were supposed to do). If you find yourself struggling to fill up the "Work Experience" category, emphasize your skills in other ways. Maybe you led a team on a semester-long project or organized a charity race in your town. Feel free to mention something from school or activities you have done in the past. The bottom line is that you are trying to sell yourself as trustworthy and capable. If you don't have a job or internship to speak for you, that doesn't mean your relevant talents shouldn't be noted.

Skills. List any specific skills that can be utilized in the job that you seek (but remember to be honest).

Interest and Other. This is your chance to highlight any other talents or achievements that you believe might impress your potential employer.

Getting Hired

Sample Resume

JANE DOE

1234 Pine Avenue, Apt. 1 • Beverly Hills, CA 90210
(301) 555 5555 • jdoe@gmail.com

OBJECTIVE [Optional]

Detail-oriented Computer Science graduate seeks position as member of a software engineering team in a fast-paced, challenging work environment [Highlight relevant skills or strengths]

EDUCATION

University of California, Los Angeles (2007 – 2010)
Bachelor of Science in Computer Science, with Minor in Electrical Engineering
GPA in Major / Overall GPA: 3.79 / 3.54 [Show GPA in Major if higher than overall GPA]

Relevant Coursework and Projects
- Coursework heavily focused on practical aspects of Computer Science, including *C++ for Programmers*, *JAVA for Programmers*, and *Machine Structures* [Technical skills]
- Head of the Berkeley Machine Learning Project Group, leading a team of eight undergraduates in the design and development of an original machine learning algorithm [Leadership, Intelligence, Passion]

Redondo Beach High School (2002 – 2007) [Optional]
Valedictorian, June 2007

WORK EXPERIENCE

[Focus time spent on relevant jobs and qualities]
Google Inc., Mountain View, CA   2010 - Present   2006 – Present
Intern
[Describe the company and position, especially if it is not well known]
- Selected as one of 100 summer interns in the highly competitive Search Media Group at the world's leading internet search company

[Projects & Accomplishments – Focus on relevant responsibilities]
- Designed and developed source code for a variety of projects focused on search-based product offerings [Relevant programming experience]
- Built large scale distributed file systems and other infrastructures to reliably and efficiently manage and process hundreds of terabytes of information [Technical skills]
- Part of a team of six software developers responsible for optimizing performance of major database containing over 10 billion cached websites [Teamwork]
- Achieved proficiency in COBAL without any prior experience and successfully tested and debugged over 60,000 lines of legacy software code [Fast learner, attention to detail]

[Do not spend too much time on less relevant work experience]
Reborn Computers, Los Angeles, CA   2009 – 2010
Computer Repair Technician
- Repaired all brands of desktop and laptop computers and performed diagnostic services on computers and peripherals [Technical skills]

SKILLS

- Sun certified Java developer and fully proficient in a wide variety of other programming languages including Unix, Linux, C, and C++ [Technical skills]
- Fluent in English and Spanish, proficient in French [Be careful not to exaggerate]

INTERESTS AND OTHER

- President of the UCLA Computer Science Student Association (CSSA) [Leadership responsibility]
- Vice-captain of Barrack House softball team [Teamwork]
- Avid scuba diver with Advanced PADI Openwater certification [Include something interesting!]

Getting Hired

Cover Letter

Though the cover letter should logically be an introduction that says, "Hi, here are some things to know about me before you look at my resume," the reality is that it's probably going to be the reverse. Most employers just don't have the time to read a bunch of cover letters. Thus, the cover letter is the icing on a well-baked resume.

With that realization in mind, the main objective of a good cover letter should be to explain why you should get the job. It should tell a story of where you've been and where you are hoping to go, so you should spin your experiences specifically toward the job in question. This is particularly important if you appear to be shifting gears (e.g., you're a chemistry major interested in PR or you're dropping out of med school to do finance). A cover letter is a test of your personality and your written communication skills, but mostly it's a personal sales pitch. Stay focused—anecdotes and tangents, no matter how hilarious, should be kept to a bare minimum.

Thankfully, there is a basic, three-paragraph formula for a strong cover letter. Follow these guidelines (in conjunction with the sample cover letter on page 101; or check out a downloadable version online at gradspot.com/book) to ensure that you make a good first impression on paper.

Heading: Whenever possible, you want to address your cover letter to an actual human being. Headings like "To Whom It May Concern" and "Dear Sir or Madam" should be used only as last resorts. If you aren't given a name off the bat, do a little research. Applying to a magazine? Check the masthead for the editor's name. If it's a large office, try calling HR, telling them what job you're applying for (you don't have to say who you are), and asking for a specific name within the department. The personal touch will show that you're resourceful and that you care enough to figure out whom you are dealing with.

> *Hazard:*
> **Naming electronic files**
>
> When naming your resume and cover letter files, make sure they are distinctive. Recruiters get hundreds of documents via email titled "resume10.doc" or "myresume.pdf"—make it easier for them to find your information later by saying who you are in the filename (e.g., "Jacob_Sills_Resume.pdf"). It will be more searchable and your name will be more memorable.

Paragraph One: What are you applying for and why? The cover letter is, in essence, an introduction to a stranger. So what do you do when you meet a stranger? You find some common ground. You announce your purpose for addressing him or her. You figure out if you "know the same people." This doesn't mean that you find out your potential boss went to Stanford and say, "OMG, do you know my friend Brittany?" It means covering a few basics:

- What position are you applying for?

- How did you find out about the job?

- Do you have a networking connection? (If so, mention this as early as possible.)

- Why, in a sentence or two, are you interested in and a good fit for the job? (This is like the thesis statement of your cover letter that will be illuminated in the subsequent paragraphs.)

Second Paragraph: What have you accomplished in your life that is relevant to this job? You'd like people to "read between the lines" of your resume and realize you are a wonderful person with great perspective. But if they didn't even realize that Dumbledore was gay, you've got to keep your expectations realistic. Here's where you expound upon your experience and spell out the subtext for them. For example, you can talk about a specific project that you handled well but weren't able to fully convey in a simple bullet point on your resume. Or you can talk about the type of feedback you got from your boss and coworkers. Remember to be specific: Only highlight things that are relevant to the position you're applying for. This is one occasion where you can toot your own horn. That doesn't mean you should sound arrogant, but you should sound convincing.

Third Paragraph: How do you match up, why do you want the job, and why should you get it? If you were playing *NBA Jam: Tournament Edition*, this is where the announcer should be yelling, "That's the nail in the coffin!" Tie up

your experiences and interests to convince the reader that you are the woman or man for the job. Show the employer that you are enthusiastic and passionate. Don't say, "If I don't get this job, I will literally kill myself!" But do give a strong indication of why the job interests you and what unique contributions you would bring to it.

Closing Statement: Mind your Ps and Qs. When closing out a cover letter, remember a few key things:

- Reiterate your contact information.

- Thank the reader for taking the time to consider your application.

- Sign your name if you are not sending electronically.

Sample Cover Letter

JOHN DOE

john.doe@gradspot.com

8888 W. 16th St., Apt 5B   (215) 555 5555
Philadelphia, PA, 19147, USA

Derek Anderson
Head of Undergraduate Recruiting
Diamond Group
222 Malone Street
Houston, TX 77007

Dear Mr. Anderson,

I am writing to apply for an Assistant Strategist position with the Diamond Group. After speaking with Daniel Kelly and conducting my own research, I know that Diamond would be a perfect match for my talents and aspirations. I recently graduated from the University of Michigan, where I maintained an overall GPA of 3.85/4.00 with a major in Marketing and a minor in English Literature and Language. Through a diverse range of professional experiences, including internships at *The Milwaukee Journal Sentinel* and Morgan Stanley, I have consistently been intrigued by the way in which companies both predict and shape the desires of consumers as they build their brands. By joining the Strategic Planning team, I hope to pursue this interest and further develop my knowledge of the industry as a whole while producing for your company.

While working on the arts desk at the *Sentinel*, my coverage of commissioned music in Nike's viral marketing campaigns garnered the interest of the business editor, who asked me to write a piece about the role of authenticity in the company's branding strategy. I continued to follow this trend on my blog, eventually leading to a successful pitch to Slate.com last year. Meanwhile, my internship last summer at Morgan Stanley offered me an intense immersion in the basic mechanics of M&A corporate advisory, as well the investment banking industry in general. I acquired a great deal of business acumen from being part of such a hard-working environment, and I greatly enjoyed researching the potential for market growth in a variety of industries. However, while I received encouragement from my supervisors to pursue a full-time position with the company, I did not find that the job played to my creative strengths.

At Diamond, I hope that I can pursue my passion for corporate branding and marketing strategy within the context of a more focused and creatively challenging environment. My background in print and online media provides me with a lens through which to analyze a brand and assess its marketability, while my investment banking experience has helped me develop a high level of professionalism, attention to detail, and analytical skills to review businesses. I especially hope to apply these skills to aid Diamond's shifting focus toward digital advertising. I am extremely excited by the prospect of translating my skills into a market strategy role, and I look forward to speaking with you about the possibility of joining your company. If you have any further questions you can reach me by email (john.doe@gradspot.com) or via phone at (215) 555 5555.

Thank you for your time and consideration.

Sincerely,
John Doe

Salary Requirements

Many jobs will ask you to include salary requirements with your application. While it might sound awesome to say you require, "Cheddar, gouda, and other denominations of cheese," this is actually sort of a no-win situation. On the one hand, the company may be using the salary requirement as a screening process—if you are too high, you might not be considered. On the other hand, it might be trying to save money by finding people who will work for cheap. There is no cure-all to this irksome malady, but here are a few suggested remedies:

Do your research. Look into the industry in which you're applying for a job and find comparable positions. Visit Salary.com to gauge ballpark figures, talk to people you know in similar positions, or cold call a competitor and try to find out what they offer.

Give a range. You really don't need to say, "I hope to receive $34,553.78 per annum." Figure out the industry standard and say something like, "I hope to receive a salary in the low- to mid-thirties." Covering the basics without being evasive shows that you are a diplomatic wizard.

Stall. Say you would prefer to discuss compensation in an interview, but you don't imagine it will be a problem.

Don't forget benefits. Make sure you know what benefits are offered, such as health care and 401(k) plans. When the time comes, it may be easier to negotiate for wider benefits than a higher salary. Assess your own needs to figure out if a $35K salary with full benefits is better than $40K with none (hint: it probably is).

Emailing Your Job Application

In this day and age, it's rare to physically mail in an application. Often there will be an online application where you simply plug in your info and upload your resume and cover letter. However, sometimes you will be asked to email your materials. While this system is supposed to make things easier and more efficient, it also adds new trauma-inducing variables to the equation. What do

I put in the subject line? What do I put in the body? Take a deep breath, young grad. It's basically a matter of common sense and following directions.

If there are no instructions for the subject line, include your name and the title of the position. A catchy or offbeat subject line (e.g., "Will Work for Food") is rarely appropriate, though it's up to you to judge the attitude of the organization. Don't be afraid to paste your cover letter directly into the body of the email as well as attaching it. This is the one document you really want someone to read, so serve it up on a platter. Also, **we strongly recommend that you convert all your documents to PDFs** to ensure that anyone is able to read them and to prevent extraneous markups from appearing.

Below we've provided a sample application email (which can also be found online at gradspot.com/book):

From: Samuel Bentley <sbentley@gradspot.com>
To: Mrs. Daniels <Mrs.Daniels@fakeweb.com>
Subject: WX957 – Production Assistant
Attachment: Sam_Bentley_resume.pdf,
Sam_Bentley_coverletter.pdf, Sam_Bentley_clips.pdf

Dear Mrs. Daniels,

I am writing to submit my application for the role of Production Assistant, which I learned about through your listing on Media Bistro. Attached you will find my résumé and cover letter, as well as a PDF of my writing clips. For your convenience, I have also pasted the text of my cover letter below.

If there is any other information I can provide, please do not hesitate to contact me by e-mail (sbentley@gradspot.com), or by phone at 646 555 5555.

Thank you for your consideration,
Samuel Bentley

Getting Hired

References

Hiring is always about trust. Unfortunately, the prevailing code on the streets is "don't trust anyone," so you'll often need to bring in some backup to vouch for your good name: a reference.

The most important thing to note about references is that a personal relationship speaks louder than a fancy name. If you had a great rapport with your thesis advisor and never spoke with the dean, go with the thesis advisor—he or she will know a lot more about your strengths and will have a genuine interest in promoting them. Maybe you want to get into trading and your second cousin's great uncle is T. Boone Pickens—utilize this connection for networking, but don't ask for a meaningless reference. You don't want HR calling up someone who barely knows you. This makes you seem like you haven't cultivated meaningful relationships with people who are willing to vouch for you.

While you should line up your references before applying for a job, you don't need to include them in your initial application (unless specifically instructed to do so). Generally, references come into play once you are being seriously considered for a job. Upon request, provide a PDF document with the name, title, company, and contact information (work phone and email) for each of your references (usually three to four). No major formatting is required, but make sure the file name is easily identifiable, and remember to list your name and contact information on the page. In addition to the attachment, it is appropriate to paste this information into the body of an email.

Below you'll find some suggestions for the type of people you should be considering to use as a reference:

A former boss

A professor or a dean

A coworker

A coach

A family friend in the industry

Someone who already works at the company you are applying to (money in the bank)

Networking

Once you've got your career story down on paper, it's time to put yourself out there in order to leverage any connections you may have to potential jobs and to create new ones. No matter how great a candidate you are for a position, you may never get an interview without the help of someone on the inside who can make sure your application finds its way to the top of the pile. And, you might not even know about a job in the first place until you meet the right person who thinks you can do it. In fact, far more positions are filled through referrals than through a job hunter applying blindly to a posting. Thus, it's no surprise that just about everyone on the planet—from corporate execs to skateboarding pros to acupuncturists—ranks networking as one of the most important parts of career building.

To understand how the real world works, consider the following situation: You're applying for a job and are up against one other candidate. The two of you have the same credentials, and you both come off well in social situations. But now for the X-factor: the other candidate is best friends with the interviewer's daughter. Peace out! Another of life's bitter herbs, but that's just the reality of the job market. Rather than crying about nepotism and pursuing some sort of proto-Marxist vendetta, get out there and network. As annoying as it is to get passed up for a job because someone else has a relationship that you don't, it's awesome when *you* are the one with the relationship. It's not a perfectly meritocratic system, but you have to accept that companies are much more inclined to go for a known entity than a wildcard (so much so that many even pay employees for referring friends to fill new positions).

This is not a *carte blanche* to shamelessly social climb your way to the top. In fact, networking is not all about kissing butt and taking names. Good networking involves being friendly, polite, proactive, and reasonably adept at expressing your interests to people. You do not have to be a slimy, shallow a-hole. At the end of the day, the more you network, the less "net work" you will end up doing in life. Doors will begin opening for you. Exciting opportunities will materialize out of thin air. And you'll have a lot of coffees with semi-interesting people.

Networking doesn't start with your dream employer. If you were talking to the employer of your dreams, then you wouldn't need to be networking in the first place. Networking starts by interacting with anyone. The key is understanding that just because you aren't talking directly to the CEO of the company you hope to work for doesn't mean that another person can't help you get your foot in the door. Ironically, the CEO is probably not the one who would ultimately be making the decision to hire you, so instead shoot for the people who would be your immediate superiors or coworkers.

Leave no stone unturned. Networking is a 24/7 endeavor. You're just as likely to find out about a potential job while socializing as you are while seeking advice from professionals. That doesn't mean you should only befriend rich kids with powerful parents. But it does mean you should look for networking opportunities all around you. Meet-up groups, recreational sports teams, and volunteer activities all provide settings in which you could meet someone who might know of a job lead. Chat up that guy in the corner of the café where you hang out—while he may just be a wannabe screenwriter, he might also be the favorite nephew of Steven Spielberg.

Don't underestimate the influence of other recent grads. Don't turn your nose up at networking with people who are one to three years out of college. They are often asked to review resumes submitted by applicants from their alma maters.

Don't expect to get a job right away when networking. While networking is the art of getting the job before the interview, that doesn't mean you're going to get the job immediately. Be patient.

Be friendly; it's about finding commonalities. Don't launch into a conversation with people

> **Tips & Tricks:**
> **Networking to recruiters**
>
> Some industries never use recruiters for entry-level jobs, but many companies that hire a lot of recent grads each year use recruiters as a filter between the company and the field of potential candidates. "The best place to start at a large company is with a recruiter," says Holly Paul, the National Sourcing Operations Leader for Campus and Experienced Recruiting at PricewaterhouseCoopers. If you're lucky, a recruiter from a company where you want to work visited your school during a job fair. But even if you didn't encounter one through campus recruiting, you can still use them to get a foot in the door. You can find company recruiters through networking or you can ask your school's careers services office if it has any hookups. You can even just call the company and ask. Within the recruiting industry, however, there's also an allure to going out and finding great candidates. And guess what? From our conversations with people in the industry, it's clear that Facebook (p. 115) and LinkedIn (p. 110) are very much on the radar, so be sure to maximize your presence on those platforms.

you're networking with by asking them whom they know or if they can help you land a job. Try to find some common ground—if need be, feel free to talk about something completely non–work-related (e.g., current events, sports). If you establish rapport first, the conversation will eventually turn toward what you want to do (or you can politely nudge it in that direction). And when that happens, you're effectively networking.

Keep track of your connections. After you make a new contact, jot down notes about your encounter on the back of his/her business card. Then create a networking spreadsheet with columns for "name," "company," "contact information," "how we met," and "correspondences/meetings." You can really stand out (particularly when networking with someone you've only met once or twice) by remembering specifics about your discussions. So also add a "notes" column for details (e.g., "Mary loves *Curb Your Enthusiasm* and started out as a waitress before she got into the PR biz"). Lastly, remember to stay up-to-date with your correspondence by putting things like, "Sent resume 7/19/10. Told to follow up 9/1," in the notes column.

The Informational Interview

Informational interviews (or as we like to say, "Infoviews") are the perfect way to get your foot in the door because they're easier to score than job interviews. An informational interview is an opportunity to talk with someone in an industry or at a company you find interesting. It's not an interview for a job, but rather a way to become more informed about potential opportunities, ask questions you wouldn't otherwise ask during an actual interview, and to make yourself known. This approach will provide you with two advantages: it will enable you to be more knowledgeable when the real interview rolls around, and it may actually turn into an interview. Remember that anytime you're talking with an employee of a company you one day hope to work for, you're being interviewed (even if they don't say so), so look alive! For a sample informational interview request, keep reading.

Getting Hired

Sample Informational Interview Request

The first sentence of your request should both introduce who you are and explain your connection to the individual you are contacting. Maybe he or she is a friend of a friend (as per the example below, as well as the sample found online at gradspot.com/book). Or maybe this is just a cold call and you pulled the name from a newspaper article. Next, share any pertinent experience you may have and also let the recipient know what you're hoping to accomplish via the informational interview. Lastly, leave your contact information.

From: Michael Humphrey <mike@gradspot.com>
To: Mrs. McGregor <McGregor@fortune500.com>
Subject: Interview Request

Dear Mrs. McGregor,

I recently graduated from the University of Miami, and after my good friend, David Johnson, learned that I was interested in a career in marketing, he suggested I contact you to request a brief informational interview.

While at the University of Miami, I majored in marketing. In addition, I had an internship last summer at Razor Corp, where I assisted media buyers on several high-profile interactive marketing campaigns. I now plan to apply both my education and my work experience to a career in marketing. At your convenience, I was hoping to learn what types of positions you suggest for a recent college graduate, and also to hear your thoughts on the future of the industry as a whole.

Thank you very much for your time. If you are available to speak with me, we can talk over the phone, or I can meet you at a location of your choosing. I can be reached at 305 555 5555 or by e-mail at mike@gradspot.com.

Appreciatively,
Michael Humphrey

While most people will choose to email their potential interviewer, if you only have a phone number, try the script below on for size:

"Hi, my name is Michael Humphrey. I was fascinated by the recent article about you in the New York Times, so I thought I would get in touch because I'm very interested in pursuing a career in marketing. I was hoping you might be willing to spend a few minutes talking on the phone or in person to provide me with some advice based on your experience. Would it be possible to set up an informational interview at your convenience? Thank you very much for your consideration. You can reach me at (212) 555-5309 or via email at mike@gradspot.com."

Spot Check:
Prepping for the "Infoview"

If you've managed to find someone willing to chat with you, kudos. Now don't screw it up! We kid, because as long as you follow this helpful checklist, everything will be fine and dandy.

Pick a chill place to meet. Assuming it's not someone you have a prior relationship with, don't ask to meet over dinner or "drinks," unless they offer. Instead, ask if they would be willing to talk over a cup of coffee, or during a quick breakfast or lunch. Other options include meeting at someone's office, or finally, talking on the phone. Of course, an in-person conversation always has more impact, but you should always meet at a time and place that is convenient for the other party.

Treat your meeting as if it were an actual interview. This means reading up on the person whom you're meeting with, the company they work for, related recent news, and the industry as a whole (thank you, Wiki-Google). This will help with conversation topics, and your preparation will convey your enthusiasm. That said, don't go wild with displaying your knowledge of someone's personal history—you don't want to transform from "job candidate" to "restraining order candidate."

Come armed. Always bring some type of notebook and a pen. If you can do so discreetly, bring a resume in the event the person you're meeting with asks for it—though you can always email it afterwards. If you are networking over the phone, you can compensate for the lack of face time by being extra organized. Spread out your notes in front of you or keep a Word document open—the person you're speaking with will never know and it can make you look extremely knowledgeable.

Don't forget etiquette. You'll never get yourself in trouble by being too polite (at least at first). Call people Mr., Ms., Mrs., etc. Always meet/speak with people at their convenience. If you're getting coffee or food, offer to pay even if you think they'll insist on picking up the tab. If they do insist, you can give in and let them pay at that point. (Check out page 163 for a whole discussion of meal etiquette.) As your interactions move along, you can get a vibe from the other person and loosen up accordingly. For example, if they tell you to call them by their first name, it's most likely not a "test," so go ahead and do it. If it is a test, they're creepy and you may be networking up the wrong tree.

Always send a thank you note after every networking meeting. So, you've spent an hour talking with someone about a job, and that person has been kind enough to share her career insights with you. She did you a favor. Acknowledge it by sending a thank you letter (or email, as the case may be these days). Depending upon your relationship with the person with whom you just spoke, the letter can be formal or just a few sentences. Referencing something you discussed during your conversation goes a long way. You can even ask a follow-up question, and if the person requested to see your resume, this is an opportunity to send it along. For more information on crafting your resume, see page 94. ■

Web Links:
Professional Networking Sites

While it's wise to protect yourself from prying employers online (see page 91), the Internet is also a great place to self-promote, get your name out there, and network your way toward great jobs. Online career networking is growing rapidly as the first web-savvy generation of workers begins to make its mark on the professional world.

LinkedIn

LinkedIn.com was the first online career network to gain widespread popularity, and today it boasts a user base of 48 million "professionals." Basically, it's like one massive cocktail party, minus the cocktails and the human interaction. (If you want to set the mood, however, just whip up a gin and tonic and play some light jazz on your computer.) All online career networks have the basic features you'd expect, so we're going to assume that you can figure out the basics. What we want to explore here are ways to make your profile stand out and get exactly what you want from the site.

* **Make your profile public.** This means anyone can view it, and Google will even display it as a search result when people Google your name (see page 93). To do so, go to your account section and edit your "full profile." While you're at it, choose a custom URL (e.g., linkedin.com/in/snooki). One caveat: Before you plaster your name all over the 'net, make sure that you've fine-tuned every part of your profile.

* **Dig deep for connections.** Found someone who works at the company of your dreams but don't want to cold call? Check his or her LinkedIn profile to see if you have any connections. LinkedIn shows connections that have up to six degrees of separation—you could probably even find a way to holler at Kevin Bacon! In a bind, you can have your friend ask her friend to put you in touch with a friend's friend. Again, it may not sound ideal, but it's better than sending a random email to a potential employer before you've laid any groundwork.

* **Ask questions.** LinkedIn enables you to send a message to your entire network in the form of a question. So, once you've built up your LinkedIn buddies, ask a question like, "Is anyone connected with a friend who works at Macy's?" to start the ball rolling on your job

search. You may be surprised to find several responses from friends who know someone who knows someone else who works at Macy's. Even if you only have a second-degree connection, it's better than blindly submitting a resume.

* **Post a status update.** Just like with Facebook, you can post status updates that will appear on peoples' LinkedIn news feeds and your profile page. Just remember to be careful what you post, particularly if you've set your profile to be publicly accessible.

* **Consider going "Business" for even more connections.** Once you find someone you want to talk to, you can't directly message that person unless you are connected. However, if you sign up for a "Business Account" (starting at $24.95 per month at the time of printing), the floodgates will open and you can contact whomever you like. The best way to holler at someone out of the blue is through the option called "Expertise Requests" (a.k.a., informational interviews), in which you appear to be asking for advice rather than a job. (Don't worry, these interactions can often turn into interviews if you impress the contact and the company is hiring.)

* **Don't be shy about asking people for LinkedIn recommendations.** LinkedIn enables former bosses, coworkers and other connections to add letters of recommendation to your profile, similar to traditional references. There's nothing better than an objective source lauding your talents. And don't forget about karma—you may need to return the favor one day, so be careful about whom you ask to recommend you and whom you're recommending.

* **Don't accept everyone and every offer you get at face value.** More and more, recruiting companies are popping up on LinkedIn. When you think you're networking your way to a job at Nike, you might just end up networking your way to chatting with a recruiter. This isn't necessarily a bad thing—just something to be aware of.

* **Expand your network.** If you don't opt for the "Business" account, the best way to leverage LinkedIn (aside from optimizing your profile so that a recruiter can find you) is to grow your network. The easiest way to do this is to import your contacts from your Gmail or other email accounts. You can do this when you first create an account or by going to the "Contacts" section.

Getting Hired

111

Ask The Expert:
LinkedIn Tips for Recent Grads

Lindsey Pollak is one of our favorite career gurus for recent grads. She's the author of Getting from College to Career: 90 Things to Do Before You Join the Real World *and a frequent contributor to FastCompany.com and the Huffington Post. She also happens to be a Campus Spokesperson for LinkedIn, so we figured we'd pick her brain for some insider tips for recent grads dipping their feet into the career networking pool.*

What one LinkedIn feature should every recent grad job hunter know about and leverage?

Though it may seem obvious, the most important LinkedIn feature is your profile—specifically your use of keywords, profile picture, and recommendations.

It's extremely important to include keywords in your summary statement. The summary portion of your profile provides a chance to share the highlights of your bio in your own words. It's also a place to include keywords and phrases that a recruiter or hiring manager might type into a search engine to find a person like you. The best place to find relevant keywords is in the job listings that appeal to you and the LinkedIn profiles of people who currently hold the kinds of positions you want.

Keep in mind that you should list all experience (including unpaid or volunteer work) in your summary, as it provides a full view of your experience and will help former colleagues and classmates find you on LinkedIn. If you are a current student or recent grad, you can include relevant coursework and extracurricular achievements as well.

Finally, nothing builds credibility like third-party endorsements. The most impressive LinkedIn profiles have at least one recommendation associated with each job a person has held. If you feel awkward soliciting recommendations try recommending someone else's work first—in hopes that he or she will kindly return the favor.

Is there a best practice for cold-connecting/emailing people on LinkedIn?

Once you've connected with people you already know from "the real world," LinkedIn provides you with tools to connect, degree by degree, with the connections of your connections for mutual benefit.

Note that the way LinkedIn is set up, you can only connect to someone via an introduction from a mutual connection. This ensures that the connections on the site are trustworthy and there is very little spam. Other than paying for a "Business" account, the best way to connect with people you haven't met is to ask for an introduction through a mutual connection. If you don't have a mutual connection but belong to the same Group, you can send a message to a fellow member.

If you do ask a mutual connection for an introduction to someone new, be sure to be polite, professional, and proactive. Customize the message and use proper grammar and professional etiquette. If you demonstrate your interest in the person's career and show that you've done your research, the cold connecting won't feel quite so frigid.

Should I join groups? Any recommended groups for recent grads?

Absolutely! Groups are at the heart of LinkedIn and are a great way to become active on the site. LinkedIn Groups are communities of professionals based on common interests, experiences, affiliations, and goals. University alumni groups are among the most popular and active on LinkedIn. I definitely recommend that recent grads join their alumni group to get access to interesting members, discussions, job postings, news postings, and more. If you're part of a professional organization or a Greek organization (business or social), it's a good idea to join these groups too. There may be national or regional groups as well as groups for your school's alumni. LinkedIn groups—especially the well-established ones— can serve as an additional communication tool, a community builder, and a research tool to boost your job search and expand your network. ∎

Getting Hired

Sample LinkedIn Profile

Summary

Versatile writer/editor with experience in both print and online media. Particularly interested in entertainment coverage and reviews.

Specialties

Restaurant and bar reviews; music coverage; copywriting; CMS administration; Search Engine Optimization; and HTML

Experience

Associate Editor

Hang Ten Media
Writing and Editing industry
June 2009 – Present (9 months)

* Review bars, restaurants, and live music shows

* Develop story ideas with editors and freelancers

* Copy and style edit online and print submissions in preparation for publication

* Manage database of establishments

Doostang

The "Doo" is a lot like LinkedIn, except with a much smaller user base (it began as an "invite only" network and still maintains a certain air of exclusivity). Initially, Doostang leveraged its "high quality" users to attract companies that did not list jobs on other sites. Now that it is an open network, most of its cachet has worn off, but its job listings still contain a higher percentage of the more sought-after (and thus competitive) positions. So while LinkedIn is larger and will afford you access to more people and companies, Doostang may very well provide access to a gem that you won't find on LinkedIn. The only kicker is that in order to apply to Doostang's premium jobs, you have to pay $39.95 per month (which to be fair, is a small price to pay if you actually land one). Savvy job hunters might consider using LinkedIn to build a large network and Doostang to search for diamonds in the rough.

Facebook as a Career Networking Tool

Don't forget Facebook (as if you would, you Facebook FREAK). Although not focused exclusively on career networking, Facebook has over 500 million users, many of whom list their employer. Expand your network and scan it to find people in the industries that interest you or, better yet, people who work for the companies you want to target. Facebook is also useful for letting people know what you are after. For example, you can post notes or use your status to alert your friends to the type of job you want; with any luck, they'll holler at you when they come across something they think might be of interest. Just don't sound too desperate—networking, even online, is a lot like dating.

Twitter

While it would be a stretch to think that you can get a job on Twitter by doing X, Y, and Z, creating a presence on the site can be another effective weapon in the twenty-something job hunter's arsenal. The reasons are twofold. First, it's a great networking tool with one advantage over Facebook: because it's more public, it's easier to connect with new people and even gain access to brands and companies. Second, because of the combination of individuals, websites, and companies using Twitter to communicate, you can essentially use it like a news feed to stay on top of industry chatter. Here are some tips:

Find people to follow and search for what you want. Start out with the "Find People" tab on the top navigation and use the tool to find people and companies that you think might be interesting. This tool will sift through user names and Twitter profiles for you, so if you're inclined to work for a skydiving company, search for "skydiving" and see who (and what) comes back.

In addition to skydiving resources and companies, you can also find a whole slew of individuals who might be interested in the same things you are, professionally and otherwise. Head on over to search.twitter.com and you can search individual keywords as well as any user-generated hashtags. If "#career" proves too broad (and it will), try narrowing down to specific industries (like #skydiving, #basejumping, #parachuting), companies you want to know about, or even specific people who work at those companies. You might find someone who works for the company you've just sent your resume to but who doesn't list their company inside of their biography or name but does have it in their tweets. (Otherwise, they would have appeared in Twitter's "People Search" tool.)

Another way to find relevant tweeters is to search an external Twitter directory like Twellow.com or Wefollow.com. When you find people talking about the topics you're interested in, start following them (when you're signed in, a big "follow" button will show up under their names). Take note of whom they tweet at, and follow those people as well.

Get involved. As with any social networking tool, the mountain won't come to you just because you created an account. There's no need to become a Twitter fiend who can't sit through your cousin's rehearsal dinner without feeling the need to post 35 updates detailing the chef's choice of garnish on the baked potatoes; but, you will need to spend a little bit of time with it if you want to see the benefits. When someone asks a question you think you have a good response to, "@" them and respond. They'll likely write you back to thank you, or ask for more information.

Most importantly, post good content. The better the content, the more likely others will re-tweet it—providing useful links or saying funny things tend to be the most successful approaches. You should also re-tweet other posts—it feeds people's egos and makes them like you! Of course, you can also just follow a bunch of people in silence and use the site like an RSS reader, but if you want to garner any attention, you'll have to contribute to the "conversation." At the very least, it's worth spending five to ten minutes a day checking on what the people you follow have to say. You never know—they may mention a job opening that hasn't been formally announced yet!

Getting Hired

Our friend Michael Gruen (who co-authored the *Dummies Guide to Twitter*) helped us to further understand the ins-and-outs of extending your job search to the Twitterverse. Here are some more savvy maneuvers to get you started:

* In your Twitter bio, link to your LinkedIn profile, your personal website or portfolio, or anything else you'd like people to see when they check out your Twitter feed.

* Before you start following people, make sure your profile is as refined as it can be (i.e., has a link to your resume, includes a compelling description, has a good nickname, uses a neutral background or one appropriate for the type of job you want).

* The #tweetmyjobs hashtag is a great source of job listings (and it also has an accompanying website at tweetmyjobs.com).

* Twitterjobsearch.com is a pretty good search engine to find job tweets.

* Follow the right people—in addition to the techniques already mentioned, search Twitter and Google for headhunters and recruiters. Feeds such as @freelance_jobs, @jobsforkarma, and @kellyjobs are a good starting point for finding job listings.

Interviewing

Now that you've prepared your application materials (see page 102) and mixed and mingled (both online and off), the real fun begins. It's time to show your face at the companies that would like to interview you. But keep in mind that there may be a bit of a lull between sending in your application materials and actually being summoned for an interview. One of the most frustrating parts about applying for jobs is that sometimes (quite often, in fact) you never hear back. Even though you spent six hours perfecting the cover letter and sent an extremely gracious follow-up email a month later, you might get straight up blanked. Companies receive too many applications to muster the humanity it would require to respond to all of them. For this reason, it's advisable to cast a wide net—you may catch some unwanted things like diseased crustaceans and discarded diapers, but you'll also increase the odds of finding something you want.

The best advice we can give, particularly for newcomers to the job market, is to accept every interview you're offered. Even if you are 99% sure you will

Getting Hired

Tips & Tricks:
Phone interviews

 Phone interviews are often a critical first step toward landing an in-person interview. In rare cases, they can be the only interview you'll get. Since you can't read the various social cues of a face-to-face conversation, you have to rely solely on what you say and how you say it—use enthusiasm and intonation to sell yourself, and avoid chewing gum, smoking, or eating. Be prepared for the call, find a quiet place where you feel comfortable chatting, and find a landline to avoid a cell-related snafu. Tell family members or roommates they are forbidden to touch the phone while you're interviewing. Finally, take advantage of the best part of phone interviewing—no one can see you, so you can lay out all of your notes in front of you and nail all your talking points. You can also wear your pajamas—score! Some people feel that standing up during a phone interview helps them feel (and sound) more energized. Just remember that standing does not mean running laps around your living room. Being out of breath will make you sound frazzled, creepy, or both.

not want the job, interviewing is an acquired skill, and any chance to practice will pay off down the line. Each time, you'll learn how to manage your nervous tics, expose yourself to new questions, and perfect your handshake until it hovers playfully between dead fish and vise grip. You might even learn that you do actually want the job. The whole process of interviewing can be extremely nerve-wracking for some people, but it's also the part of the game where you can really stand out from the hordes of other applicants with comparable credentials. We hope our tips will help you shine with the intensity of a thousand suns.

Prep Work

Prepare for an interview as you would prepare for a test. That doesn't mean drink a sixer of Red Bull and stay up all night playing online cribbage. It means anticipate what's coming and make sure you are ready to knock it out of the proverbial ballpark. Research the company, the industry, and the interviewer beforehand. Start with the company website: pay close attention to major divisions of the organization, highlighted products or services, press releases, vocabulary, and who's who within the company's hierarchy. Search Vault.com for company profiles, employee surveys, diversity statistics, and more (see page 53 for more resources). Find out if the company has been in the news using Lexis Nexis (often available through your college library) or by searching the archives of major papers like the *New York Times*, the *Wall Street Journal*, or the *Washington Post*. Finally, don't forget to do some Googling, and consider checking out online career networks like LinkedIn and Doostang to find the interviewer and see if you have anything in common. (For more on online career networking, see page 110.)

After you've done your background checks, write up a list of potential questions that might pop up, including both general personal questions and those specific to the firm. Ask other people who may have interviewed with the same company or similar companies for advice on what to expect during the interview. Also, refer back to the job description to remind yourself of exactly what skills they are looking for so that you can stress them throughout the interview. Finally, know your resume and cover letter inside out; sometimes, the information on your resume is the only thing that the interviewer will know about you, so be prepared to defend its honor to the death.

Interview Dress

One of the most anxiety-inducing elements of the interview process is figuring out what to wear on the big day. The corporate culture of the company you're interviewing at plays a large part in how you should dress for your interview, but gauging this culture ahead of time is not always easy. There are however a few things you can do to prepare. First, if you know people who work at the company (or at a similar company/in the same industry), ask them what they wear to work and what they think would be appropriate. Second, scan the company's website for photos. If there are images of employees happily working away, take note of what they're wearing. And if those two routes fail, call the company and ask the receptionist what the standard dress code is. You don't have to reveal who you are—just say you have a meeting coming up (or, if you're really paranoid, have a friend call up for you...from a payphone...in a different state).

> ### Tips & Tricks:
> ### Ironing Your Clothes
>
> Making sure your clothes are as crisp as Jay-Z's may seem minor, but when it comes to the job hunt, every little detail counts. Though ironing is in theory simple, don't try it for the first time right before your interview. Do a test run and don't forget to always read the tag inside a garment to check whether it can be ironed. Now instead of boring you with ten pages of badly drawn diagrams, we figured we'd just suggest you head over to YouTube for more "How to Iron" videos then you'll ever want to watch.

Getting Hired

Golden rule: No matter what you decide to wear, make sure that it is clean, pressed, newish looking, and well-fitting. Also, always err on the conservative side of the wardrobe spectrum. For advice on wardrobe staples, where to get them, and then how to clean them, see the "Office Dress" section on page 153.

Men. If you're interviewing in a more conservative industry (or in an industry where you will be in the public eye, like hospitality or sales), you should wear a suit. Navy and grey suits are flattering and work well with accents, such as pastel-colored collared shirts or colorful ties. Just remember that anything too flashy will distract—and you don't want to be remembered as the guy with the blindingly bright shirt, or the guy with the novelty tie that plays "Take Me Out to the Ballgame," for that matter. The safest bet is always a dark blue or grey suit (two or three buttons with the bottom button always left unbuttoned), a white shirt, and a conservative tie. If your suit doesn't fit well, it's worth spending the money to have it altered ($25 to $150 depending on how much of a disaster it is). Wear dark socks and invest in a nice pair of (recently polished) shoes. For other types of industries such as IT or publishing, business casual attire will be sufficient. This generally means nice pants, a belt, a collared shirt, and a sweater or nonmatching blazer, no jeans.

One frequent trap male interviewees fall into is being poorly groomed. This is a huge issue and one you can easily avoid with some basic prep work. We don't doubt that you look sexy with three-day scruff, but you also look a little bit like a caveman. And unless you're interviewing at Geico, that's probably not the look you want to achieve. Shave, shower, and do multiple mirror checks before marching into the line of fire. You're more likely to nail the interview if you're confident that you've nailed your look.

Women. The same basic ground rules apply for women. If you're interviewing at a more traditional company or corporation (e.g., a bank, a law firm, or a company's corporate headquarters), a conservative pant or skirt suit should do the trick. Wear closed-toed shoes and, if you wear heels, make sure they aren't distractingly high. Tripping down the company stairs will make an impression—but probably not the one you were going for.

If you are interviewing at a more creative or casual company, a suit is probably overkill, but you should still look like you made an effort. A conservative dress or knee-length skirt with a nice blouse and/or nonmatching blazer is a safe bet. When in doubt, err on the side of formality. And no matter what you wear, remember that carrying yourself with confidence makes *any* outfit look that much better.

Keep flashy accessories and colorful pieces to a minimum during the interview. Once you land the job, you can start to live it up. Same goes for handbags: If you tend to carry a bag with a blatant brand logo, be aware that it will be noticed (for better or worse).

Game Time: Day of the Interview

If you played sports in school or were on the debate team you know how nerve-wracking it can be to anticipate an event where you have to be 100% on the ball. Game day readiness is all about routine and preparation; quell anxiety by avoiding last-minute problems. Print out multiple copies of your resume and any other materials the night before and put them in a nice folder. Make sure your outfit is pressed and looking sharp. Don't eat anything that will upset your stomach, pop an Icebreaker, and don't drink too much caffeine if it will make you jittery. Finally, make sure you know how to get to the interview, and plan to arrive early. A late showing is a surefire way to ruin your shot at the job. If you *are* running late because of an Amtrak strike or legitimate emergency (catching the end of *Pirates 3* on TV doesn't count), call ahead to let them know what is going on and when to expect you.

Spot Check:
In the Interview War Room

When the moment of truth arrives, be prepared to cock back a fully loaded clip of wit, charm, and illuminating-yet-humble tales about why you are awesome. Here are some things to remember:

✔ **Check your body language**. Sit up straight, avoid nervous fidgeting, and make eye contact (though not to an awkward extent). If you are not a very expressive person, try your best to smile and display enthusiasm—someone who does not know you may mistake your demeanor for boredom or apathy.

✔ **Go in with a game plan.** Figure out how you are going to pitch yourself for the job at hand, and know what talking points you definitely want to hit. Even though the interviewer is asking the questions, you can still "topsy-turvy" the situation and put yourself in the driver's seat.

✔ **Speak slowly and clearly.** Unless you are interviewing to read off the side-effects at the end of a Lipitor commercial, speaking a mile a minute will make you seem insane, incomprehensible, or nervous—in any case, not the impression you want to make. Before fielding each query, steady yourself with a deep breath, which will have the added benefit of making your answers seem less rehearsed.

✔ **Don't panic.** If a question throws you off, don't stare at your feet for five minutes or go into an epileptic fit of "uhs" and "likes." Utilize stalling techniques like repeating the question out loud or asking for a clarification. If you are offered a drink at the beginning, accept even if you're not thirsty—a well-timed sip can be a lifesaver when you're flummoxed. When all else fails, thinking out loud is always better than silence, no matter how much you think you're bombing.

✔ **"What is your biggest weakness?"** You will almost always be asked this question, because everyone in the world thinks it's revealing, when in fact it is not at all. Most applicants pursue the same tactic: take a strength and then frame it as a weakness. This approach can work, but realize that "I'm a perfectionist" is getting a bit tired. Instead, you might try an honest yet strategic approach: state an issue that is not horrendous, explain how you confronted the issue, and show that you have taken proactive steps to improve. Something like, "I have gotten bogged down in the details of large projects in the past, but after realizing this about myself I have been consciously stopping to take a step back and look at the bigger picture." Never say you are lazy or tend to make mathematical mistakes, even if it's true.

✔ **Don't be negative.** Badmouthing ex-bosses or past experiences makes you sound high-maintenance and pessimistic. Rather than talking about what you hated about your previous jobs, find a way to describe what you learned and what your new goals are.

✔ **Ask questions.** It's safe to say that 99% of interviews end with an invitation to ask questions about the job and the company. An original question will demonstrate that you've thought deeply about the job/company/industry and will make you stand out from those other drones being interviewed. Refrain from asking about salary, benefits, vacation time, and so on. You can handle that with HR, or after you actually get an offer. For some example questions, see page 124.

✔ **Request a response.** To give yourself peace of mind, don't hesitate to ask when you can expect to hear back. Ideally, doing so will save you some sleepless nights spent worrying why you haven't received a response yet. Be aware, however, that sometimes hiring schedules can shift. If you haven't heard back within the timeframe indicated, feel free to send a polite follow-up email.

✔ **Ask for business cards.** Request a business card from each person you meet during your interview, otherwise you'll be kicking yourself when it comes time to send thank you notes and you can't remember anyone's name. If possible, make notes on the back of each person's card about specific points you can reference when you write to thank them (see page 126). ■

Sample Interview Questions

Thankfully, not every interviewer is as creative as Jimmy Fallon, so it's not uncommon to hear the same general questions time and again. No matter how suave you are, it's worth taking a moment to prep your answers. Grab a friend and run through the list of questions in order to become comfortable with the process. You don't need to memorize your answers (after all, you have to be able to think on your feet), but after this exercise, you'll have plenty of coherent thoughts in the chamber.

Questions You May Be Asked

* Tell me about yourself. (Another variation: Walk me through your resume.)

* Can you share some experiences that you think prepared you for this opportunity?

* Why do you want to work here?

* What interests you about this industry?

* Describe some experiences in which you had to work as part of a team. What was your role? Did you like it?

* Can you describe a situation in which you successfully multitasked?

* Can you remember a situation in which you held a lot of responsibility? Solved a problem? Rose to a challenge?

* What are your goals in pursuing this job?

* What are your interests outside of work?

* Do you consider yourself detail-oriented or more of a "big picture" person?

* Traditionally, what does your decision-making process entail?

* Can you share a situation in which you had to make an ethical choice?

* Share with me a time when you were disappointed in yourself. How did you improve?

✳ Describe a situation in which you had to be insistent to make your point. How did you make sure your voice was heard?

✳ Are you self-motivated or do you prefer to follow directions?

✳ Have you ever had to resolve an issue with a superior? If so, how did you do it?

✳ How do you manage your time?

✳ Do you have any questions for me?

Don't forget to come up with some questions to ask your interviewer to demonstrate your interest in the company. When constructing these questions, go to the company's website, browse the recent news, and develop a question from there. For example, you could ask, "How is this company taking advantage of new opportunities in digital media?" However, it's probably safer to steer clear of asking about salary (see page 102) and benefits unless the interviewer broaches those topics.

Questions to Ask Your Interviewer

✳ What is the most rewarding thing about working here?

✳ Can you tell me a bit more about the company culture?

✳ How is success measured?

✳ What are the opportunities for advancement for the position I'm applying for?

✳ How many people work in the department where I would be, and how is the department structured?

✳ Is there a "typical day" for the job I'm applying for?

✳ What's a typical first-year assignment?

✳ What are the organization's plans for change and or growth in the future?

✳ What are you looking for in a new hire?

Getting Hired

Follow-Ups

A follow-up thank you letter is not just polite; it is also a chance to reiterate qualifications, reemphasize your interest in the position, or bring up something you didn't get to mention in person. Within 24–48 hours of interviewing, write a brief note to each individual who spoke with you. If there is any doubt about correct names, spelling, or titles, check the business card or call the office to double-check. After that, wait until the timeframe that you were given for a response has passed before calling or emailing again. An overly eager beaver is no one's favorite type o' beaver. Check out a sample thank you note below or online at gradspot.com/book.

> Dear Mr. Alexander,
>
> Thank you for taking the time not only to interview me, but also to share your insights into and experiences at Smithfields with me. It was exciting to hear you discuss how the meritocratic culture truly pervades every facet of the firm. I also enjoyed learning about the lean project teams that enable new hires to assume lots of responsibility very quickly. After meeting with a number of employees on Monday, I feel certain that I would like to become part of the Smithfields community. Thank you again for your time and I hope to be hearing from Smithfields soon.
>
> Sincerely,
> Blair Stevenson

Making a Decision

Congratulations! After months of begging and pleading at the feet of employers, the offers are rolling in. Now you've got some swagger! If you get two or more offers, all we can say is take into account all of the issues we've brought up throughout the last two chapters: geography, salary, benefits, office vibe, and so on. Go with your gut, and if you got job offers in different industries, don't feel that by choosing one you have to stick with it forever.

So there you have it, the Gradspot guide to landing your first job. Before we move on, there's just one more set of demons to lay to rest…

Should I Take a Job I'm Not 100% Sure About?

We won't go so far as to say that starting your first job will cause another existential crisis, but let's be honest: it could. Taking a job that you don't feel is perfect for you can be a tough pill to swallow. Like the pilgrims of yore, today's "settlers" may wonder why they gave up a mediocre life of unemployment and mild persecution for "the New World."

Settling is all about perspective. On the one hand, there's a dark storm cloud in the post-grad forecast: 99 times out of 100, your first job is not going to be your dream job. But there's a silver lining as well: The majority of recent grads hold three or four jobs in their first five years out of college, so you don't have to stick with anything you hate for long. Still, feeling like you've sold yourself short can definitely keep you up at night. There are no simple answers, but it's important to develop a more holistic view of your entry into the work force. (See our interview with Alan Pickman on page 129 for thoughts on "false feelings of irrevocability.")

Why Do You Feel Like You're Settling?

There are a lot of factors that go into the decision to settle for something that isn't fully "you"—your economic situation (often based on how long Mom and Dad will pay your way), the difficulty of entry into a given industry, and the likelihood of other opportunities arising. Not even the great mathematician Leonhard Euler could reconcile those variables, so you probably can't either. Try to pinpoint exactly why you feel like you're settling—by necessity (you need to pay the bills or take a job in Wichita to be near your sick grandmother), by ambition (you have big dreams and will not be satisfied until you run your

Getting Hired

own company), because it's the easy option (laziness), or because you don't yet know what your dream job is (lack of clarity at this point is totally normal).

Make a Commitment

Once you've made a decision, it's important to commit to it rather than constantly wondering what could have been (at least at first). It's sort of like how finding a boyfriend or girlfriend is as annoying as having one, but at some point, you have to stop playing the field and commit (for a bit). You may be surprised—what seemed like trivial busy work could evolve into real responsibility (in the same way that a one-night stand could evolve into a meaningful relationship). In addition, you can look for other jobs/partners while you're at it, but your hands are going to be tied because if you get caught, it's pretty awkward.

Okay, this analogy is pretty much aces so far except for one important fact: getting out of a relationship sooner rather than later will make things easier, but when you start a job, a certain level of commitment is expected (it varies, but generally a year is considered the minimum, and two demonstrates a strong commitment). Here's the thing, though: Just as being in a relationship makes you more attractive to other people (the old "I want what he/she has" phenomenon), holding a job will boost your status in the eyes of other employers, as well as provide you with new skills and experiences. Moreover, if you perform well, they'll be more likely to speak highly of you to others when you move on (rather than badmouthing you 'round the block and on the Interweb).

Should I Take a Job That Pays Less than I'd Hoped For?

This is a whole different type of settling—forgive us for not feeling bad for you. Presumably, you can either slave from "8 'til late" every day doing something you don't love, or make a significantly smaller salary doing what you really want to do. Either way, it's nice to have options. We'd like to say go with your heart every time, but we realize that things like student debt and rent are real concerns. If you are fortunate enough to have a little bit of financial cushioning, think twice before buying into the allure of a six-figure salary. Even though parents and grandparents love to recount their days of "paying dues" in terrible first jobs, it's a slippery slope toward a breakdown when the only thing getting you out of bed in the morning is the paper chase.

See page 171 for more information on deciding when to move on from your first job.

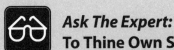

Ask The Expert:
To Thine Own Self Be True

Admittedly, it's more than a little daunting to consider planning an entire career when you don't even have your first job yet. To help keep the demons at bay, our friend Alan J. Pickman, a career management professional and psychologist, shared some wisdom about how recent grads can channel their skills and interests into fulfilling work lives.

I graduated. What do I do with myself now?

In terms of self-assessment, you should not only consider your skills, strengths, and interests, but also your values, hopes, dreams, and drivers.

To get to know the job marketplace, you can gather information from electronic and printed sources, but at some point, you must talk to people who work in the fields that interest you to explore what different working environments are like, what the people are like within a given profession, how they are rewarded, and how their careers have developed.

Slight problem—I didn't do so well in school. Am I doomed as a professional?

If you didn't do well in school, it doesn't mean you don't have interests, values, and things that you're good at; you simply have to be self-aware and mindful of those other elements. In thinking about a career, you should consider the activities you were involved in, clubs you might have joined, things you did during your summer vacations, and the type of people you surround yourself with. These are all indicators of what's important to you; academic excellence is only one piece of the larger puzzle.

What if I make a mistake?

This worry is often based on a false sense of irrevocability—"if I choose Path A, I am saying goodbye forever to Path B." Today, it's appropriate for young adults to hold a number of different jobs in the years after they graduate. Your early jobs are really mechanisms by which you can help to form and sharpen your sense of career identity, so as long as they are increasing your self-awareness, they are useful. If you don't go through this exploration as a young adult, it's very possible that you'll end up needing to go through it much later in your career.

What are some common traps I should avoid?

The biggest trap I've seen among young adults is that your own voice may be less clear (and given less weight) than the voices of those around you. Whether it's peers or parents who are influencing you, it's often difficult for young adults to have a high degree of self-knowledge and the courage to attend to their own voices. I would strongly advise you to run with your interests and passions when you're starting out, because there will never be a better time to do so. ■

Getting Hired

Chapter IV: Working Life

Working Life

When you get that call or email telling you that you've got a job or internship, relief will wash over you in an awesome wave. Maybe you'll have a celebratory drink or go to Six Flags. But as the big first day draws nigh, a creeping sense of dread can begin to sully even the most buoyant of dispositions. "What if I am bad at the job? What if it is miserable? Is this really what I want to be doing? Are they going to find out that I don't technically know how to use Excel?"

It is, indeed, one of the great ironies of the employment process. While devoting countless hours to the job hunt is unquestionably a worthwhile endeavor, many recent grads take for granted the preparation time necessary to ensure you are actually ready to go to work.

In this chapter, we'll help you ace your first day, avoid the booby traps of office politics, dress the part, instant message with old people, and much more. Office life is not always intuitive, so it's important to prepare yourself. You'll be running the place in no time, we know it.

 First Jobs of Famous People

Few careers begin at the top, and many of the people we now idolize started their working lives with some pretty suspect first jobs.

Bill Gates: Congressional page

Bill Murray: sold chestnuts outside of a grocery store

Jerry Seinfeld: sold light bulbs over the phone

Madonna: worked behind the counter at a Dunkin' Donuts

Stephen King: janitor (inspired to write *Carrie* while cleaning a girls' locker room)

Walt Disney: ambulance driver

Coolio: fireman

Danny DeVito: hairdresser

Ellen Degeneres: shucked oysters, painted houses, sold vacuum cleaners

Rod Stewart: gravedigger

Sylvester Stallone: lion cage cleaner, porn actor ∎

Surviving Your First Day

Starting work can be one of the most awkward things you've ever done in your life. Waiting to be told where to sit, how to log into your email, and who (if anyone) is going to go to lunch with you can make you feel like a helpless infant waiting to suck from the teat of responsibility. The thing to remember is that adults in the workforce can be as awkward, lazy, and self-absorbed as the people you knew in college, and, unfortunately, not everyone is going to make an effort to help the new person feel welcome. You have to slowly work your way into the fold—don't force it. Be polite, enthusiastic, and friendly, and give yourself time to feel out the office vibe. Here are a few tips to facilitate your entry into the workplace.

Don't Be Late

The cardinal rule of your first day is to be on time. If possible, take the trip from wherever you're staying to the office beforehand to gauge how long it will take. Or at least time it out using HopStop.com or Google Maps. Then add an hour to that. If you're there early, grab a coffee. Maybe you'll have time for a few. But it's worth it, because being late will set a horrible precedent.

The Name Game

Most likely, you'll meet a bunch of people on your first day, from mailroom employees up to your boss. No one will fault you for taking a few weeks to get acclimated and acquainted with the office, but quickly learning people's names can help you make a great first impression. After you've been shown around, try making a quick chart of who people are and where they sit. If you do forget, don't be afraid to ask again—"I'm so sorry, I've been meeting so many people and managed to forget your name. Could you remind me?" Eventually, however, you will not be able to use this line anymore, at which point you'll find yourself in the extremely awkward situation of mumbling the name of someone you've seen every single weekday for six months.

State Your Purpose

Sometimes you will meet your boss or supervisor for the first time the day you arrive for the job. Don't go barging in with the wild ideas you came up with on the ride over, but do be forthcoming with your goals and expectations. Let your boss know what aspects of the company interest you most and where you'd like to get involved. If the response to that is, "Actually, you will just be buying me Frappuccinos and doing my son's homework," then go with the flow. Nonetheless, it will still be useful to give your boss a sense of your aspirations, even if he or she appears to ignore them. For more mundane run-of-the-mill issues like hours, vacations, and reimbursements, it may be more prudent to check in with HR. However, feel free to bring these topics up with your direct superior (not necessarily the boss of all bosses) if there is confusion, but don't do it during your first day and make sure you take an approach that does not bear hints of an "I want to work as little as possible and go on vacation next week" attitude.

Start Strong

You know how whenever you meet people you immediately size them up and sometimes text your best friend about how they have a big forehead or super wet hands? Well, that's admittedly a bit superficial, but everyone makes those snap judgments. In the case of starting a new job, the point is not to try to be cool but rather to put your best foot forward in a professional sense, because each of your coworkers and certainly your manager will develop an impression of you early on—as hard-working or lazy, smart or not-so-smart, and so on and so forth. Impressions stick, so be ready to go the extra mile while it really counts. Get to work before everyone else and be the last person to leave... at least in the beginning.

Get Your Bearings

At larger companies, offices can be like labyrinths, with more barriers to entry than Cuba. If no one shows you, be sure to ask around to locate the following essentials: bathroom, kitchen, mailroom, office supply cabinet, and the fire exit. You may also need to get an ID card made, so try to look presentable (though the photo will be terrible anyway). It is advisable to get on

> *Smart Money:*
> **The company cell phone**
>
> If your company is willing to pay for your cell phone plan, why not let it? Low-balling it, that's $600 per year of extra cash in your pocket. It would be a no-brainer, but, of course, all corporate generosity comes with baggage—in this case, full disclosure of your minute usage and call logs. The company is compensating you for all the business calls you are hypothetically making, which, believe it or not, does not include calling your boyfriend in London. Some people take the company plan and then get an additional phone with a scaled-down plan for their personal use. However, many companies probably don't really care what you do with the phone, so talk to coworkers to find out how lenient things are before running in fear.

the good side of the security guards, who are like the Minotaurs of your office. If they decide that they don't like you and you forget your ID, they'll pretend they've never seen you and make you contact your supervisor to get in, thus causing embarrassment and annoyance all around.

Write It All Down

During the first weeks and months on the job, you will be the recipient of a nonstop deluge of information, ranging from the menial (e.g., how to sign in guests, where to find post-it notes) to the monumentally important (e.g., how to get paid, who is your manager). Even if your superiors don't expect you to take it all in the first time around, you will come out looking on the ball and ready if you do. For this reason, it's important to take copious notes about the who, what, why, when, and how of the office as you go along. You might feel silly writing down something as simple as "BCC Geraldine on all client emails," but you will feel even sillier if you mess it up. As a general rule, always bring a pen, pad, and if appropriate a calculator to all meetings—even if you just draw pictures of beagles wielding grenade launchers; at least it will look like you are trying.

Smart Money:
Reimbursements

 While no one complains about a free dinner at work, it's important to realize that the "free lunch" is still elusive. Sure, you can get a filet on "the Man" every now and then. But if he's paying, that only means that it's late at night and you're at the office when you could be home or out with friends. Nonetheless, don't look a gift-horse in the mouth. Get everything reimbursed: cell phones (p. 135), transportation, food, and whatever else the company is willing to cover. Most likely, you'll have to spend cash up front, and then your expense department (after approval by your boss) will reimburse you. But there's a silver lining to this cloud. If you pay for everything on a rewards credit card, you're banking the points without spending any money of your own. Jackpot! Usually, to get reimbursed, you'll have to hand your receipts to someone in the back office. One caveat: The reimbursement might not come immediately, so make sure you will have the money in your account to pay your credit card bill when it's due.

Be Prepared to Fill Out Forms

Over the course of your first few days you will probably be presented with a number of forms to fill out, many of which will require your Social Security number (worth memorizing if you haven't already). They include:

W-4 Form. This will allow your employer to determine the correct amount of tax to withold from your wages. Don't want them taking any of your money? Unfortunately, it doesn't work like that. If your employer did not withhold these taxes from you, then you would have to pay them all in one enormous lump sum at the end of the year —better to just play it by the books and avoid extra hassle. When filling out the form, you will have to note any tax exemptions that you will be eligible for that year. But since most of us are unmarried with no kids or house, it's pretty straightforward—you'll just file as a single person with no dependents. If you think you may be eligible for any exemptions, check out the "IRS Withholding Calculator" online (IRS.gov) before your first day of work. It provides a series of simple prompts that will help you figure out your filing status.

Benefits. Landed a job with a 401(k) plan and health care coverage? Back of the net! But choosing a doctor or deciding how much of your monthly paycheck you want to put into savings can be confusing (particularly if you've never done it before), so don't feel you have to pick on the spot. Take these forms home so you can do some research and seek advice from parents and friends. HR's job is to help you understand your options, so feel free to schedule as many explanatory meetings as you want. Believe it or not, some grads feel timid about taking advantage of benefits when they know they don't plan to stay with a company for very long— don't be! You are working hard and they're part of your compensation; they are meant to be used. They're also easily transferable. (For more on retirement funds see page 263 and for more on health care, see Chapter 8.)

Direct Deposit. Assuming you have a bank account, sign up for direct deposit of your paycheck so they will be dumped straight into your account and you won't have to worry about losing checks or waiting for them to arrive in the mail. To do this you will need to bring a voided check to the office. (To learn how to void a check, see page 244.)

Noncompete and Non-disclosure Agreements. If you are working at a start-up or a company that deals with proprietary information, you may be asked to sign legal documents stating that you won't share confidential information or offer your services to other companies that are deemed competitors. Often, you either sign or don't take the job and that's the end of the story. However, sometimes there is some wiggle room, and at any rate, it is advisable to at least take some time to review the documents (and ideally show them to a lawyer) so you know you are not shooting yourself in the foot. The last thing you want is to finally get a job at the company of your dreams, only to realize that you have agreed to not work in the media industry for at least two years after leaving your current gig.

Working Life

Ask the Expert:
Women in the Workplace
by Hannah Seligson

Hannah Seligson is a recent grad after our own hearts. In her book New Girl on the Job, *she addresses the difficulties of being a young woman in the workplace from the Gen Y perspective. It's a great supplement for any females reading this book, as well as males who want to appear sensitive to their friends or romantic prospects. Here, she provides some essential tips for "new girls" trying to find their footing in a first job.*

As a Gen Y, I've grown up with the protection of Title IX, witnessed women make inroads in every imaginable field and profession, and have never been told I couldn't do something because of my gender. In fact, it was quite the opposite. So why, with all these doors swinging open, did I write a book offering advice to young working women? Because, distressingly, there is very little advice directed toward young women about how to "make it" during their formative years of employment.

As both the AAUW's "Behind the Pay Gap" study and NACE's "2007 Graduating Student Survey" confirm, workplace inequities don't settle in five years after graduation, when you've bumped your head on the glass ceiling for the first time, or even once you've reached the executive suite—they kick in immediately.

The good news is that Gen Y women have the power (we are 35 million strong) to exact some real change in the workplace. Here's how we can make it happen.

Think career, not job. When people talk about what you are going to do postgraduation, the question is typically framed in terms of "finding a job." You don't hear people say, "Julie, find a career." But they should. While it might be daunting to think that way in your twenties, it's imperative. Jobs are not as lucrative or satisfying as "careers." In practical terms, think about how your first few jobs will help you achieve your career goals. Map out where you want to be in five years and work backwards in terms of the steps it will take to get there.

Don't get assistant-ized. Tory Johnson, the CEO of Women for Hire, puts it like this: "It's very easy for young women to get stuck in support roles... After a year or so you become pegged and it's more difficult for your employer to see you in a different light." Ilene H. Lange, president of Catalyst, attributes the glaring absence of women at the top to the fact that women are two and half times more likely to be channeled into staff jobs like Human Resources and Communications than into operating roles where they would generate revenue and manage profit and loss. So use an assistant position as a springboard to bigger opportunities, not as a place to incubate.

Self-promote, because no one will do it for you. Too often, working women's desire to "please" and to "be liked" prevents them from receiving recognition for their hard work. A recent survey by Women Unlimited found that 56.4 percent of women took credit for their work "rarely" to "sometimes." This, unfortunately, doesn't jibe with the advancement paradigm in the American workplace. Whether you are a man or woman, just putting your head down and doing a good job won't put you on the path to advancement.

When you get accolades from a client (or anyone for that matter), make sure to inform your boss. Keep a work journal and note your contributions to projects so you'll have a concrete list (read: bargaining power) when you need to negotiate for a raise or a promotion, and always take credit for your work—or someone else will!

Grab a mentor, or a few. According to a 2002 survey by the Simmons School of Management, women who had informal mentors reported greater numbers of promotions and a higher promotion rate than those without mentors.

Think about it as if you are building a team. You want to seek out relationships with a broad range of people, both within and outside of your office, so you can strengthen different skill sets. Don't ask a would-be mentor, "Will you be my mentor?" It's the office equivalent of, "Will you be my boyfriend?" Instead, approach him or her with specific requests and questions. For example, "I really admired the way you pitched that client on. Can we sit down for ten minutes on Thursday and go over the client presentation I'm giving next week?" And when you're in a position to mentor, you can pass the favor on. ∎

Working Life

School vs. Work: **What's the Difference?**

There's a natural inclination to think that whatever job you take will be a lot like school. If you were a good student, it's logical to assume you'll be good at work. Unfortunately, school and work bear very little resemblance to one another, and the recent grads who enter the workforce each year thinking otherwise are pretty much responsible for our generation's bad rap as entitled know-it-alls. So what's the difference? For one thing, you pay schools money so they have to pretend to care about you, whereas companies pay you money and are more inclined to be bitter if you don't live up to expectations. But beyond that obvious fact, there are many differences that can be leveraged to your benefit if you're ready for them. To help you prepare, we've laid out some of the key aspects of college that will probably no longer apply on the job, as well as tips for acing the transition.

IN COLLEGE... It didn't matter if your professor liked you. Sure, you might have brownnosed your way from a B to a B+ a couple of times, but more often you barely interacted with your professor, and he or she may not have even known your name.

IN THE WORKFORCE... If your direct boss doesn't know your name, you're in trouble.

> *TIP: Make sure your boss likes you. If he or she isn't on your side, making your way up the ranks will be infinitely more difficult.*

IN COLLEGE... It didn't matter what your classmates thought of you (at least in terms of classes—social life was a whole different viper's nest). As long as you had a friend or two to mess around with in the back of the lecture hall and some poindexters to crib notes off of for the final, you were fine.

IN THE WORKPLACE... If you don't get along with your colleagues it's tough to succeed, especially since there are many more buses you can get thrown under at work than in school.

> *TIP: Be nice to your colleagues, even the ones you don't like.*

IN COLLEGE... You could get your work done by yourself most of the time, aside from the infrequent group project.

Working Life

140

IN THE WORKPLACE... You'll likely find that much of your work relies on other people in some way (e.g., boss, colleagues, supporting departments/staff, vendors, clients). Teamwork is critical in most professions—not just for getting the job done, but also so you've got soldiers who will ride for you when things get real.

> **TIP:** *Don't hesitate to take up the slack of another team member; it will help you in the future. And don't be critical of other people's work. Be constructive.*

IN COLLEGE... There were long periods of chilling punctuated by short and unhealthy bursts of intense effort.

IN THE WORKPLACE... The "daily grind" says it all. Not to suggest you won't love what you do (hopefully you will), but there's definitely a Sisyphean element to a full-time job. You work like a maniac on a big project, then as soon as you're done, another shows up. Then another. Then another.

> **TIP:** *Again, if you're going to work hard at any point, put in a strong effort for the first three months immediately after arriving at a new job. Everyone will form an impression of you as a hard worker, thus buying you padding to slack off later down the line.*

IN COLLEGE... You receive months-long breaks.

IN THE WORKPLACE... You pretty much have to lose your job to get a break that long (unless you're a teacher/ professor-type).

> **TIP:** *Plan vacations strategically and become a vacation magician. Turn three-day weekends into four-*

Tips & Tricks:
Never stop looking for opportunities

 When you finally land a job, there's something to be said for giving it your full attention and not being distracted by the "what if" demons. Better jobs than yours certainly exist, especially when you are young and inexperienced, but doing well now will help you get to those eventually. That said, working hard shouldn't put up the blinders on career opportunities. Take an hour each month to scroll through some job sites (while at home, never in the office!), check up on openings at your dream companies, have coffee with an old boss, or read up on your industry to see what's new and exciting. Networking doesn't just have to be done a few weeks before you apply for a job—building contacts will always come in handy when you decide to make your next move.

Working Life

141

day weekends and weeks off into ten-day vacations with the aid of major holidays. Also, it's key to take full advantage of any free time you have before finding a job, or when you're in between jobs. Once you're working, you'll daydream endlessly about having that kind of free time. Check out page 6 for travel ideas, as well as jobs and volunteer opportunities that allow for travel.

IN COLLEGE... There are grades and clear feedback cycles for your work.

IN THE WORKPLACE... It's often somewhat difficult to figure out precisely how you're doing, where you stand, and where you're going, even if the company makes an effort to schedule regular reviews.

> **TIP:** *Every once in a while ask your superior how you're doing, particularly if you've just delivered on a project or task. Don't overdo it though, as you can easily be marked as high maintenance.*

IN COLLEGE... You knew you had four years, and most people stuck it out in the same place without transferring.

IN THE WORKPLACE... People come and go all the time, especially at our age.

> **TIP:** *Try and figure out how long you want to be somewhere, and plan accordingly. But remember: Best-laid plans don't always work out, so you should act like you're going to be at your job forever until the day you actually leave. When you do bounce, try not to burn any bridges on your way out—unlike some of the less savory characters at college, your workmates could be useful networking contacts down the line (and they might even be called as references).*

IN COLLEGE... Dropping out wasn't much of an option.

IN THE WORKPLACE... Quitting is *always* an option.

> **TIP:** *Here's a good test to run: If you look around and there's no one in your workplace with a career and lifestyle that you'd like for yourself personally and professionally, that's a great sign that you're not a long-term fit for that organization. If you see someone who fits that description, that's awesome. Go make friends with that person now!*

IN COLLEGE... Literally everyone was fair game to hook up with on any given night (hypothetically).

IN THE WORKPLACE... Every cutie is a potential landmine.

> **TIP:** *Tread very, very carefully. For more tips on office romances, see page 150.*

Office Politics

Office politics are one of the mythical aspects of working life that most people cannot truly appreciate until they have experienced their effects first hand. They are the basis of huge debacles like Monica Lewinsky giving the "Head of State," as well as great works of art like *The* (British) *Office*. Indeed, as long as you stay out of hot water, office politics are one of the best parts of a job, if only because a classic workplace faux pas can be pretty hilarious.

Despite their mystique, office politics can be easily navigated with a bit of common sense, confidence, and composure. At the end of the day, most disasters boil down to ambiguous power structures, judgment lapses, and the general awkwardness of human beings. Here's a quick field guide to social and professional interactions in the workplace.

GOSSIP FOLKS. If office romances are a "play it by ear" situation, office gossip is firmly in "don't play it at all" territory. Listening to the resident gossip-mongers dish the dirt is all very well and good, and you should feel free to take that information home and laugh about it in private. But once you start soliciting or dispensing gossip yourself, Pandora's box will creak open and unleash a minefield of potential hazards to your good standing in the office. As with life in general, your safest bet is to employ a "don't trust anyone" strategy. Even if others are making fun of your boss or sending around incendiary emails, resist the urge to join in with a zinger of your own. Some people talk recklessly, while others consciously backstab—either way, whatever you say will mysteriously find its way back to you.

BRINGING BAGGAGE TO THE OFFICE. Everybody has problems. But if you don't hear grown folks complaining about divorces and mortgages, why do you think it's appropriate to whine about your boyfriend or messy roommate? Water-cooler chatter is one thing, and if you make a friend at work who is willing to listen to your moaning then all the better. Just don't let non–work-related issues affect your productivity or attitude. "Professionalism" means ignoring your emotions and acting like work is literally more important than your own life. (Also, unless people know you are going on vacation,

don't bring literal baggage to the office, either. It will be a dead giveaway when you call in sick the next day.)

SOCIALIZING WITH COWORKERS. The sociability of an office varies quite significantly from place to place (and, often, from industry to industry). Some investment banks have a fratty "work hard, play hard" approach that is fueled by popping bottles and sometimes ingesting class-A drugs. Other offices have training programs or "class" systems that attempt to foster strong bonds between coworkers through retreats, volunteer outings, and parties. And, once in a while, people befriend coworkers at normal offices because they actually like them or are just very bored.

The thing to remember is this: Just because you work with someone does not mean you have to be best friends. Nor does it mean you have to invite him or her to your birthday party. Pay attention to the social dynamics of your office, but realize that you are free to set your own standards and boundaries. Once you've proven to be a good worker, only a huge jerk will begrudge you for having your own life outside of the office.

PUSHING BACK ON YOUR SUPERIORS. The first time you feel you are disrespected or mistreated in the workplace can be a shock to the system and make you want to run to your mom crying. But, depending on the severity, it might be advisable to let it slide before you've gauged your boss's style and expectations. If it becomes habitual and makes you feel uncomfortable, then it is time to talk to HR or speak with a superior. We understanding how it can feel like you are admitting weakness if you say your workload is too heavy. But again, there comes a time when your boss's expectations need to be in line with your own.

At the end of the day, most people would rather you speak up and say that you are overwhelmed than end up with an unfinished or shoddy product when the due date arrives. Over time, you'll get a sense of who will value and reward your hard work and who is just looking to pawn off all the dirty work on you. But when you're a newcomer, the best course of action is to stiffen that upper lip and work hard enough to earn a good reputation. A good rep, in turn, will allow you to push back down the line without being looked upon suspiciously.

OFFICE PARTIES. The company Christmas party is a tried and true tradition in most offices around the country, but it is just one beast in an odd menagerie of social events at work. Whether it's a holiday shindig, Friday happy hour, or a farewell party for a retiring fossil, the same rule applies: Don't get wasted. It seems as though it would go without saying, but you'd be surprised at how many bright, hard-working recent graduates embarrass themselves by going hard on mixed drinks or failing to gauge their limits. You can drink, and in some cases even get a little bit tipsy if that's how other people in your company get down, but just don't overdo it because it's not worth the risk of saying or doing something that will affect your standing in the office.

Once you've passed the "are you an alcoholic?" litmus test, office party etiquette pretty much boils down to basic standards of sociability. Avoid the obvious taboos in conversation—sex, religion, politics, and off-color jokes. However, don't feel that you have to only talk about job stuff. Office parties are a great opportunity to interact outside of the structure of work, which is often not very conducive to getting to know people. Being sociable at a work party can put you on the radar of someone you don't know very well or help you impress your boss, both of which can pay dividends back in the office. (If the party involves a meal, see page 163 for more on business meal etiquette.)

TAKING RESPONSIBILITY AND GETTING CREDIT. At school, you hand in a paper and you get a grade. Sometimes you do group projects and end up doing all the work while your pothead partner reaps the benefits, but at least you still end up with the results on your report card. At work, there is a lot more ambiguity not only in terms of the feedback you receive, but also in who takes credit for what. Sometimes a boss might simply make a false assumption about who has completed the work that he or she is receiving, while at other times your superiors will just take credit for your labor in order to make themselves look better.

Either way, you've got a tricky situation on your hands. Demanding credit for everything you do might not be realistic or even necessary. However, if you are being systematically overlooked, you may want to address the issue head-on. If you go this route, do so calmly and don't storm in with guns blazing. Ask a mentor or a senior person you have a good relationship with for advice. Meanwhile, don't be the perpetrator of poor professional etiquette—give credit where credit's due, and take responsibility when your work is queried instead of passing the buck.

Working Life

Lingo:
Business Speak

Sometimes walking into an office can be like touching down in a foreign country. The local uniform is borderline fascist, and people speak a dialect that you've probably never heard before. But while the garments are unnecessarily uncomfortable and expensive, the language has fewer words than Esperanto and is pretty easy to pick up. Here's a crash course:

> **CHICKEN & EGG SITUATION**
>
> *Corporate meaning:* There is an unclear causality at work.
>
> *What it really means:* There is probably some sort of logic to the data that you are presenting to me, but it would require too much thought to figure it out. I will just artfully dodge the entire issue with a meaningless cliché!

> **GRAB THE BULL BY THE HORNS**
>
> *Corporate meaning:* Take control of the situation.
>
> *What it really means:* No one grabs the bull by the horns, not even a bullfighter. It's just dangerous. The better move is to wave a colorful sheet around to annoy it, then jab spears into its spinal column.

> **SUBOPTIMAL**
>
> *Corporate meaning:* There is a better path or solution.
>
> *What it really means:* What we're talking about is terrible.

> **IT IS WHAT IT IS**
>
> *Corporate meaning:* We're all underwhelmed by the situation at hand, but I have no intention of fixing the problem.
>
> *What it really means:* Literally the most meaningless phrase in the world.

COMPARE APPLES TO APPLES

Corporate meaning: When doing analysis, only compare like things.

What it really means: Apparently, it would sound too negative to say "don't compare apples and oranges" like a normal person would. That said, we'd love to meet the person who can objectively compare a Granny Smith to a Red Delicious.

DON'T REINVENT THE WHEEL

Corporate meaning: Let's not try to fix something that isn't broken or come up with new solutions to problems that have already been solved.

What it really means: I am far too lazy and uninspired to think of a creative solution. (Unfortunately, this fear of taking on the wheel has slowed GDP growth by at least 10% per year. Maybe there really is a better solution.)

DELIVERABLE

Corporate meaning: A tangible piece of work that can be handed in and reviewed.

What it really means: I don't trust that you are actually doing any work so I will force you to waste time by turning it into a grown-up homework assignment.

DRINK THE KOOL-AID

Corporate meaning: You have to buy into the corporate culture and believe in the company.

What it really means: Working is miserable, so you must trick yourself into thinking that it is awesome, mostly by pretending that Ultimate Frisbee outings and happy hours are better than not doing those things and actually following your own social calendar. Oh…and this phrase originated from a mass suicide orchestrated by Jim Jones— the zealot, not the rapper. Baaalllllliiiiinnnn'!

Working Life

Ask The Expert:
Do I Have Imposter Syndrome?

When you are at the bottom of the age and experience pile, adjusting to the workplace can be par-ticularly tough, and it's not uncommon for recent grads to harbor fears that they are not really as bright as their resumes suggest (and their coworkers assume). To get to the bottom of these feelings of inadequacy, we called Dr. Valerie Young, who studies a phenomenon that she calls "Imposter Syndrome."

What Is Imposter Syndrome? Imposter Syndrome is an often unconscious feeling deep down inside, the idea that [you are] not really as bright and capable and competent as everybody seems to think. People who typically experience Imposter Syndrome have achieved some mea-sure of success, whether it's getting into college or graduate school, getting good grades, and so on, but they just have a hard time internalizing that success. They kind of explain it away.

What would be the telltale signs that one is really suffering from Imposter Syn-drome, as opposed to just general anxiety about life? I have heard people say, "I figure, if I can get a Ph.D. in Astrophysics from Cal Tech, anybody can." Constantly being sort of dismis-sive of your compliments—that would definitely be one sign. If there is a certainty that every time you do succeed you feel like, "Phew, got through that one, but the next time I'm not going to be so lucky," then that's something you need to pay attention to.

What do you suggest people do on a practical level to address it? I think the first step is to break the silence and realize that there is a name for these feelings. The problem is that people think that they are the only ones who feel this way and that's where the fear and the shame of stigma kicks in. Also, I think a lot of it is keeping entitlement in perspective. I think of entitlement as saying to yourself, "Aren't I entitled to make a mistake? And aren't I entitled to not know all the answers?" Finally, redefine competence not as knowing how to do everything yourself, but rather knowing how to identify the resources that you need to achieve the goal.

Is it possible to express to your superiors that you are feeling like a fraud and that it affects your job execution and/or enjoyment? You know, I don't think I would bring up to your boss that you feel like a fraud. Give yourself permission to feel really off base for the first six months or nine months, but recognize that this is how people feel when they start a new job because you are learning new systems, new acronyms, and a whole institutional history that other people know about and you don't. So, you go into this new job and you don't know what's going on and it's not like if you were any smarter you would know what was going on. It's not an intelligence thing, it's looking at it differently and saying, "Well, why would I know what's going on?" ∎

The Importance of Mentors

We've established that the working world is a lot different from college, but one thing that remains the same is that it's useful to have someone older and wiser on hand to help you navigate tricky situations. In college, an advisor or dean probably helped you (or at least should have helped you, theoretically) when your roommate urinated on your term paper or you needed guidance on which major to choose. In the "real world," however, an adult whom you trust and who cares about your career development can be a godsend. Holly Paul, National Sourcing Operations Leader for Campus and Experienced Recruiting at PricewaterhouseCooper, puts it bluntly: "If you don't [have a mentor], you need to find one as soon as possible. Someone who knows you well and who you can trust to give you candid feedback is indispensable when you're starting your career." So unless you've got mentors flying out the wazoo already (lucky you), check out these tips for tracking down that special someone.

Two Mentors Are Better than One

A mentor doesn't have to work in the same office as you—indeed, it's often better to have a third party you can address freely without stepping into the mire of office politics. Different people can help you with different aspects of your professional growth, so don't feel you have to limit yourself to one all-encompassing mentor. That said, sometimes it's useful to have a mentor within the office as well, since every company has its idiosyncrasies, and you may need someone who understands the specifics of your situation. Also, if you have someone looking out for you in the office, it can make a huge difference with regards to decisions like year-end bonuses, vacation time (when someone else wants the same days), and getting staffed on good projects.

How to Find a Mentor

Whether you gravitate toward your Uncle Larry or a woman you met at your first internship, the trick is to find someone with whom you share common ground (e.g., you grew up in the same town, went to the same school, share similar interests). Lots of people are happy to help a young person just beginning his or her career, but the right person is one you feel comfortable with and who has experience in your industry of choice. As Paul explains, "You can also try to find alumni through your school (or if you've been hired, you can reach out to people at your future employer via LinkedIn). The trick is to start asking proactively for targeted guidance, since it's unlikely that someone will just suddenly want

Working Life

to be your mentor." Another strategy is to utilize your company's mentorship or "buddy" program, if it offers one. Also, how about contacting old professors who might know someone in your field? Along the path to the perfect mentor, gather advice from anyone with whom you develop a friendly relationship. It's free, so why not listen, right?

What Do You Hope to Gain?

It's best to ask for your mentor's advice on a particular topic, such as the pros and cons of getting an MBA or figuring out how to ask for a raise. Furthermore, the more you share about yourself, the easier it will be for mentors to specifically address your personal goals, interests, motivations, and background. A mentor who really knows you can give the most meaningful advice during times of transition, especially if you are struggling to figure out what it is you really want to do or how you can best grow in the industry you've decided to focus on.

Make It a Commitment

Once you have found your mentor(s), establish a specific time commitment from the onset that you're both willing to make, because without a schedule, you're less likely to have regular contact with each other. Will you be meeting monthly for coffee? Catching up on the phone every couple of weeks? Be sensitive to your mentor's schedule and make it easy for him or her. Investing time and energy into your mentor relationship could potentially have a positive, lifelong effect on your career and your life, so take advantage of those who want to help you—you never know when you'll need sage counsel. And if there's one thing that's really hard to track down at the last minute, it's sage counsel!

♥ Office Romance

Ah, the fresh hunting grounds of a brand new office... Excited to hook up with all your colleagues? You should be. But you need to tread carefully—no matter how "progressive" companies claim to be, some HR departments will still come down on you like a ton of bricks if they think you're using the terms "spread" and "sheets" in a context that doesn't involve Excel. Some may even fire you.

That said, the taboo of the office romance is fading to some extent. Yes, there was a time when a little cubicle copulation was considered anathema to a successful career. "Business and pleasure don't mix," said the conventional wisdom. "Sex in the office is harassment, even if it's consensual." But while many people profess a "don't poo where you eat" philosophy with regards to a little flirty flirty in the workplace, the stats show that at least 40% of workers have tried it.

Young people are working longer hours, and as the work-life balance shifts further toward the "work is life" end of the spectrum, the office has become the new bar (with the only difference being that you have to wear headphones when you listen to "Living on a Prayer"). Before you dive in head first, consider a few crucial questions: Will an *affair de cubicle* alienate you from the rest of the office? Can you hide embarrassingly red cheeks with some concealer? Will your suit accommodate a surreptitious Texas tuck when the CEO rounds the corner? Do you really have no other prospects?

If you do decide to play with fire, here are the different scenarios you might run into:

♥ **DATING AN EQUAL.** If you are dating another newb, it's mostly up to the two of you to decide if competing for the same promotions, raises, and projects will breed ill will. Most other people won't care as long as there's not too much repulsive canoodling in the break room. However, think about your work-life balance—at the end of the day, the last thing you want is a reminder of work, even if that reminder has great abs.

♥ **DATING A SUPERIOR.** Let's be blunt: Sexing your boss is almost always a bad idea. Even if you successfully pull off an unethical plan to get ahead through sexual favors, the rumor mill is quick to spot an unjust promotion. If you really "like" your boss, check your feelings to make sure they are genuine. Then check his or her hand for a wedding ring. Then quit the job and pray it works out.

♥ **DATING AN INFERIOR.** Most of us don't have to worry about this right now because we are the inferiors. But again, the issue that arises here has to do with maintaining "professional integrity." Of course, the interns are always fair game, regardless of age—they can't find the paper for the printer, let alone HR! Just kidding. In all seriousness, this is also a horrible idea, as the last thing you want to be known as is the manager who hits on subordinates. Check yourself before you wreck yourself, because those texts you thought were "playful" could quickly get you sued.

♥ **DATING A CLIENT.** If your job involves going to a lot of dinners or entertaining clients outside of the office, you never know what might develop once the vino starts flowing. Know your own limits and re-member that your job is not to jump people's bones (at least we hope not). If your boss finds out, your actions will not be looked upon favor-ably. If he or she is the one cajoling you to flirt for business, ask yourself why you decided to work for Don "Magic" Juan.

♥ **DATING SOMEONE IN A DIFFERENT DEPARTMENT.** "Cross-pollination" is probably the safest bet, but remember that it has also bred some of nature's biggest freaks, like the liger. Lindsey Pollack, au-thor of *From College to Career: 90 Things to Do Before You Join the Real World*, flies a cautionary flag: "When I was working at a dot com several years ago, I went on a few dates with a cute guy in the IT department. After it ended, I was too embarrassed to call IT support again, even when my computer got a serious virus!" The lesson is simple: Never date someone who has access to your computer.

♥ **WHAT ABOUT THE JANITORIAL STAFF?** The janitor has access to three important things: keys to the supply closet, a late-night sched-ule, and the wherewithal to quickly clean up the "scene of the crime." Worth considering, perhaps.

♥ **FINAL PRECAUTIONS?** In all cases mentioned above, avoid P.D.A. like the plague. Petting, kissing, and even subtle hand-holding will alienate both of you and make work uncomfortable for others. Be wary of swapping love notes over company email or treating the Christmas party like Freaknik. And finally, always be prepared to deny every-thing when the crap hits the fan. An office tryst may literally be against company rules, so you'd better check that employee handbook to know how serious the situation could get.

At the end of the day, office romance is a Pandora's Box that's probably not worth opening. But when the juice is worth the squeeze, you'd better believe that no pantsuit or necktie is going to stop nature from taking its course. Just remember that work is stressful enough without exes lurking in the corridors and people asking why you "never call IT" anymore. Be smooth, be smart, and always protect your assets.

Office Dress

Unless in college you were a certain type of person (i.e., a terrible one), you probably didn't roll around campus on the business casual tip. More than likely, you dressed in the collegiate uniform of sandals, hoody, jeans, sweatpants, Uggs, or some combination thereof. We forgive you for the Uggs (and Muggs, if you were *that* guy), but it's time to step up your wardrobe. Now that you're employed, you've got to figure out how to dress the part. This is no simple task, as today's office dress code is not as clear-cut as it once was. Hipster chic? Creative corporate? What does it all mean?

General Style Cues

Some companies have explicit dress codes, while others may not. Megan Schuster, a Public Relations Associate at Gucci, notes that even in her chic industry, it's important not to try too hard. "Office fashion is about having personal style; there is no need to look like you fell out of a page in *Vogue*. Be comfortable. The key to looking good is feeling good."

In building your work wardrobe, versatility, comfort, and style should be your top priorities. (Remember, you have to wear these clothes for an entire eight-hour work day, if not longer.) Choose fabrics you can wash at home to save on dry cleaning costs (wool and cashmere are comfy, but they will definitely run up the bill).

If you're on a tight budget, try to choose colors that you can easily mix and match (black, white, and neutrals) so you can maximize every piece of your wardrobe. Owning one or two really nice pieces (e.g., a blazer and a pair of shoes) that you can mix and match with less expensive articles will give you the air of dressing well without having to spend a lot of cash to get there.

Finally, there's the joy (or trap, depending upon if you pull it off

> *Hazard:*
> **Dressing for the first week**
>
> If you're completely unsure about the dress code before starting a new job, call HR and inquire about appropriate attire. Then, make sure you have enough clothes to get you through the first week, but wait until you've seen what other people wear before going on an all-out shopping spree. If it turns out things are a lot more casual or formal than you'd expected, you don't want to be left with a pile of clothes that you won't actually wear to work and probably don't want for your personal life.

Working Life

correctly) of Casual Fridays. They may seem like an excuse for grown men to wear Crocs and women to wear liquid leggings, but don't let these outliers fool you into a false sense of security. As a young employee, you are constantly fighting to make sure people take you seriously, so avoid the temptation to roll to the office with bed-head and a COED NAKED TRUCKING T-shirt ("We go all night!"). Instead, make sure that whatever office attire you choose is something you'd be comfortable wearing when meeting, say, your girlfriend's or boyfriend's parents.

Industry Norms

Different industries have different norms when it comes to office fashion. Here are some basic industry-specific guidelines for looking your best.

- **CORPORATE ENVIRONMENTS (LAW, CONSULTING, BANKING).** Keep it conservative. You don't have to wear a suit (unless you have a meeting or dress code that requires one), but choose classic pieces that say, "I mean business."

- **ADVERTISING/PR/PUBLISHING.** Keep it classic and professional, but feel free to mix in some trendier pieces, colors, or accessories.

- **FASHION/RETAIL.** If you work for a specific brand, you will likely be expected to wear pieces from the brand. Otherwise, try to incorporate the brand's style with classic pieces to remain fashionable yet professional. Just remember, it's an office, not a runway.

- **MEDIA/CREATIVE ARTS.** If it's a less traditional environment, jeans may be okay, but make sure your overall look is neat and put-together.

- **EDUCATION.** Remember your crazy sixth grade drama teacher who wore denim skirts hiked up to her boobs and floral-patterned blouses with lipstick stains on the collar? Don't dress like that. Instead, aim to wear classic, comfortable clothes that won't distract horny adolescents.

Work Dress for Men

Work dress for men is not that complicated, though there are some rookie mistakes that are easily avoided. Where many recent grads stumble is not so much in figuring out *what* to wear, but more so in failing to adjust their standards for "put-togetherness." Perhaps the biggest source of blunders is in fit—a lot of guys come out of college with no sense of what fits well and what doesn't, so it's worth making an honest assessment of any "dress clothes" you already own and deciding whether or not they really fit well. Baggy pants and oversized shirts can easily make otherwise suitable items look a bit sloppy. Another common pitfall is mistaking "going out" shirts for nice shirts. The difference is sort of difficult to describe, but if it's black or has extremely colorful stripes, you might want to reconsider. Finally, it's time to invest a little bit of that salary into dry-cleaning. Peeling clothes off the floor and giving them a quick *eau de toilette* misting won't cut it anymore. Keep items freshly laundered and pressed. Brooks Brothers makes great no-wrinkle shirts that can ease a lot of the hassle.

MEN'S STAPLES. According to Michael Williams, a fashion PR pro and author of the men's style blog AContinuousLean.com, anyone who works in a professional office environment should start building the following staples into his wardrobe: "Two grey suits (a summer weight and a winter weight), two sport coats (corduroy and wool), seven collared woven shirts (white, blue, yellow, etc.), five pairs of non-denim trousers (khakis, wool, etc.), ten white tee shirts, ten pairs of dark socks, a khaki rain coat/trench coat, a dark overcoat, and three pairs of shoes (brown, black, and boots for winter)." Clearly, you won't buy all of these things at once. But if your office is on the formal side, a good start would be one pair of dress khakis (no cargo pockets!), grey wool slacks, a dark suit that's been tailored, four or five long-sleeve button-down shirts, and dark shoes. A good black belt will go a long way, as will a couple of versatile blazers and ties.

GROOMING. At the beginning, you should assume you need to be clean-shaven. No goatees, no two-day stubble—not even a subtle flavor-saver. A fresh haircut is also a worthwhile investment before your first day. Once you get a sense for what's acceptable, you may be able to

> ### Tips & Tricks:
> ### Dress for the job you want
>
> Have you ever heard some-one say, "Dress for the job you want, not for the job you have?" That doesn't mean you should come into work dressed as an astronaut, nor does it mean you should cultivate a rotation of Nancy Pelosi–inspired red power suits. It does mean you should show up prepared for any situation that might arise—even if you spend most days daydreaming at your desk. You never know when a last-minute meeting might come up, and your chances of being asked to attend will skyrocket if you're looking sharp. If you plan on having a successful career, take pride in your appearance and the people that matter will notice.

Working Life

throw a little facial hair into the mix, but keep it clean and neatly trimmed. Also, while it should go without saying, brush your teeth before going to work—you may have brushed once a month in college, but it's no longer optional when you're working closely with people in the office.

SHOES. "Comfortable and classic is the way to go," says Williams, but don't think that means you can wear your "fancy" sneakers. "Footwear is the one place that it really pays to invest in. Buy well-made Goodyear Welted shoes in brown and black (this means that the upper and the sole are two separate pieces that can be easily resoled). Break them in once and then have them resoled again and again, thereby saving money and still looking smart."

WHAT THE HELL IS BUSINESS CASUAL? No one really knows, even if he pretends to. A good rule of thumb is to err on the "business" side rather than the "casual" side. Better to look a bit stiff but respectable than to stand out for being overly relaxed. If you're looking for a general sense of what a business casual outfit might look like, it's basically somewhere between wearing a suit and wearing jeans and sneakers. Think wool pants, a collared shirt, and leather shoes. Maybe a blazer without a tie if you want to be extra spiffy.

WHERE TO GO. J. Crew, Banana Republic, Brooks Brothers, Gap, and Men's Wearhouse. Department stores are good for variety, and you can always look for discounted gear at Target, T.J. Maxx, Ross, and Marshalls.

Work Dress for Women

Office dress for the ladies is a whole other box of chocolates—the options for women are both more fun and more nuanced than those for men, but as a result they're also more overwhelming. The key is that you're not Lady Gaga, so you probably don't want to be defined by your clothes (or lack thereof). Instead, strive to be age-appropriate, office-appropriate (i.e., stylish but not sexy), and industry-appropriate. Not an easy balance to strike, but it can be done!

Depending on what industry you work in or what your work environment is like, the norms of office dress can differ quite drastically. A good rule of thumb is to take your style cues from your female superiors and co-workers. As you become more comfortable in your job, you'll get a feel for how much leeway you have when it comes to office dress. Just remember: Looking put together should trump any attempt to be "stylish." Not to get too Emily Post on you, but nicely styled hair and nails can take you from "presentable" to "chic" in no time flat.

WOMEN'S STAPLES. Do as the French do and come up with your own "uniform" that you don't have to think too much about. Here are a few key pieces that will get you through the workweek:

- Dress pants (black or grey)

- Pencil or A-line skirt (no minis)

- Tights (a great way to extend the life of your skirts into winter)

- Blouses or collared shirts (avoid "going out tops," or anything low-cut)

- Cardigans to pair with skirts or pants

- Office-appropriate dresses (nothing too short or sleazy)

- Blazers

- Pant or skirt suit (if necessary)

SHOES. Stylish shoes can dress up a very basic ensemble, but make sure you can last the whole day in them. Hobbling is never a good look, and your five-inch stilettos will likely be more of a distraction than an asset, so save them for your post-work cavorting. Instead, pick up some cute flats and comfortable heels that you can wear with a variety of outfits. If you can wear jeans to work, low heels are a great way to dress them up.

GROOMING. Accessories are another place to get creative, since it's easy to add a little flavor without drawing undue attention. As for hair, nails, and makeup, the best advice we can give is to keep it classy and observe what others around you are doing. If your boss is sporting this season's vampy nail polish, go for it, but stay away from acrylics or anything that needs to be glued or sprayed on.

GET YOUR FLAIR ON. Even if you work in a traditional corporate setting, there's no reason why you can't have fun with your wardrobe and show off some of your personal style. Shoes and accessories are areas where you can do this, as well as occasionally whipping out your jazz hands. Adding colorful flats or some chunky jewelry to your black basics can provide you with that creative touch that will keep you from blending into your cubicle.

Working Life

WHERE TO GO: Banana Republic, Gap, J. Crew, Ann Taylor, Club Monaco, Old Navy, and Ross. Department stores offer a lot of merchandise all in one place, and many of them sell clothing manufactured under their own moniker, which can be cheaper than name-brand items. Stores to check out include Bloomingdales, Nordstrom, Saks, and Lord & Taylor. You can also score some great finds by combing the racks at Target, T.J. Maxx, and Marshalls. For more fun pieces and accessories, check out Zara, H&M, Anthropologie and Express. Visit BlueFly.com for designer items at discounted prices.

Internet, Email, and Phone

For most people, one thing that remains constant between unemployment and employment is that they spend most of their time online and on the phone. But while it used to be just Big Brother and "Net Nanny" on your case, you've now got to contend with company HR departments and nosy bosses. You're still surfing the 'net, but there are sharks in the water. Here are some tips for remaining above board.

Internet

Depending on what your job is, you may be able to explain frequent sessions on YouTube or TMZ, but sometimes your company will block certain sites. In general, let common sense be your guiding light and remember that you can surf to your heart's content once you get home. Also, be considerate of your friends who are starting new jobs. If you have unfettered access to the Web but know your bestie is heavily monitored, think before sending out links and be sure to add a lame but useful "NSFW" ("Not Safe For Work") caveat.

Instant Messenger

One of the most upsetting realizations about many offices is that IM is the prevailing mode of intra-office communication. It's sort of odd to IM with someone sitting literally a few feet away from you, and it is *very* odd to IM with someone 30 years your senior. While you may have grown up using IM to gossip and flirt with sexual predators online, your older coworkers were likely introduced to it solely as a business tool. Don't get caught in the trap of treating IM as a green light for being unprofessional. Here's how *not* to do it:

> **SeXyNeWb:** wazzzzzupppppp, suckaaaa!!!!
>
> **LeRoyJenkins:** Hello, could I ask who this is?
>
> **SeXyNeWb:** im the new asst. can I ask u sumthin? i am so lost! LOL
>
> **LeRoyJenkins:** Oh, hi Karen. I didn't know that this was your screen name. What can I help you with?
>
> **SeXyNeWb:** i don't know where the stapler is. i would ask jon but he's sorta weird, right? LMAO! he smells like full-court basketball.
>
> **LeRoyJenkins:** You can check in the supply closet in the hallway. There should be a few in there, but if not you'll have to order a restock. I believe your orientation packet has a map that points it out.
>
> **SeXyNeWb:** yah i think i lost that! i am a little hungover ;)
>
> **SeXyNeWb:** my boyfriend and I got in a big fight and I got a little frisky with the pinot... hehe
>
> **SeXyNeWb:** brb... sum weirdo from my middle school is IMing me... wt fuuuu
>
> **SeXyNeWb:** u there???? I still can't find anything!
>
> LeRoyJenkins is idle (4:35pm)
>
> **SeXyNeWb:** lataz
>
> SeXyNeWb is away (OMG this is CRAZY guuurls!!! www.twogirlsonecup.com)

What went wrong? Ah, so many things. This conversation has more mistakes than Sinbad's Wikipedia page. Let's assess the damage.

- 🖑 **CHANGE YOUR SCREEN NAME.** Whatever you thought was hilarious in fourth grade is probably wildly embarrassing or inappropriate now.

- 🖑 **ANNOUNCE YOURSELF.** Don't just jump straight into a question or a demand—write something like, "Hi, sorry to bother you. Got a second?" If you've never IM'ed a person before, say who you are. Figure out what screen names you will need in order to correspond with everyone in your department.

Working Life

- ⌐ **AVOID IM LINGO.** If your coworkers are dropping "LOLs" and "brbs" all over the place, feel free to join in. But don't assume that everyone knows all the acronyms.

- ⌐ **BE AS CLEAR AS POSSIBLE.** Take hormones and booze out of the equation and IM is still a hot zone for mixed messages—get to the point and say what you mean. Similarly, if you've got something lengthy to say, it's better to send someone an email, pick up the phone, or go talk to someone in person.

- ⌐ **DO SOME BUDDY LIST HOUSEKEEPING.** If you're rocking a screen name from way back in the day, you might want to change it or consider deleting some of the 400 buddies you've accrued since middle school. You don't want your past sneaking up on you in the workplace, so take precautions.

- ⌐ **SHOW YOUR STATUS.** SeXyNeWb wasn't the only one making mistakes (though we can't blame LeRoy for taking a breather from that convo). If you are away from your computer, let people know. Word of warning: "I am here but am playing a computer game that takes up my whole screen" will not be looked upon favorably.

Email

First things first: If the company you work for doesn't block personal email sites (like Yahoo!, Gmail, etc.), then there's probably no reason to give your work email to your friends and family. Mixing business and pleasure in your inbox could be risky, and it can also garner you some incredibly weird spam. Worst of all, things that you don't even send can get you in trouble, so be wary of letting your friends recap your weekend behavior over company email. Bear in mind that anytime you use a company email account, you are technically representing the company in public and they can access your email at will.

Once you've figured out the conundrum of staying on top of personal email without getting too loosey-goosey in your work account, you've also got to deal with intra-office email etiquette. Here are some tips for switching up your email game to remain work-appropriate and professional:

- ✒ **FORMALIZE YOUR LANGUAGE AND TONE.** Once you get to know your boss and coworkers, you can gauge how they correspond over email and begin to adapt a bit. But part of professionalism is cleaning

Working Life

up the language and grammar of your emails. No IM abbreviations or other tics you might have developed!

🖙 **PROOFREAD, PROOFREAD, PROOFREAD.** Read over everything before you send it and check the spelling of names against the address you are emailing.

🖙 **DON'T INUNDATE PEOPLE WITH CCs**. If someone doesn't know why he or she is receiving a copy of an email, you have erred.

🖙 **BEWARE OF THE REPLY-ALL.** One of the biggest pitfalls in the entire office environment is the "reply-all" button. Everyone from government officials to CEOs to interns can fall victim to an inadvertent "reply-all," or a reply that was supposed to be a forward. Usually, replying all is just annoying for other people, especially if you are replying to the entire office. But when you reply to an email that your boss wrote and you say, "WTF, does he really expect us to do that?" then you're flirting with job termination. Best to make a recipient list and check it thrice before sending an email.

🖙 **FORWARD THINKING.** Beware of forwarding confidential documents, even if it's to your dad or best friend to ask for help with deciphering them. A company could easily fire you for this, and someone on the other end could also get in trouble (especially if the FCC catches on).

🖙 **DON'T JUMP THE GUN.** Make sure you have read through all the replies to an email before adding your own commentary. No one likes to hear the same thing five times.

🖙 **STEP UP YOUR SUBJECT LINES.** Titling every email "yo" will no longer cut it, not only because it is too informal, but also because most people receive an absurd amount of work email and need to be able to search their inboxes easily. Something along the lines of "January Expense Reports" is better.

🖙 **DON'T BE A STICK IN THE MUD.** Socializing isn't what it used to be, and people have become accustomed to interacting almost exclusively via the computer even though they work 50 feet away from one another. This is not an excuse to be a recluse (on the contrary, it's important to have real contact with people). You can, however, use email to your

Working Life

advantage in the office. Send a link to a coworker if you think he or she will find it interesting. Email someone in another department if you'd like to grab coffee and learn about other things the company does. Or join in the joking around if you think it's appropriate—avoid racial or sexual jokes and other blatantly offensive things, but don't feel you have to be completely humorless.

✎ **Stay Organized.** You will get crazy amounts of email at work from tons of different people. Some messages will contain tasks you need to complete right now. Others will pass along information that won't become relevant until three months down the line. If you're using "Outlook" (the most popular office email client), make some folders and figure out a system for keeping track of everything.

Phone

Being professional on the horn is something for which many recent grads are woefully under-prepared. Still, as the new kids on the block, many are forced to act as stand-in secretaries. Some positions have a specific protocol you need to learn, and if you work on a desk at a talent agency (think Lloyd in *Entourage*), you may even have a script that you have to follow to the tee. Get familiar with the standards expected in your office and learn to take down the necessary details. Few things are as embarrassing as calling back a client and asking them to remind you of their name and vital stats.

One rule that applies everywhere: Answer the phone by saying, "This is [insert name here]." Even if you're 100% sure you know who's calling you, answer like it's your boss (guaranteed, it will be sometimes). If you're in a conference room or somewhere other than your desk and you pick up the phone, say, "Conference room."

When it comes to personal phone use in the office environment, a certain degree of common sense and decorum is required. Ever wonder what it's like to have a wiretap? To find out, you can either sell drugs on a massive scale, or you can work for a big company. As messed up as it sounds, someone might be listening in (especially if you're in a sales position), so it's probably best not to talk about last night's deviance, unless you were doing your cousin's statistics homework. Even if the mysterious "HR" is not piped in, beware of coworkers lurking in nearby cubicles pretending to be listening to music—you know they surreptitiously mute it whenever you get a call. If you need to deal with a personal matter feel free to do it quietly and politely (time to master the always awkward "hushed office voice"!), but if you are going to complain to your mom about your roommates or plan a *Jersey Shore*-themed party with your friend, find the time to step outside and use your cell phone. Or wait until after work.

 # Business Meal Etiquette

Once you arrive in the business world, your success will often depend on the way you present yourself. One of the most tricky work situations to navigate is the business meal, which could be anything from a "power breakfast" (who brought the multivitamins?) to a business lunch or an all-out formal dinner. Generally, you'll either be invited as a guest or as a potential hire, or you'll tag along with your boss/coworkers to meet clients. Whether you're the wooer, the woo-ee, or even if it's just you and the boss, the basic rules of engagement are pretty much the same. Here's some food for thought.

WHAT TO WEAR. If you're coming directly from work, then you may already be adequately outfitted (depending on where you work). Take wardrobe cues from your boss and, if you're unsure, ask beforehand what would be appropriate for the occasion. If you're rolling solo, consider swinging by the restaurant in advance or calling ahead to ask what the dress code is. In moments of uncertainty, err on the side of formality, but keep it subtle (you can foster your love of ascots and Madeleine Albright–style pins on your own time.) Check out the "Office Dress" section on page 153 for general rules about how to dress for professional situations.

BE EARLY. It will give you time to compose yourself before the power players arrive. If you are the first to get there, wait for

Hazard:
Understand "the waiter rule"

 Knowing how to use a fork and knife is important, but don't get so caught up in the "rules" of etiquette that you forget to be a nice person. It's common knowledge that CEOs (and people in general) look at a person's social skills when making judgments about what he or she is really like. So when you're invited out for a business meal, it's not really about the food; it's about how you interact with the world and deal with whatever comes at you. How do you treat your waiter when everything is going well? And what about when he gives you your steak medium-rare when you asked for it medium-well? The answers to these questions could determine whether you land (or keep) the job.

Working Life

the other party to arrive before sitting down. (Note: This is *not* an opportunity to get aggressive at the bar.)

NAVIGATING THE MENU. Lobster Thermidor may be delicious, but if it's the most expensive thing on the menu, you might want to steer clear. That doesn't mean you have to order "just an appetizer" (that would also be lame), but be reasonable. Essentially, you don't want your bizarre order to overshadow your great personality. Likewise, don't order something that is incredibly messy or complicated to eat. You're here to further your career, not to fling food chunks across the table. If you get put on the spot, politely ask the server to come back to you and then make a decision based on what others have chosen. If you want to play it really safe, you can always go with, "I'll have the same, please." Just don't be too overtly sycophantic about it.

POWER DOWN. Switch any mobile devices to silent mode, and then ignore them until you've left the restaurant. Even if others at the table are texting incessantly and checking BlackBerries, maintain your quiet dignity—they can get away with it, but you might look rude or distracted. Double standards—deal with it.

EASY ON THE SAUCE. This is a no-brainer, but it's worth noting that business and booze mix dangerously. Some companies have policies against drinking in a business setting, while others are a little more relaxed. We're not saying you must abstain completely (if everyone's "trying the sake," there's no need to be prudish), but don't plan on spending the afternoon swilling martinis. A good rule of thumb is never order a drink first, which ensures that you're never the only one drinking. (If you are, beware that you may come off as a total lush.)

MR. OR MS. CONGENIALITY. In essence, the key to etiquette is avoiding controversy and doing your best not to embarrass yourself. Fun, right? Set yourself up for success by dressing appropriately, being polite to waiters (see "the waiter rule" p. 163), and generally going with the flow (i.e., don't throw a fit if they're out of pork belly). You'd also do well to avoid controversial topics in conversation (the time you pounded an entire bottle of Malibu is unlikely to impress a potential employer or client). Act as you would if you were out with a friend's incredibly intimidating parents, and let the host (or your boss) be the one to determine when the conversation turns to business.

PAYING THE BILL. In most cases, you won't have to worry about this. For business meals, the rules are pretty easy: If you are invited, you should not be expected to pay, and it might be considered inappropriate if you offer. If you're just out with other coworkers bonding, offer to split the bill (they might pick it up depending on the age and status difference, but it's still best to ask). And if you're the host (e.g., you've invited someone out in order to network), you should offer to pay.

AFTER THE MEETING IT'S THE AFTER-MEETING. Going out with a boss or potential client can catapult the night into uncharted waters of business/ pleasure awkwardness, and it is perfectly reasonable to gracefully decline. If it's an important client or your boss urging you to go out, you should probably suck it up and go, but know your limits. Having to work early the next day is a good excuse that will get you out of partying *and* make you look responsible (bonus!). Then again, if you're out with coworkers who know you don't roll in 'til noon, this maneuver may not work.

Business Travel

Getting invited on a first business trip can put a well-justified spring in a recent grad's step. The fact that your company values your contribution enough to put you on a plane and pay for a hotel room is a nice vote of confidence. However, a lot of people have no idea what to expect from a business trip, and expectations quickly turn to disappointment when they realize it's not all piña coladas, complimentary mints, and deals inked in front of the Taj Mahal. More often than not, it's just like a regular workday, only much more stressful because of the new environment and logistical challenges of doing business outside the office. But where a complainer sees an exhausting challenge, a savvy recent grad sees a chance to impress his or her boss. Performing well on a business trip speaks not only to your ability to represent your company on a client's turf, but also to your aptitude for navigating new situations smoothly. Whether you're a traveling salesperson heading to Cincinnati or a fancy consultant jet-setting to Germany, here are some tips for the road—play it right and you might just get those 15 minutes at the pool after all.

TRAVEL ARRANGEMENTS. Prep work is crucial, as is knowing the company's reimbursement policies. What budget do you have for the flight and hotel? Can you rent a car or are you expected to use public transportation? Do you book your trip through a company travel agent or pay for it yourself (credit card reward points, what what!) and get reimbursed? If you're traveling with your boss, it's best to plan the trip together or with his or her assistant to make sure you meet any special needs (e.g., a hotel that's walking distance to meetings, yellow M&Ms upon arrival). If you're responsible for booking the accommodations, make sure there is a business center on the premises. You just never know when you're going to need to print a last-minute document, send a file, or even fax something (old school!). Prior to booking a flight, it might be worth checking Flightstats.com to make sure you aren't cutting a meeting close on a flight that's always 20 minutes late.

PREPARE EVERYTHING YOU'LL NEED IN ADVANCE. A few days before you leave, print out any important documents and copy all relevant files (and even tangentially relevant files) to a USB thumb drive. If you are giving a presentation, consider copying your Power Point slides and other materials to a CD, DVD, or other storage device. In the event that you're visiting multiple companies, split up the materials regarding each one so you don't fire up a CD at Company B and accidentally open up proprietary information about Company A, which just happens to be Company B's biggest rival (whoops!). In addition, don't get so caught up in the logistics and practical stuff that you forget to actually prepare to meet the client. If you've done your research and gone a step beyond what's asked of you, the chances of impressing your boss on the road will be much higher.

FIND SOMEONE TO HOLD DOWN THE FORT. No matter how prepared you are, you'll probably leave something behind or realize you need a random file only after reaching your destination. To avoid a mad scramble, it's always helpful to have someone in the office covering your back. Show this person where all of your files are located (digital and printed) and make sure he or she is working on the days you're traveling. We're sure you'll be happy to return the favor, especially if your office bud helps you avert a disaster.

DO YOUR RESEARCH. Depending upon your company's style, you might want to research restaurant and entertainment options before leaving, especially if you're expected to go out with a client or you're attending a conference where you might meet people to network with in the evenings. More practically, be sure to locate a local copy shop or Kinkos in the event you need to print documents and your hotel's business center is closed. And since we're guessing you can't do your job without Internet, you might want to check out Jiwire.com and Wifinder.com ahead of time to find a few Internet hot spots (though maybe your company has those handy-dandy wireless Internet cards).

PACKING. The art of packing is crucial for any trip, but particularly for a business trip. You want to travel like a ninja—stealth and maneuverability are important, but you also want to be prepared for the unexpected. Don't show up with a summer-camp style trunk, but give yourself a back-up plan in case you spill in-flight chicken piccata all over yourself. Check in with your boss or colleagues to

Working Life

see what the expected "away uniform" is. If you're given no guidance, you can always call up reception at your client's office and inquire about dress standards. "No-wrinkle" shirts are a traveler's best friend, and packing carefully can make the difference in how articles of clothing come out on the other end. In addition to clothing, be sure to pack a travel alarm clock, toiletries in a plastic bag (just make sure no liquids exceed three ounces and you have a zip-top, quart-size bag to fit them in to conform to TSA guidelines), a phone charger, and a laptop charger (plus AC adapter if you're going abroad). Last but not least, bring a stain stick—ones made by Tide work well—to ensure that you're prepared for any emergency, as well as some extra cash in the event you need to pay for a last-minute cab or something else.

DON'T CHECK YOUR BAGS. If your boss isn't checking bags, you shouldn't either. It just takes more time upon disembarking from the plane, and there's always a chance they'll get lost. Going carry-on will force you to pack smarter, which always lends to easier business travel.

STOCK UP. While your company is apt to pay for most of the incidentals on your trip, the less money you spend, the better. Instead of cracking open the mini-bar upon arrival, consider making a convenience store the second stop after your hotel for any drinks or snacks you need to keep you going. Can we hear you say Red Bull and Gushers?!

SET MORE ALARMS THAN THE FEDERAL RESERVE. Well, at least two. Nothing is more embarrassing than missing a morning meeting with a client. Whether you use your cell or BlackBerry and an alarm clock, or an alarm clock and hotel wakeup call, you should always "double up." We'd even recommend setting two wakeup calls 15 minutes apart just to be sure. And if you're going to use your phone or travel clock, make sure the time zone is correct. Ultimately, when it comes to alarms, being freakishly OCD is a good thing.

SAVE ALL RECEIPTS. You'll almost always need to hand in your receipts to get your money back at the end of the trip. When traveling, make sure to hold onto your receipts like they're worth the amount that's printed on them. If pretending you are literally holding a $75 bill makes it more fun, go for it.

Working Life

Ten Steps to Take If You Lose Your Job

A lot of this book focuses on how to find your first job, but the unfortunate truth is that some readers are going to have to deal with a layoff (or firing) at one point or another. In a deep recession, the "next round of cutbacks" looms over companies like the grim reaper. Even during the best of times, no job is ever guaranteed—downsizing, new management, buyouts, and all sorts of other factors can leave you out on the chopping block. If it happens, don't despair. First, thank your lucky stars that you're a recent grad starting out your career and not a 50-year-old with a house and a down payment on a BMW. Then, make sure you take the following steps to mitigate the short- and long-term effects of a job loss.

1) If you were fired... The first step is to understand the firing. If you know deep down that you deserved to be fired, think about how you got into that situation and how you can avoid it next time. If you think there's foul play at hand (e.g., office politics, discrimination), now is the time when having a mentor (p. 149) could be crucial. If you really think you have a valid complaint, check in with the U.S. Equal Employment Commission (eeoc.gov) or see if you can speak with a lawyer. For most people, the main question is how to move on. As you start job hunting again, it's important to get your story straight. Depending on how long you were with the employer, you may consider leaving the job off your resume entirely—after all, you're a recent grad and there are plenty of other things you could have been doing during that time (like maybe you also volunteered, and you can make the volunteer work seem like a bigger commitment). If you do put it in on your resume or bring it up in an interview, be honest and straightforward. Don't dwell on it and don't be negative about your past employer. More than likely the company interviewing you will look into the firing, so a web of lies is the last thing you want to leave in your wake.

2) Prepare for an exit interview, and be wary about signing anything. The reasons for your dismissal are crucial to your ability to receive unemployment benefits (see #3), as well as your story moving forward. Stay calm and use your final meeting with your (now ex) employer to clear up any grey areas about why exactly you're being let go. You may be handed a severance/termination agreement to sign, but don't feel you have to do so before taking a very close look and, if possible, running it by a lawyer. It is equally important for you to be cognizant of any terms that could potentially limit your prospects moving forward, such as "noncompete" clauses regarding your ability to work for other companies in the same field.

3) Find out if you're eligible for unemployment benefits. If you were terminated through no fault of your own (i.e., you weren't straight-up canned for negligence) and you meet other eligibility requirements, you may be able to collect unemployment benefits. You can find out by contacting your state unemployment office. You should do this immediately because benefits generally last for a maximum of 26 weeks, and it may take a couple of weeks (or months—there are horror stories) for a check to start arriving. When you go to file for unemployment, you need the following information: your social security number; a mailing address and phone number; and the names, addresses, and dates of employment of all your past employers for the last two years.

4) Don't let your health insurance slip away from you. Losing your benefits sucks, but it doesn't mean you should let yourself become an uninsured, devil-may-care lunatic. In most cases, you can sign up for COBRA, which will allow you to maintain your employer-sponsored health plan at your own expense. However, most healthy twentysomethings can find a better deal on an individual plan they find themselves. The key is to maintain insurance somehow, as a large gap in coverage (over 60 days) could make it harder for you to get your next policy. Go to Chapter 8 to learn more about the importance of maintaining coverage, as well as ways to get health insurance when you don't have a job.

5) Avoid the temptation to go out in a ball of flames. Getting laid off definitely qualifies as uncool, and your first reaction may be Hulk-like anger or an overwhelming desire to slink off quietly and never speak to anyone from work ever again. But in the long run, the much more constructive course of action is to make nice with all your bosses and coworkers, because they can be crucial networking contacts down the line. If they walk you out with your belongings in a paper box, resist the urge to cry and/ or yell, "You haven't seen the last of me! I am going to take you all down. Down to Chinatown!!!!!"

6) Gather all your files and any other work you don't want to lose. HR will probably say something to you on the last day about handing over any company property and not taking "proprietary" files out of the office. And yeah, you shouldn't take in-house documents and spread them all over the Internet in some sort of insane act of vengeance. But if you just want a file for your own personal use in the future, go for it. After all, you did the work, and it could save you a lot of time in the future if you end up working on similar things. Any contacts you made while at work may also be valuable for networking, so make sure you make a record of your work address book.

7) Tell everyone you know you're back on the job hunt. It can be embarrassing or painful to tell people you got laid off. But honestly, most folks are more likely to be sympathetic than they are to call you a loser. And more importantly, if your network doesn't know you're looking for a job, the hunt is going to be a lot harder. So first things

Working Life

Ten Steps to Take If You Lose Your Job continued...

first: Throw up a Facebook status message letting people know your situation. Feel free to make it lighthearted. Here are a few examples:

Got the axe this week. Timberrrrrrr!!! Seen any job openings in publishing?

Anyone catch the front page article about me in USA Today? "600,000 workers laid off in February." Misery loves company! Anyone got tips for applying to business school?

Remember when I worked for that car company? Yeah, me neither! Looking to switch modes—interested in marketing and branding. Holler if you've got any advice.

8) Start making some money. The thought of ramping up for another job hunt may be overwhelming. The bad news: Any savings from the last job aren't going to last you that long (plus, they're supposed to be *savings*, remember?). The good news: There are plenty of ways to stay afloat before diving back into the fray. Check out page 77 for ideas on making money when you don't have a full-time job.

9) Don't feel sorry for yourself. Seriously, as weird as it sounds, there's no better time to lose a job. You have the least to lose at this stage in your career, so roll with the punches and get excited about the next adventure rather than wallowing.

10) Have a little fun. One of the toughest parts about transitioning from college to working life is severely decreased time off. If you're in a financial position that allows you to put off working for a bit—whether that's a couple of weeks or a few months—check out Chapter 1 for ideas on how to spend your time. ∎

On Work and Boredom

According to *The Quarterlifer's Companion*, well over one half of recent grads in the workforce complain about severe boredom on the job. In fact, that number is far higher than those who complain that they are stressed out by their workload. Since fresh-out-of-college employees lack experience, many supervisors are careful about putting too much on their plates. However, sometimes whole offices are just sluggish and inefficient. If Internet caches could talk, they would weave a tale of monumental inefficiency across the Webisphere. According to a survey by AOL and Salary.com, the average American worker wastes 2.09 hours per eight-hour workday, mostly by hanging ten on the 'net, socializing with coworkers, and attending useless meetings.

Working Life

The point is, being bored at work is normal, but you need to figure out whether it's the job as a whole that bores you or the fact that you're not getting enough challenging work. The latter situation can be rectified if you are proactive. Ask bosses and coworkers if they have any side projects that you could help out with, or pitch your own ideas when given the opportunity. Don't expect everything to come to you—go out and get it, and eventually you'll earn people's trust and they will feel comfortable giving you more responsibility. And then you will be extremely busy, and you'll probably complain about that too!

If, however, the whole place just feels like somewhere that dreams go to die, perhaps it's time to start putting out the feelers for something new.

Beyond Your First Job

Depending on when you've come across this book, life beyond your first job might seem way too far off in the future to even begin contemplating. But since the Bureau of Labor Statistics reports that the average American works ten jobs between the ages of 18 and 40, it's likely that sooner or later, you'll get to the point where you will think about moving on to new pastures. Whether you are considering switching jobs within the same field or trying something completely new, it can feel daunting (and sometimes a bit awkward) to get out of an existing gig that pays the bills. However, it's important to remember that now is a perfect time in your life to take calculated risks. Unlike cutting your own bangs or sledding alone, some risks have potential benefits.

If you can't afford to quit your current job until you've found a new one, job hunting can be a bit of a struggle, especially if you don't want your current employer to know you are looking elsewhere. In order to play it extra smooth, schedule interviews during your lunch

> **Tips & Tricks:**
> **When to admit you hate your job**
>
> Does it feel like work is throwing you into an emotional rut? Be sure to assess the source of any negative feelings about your job. If you are just frustrated because you think you should be running a company, dating a model, and vacationing in Bora Bora, then give yourself time. However, if every day fills you with dread and you often consider staying in bed instead of going to work, maybe you are in the wrong job. If you've been there a year and feel discontent, now is the perfect time for a change. For tips on switching jobs, see the next page.

Working Life

break or take strategic vacation days to accommodate any traveling or interviewing that you might have to do. You can also utilize phantom doctor's appointments (be ready to explain what the hell's wrong with you) or squeeze in early morning breakfast meetings before work.

As for the interviews themselves, prepare yourself thoroughly for one inevitable question: "Why do you want to leave your current job?" The real reason might be that you despise your boss and feel degraded when he makes you expense his trips to the strip club. But being positive will leave a much better impression—say that you feel you've outgrown your current position, or that you are looking for a new challenge. However, don't forget to talk up all the stuff you've learned at the job you want to leave. You are evolving from a smart but untested college grad into a smart and semiexperienced twenty something. And believe us, employers know the difference.

Five Good Reasons to Leave Your Job:

✓ You are chronically tired or depressed.

✓ You are being harassed.

✓ You are 100% sure you are in the wrong industry.

✓ You want to move to a new city.

✓ You don't think you would like doing what your boss or boss's boss does.

Five Bad Reasons to Leave Your Job:

✗ You just don't like working in general.

✗ You are in an office relationship that has turned sour.

✗ There is not a Starbucks close enough for your liking.

✗ You have done something illegal.

✗ Other offices have better vending machines. ∎

Chapter V: Housing

Housing

Do I need a solarium? Billiards table in the rec room? Pool, Jacuzzi, or both? These are questions that 99.9% of you won't be asking when looking for a new place to call home. Yes, it's true, your first place is not necessarily going to be palatial. If it is, well played. But if not, don't fret. The important thing is that by moving to a new city and/or renting your first place, you are taking a huge step toward independence and personal responsibility. Having your own space will give you the breathing room you need to thrive socially and creatively. Furthermore, it will force you to become more self-reliant as you learn to deal with landlords, pay utility bills on time, buy your own groceries, and maybe even clean up after yourself once in a while.

In this chapter, we'll provide you with all the know-how you need to transition to life beyond the nest and into a crib to call your own, from choosing a city, to finding the right pad, to maximizing your living situation.

The Other Option: Moving Home

One of the most immediate issues facing the recent graduate is where to seek shelter after getting kicked out of the dormitory. If you're like most of your contemporaries (about 60%, according to a Monster.com survey), the default solution is your parents' house. And why not? Home provides many creature comforts, the rent is usually pretty competitive (i.e., $0), and cable is free. What's not to like?

Apparently, not everyone thinks it's such a no-brainer. If you believe the Baby Boomer-biased media, you'd think America had an epidemic on its hands. Yes, it's true—more and more college grads are moving home after graduation than ever before. As the naysayers like to point out, young people are making financial sacrifices early on in their adult lives while forcing their parents to postpone retirement to support them. In her book *Generation Me*, sociologist Jean Twenge even goes so far as to suggest the underlying motivation for this trend is selfishness. Apparently, we are a generation of narcissistic daydreamers who would rather lounge at mom and dad's house thinking about our passions than worry about a mortgage. Sounds like the end of the world!

Ms. Twenge is entitled to her opinion, but the rulebook has changed since our parents first left college. The old paradigm of "graduate college, move out, start a career, get married, have some kids" no longer holds. Career paths are more varied but also more complicated than they once were, and it takes the average graduate several months (if not longer) to find a job.

If you're 35 and still getting yelled at by your mom for leaving the toilet seat up, then you might have cause for concern. But for now, don't beat yourself up about settling back into the nest, whether it's for a summer or a year. As long as you treat it as a temporary solution and show a little initiative to do *something* (see page 41) other than sit around reading *Twilight*, things will eventually work out. Here are some tips for navigating a potentially thorny situation.

Smart Money:
The economics of living at home

$ It's undeniable that the number one reason grads move in with their parents is money. So whether you're trying to break into a low-paying industry or you haven't quite figured out what you want to do after college, check out the potential monthly savings that are available: $500 to $1,500+ on rent, $300+ on food, $65+ on cable and Internet, $50 on electricity, $50 on coffee, $10 on renters insurance… and those are just the basics. Unless your parents are asking you to shell out some extra cash (even then it's still a great deal), you could end up saving somewhere between $1,000 and $2,500 per month. Maybe living with mom and dad won't be so bad after all.

Don't Fall Back into Bad Habits. Presumably, at least four years have passed since you really lived with the 'rents. They got used to daily life without you, and they probably liked it. Even if you have younger siblings, your departure to college meant one less mouth to feed, one less load of laundry each week, and far fewer ornery teenagers displaying horrible posture throughout the house. You'll do yourself a favor by seeing their side of the story and easing your way back into the Matrix. It's amazing how quickly that feeling of youthful entitlement can creep back into your psyche when you enter the house, but you don't want your selfish demands to come crashing down on your parents like a ton of bricks. Clean your clothes, wash the dishes, offer to buy (or at least fetch) groceries, and do some cooking. You can annoy them all you want and make them worry day and night, but don't make your return to the house feel like more *work*.

Make the Most of the Time with Your Family. Tempers fray easily in the pressure cooker of post-college life. As if job hunting wasn't aggravating enough, being forced to give Ma Dukes a nightly recap of your progress can become extremely irksome. And ironically, it can be even harder if you've got a job. The last thing you want to do when you come home tired at the end of the day is to tell your mom all about the papers you filed and the copies you made—it salts the wound liberally. That said, it's wise to fight past the feeling of being smothered by your parents. Whether it's two weeks, six months, or a year from now, eventually you'll be on your own. Careers will force you to move around, significant others will demand that you go to their house for Thanksgiving—all sorts of things will ensure that you see your parents less frequently. Have dinner together, hang out with younger siblings, and make some memories while you have the time. Trust us, you'll feel better for it in the long-run. And if peace of mind doesn't motivate you, then just think of your civil behavior as remuneration for your room and board.

Dad-uation (and Mom-uation). Parents also go through a transition after you graduate, so it's important to keep their interests in mind when you re-infiltrate their home. If they helped finance your education, they are probably pretty pleased about not having to pay another semester's tuition. Don't rain on the parade by finding new and less justifiable ways to be a financial burden. Give them space when they want to have friends over instead of sitting in the living room playing Xbox Live with headphones on—that's embarrassing for everyone. Overall, try to avoid giving the impression that your college career was a complete waste of time and money.

Save As Much Money As Possible. Whether you're jobless, interning, or stuck at a starting salary that can't support you month to month, the luxury of not paying for rent, utilities, or food can make a huge difference. However, if you go and blow any loot that does come into your hands on unnecessary extravagances, you will be doing yourself a huge disservice for the day when you do actually need to pay for things. Adopting a frugal lifestyle should not be that difficult, because let's be honest, living "la vida loca" (whatever that means) and staying with your parents don't necessarily vibe. Do you really want to be hitting the bar and playing tonsil hockey with strangers in your childhood bed? Save the money for a time and place when you can live a little more loosely. Who knows—the good budgeting and saving habits you start now might even translate to life beyond the nest.

Set a Schedule. Being semi-productive every day—or at least constructing an elaborate façade of industriousness—will help to get your parents off your back and make you feel more motivated. If you are already working, this shouldn't be too difficult. If not, wake up at the same time every day, and try to make sure that it's before noon. After that, try to do something useful. In *The Quarterlifer's Companion*, Abby Wilner and Catherine Stocker suggest scheduling at least one activity each day to help you on your job search: "It can be an interview, a trip to the library to do research, a trip to Kinkos to copy resumes, anything." It doesn't really matter what activity you choose to schedule as long as loafing around and being cantankerous does not become your *modus operandi*.

Enjoy the Fairies. Sometimes you will leave your room covered in soiled clothing, only to return later in the day and find it neatly ironed and folded on your bed. That is the Laundry Fairy. Or maybe one day you will be watching reruns of *Who Wants to Be a Millionaire* and suddenly dinner will magically appear in front of you. Thank you, Dinner Fairy! Some of us are lucky enough to have parents who, in spite of their better judgment, can't help but spoil us when we are around. Maybe your moving home is not cause for celebration, but you've still been gone long enough for your parents to miss you a little bit, and you also just achieved a great milestone by graduating. In other words, you are in good standing! Milk this situation as much as your conscience will allow you to, because when you move into your own place, those fairies will be slaughtered and subsequently resurrected as ruthless demons that will make your life infinitely more difficult.

Making It Long Term. Some people end up working or going to graduate school in the city their parents live in, and financially it might make sense to create a long-term arrangement that could span several years. This is a trickier situation that depends a lot on your relationship with your parents. If they let you do the things that you need to do to feel sane and you don't step on their toes too much, it can work out nicely and allow you to save money that you would otherwise be pouring down the drain unnecessarily.

At the end of the day, you need to be honest with yourself and make sure you are not stifling your potential by staying shacked up in the house. If you realize you need to spread your wings a bit more, you'll find a way to make it out. ■

🌐 Location, Location, Location

Housing

So, you've made the decision to move out of the nest and go your own way. Go your own way! Subject to a few restrictions, you now have the world at your fingertips. Close your eyes, spin the globe, and point. Gary, Indiana! Okay, forget that plan. A more logical approach may be in order.

Let's start with some real talk. The first city that you move to after college isn't necessarily the one you'll end up in for life. So go sow your nomadic oats. Always wanted to live in Austin before settling down in Philadelphia? Or how about Beijing before Kansas City? (Who said you have to settle "Stateside" right after college? Check out page 5 for ideas on how to take yourself international.) Now's the time to explore and experiment, when your responsibilities are at an all-time low and all you need to worry about, in most cases, is putting a roof over your head, eating food, and possibly repaying student debt (but no kids, mortgage, etc.). And if you end up somewhere you don't like, just move on to the next place. In the worst-case scenario, you move in less than a year. We promise, it's not a big deal.

When it comes down to the process of city selection, there are really two approaches: picking a city because you want to live there, or picking a city because you think it will maximize your job prospects. These aren't mutually exclusive, but it's worth considering the thought process behind each as you weigh your options.

Find a City (Find Yourself a City to Live In)

If you aren't the type that's rushing to make the "millionaires under 30" list (or you are that type but think you can do it without being in a business hub), you've got a ton of options for your first post-grad city. Is there a place where you've always seen yourself living, or a city that appeals to your gut for no particular reason? Some criteria to consider include the following:

- 🏙 **Friends and Family:** Do you need to be around your friends and family, or do you want to blaze your own trail for a bit?

- 🏙 **Cost of living:** This factor can be the difference between squatting and living (relatively) large. We recommend using Sperling's Best Place cost of living calculator (BestPlaces.net/COL), which allows you to plug in two cities and compare the cost of key expenses like food, transportation, health services, and more. And for a really comprehensive statistical overview of the city you're researching, check out City-data.com.

Weather: Are you a surfer, a skier, or someone who avoids going outside at all costs?

Demographic: Do you want to be surrounded by other recent grads, stroller-pushing newlyweds, or incredibly old people?

Culture: Do you want a city that has nonstop entertainment in the form of art and museum exhibitions, classical music, opera, Jonas Brothers shows, and other concerts?

Attitude: Do you like a fast-paced or laid-back vibe?

Nightlife/Bar Scene: Do you want to club hop, frequent the local speakeasies, or drink Trader Joe's wine at home while tearing through your Netflix queue?

Pick a City for a Job

If the "right job" is at the top of your priority list, we salute your self-starting 'tude and offer one piece of advice: Seriously consider what job you want before you pick your city. That's because once you choose the industry you want to break into, your city may be picked out for you (assuming you want to be in the hub). Richard Florida's *Who's Your City?: How the Creative Economy is Making Where to Live the Most Important Decision of Your Life* is a great resource for comparing post-college cities and getting a feel for which industries thrive in each.

 ## Gradspot's Ultimate (Abridged) City Guide

Below, we've included a snapshot of five of the most popular cities for recent grads. If these fail to suit your social or occupational needs, check out Gradspot.com for a more comprehensive list or use the criteria above to selecy the city that is the best fit for you.

WASHINGTON D.C.

Ever the town for movers and shakers, DC is riding the wave of excitement ignited by the election of Barack Obama. It's often said the dynamics of the town shift according to who's in office, particularly during the summer when the nation's capital is flooded with party-hardy interns. If you are coming from a large city, D.C. can feel comparatively small and segregated, but it is also rife with young people in politics, academia, and journalism (a plus for guys: women outnumber men by about five to four).

Housing

KEY STATS

Major Industries:	Government, Non-Profit
Climate:	Four distinct seasons with hot summers (Winter—30°F, Summer—80°F)
Transportation:	The DC "Metro" system is famously clean and efficient, and it will get you most places you need to go. However, stations close at 3AM on the weekends (midnight during the week) and cabs are expensive, so some complain that going out can be a pain.
Avg. Price of a One Bedroom Apartment:	$1,535
Cost of Living Index Value:	166
Closing Time:	Su-Th 2AM, F-Sa 3AM
Professional Sports:	MLB—Nationals; NFL—Redskins; NBA—Wizards; NHL—Capitals
Famous Foodstuffs:	Chili half-smoke (made famous by Ben's Chili Bowl)
You'll love it if...	You're an aspiring politician or academic who thrives on youthful naïveté
You'll be miserable if...	You can't stand arguing and want a "big city" feel
Best Thing Ever:	Bountiful green space
Worst Thing Ever:	Political blowhards and people who use the phrase "inside the Beltway"

LOS ANGELES

Everyone in L.A. thinks his or her life is like *Entourage*, and for a select few, that's actually true. Others do their best to fake the funk, talking their way into various parties and hoping against hope that they are seconds away from "blowing up." But L.A. stands as a testament to the idea that weather really does matter—people are happy, beautiful, and relaxed. They leave work early and go to the beach year-round. So can anyone really blame them for loving their mirage of a city?

KEY STATS

Major Industries:	Entertainment, Fashion
Climate:	Not too hot, not too cold, but just right all year (Winter—58°F, Summer—75°F)
Transportation:	Car culture rules
Avg. Price of a One Bedroom Apartment:	$1,240
Cost of Living Index Value:	156
Closing Time:	2AM (but many after-hours spots keep going 'til 6 in the mornin')
Professional Sports:	MLB—Dodgers, Angels of Anaheim; NBA—Lakers, Clippers; NHL—Kings, Anaheim Ducks
Famous Foodstuffs:	Burritos; Korean BBQ; the latest celebrity diet fad
You'll love it if…	You're a laidback, sun-loving cat who just wants to chill
You'll be miserable if…	You're obsessed with ideals of authenticity and don't embrace casual friendships
Best Thing Ever:	A-list celeb sightings ain't a thang
Worst Thing Ever:	People rarely act their age

BOSTON

If you like sports and fratty behavior, Beantown may be the place for you. With tons of history and a recent spate of championships, the town's sports teams drive the daily conversation, which generally involves the use of strange accents. Moreover, "America's College Town" is packed with students who populate the bars and/or drink terrible beers in dorm rooms throughout the city. Though not always the most vibrant of cities, Boston is very livable. There are some wonderful museums and historical sites, and few things beat a run or walk along the banks of the Charles River in spring.

Housing

KEY STATS

Major Industries:	Consulting, Venture Capital
Climate:	Four distinct seasons with cold winters (Winter—30°F, Summer—72°F)
Transportation:	The "T" system and buses will get you most places, but most lines shut down by 12:30–1AM. A commuter rail serves the 'burbs. (Subway fare: $1.70)
Avg. Price of a One Bedroom Apartment:	$1,950
Cost of Living Index Value:	128
Closing Time:	2AM
Professional Sports:	MLB—Red Sox; NFL—Patriots; NBA—Celtics; NHL—Bruins
Famous Foodstuffs:	New England Clam Chow-dah
You'll love it if...	You're a beer-swilling, sports-loving type with a blue-collar streak (aka you like Dunkin Donuts more than Starbucks)
You'll be miserable if...	You hate being cold and can't stand college students (because they remind you of all your regrets!)
Best Thing Ever:	The Boston Marathon
Worst Thing Ever:	Red Sox fans

Housing

NEW YORK

New York City is Mecca for many recent grads looking to live the Twentysomething Dream. "Work hard, play hard" is the motto many live by, putting in long hours at the office and partying when the average person would wisely choose to go to bed. The yearning for success—that old "if you can make it here, you'll make it anywhere" attitude—is almost tangible, and while some feed off the energy, others find it exhausting. The transient hordes and uber-competitive real-estate market contribute to this restless energy, but if you can keep your own goals in sight, New York can be whatever you want it to be. Being bored is not an option.

KEY STATS

Major Industries:	Finance, Fashion, Advertising/Marketing, Publishing
Climate:	Temperate spring and fall; stifling summer exacerbated by crowdedness and scarce air-conditioning; cold winters (Winter—34°F, Summer—77°F)
Transportation:	Subway and cabs are a way of life. Parking fees are sky high and cars are essentially useless within the city. (Subway fare: $2.25.)
Avg. Price of a One Bedroom Apartment:	$2,249
Cost of Living Index Value:	165
Closing Time:	Bars close?
Professional Sports:	MLB—Yankees, Mets; NFL—Giants, Jets; NBA—Knicks, Nets; NHL—Rangers, Devils, Islanders
Famous Foodstuffs:	Pizza on every block; chicken cutlet sandwiches from the bodega; delicious (but often overpriced) meals of every cuisine imaginable
You'll love it if…	You're a motivated, energetic type who doesn't mind living beyond your means in the name of "being young"
You'll be miserable if…	You're a penny-pinching homebody who hates noise, people, and staying up late
Best Thing Ever:	24-hour everything
Worst Thing Ever:	Various bridges and tunnels to NJ, Staten Island, and Long Island

CHICAGO

The jewel of the Midwest combines cosmopolitanism with a refreshing dose of hospitality, catering to those who like city life but don't like the "f*&k you, a*^hole!" mentality of places like New York. There are few big cities that are prettier than Chi-Town, which offers a mix of leafy neighborhoods, an architecturally stunning downtown, and a gorgeous lakefront. Tons of bars, live music, and museums keep recent grads entertained, but beware—the winters are not for the faint-hearted.

Housing

KEY STATS

Major Industries:	Aerospace, Finance, Consulting
Climate:	Four distinct seasons, but beware of freezing winters (Winter—28°F, Summer—74°F)
Transportation:	The 'L' and buses will get you where you need to go (Fare: $2.25)
Avg. Price of a One Bedroom Apartment:	$1,106
Cost of Living Index Value:	126
Closing Time:	Su-F 3AM, Sa 4AM
Professional Sports:	MLB—White Sox, Cubs; NFL—Bears; NBA—Bulls; NHL—Blackhawks
Famous Foodstuffs:	Hotdogs with the works and deep-dish pizza
You'll love it if…	You like your big city flavor tempered with a dash of Midwestern hospitality
You'll be miserable if…	You are suspicious of nice people
Best Thing Ever:	The coolest architecture in America
Worst Thing Ever:	The wind off Lake Michigan

Top Five Tips for Moving With and Without a Mover

Whether you're moving out of your college dorm or into your new place (or both!), you are going to have to deal with the arduous task of transporting all of your stuff from point A to point B. Here are some tips for moving solo, or with the help of a professional mover.

Moving with a Mover

1) Prepare. Figure out what you'll need (e.g., boxes, tape, truck) and secure it before moving day so you won't have to scramble. If you wait until the last minute like every other kid in College Town, USA, you may be stuck riding the Greyhound. This eventuality, in turn, will give new meaning to the word *depressing*.

2) Get help. Ever tried to load a mattress into a car/truck on your own? Now imagine trying to repeat this process with all of your furniture. Ask friends and family for help. If that backfires, then scour Craigslist for freelance strongmen. You don't need to be a hero.

3) Pack smart. Save some cash by getting your packing materials online or from a hardware store. Also, put some thought into what goes in each box and how to avoid wasting space. Storage/packing is an art form that should be treated with due respect.

4) Wheels. Check U-Haul, Budget, and Penske to see what kind of ride you will need and compare prices. On pickup day, arrive early to get first dibs. When loading up, remember to distribute weight evenly. If you are renting a trailer, make sure the truck and/or your car has a hitch to attach it to.

5) Assume it will be annoying. I don't care what people tell you; moving yourself is a big pain in the butt. If you have the cash, do yourself a favor and spend it to hire movers.

Moving with a Mover

1) Make a reservation. This is not your Intro to Philosophy term paper—just because you are paying someone else to do it for you doesn't mean you don't have to give it any thought before the date of pickup. Most moving companies recommend making a reservation two to four weeks ahead of time.

2) Comparison shop. In comparing movers, you will naturally want to consider pricing, but you also want to learn a bit about the company that will be sending someone to pack all of your worldly goods into a truck that could double as a getaway vehicle. Make sure your mover has insurance and uses fulltime staffers that will be mindful of their own job security when moving your stuff.

3) Check the fine print. Once you are given an initial estimate, it is helpful to rattle off any potential obstacles you envision to ensure the movers don't hit you with any hidden fees. Do they charge an additional fee for large items like an armoire? Will the company transfer your goods mid-move to a different truck (thus increasing chances of breakage)?

4) Get directions. If you are at a point of indecision about where you want to live, hiring a mover in the hopes that they will make the decision for you is probably not the way to go. Printing out specific directions ahead of time will save time and money. It will also force you to pick a place to live and thus prevent the possibility of homelessness.

5) Pack yourself. Not only do movers generally charge by the hour, but they also won't care if all of your belongings are supposed to be sorted by "awesomeness factor." Moreover, they will charge a premium for packing supplies, and use way more boxes than is necessary. Handle this part of the process on your own and then use the pros for what they do best—heavy lifting. ■

Housing

Neighborhood, Space, Cost: Two Outta Three Ain't Bad

Once you've chosen a post-college city to live in, it's time to set some criteria to guide your hunt. To do so, it is necessary to balance the three main criteria for judging places: neighborhood/location, space, and cost. Realistically, it is best to select two of these three and focus on getting the most out of those. Otherwise, you might find yourself living in a pipe dream.

Neighborhood

In most cities worth living in, there exists a wide range of neighborhoods, each boasting its own inimitable flavor. Some are filled with hipsters who aspire to be starving artists even though their parents work for Fortune 500 companies. Some are filled with octogenarians, while others are havens for young families. If you are new to a city, get a sense of the landscape by reading guidebooks, grabbing local magazines and newspapers, and talking to people who have lived there. Walk around neighborhoods during the day and then go back at night so you can see what you can do and whether or not it feels safe—saving money is great, but if you are going to end up getting the shirt stolen off your back twice a month on the way home from work, maybe it's not worth living on "the wrong side of the tracks." Aside from safety for your body and belongings, think about whether or not you feel comfortable. Is the neighborhood diverse? Do you feel like you stand out in a way that doesn't feel right? Trust your gut, because as much as you think it might motivate you to work harder, it sucks to live in fear and dread of returning to your own pad at the end of the day. Here are some more pressing concerns to consider:

☞ **PROXIMITY TO WORK.** Will an hour commute to and from work make you want to impale yourself on a rusty spike? If you drive, what will the morning traffic be like? Would you rather wake up half an hour later every weekday or be closer to your friends on the weekends? A good way to estimate your commute is to get transit directions from your potential neighborhood/pad using HopStop.com and Google Maps.

☞ **PROXIMITY TO TRANSPORTATION.** The added convenience of having a bus, train, or highway nearby can pay off huge in the long run.

☞ **SAFETY.** We'll just mention it again so we don't get sued. (Just kidding—we really do care about you!) Use sites like

NeighborhoodScout.com, City-Data.com, and Homefacts.com to get safety info on the neighborhood.

☞ **CONVENIENCE.** Grocery stores, banks, and pharmacies should be easily accessible, or else you might get aggravated and/or hungry.

☞ **OTHER.** How much do you value being close to friends, restaurants, bars, parks, and anything else that will make your life more convenient and enjoyable?

Space

As the fictional British broadcaster Alan Partridge once pointed out, "People always go on about space. But people forget, you can get lost in space!" Though your getting lost in your first pad is about as likely as Baghdad winning the next Olympic bid, the fact remains that space is not always all it's cracked up to be, particularly when it comes at a high premium.

We should note that you could probably rent an old farmhouse in Mississippi for the same price that it costs to live in a cramped Manhattan studio, and in many ways that's an awesome idea. But for now let's assess the realities of city living.

When looking at an apartment or house, think about how much natural light it gets and how important that is to you. If you end up renting a convertible, will the added room block out most of the light? Next, assess the floor plan, which is generally much more important than the square footage number quoted on the listing. Do you have

> **Smart Money:**
> **Flex/convertible apartments**
>
> One concept that is particularly relevant to recent grads living with roommates is that of a flex apartment, also known as a convertible. These terms refer to apartments that have the space (generally in a large bedroom or off the living room) to add an extra bedroom by putting up pressurized walls. So a "flex three" or "convertible three" is a two-bedroom apartment with room for a third. It does not mean that it is a three-bedroom that can be flexed or converted to four, so if you have more than three people look elsewhere. Like a convertible car, these apartments are usually pretty cramped, and unfortunately you can't pop the roof to get more sunlight. However, this type of arrangement can make the rent much more manageable for recent grads on tight budgets. (For more real estate lingo, see page 194.)

to walk through another bedroom to get to the bathroom? Are the hallways awkwardly narrow? Finally, think about your unique lifestyle and needs. If you live with a social group of friends and you plan to spend most of your free time at home together, then maybe it's worth sacrificing large bedrooms for a bigger living room and kitchen. But if you want to spend your evenings watching (and then re-watching) *Eat, Pray, Love* in peace, hold out for a suitably comfortable bedroom. Finally, if you have worked out a rental scheme in which you and your roommates will pay different amounts, make sure you look for places where the rooms match their respective price tags.

The Big Issue: How Much Is This Going to Cost Me?

How much you are willing to pay is pretty much up to you, though we encourage you to think about saving your money rather than blowing it on an unnecessarily extravagant pad. In economic terms, rent is a *sunk cost*, meaning it cannot be recovered once you've paid it. It is not an investment that will accrue value over time (unlike buying a place, which you can learn more about on page 220).

The key question is how much is reasonable when it comes to rent. Property prices vary so drastically from place to place that geography plays a huge role in this decision, but a wise recent grad budget (p. 255) would have you spending around 35% of your monthly income on rent. That might not be possible in the most expensive cities, but you should never spend more than half of your salary on rent and utilities (so if you make $35,000 a year and bring home $2,000 a month after taxes, Social Security, and health care, your rent should be a maximum of $1,000 per month).

It's important to settle on a range before you start hunting to avoid wasting time looking at places you can't afford. To set that range, you need to get a sense for the average rents in the place you're hunting so you don't get swindled or go in with an unrealistically low budget. Just scour Craigslist listings, review RentBits.com averages, talk to friends and coworkers, and call up a few brokers for an overview of the market (you don't have to commit to work with them). When you actually start seeing places, be very explicit in asking about the average cost of utilities and the services each provides (generally trash removal, water, and maintenance).

Perks and Special Needs

If you require wheelchair-accessibility or you own a pet, you'd better make sure that any building you look at can accommodate these needs. Beyond the essentials, you need to determine how much you value the various "bells and whistles" of the living facility.

👍 **LAUNDRY.** A laundry room (or better yet a washer and dryer in the apartment or house) should be a major point of investigation. However, bear in mind that laundry rooms cost money, so look around the neighborhood before ruling out a laundry-free building—there may be a Laundromat next door that will wash, iron, and fold your clothes for little more than it would take to use the machines.

👍 **KITCHEN.** A refrigerator, stovetop, and oven are basic, but a dishwasher can be a godsend to a busy and lazy grad. That said, if you never cook at home (let alone eat outside the office), maybe it's irrelevant. Determine your cooking needs and aspirations, then proceed accordingly. You can also roll with paper dishes and plastic silverware to make things easier. Just don't expect Al Gore to show up at your dinner parties. If you're subletting or joining an existing house share, ask about whether the kitchen is already equipped with shared items or whether you would be expected to contribute your own dishes, pots, pans, and so on.

👍 **GYM.** Having a gym in your building, community, or house is pretty fresh, but again, assess your actual schedule and habits. Does your job provide a gym membership somewhere better? Would you prefer to work out at home or closer to work? Have you even worked out since '99? Maybe it's not so crucial after all…

👍 **DOORMAN AND/OR SECURITY.** What kind of security is in place for residents? Is it a gated community? Are there night patrols? (And if so, is it because the surrounding neighborhood is a warzone?) In cities, a doorman apartment is not only safer, but also more convenient when it comes to dealing with packages, guests, and other building-related issues. However, if packages are your main concern, remember that you may also be able to get them shipped to your office. If it's not a typical "doorman building," is there security on hand or a number you can call in case of emergency? Needless to say, having this type of staff on the premises almost always means higher prices, so decide how much these services are worth to you.

👍 **PATIO, BALCONY, OUTDOOR SPACE, OR ROOF ACCESS.** If you like "grilling and chilling" as much as Bobby Flay does, a little deck space can be very agreeable, but that doesn't mean you have to splurge on the penthouse. Many apartment buildings offer shared roof or garden space, and some apartment and condo complexes have interior parks and/or lawns where you can commune with nature to your heart's content.

👍 **PARKING.** Do you need it, and are there cheaper alternatives?

👍 **HOUSES.** In some cities, it's more common to rent houses (or "apartments" within individual houses) than it is to rent an apartment or condo in a managed building or complex. The process of searching for a rental house is much the same as searching for other types of housing, but once you find one, there are a few new variables that go into the mix (got your snow shovel?). If you're considering this option, check out "Specifics of Renting a House" on page 204.

The Real Estate Hunt

There are essentially two ways to find housing: get a broker or search on your own (or do both simultaneously). Depending on where you live and what type of living situation you seek, working with a broker may or may not be an option. Brokers are more prevalent in certain cities (e.g., Boston, New York, Chicago), and they tend to work directly with management companies that oversee specific apartment buildings or sometimes with the Homeowners Associations of condo complexes. Whether you decide to work with a broker or not, brace yourself for a healthy dose of stress and annoyance. Hunting down your own dwelling can be an all-consuming process, but once it's settled, you can throw a housewarming rager and you'll soon forget what a pain in the ass it was. Here are some of the pros and cons of using a broker versus hunting on your own.

Hunting Option #1: Do It Yourself

Conducting an independent search is a good idea if: 1) You have the time; 2) You want to save money by avoiding brokers' fees; 3) You're planning to move into an established house share or a sublet; or 4) You're looking to rent a condo or apartment directly from the owner or a management company. (Management companies usually run big buildings or apartment complexes, and they'll almost always have a central office you can visit or call to inquire about open units.) While looking for "no fee" housing requires a bit of creativity and a lot of perseverance, it is an entirely viable option and a good way to save cash at this fiscally precarious moment in your life. To ensure that the hunt goes as smoothly as possible, check out these savvy hunting tips.

⚲ **SOUND THE ALARM.** Let family, friends, and coworkers know you're in the market for a new place. Ask friends about their search to get a list of good websites and management companies. Also, if you like a friend's building, have him or her ask the super if there are any apartments up for rent. Some buildings and management companies offer "Refer-a-Friend" rewards to tenants who bring others in, so you may help your friends cash in. (If you end up renting a place with this policy, don't forget to take advantage in the future when you hear of someone who is looking—or at least demand that your friend who referred you buys you a burrito.) Word of mouth is especially useful when it comes to subletting (p. 211), as people often seek to sublet to friends or friends-of-friends before making a public announcement. Use your social networks (e.g., Facebook, Twitter) to let people know you're looking and to see if they have ideas.

⚲ **GO TO THE SOURCE.** This is often the best strategy. If you've narrowed down your search to a neighborhood, visit each building in the area and ask people going in or out whether there are apartments available, or find the number of the management company (sometimes found on a plaque in the entranceway) and call directly. Even if they don't have an apartment in the building you're calling about, they might have one nearby. If you're looking for a house, cruise around the neighborhood looking for for rent signs.

⚲ **CRAIGSLIST.** In most cities in the United States, Craigslist reigns supreme as the go-to resource for housing. Everyone should start here, if only to get a sense for the market. If given an option, begin by searching under the "No Fee" section, where you will find apartments being rented directly by management companies or condos being rented directly by owners. Occasionally, brokers may list apartments in this section with the caveat that they will absorb any fees, therefore making them "No Fee" from the standpoint of the tenant. As always, beware of Craigslist fraud—if it seems too good to be true, it probably is.

⚲ **OTHER RESOURCES.** Beyond Craigslist, different cities have their own local resources, such as Rentvine.com in Denver and RentersResource. com in Houston (a comprehensive list is available via gradspot.com/book). Ask friends and coworkers what they used. In addition, scour classified ads in local publications (or on their websites). If your city has a college or university, check with their housing office to see if you can tap into any listing services or resources they provide for grad students and/or faculty members. Some schools even lease rooms to interns on a short-term basis, especially during the summer.

Housing

 Lingo: **Ad Speak in Real Estate Listings**

When you start hunting for an abode, you will quickly learn that real estate listings are a veritable study in the art of the euphemism. The more fluent you are, the more efficient you will be in your search. As a rule of thumb, avoid any online ads that feature flashing lights, size 98 font, or exclamation mark abuse. Beyond that, here are a few translations to help you on your way. Note that use of these words does not always mean you can yell "You lie!" at your computer. But if you have a bad feeling about a listing (or, most important, there are no photos accompanying the listing), they should be viewed with healthy suspicion.

> **Cute / Cozy / Adorable / Intimate**—It's tiny and may lack basic features like closets and storage-space. Your bed (if you can fit one) may very well take up the entire bedroom and/or apartment. On the upside, it will be cheap to heat (just add more fiber to your diet).

> **Full of Character / Charming**—Dirty, rundown, decrepit, and potentially located in a poorly maintained building.

> **Bohemian / Funky**—Indicates there is something "different" about this place. Could be anything from lingering marijuana fumes coming from the neighbors' apartment to pornographic murals on the living room wall. Be sure to ask for details.

Never Lived In / State of the Art—It will be freshly painted, and the appliances will be new, but don't confuse newness with high quality. You may encounter even more maintenance issues in a brand new place than you would in a more weathered spot.

Quiet Neighborhood—Sometimes known as a "boring" and/or "secluded" neighborhood. Might make you feel like you're living in a slasher flick.

Lively / Animated Neighborhood—Prepare to be kept awake at night by traffic/revelers/the sports bar on the first floor of the building.

Up-and-Coming Neighborhood—Everyone loves an underdog, but you don't necessarily want to live in one. If it's really "up-and-coming," find out what's setting it back from arrival at the "nice neighborhood" promised land. Most importantly, make sure it's safe.

Great Location / Convenient To [Some Place Cool]... —Perhaps the most subjective of all real estate descriptors. Do they mean it's literally walking distance to a place you'd want to go, or walking distance to the 45-minute train that takes you to that place? Ask for a precise address and Google map that sucker.

Hunting Option #2: Real Estate Brokers

If you're moving to a city where brokers are accessible, they can be very helpful, especially if you're hunting for the first time or are completely unfamiliar with the city. The main advantage to using a broker is that they go through all of the listings for you to separate the wheat from the chaff, and they can show you a lot of apartments at once, thus saving a lot of time. They may also have exclusive access to rentals you would not find on your own, and they can sometimes get better deals from management companies than you could negotiate yourself. Traditionally, broker fees run between 10–15% of the yearly rent (though this can vary by city), but in a tough market, many brokers are willing to negotiate or waive their fees entirely—or management companies may agree to cover the fee for you. For this reason, a bad economy is a good time to use a broker, even if you wouldn't have done so otherwise.

Some brokers are great: resourceful, empathetic, and not criminal. But many are none of the three. So if you do seek their services, you have to learn how to cut straight to the real talk—it's helpful to always keep in mind that they are working for you (make them earn it!). You shouldn't have to pay anyone until you actually find a place, so feel free to work with a number of brokers simultaneously. Word of warning: They may drop you if they find out, but *c'est la vie*. There are plenty of brokers in the real estate sea. Here are some rules of engagement to keep in mind:

- **FIX A PRICE.** First figure out the highest rent your budget will allow. Then shave off a couple hundred dollars to account for the broker fee (if applicable).

- **FINDING A BROKER.** Try to find good brokers by asking friends what companies and specific brokers they used. Or do a Google search to locate brokerages in your city. Finally, peruse Craigslist, as it will often connect you to individual brokers or brokerages.

- **PLAY THE FIELD.** Work with several brokers, but be (or at least pretend to be) serious with each. If a broker senses you will come through as a potential renter, he or she will go above and beyond to seal the deal. If you think you're getting brushed aside, remind the broker (in a tactful way) that there are many others who are just a phone call away.

- **GET A SCHEDULE.** The first dirty broker trick is to try to up-sell you by showing places way out of your price range, and then bringing you to a dilapidated hut within your actual budget. Ask for an itinerary before seeing any apartments, then nix anything that doesn't fit your range. If that doesn't leave anything left to see, tell the broker to get back to work or take a hike.

- **UNDER PRESSURE.** The second dirty broker trick is to pressure you into settling on a place by mentioning the six other people waiting to put in an application. Whether those six people actually exist or are merely figments of the broker's screwed-up imagination, you may never know. Don't let the broker pressure you into a hasty decision. That being said, if you know you like it, mount up and take it—those six people may be out there after all.

- **DO SOME RECON.** The Better Business Bureau is a good place to check up on the credentials of specific brokerages.

- **NEGOTIATE.** Go for the gold. The recent economic crisis puts you in a great position to negotiate. For tips on how to go about it, see page 206.

- **BEWARE OF CONTRACTS.** If a broker wants you to sign anything, read it very carefully, and remember that the window for negotiation closes once you lay down a signature.

Sealing the Deal: Applying and Signing the Lease

If you thought *finding* a place was a struggle, you are in for a treat, *mon frère*. Actually sealing the deal is half the battle (more so in some cities than others), and in most cases it involves an infuriating mix of timing, luck, and favoritism. No matter where you are, some prep work and a light sprinkling of gamesmanship can give you the head start you need to score that sweet pad. While it's not always necessary, it never hurts to pull together the necessary documentation beforehand and bring it with you when you visit places to give yourself an advantage over others who are less prepared. You might come off looking like an over-eager spazz, but sometimes the biggest spazz gets the worm. Keep in mind that your documents may need to be notarized (the same goes for guarantor's forms, which are discussed below), and if you have any roommates they will probably need the same documentation as well.

🔒 Confessions of a Nomad: The Modern-Day Odysseus
by Gritz

After living with my mom in Washington, D.C., for the first fall after I graduated, I decided to seek fame and fortune at an Internet start-up in New York, where I shacked up with my best friend from college and his parents. Everything was going great until I was fired three weeks later, less than 24 hours after I had signed a sub-lease on a place with my buddy. Suddenly, I found myself at

the most daunting crossroads of my post-college life: Should I bail out and go back home to D.C. with my tail between my legs? Or should I soldier on with no job and zero prospects? Needless to say, my hubris got the better of me, and thus my life as a nomad began.

Over the next eight months, I would live at six more locations, including two couches, one hotel, a solo sublet that everyone I know refused to visit, and a room that leaked dirt from the ceiling—when I woke up in the morning, I often felt like someone had tried to bury me alive. Sometimes, I wished they had finished the job.

Though it's rarely easy, the nomadic lifestyle is a reality for many recent grads that move to a new city before securing employment. But while job hunting, apartment hunting, and sleeping on a different futon every couple of weeks can be an exhausting endeavor, there are many hidden benefits to the life of a wanderer.

First, a good nomad will have to develop admirable social graces if he plans to make it for very long. Be it an aunt or a friend of a friend from college, your host is doing you a huge favor by providing you with room and maybe some board, so you have to be on extra good behavior.

Clean up after yourself, keep your things neatly packed away, leave the house as often as possible, and always bring your own towel (and bedding if possible)—no one wants your grime on their linens. On a similar note, don't bring a "tenderoni" back from the bar unless you are staying with your best friend. When you're a nomad, the whole idea is to snag a spot in someone else's bed! The need for a roof over your head actually adds a bizarrely Darwinistic subtext to the act of flirting, because getting it cracking means free shelter and another night of survival in the concrete jungle. (Needless to say, I never actually achieved this level of nomadic prowess. Boo-hoo! I guess that is the price one pays for having uneven facial hair and eczema—conditions which are only exacerbated by the nomadic lifestyle.)

Next lesson: A nomad shall become extremely resourceful and knowledgeable about the city where he or she subsists. On the one hand, you may become familiar with many different neighborhoods, which will come in handy if you ever decide to get your own place. However, you will also need to develop the ability to kill time on the streets, ideally for free. Sometimes you will have to wait for your host to get home, or you'll wake up on a Saturday morning and literally not know where you are going to sleep that night. Lurking around a city is an art form that requires a little outside-of-the-box thinking. Street performers become your TV; Barnes & Noble is not just a bookstore, but also an opportunity to catch up on world affairs and use a semiclean toilet. Best Buy is the rec center, where kids play Xbox and lounge in gaming chairs all day. Help yourself out by using some of the money you're saving on rent to join a nice gym—it will serve as an unofficial clubhouse where you can shower, utilize various hygiene products, and hang out if you have nowhere else to go.

Finally, the consummate nomad shall develop an intimate appreciation of life's necessities. If you are going to be nomadic for any extended period of time, you will need to scale down your belongings to a bare minimum. A few changes of clothes, toiletries, a pillow, and a towel are really all you need—wait until you find a place before calling in the PS3s, humidifiers, and other household luxuries. When it comes to food, channel your Neanderthal lineage and learn to be a hunter-gatherer. This involves pulling moves like eating all of the free samples at Whole Foods and taking home food from buffets for dinner. (You can also become a "freegan" and literally eat out of the dumpster.)

At the end of the day, being nomadic can be an invigorating experience, because you haven't really lived until you've sat on a park bench wondering whether or not you might have to sleep there. Also, if things go well, the experience can reaffirm your faith in humanity. The modern-day nomad is a sympathetic character that people love to help, so foster good etiquette and enjoy the fruits of others' hospitality! ■

Real Estate Hunting Essentials

Not every landlord requires exactly the same items, but you will almost always need to provide some combination of the ones listed below. Once the process is done, make sure anything you handed over is returned to you.

- **Copy of Photo ID.** Driver's license or passport should suffice, no matter how unfortunate the photos.

- **Letter of Employment.** Must verify duration of employment, position, and salary. Ask your boss or your company's HR department to provide it for you and don't be intimidated to make this request as it's expected. If you don't have a job yet, you'll probably need a guarantor (see next page).

- **Two Most Recent Pay Stubs.** Get 'em from work.

- **The First Two Pages of Your Tax Return.** Some places require just the past year, while others require the past two years. Bring both just to be extra safe.

- **Most Recent Bank Statement.** Get it from the bank or online. The idea here is to look as rich (i.e., secure) as possible. If you have a savings or investment account, bring statements from those as well.

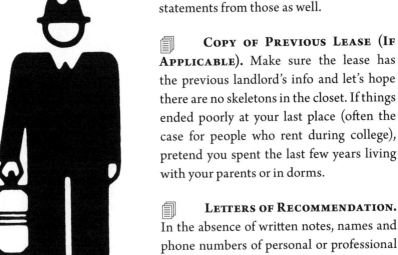

- **Copy of Previous Lease (If Applicable).** Make sure the lease has the previous landlord's info and let's hope there are no skeletons in the closet. If things ended poorly at your last place (often the case for people who rent during college), pretend you spent the last few years living with your parents or in dorms.

- **Letters of Recommendation.** In the absence of written notes, names and phone numbers of personal or professional references should suffice.

RENTAL APPLICATION AND FEE. The application will be provided by either the landlord or broker. Most often it is filled out on the spot, but occasionally it can be done in advance if there is a particular building or management company to which you are confining your search. The fee (about $50) is used to process the application and run a credit check (remember to have a blank check with you to cover this).

Guarantors

Most management companies require that a tenant's yearly income be above a minimum level, up to about 40–45× the monthly rent (income of roommates can be combined). For a $2,000/month apartment that means you have to make between $80 and $90K. If you don't stack this type of money (you're not alone), you may need a guarantor to co-sign the lease. The guarantor agreement is provided by the landlord or management company and requires some basic personal and financial information. Signing it legally obligates the guarantor (usually a family member or close friend) to pay rent if you default. He or she must earn a greater percentage of the rent—up to 80–90× the monthly rate—but combining the incomes of two guarantors is often allowed. Even if you can hack it alone, having a guarantor is never a bad idea, since it makes your candidacy that much more attractive. Take note, fair homesteaders: Some landlords won't accept guarantors from "Homestead states" (Texas, Louisiana, and Florida) because guarantors in

> ### Hazard:
> ### Read the lease (and take pictures of the apartment)
>
> Don't be lazy—this is a healthy portion of your salary we're talking about, so make sure you are not committing to anything that will bite you in the booty. For example, did you plan to leave for three months in the summer and sublet your place? Some buildings and landlords do not allow subletting, so check the fine print. If you can't decipher the legalese, try to find a lawyer to go over it with you, or let a wiser person take a look. If you can't find anyone with a good sense of the red flags to look out for, Nolo.com is a great resource for reading about renters' and tenants' rights—it's full of helpful tips and explanations of various legal components of rental agreements. Once you've actually signed the lease, take pictures (with date and time display) of the space when you first move in so that you have evidence of that giant crack on the ceiling that the landlord will likely try to deduct from your security deposit when you move out.

those states are protected if the tenant defaults on payments (and landlords don't want to deal with that).

If you don't know anyone who is willing to act as your guarantor, there are options. Websites like Insurent.com can help by acting as your guarantor (for a fee that varies depending on your credit score). If you go this route, make sure to factor the guarantor fee into your overall housing budget.

Get Your Money Right

On top of the application fee, there will likely be other lump sums of money to pay either upon application or at the lease signing. Unfortunately, you will usually have to pay a bit more than just the first month's rent—that arrangement usually only works at a halfway house. Below is a list of other charges you may encounter:

- $ **BROKER FEE.** If you go through a real estate agency that charges a broker fee, the norm is 10–15% of the yearly rent. If the management company is covering this fee for you, they will pay the broker directly.

- $ **HOLD DEPOSIT.** Used to reserve a place prior to lease signing, this fee is generally just deducted from the security deposit.

- $ **SECURITY DEPOSIT.** Paid at lease signing or move-in, this charge ensures that damages you may cause are covered. It is usually equal to one to two month's rent and refundable as long as the space is left in the same condition as when you moved in. Note: If you're renting from an independent landlord or individual owner, he or she may waive the deposit or be more lenient about the amount.

- $ **FIRST MONTH'S RENT.** Essentially another security deposit to lock it down once and for all.

Specifics of Renting a Condo

The process of searching for a condo is not so different from standard apartment hunting, but when it's time to sign a tenancy agreement, there are some distinctions you need to know. The big wildcard is the Homeowner Association (HOA) that governs the building. The HOA has no legal authority over you as a tenant, but that doesn't mean it won't have a significant presence in your life. For starters, the HOA often reserves the right to approve or reject potential tenants (which is why it may take longer for your rental application to be approved than if you were renting a house or apartment). Before you commit to a condo, make sure to read through the HOA's covenants, conditions, and restrictions (CC&Rs), which cover everything from noise disturbances to parking space allocation to tennis court use (if you're lucky enough to have scored a tennis court).

Ultimately, your landlord is the direct member of the HOA renting to you, and that person is responsible for meeting all requirements for membership. But in reality, whether it's you or your landlord who screws up, you will end up paying the price in the form of an eviction. From your standpoint, the trick is to make sure the contract clearly outlines the tenant's versus the owner's responsibilities in relation to the HOA. Keeping in mind that everything is negotiable, here are a few things to watch out for when going over your rental contract:

- Who is responsible for paying HOA fees? (Usually it's the owner.)

- Who is responsible for performing (and paying for) maintenance within the unit? (Usually a combination of the tenant and owner.)

- What about common areas? (Usually the HOA or a superintendent.)

- Who should initiate repairs/maintenance, and what is the procedure for doing so?

- Which of the complex's facilities and amenities do you have access to? What are the terms of use?

- As a tenant, are you eligible to use any external gyms, spas, or golf facilities that have contracts with the HOA?

- Are you allowed to attend events put on by the HOA (BBQs, etc.)?

- As a tenant, are you allowed to attend the HOA's monthly board of directors meetings?

- What is provided for in the condo in the way of furniture and/or appliances?

- Can you paint and/or alter the appearance of the condo?

- Rent-to-Own (see next page)

In some cases, renting a condo can be the first step towards buying a condo. When you're asking the questions above, inquire about potential **Rent-to-Own** options, which will allow the rent you pay now to go toward an eventual down payment on the unit should you choose to buy it. Consider it a test drive—rent it first, and if you think it's nice and you start to feel more financially stable, look into a purchase. If you're really serious about entering into this type of agreement, consider hiring a lawyer to help you sift through the fine print. There are huge financial benefits to this type of agreement, but you may end up paying unanticipated taxes and fees along the way. For more information on buying property, read the "Buying a Place" section on page 220.

Specifics of Renting a House

If you're in a market where it's the norm for recent grads to rent houses, there are some compelling reasons to feel like you're trumping your apartment- and condo-dwelling cronies. Bigger rooms, more privacy, a yard, a parking spot, space for awesome pets—these are all typical benefits to living in a house. But the problem with houses are twofold: more space means more stuff to deal with (lawn, driveway, a roof, etc.), and the nature of house rental agreements is that you have to accept a little more responsibility than your friend who's wedged inside a shoebox in a building with hundreds of other people. Heavy is the head that lives in a castle. So before taking on the responsibility of renting a house, make sure you weigh the pros and cons carefully. That picket-fenced pad with the basketball hoop in the driveway seems great now, but you might be singing a different tune when you're expected to deal with the giant hornets' nest that you failed to notice behind the backboard.

To break it down clearly, here are the specific issues you'll have to deal with as a house renter:

- **MANAGEMENT ISSUES.** The status of your landlord may not be as "official" as it would be in a managed apartment building; make sure you're clear on the rental terms, and discuss your tenancy rights with whoever's renting you the house.

- **MAINTENANCE.** What is your landlord responsible for, and what are you expected to take care of on your own? Consider housecleaning, lawn mowing, snow removal, garbage disposal, and routine maintenance like plumbing and electrical issues.

- ✔ **HIGHER BILLS.** Houses are big and therefore more expensive to heat and clean. That creaky farmhouse might be charming, but unless you can heat it using the residual energy from your dance parties, prepare to cough up some cash during the colder months. Same goes for air conditioning in the summer.

- ✔ **ROOMMATES.** Given the obvious size considerations, you'll almost always have a roommate—or eight—in a rented house. Whose name will be on the lease? What happens if someone doesn't cough up the rent? Check out page 207 for tips on roommate living.

Let's run through the management and maintenance a little more so you don't stumble blindly into the house from hell.

Who's the Boss?

When you rent a house—or a room in a house—you will most likely be renting from an individual owner or a landlord who owns and manages a few houses in the area. As a result, these arrangements are often less formal than those you might negotiate with a large management company that oversees apartment buildings. If you're renting a room or rooms within a house, your "landlord" might be the family who owns and occupies the rest of the house. They probably don't think of themselves as real-estate biz folks per se, just people looking for a little extra income. The benefit is you might be able to bypass all the "official" stuff like credit checks and guarantors, and if the owner is nice, you might get looked after a lot better than you would in a big building. Casualness can be tricky though, so it's good to be clear about rules and protocols before you move in so the owner isn't suddenly all up in your grill telling you to babysit her kids.

Smart Money:
Trouble paying rent? Throw a party!

In Harlem in the 1920s, tenants who didn't have enough money to cover their monthly rent would call up some musicians, invite a bunch of friends over, and then pass around a hat and ask for donations. And it worked (in fact, these rent parties are considered by some to be a driving force in the birth of jazz). Today, this harebrained scheme sounds more like the setup for a terrible movie. But if it helps you avoid eviction and people have some fun in the process, you may just end up looking like a genius. And if nothing else, maybe the art form of tomorrow will emerge in the apartments of today's unemployed grads. Or maybe everyone can just play *DJ Hero*. Whatevs.

If you're renting an entire house, it's likely that your landlord might work full-time in real estate or be a local business owner who does a little real estate on the side. When you're looking at each place, inquire about whether the landlord lives in the neighborhood—often it will be someone who owns three houses on a block and lives in one of them. And while you might want a little privacy on the day you host your Naked Slip'n'Slide Festival, it's generally nice to know the owner's close at hand if a problem arises.

Negotiating Rent

Handy with a leaf blower? Passionate about re-grouting bathroom tiles? Up for babysitting your landlord's kid? If so, you may be in a position to negotiate your rent in exchange for helping out around the property. For advice on how to do this (not only for houses, but also for all types of real estate), see below.

⊠ The Negotiator's Toolkit

You may be a recent grad on a budget, but you're no sucker. As such, you have every right to negotiate and try to get the best possible deal for yourself (even if you're talking $1,000 off the rent instead of $100,000 off a house purchase). When going into battle, be strategic—it's all about striking that balance between being too pushy and being a pushover. These real estate people are slick, but you're slicker. And particularly when the economy's struggling, you're in a great position to get a better-than-average deal. Here is some helpful info to help you negotiate your way to real estate bliss (or at least contentment).

Working with Brokers. If you're using a broker, you may have better luck negotiating their fee instead of (or in addition to) the actual rent. Many brokers will waive fees when they're low on clients. If your broker won't budge, have him or her talk to the management company to see if they will pick up the broker fee on your behalf. An empty apartment or house is a landlord's worst nightmare; he or she may be willing to cover the fee if it means locking in a good tenant (hopefully that's you).

Timing. From a landlord's point of view, a lower-paying tenant is better than no tenant at all. If you time it right, you can end up getting a great deal on a property that would otherwise have been vacant. Keep in mind that landlords are more willing to give deals at the end of the month (assuming the lease would start on the first day of the next month) than they are to give them at the beginning of the month when they still have a few weeks to find a tenant. In terms of seasonal strategy, late summer/early fall and late spring/early summer tend to be very busy times for turnover, so try avoiding the rush by hunting during the "off season." You'll have less competition, and will have a better chance of differentiating yourself in the eyes of your landlord.

Doing Your Homework. Before trying to negotiate your rent, talk to friends and do online research to try to find out how much people are currently paying for properties like the one you have your eye on. The more you know about the market, the savvier you will seem. If you find that a similar property is being rented somewhere for less than what your landlord is asking, use that price as a starting point for negotiations.

A Discount for Paying Upfront. If you can swing it, ask the landlord for an overall discount in exchange for your paying the first few months' rent upfront. She will have more money in her pocket, and you will save overall. This option requires that you have enough liquidity to pay the first few months in one lump sum; if you can, everyone wins.

Turning on the Charm. No one wants to give a deal to an a-hole. Most landlords (especially those who oversee smaller buildings or rent out their own properties) are looking to find nice, reliable tenants. If you make a great first impression, they may be more lenient about rent in order to keep you on their team.

Offering Your Services. Keep it above board, but don't hesitate to get creative and offer to help your landlord out in various ways (e.g., painting, shoveling snow, garbage removal) in exchange for a rent reduction. If the landlord feels that having you as a tenant will be advantageous to him, he will be more likely to give you a break.

Re-negotiating. After you've been in the place for a year (or, if you're renting month-to-month, for a substantial amount of time), you are in a good position to renegotiate your rent—or at least to request that your rent not be increased. If applicable, point out how you've paid on time each month, how you've made improvements/repairs to the property, and how you've been a stellar tenant overall. If they play hardball, send that sass right back at them and let them know you can take your money (and your good behavior) elsewhere.

First Month Free. Particularly in large apartment buildings and communities, it's common to get the first month free as an incentive to sign a lease. If it's not offered, ask for it. If you can find a similar apartment that's offering this deal, use it as a bargaining chip at the place where you really want to live. ∎

Roommate Living

Ah, roommates—can't live with them, can't live without them.

Actually, you can live without them, but it's more expensive and sometimes sort of lonely. If you were the type of person in college who preferred the privacy of a single room, don't overlook the fact that you still lived in a dorm full of students that you could fraternize with on a whim. Living alone in post-college life can be a bit more solitary, and sometimes it's nice to have someone to come home to at the end of the working day (or the end of the job-hunting day, as the case may be).

Sometimes, however, it is not nice at all—particularly if you come home to find your roommate smearing chocolate mousse over his naked body while listening to the *Ducktales* theme song. The sword cuts both ways, as they say (the good news: sometimes that sword cuts the rent in half). If the above image doesn't put you off and you do decide to shack up with a roomie (or eight), consider what you are getting yourself into and how to make it work.

Finding (Compatible) Roommates

In this menagerie, there are three distinct beasts: friends, strangers, and lovers. (Sometimes the first two can morph into the third, but only if you are a complete masochist.) Alternatively, try to link up with other apartment seekers via friends, family, and alumni networks. Finally, Craigslist and other housing-focused websites are useful resources if you're looking to sublet or find an apartment/house share arrangement. Always be cautious when it comes to living with strangers. Craigslist can help connect you to great people who share your interests and lifestyle, but it is also a hotbed of maniacs. Let common sense be your guide, and consider taking a friend with you when you go to see potential properties.

Friends

As long as you don't allow things to get too "college," living with friends can be a nice way to ease the transition into the "real world." However, it's not necessarily going to be all gravy, all the time. Getting kept up by a noisy roommate might have been passable the night before your noon lecture, but waking up at 7 am every day will make you a bit more conservative in terms of what you deem to be appropriate nighttime behavior. New responsibilities like getting your own food, paying rent, and trying to be moderately clean can draw unspoken tensions to the surface. However, if you are good enough friends with your roommate, you will hopefully be able to work past any problems and still find that there is a modicum of love left in your hearts at the end of the day.

Strangers

Depending on where and when you're moving, you may not necessarily be moving in with friends. Living with strangers might make you a little uneasy, but for some, it can be a smart option and a good way to expand your horizons. For instance, if you are looking to create a specific type of living environment for yourself, you might want to consider looking for others who share your vision of what makes a happy home. Whether you want to maintain a "locavore" kitchen, set up an artistic collaborative, or live by a nudity-only policy, seeking out others who are on the same page can be a great way to establish the "house vibe" you're looking for.

For some, the decision to live with strangers is dictated by your fiscal situation. In these cases, you will still want to establish a set of house rules in order to keep the peace. It's one thing when it's your friend who is meticulously picking the marshmallows from the Lucky Charms, but it's quite another when it's that random dude that you've decided to shack up with. Make sure you're all on the same page about house rules and things should run smoothly. If you become friends, then you've got a "cash back" situation on your hands, but the more realistic goal should be to get along moderately well. Stack the odds in your favor by always meeting each and every roommate before making a decision.

General compatibility issues include the following:

- *Smoking.* Will your roommate be smoking tobacco, weed, or crack on a regular basis? Probably something to broach before move-in day.

- *Pets.* Don't try to hide your ferret, they'll smell it from a mile away!

- *Lifestyle.* Is your prospective roommate more of a homebody or a 24-hour party person?

- *Work schedule.* Depending on the bathroom situation, the morning shower rush can be a real source of frayed nerves (and split ends).

- *Significant others.* Do any of the roommates have boyfriends or girlfriends who are always around? Two roommates can quickly become four when you factor in significant others.

- *Gender.* Are you cool living with someone of the opposite sex?

- *Race and sexual orientation.* Beware of racists and bigots!

- *Religious and/or dietary needs.* Kosher? Deathly allergic to nuts? Be clear about your needs, and make sure you can respectfully comply with theirs.

- *Pro-dance party or anti-dance party?* 'Nuff said.

- *Other.* Cleanliness, weird habits, etc.

Lovers

Shacking up with your boyfriend or girlfriend is definitely an aggressive post-college move. The most important thing to consider is your motivation. The only real reason to move in with your significant other is if you both think it is the right time to up the ante. Doing it to save money or because it seems convenient will probably lead to tears, so don't take it too casually. For better or for worse, living together will push your relationship to its limits and give you a stronger sense of whether you're compatible enough to build a long-term future together. Remember all those nights when you said, "Let's not sleep over," because you wanted to play *Tony Hawk's Pro Skater* or watch *Sex in the City* reruns with a carton of Chunky Monkey? Well, now you *have* to sleep over, so you'd better hope that your mate is understanding of your idiosyncrasies (like the fact that you have a nonnegotiable "underwear drawer policy").

Laying Down the Ground Rules

No matter whom you end up living with, you have to sort out paying the rent and buying the cleaning supplies. Otherwise, you'll either be evicted or carried out on your couch by an army of rats while the Pied Piper upper-decks your toilet. Here's how to keep it all in check:

- **LEASE.** The lease question is a tricky one. If you want ultimate control over the apartment you may want to keep the lease in your name, but not having your roommate's name on the lease also means you become the landlord by proxy. You'll be responsible for getting the rent together on time, or covering the whole rent yourself if your roomie decides to jump ship.

- **RENT.** Will one person pay more due to certain privileges like a bigger room or parking spot? Rooms can be pro-rated based on square footage, but you may also want to take other things into account like closet space, number of windows, or proximity to the bathroom.

- **UTILITY BILLS.** Divide the duties—if one person covers cable, the other should make sure the lights stay on. And if you only watch Hulu and your roommate keeps the cable box in her room, maybe she should pay more of the cable bill. Consider signing up for automatic bill pay (p. 245) to reduce hassle and avoid late payments.

✍ **GROCERIES.** Decide up front whether food will be separate or shared so that tension doesn't arise when someone lays a finger on your Butterfinger. There are some things the apartment will regularly need, like toilet paper, napkins, and trash bags. Will these items be bought as needed by whomever, or should there be a monthly Costco outing to stock up Y2K-style?

✍ **FURNITURE.** You may have some stuff left over from college, but chances are it's been thoroughly "compromised." Figure out what's usable and then discuss who will bring what. If items need to be bought, decide whether the cost will be split or if one person will foot the bill and maintain sole ownership. (See our tip on splitting furniture on page 256.)

✍ **VISITORS.** How late is too late and how long is too long? Does your roommate's extended family plan on flying in and forming an Aero Bed flotilla on the living room floor every weekend?

✍ **CHORES.** Keep in mind that people have different cleaning habits— some tidy up every day, while some do a big *Trading Spaces*-style overhaul once a month. If your roommate cleans less often than you do, don't try to force him or her onto your schedule. Instead, try to make a compromise with other chores or get him or her to pitch in for a maid service.

Subletting

If you need something shorter-term than a standard year-long lease, or all the aforementioned renting shenanigans just seem like way too much work, subletting might be a good move for you. In a sublease agreement, you rent directly from another renter, so the whole thing's a lot less formal. There are risks to not holding the lease (keep reading), but assuming all goes well the benefits of this practice are three-fold.

First, subleases provide greater flexibility for short-term stays. A regular lease will usually last at least one year, but you can always find people subletting their apartments for almost any amount of time, from a week to many months. This arrangement is ideal if you want to "try out" a city before signing a longer-term lease, or if you are unsure of how long you will be staying. Second, many sublets come furnished and, if it's very last minute (i.e., the sublessor is getting on a

Housing

plane in two days and needs to rent the apartment ASAP), you can get lucky and score a great deal. Finally, subletting usually allows you to avoid all the "red tape" associated with actually renting your own place (like getting a guarantor). The formality of the arrangement varies depending on the parties involved, but it's unlikely you'll have to produce all of the paperwork that is required of lease-holding tenants.

Sublets come in all shapes and sizes. You can sublet a studio or a one-bedroom and have the place all to yourself, or you can sublet individual rooms within larger apartments, condos, or houses. The latter move can be a great way to meet people in a new city, but make sure you ask the right questions and get a clear sense of the house vibe before moving in (see page 209).

Looking for a Sublet

Many of the strategies listed in the "Do It Yourself" real estate hunt section on page 192 apply to sublet hunting as well. Because sublets are flexible arrangements, they can be found in any number of ways, but here are a few places to start.

WORD OF MOUTH. A great place to start, especially if you're not psyched about the idea of living with complete strangers. It's very possible you already know someone (or someone who knows someone) who is looking to rent out his or her room for a certain amount of time. Leverage your networks to let the world know you need a roof over your head, and think outside the box. Sure, you'd prefer to move into a room in a furnished penthouse, but if your friend's grandmother has an unused guest room you could inhabit for a few months, don't turn your nose up at it. You could probably negotiate milk and cookies into the deal.

CRAIGSLIST. The Holy Grail for all things housing-related, sublets included. Check the "Sublets & Temporary" section for the city of your choice, and then start sifting! Make sure to take note of whether the sublet is furnished or unfurnished, whether utilities are included in the listed rate, and whether there are any other "special" conditions involved in the rental (e.g., will you be expected to walk your new roommate's labradoodle?).

SUBLET.COM. This site allows you to search many sublets—furnished and unfurnished, long-term and short-term. The only hitch is that you must pay for membership to find the contact information (the price for two month's access ranges from $10 to $85.) The owners of Sublet.com also own Cityleases.com and Metroroommates.com, so it's really like having a tri-membership. It's worth a shot if the first two approaches fail you.

VISITING SUBLETS. Always visit the sublet (and meet any roommates you might have) before making a decision. If you are moving across the country and can't visit, ask for detailed photos, speak to the tenant(s) on the phone, and make sure you're clear on the layout of the apartment. You don't want to find out after the fact that your roommate has to walk across your mattress to get to the fridge.

DUE DILIGENCE. In order to avoid unpleasant surprises once you've moved in, make sure you clarify the following issues.:

Circumstances. Why is the sublessor subleasing the room? If you will be moving in with roommates, how do they know each other? Have they had previous subletters?

Building and management. What's the building like? Has the tenant had any problems with the landlord, management company, or board of owners?

Rent. How much is it? Will you pay the sublessor or the landlord directly? If you are going through the person who sublet the apartment to you, what will happen if they then fail to pay the rent to the landlord on time? Does rent include utilities? How and when are utilities paid for?

Security deposit. Will you be required to cover a portion of the security deposit? What happens if you accidentally punch a hole in the wall while watching a Jane Fonda aerobics workout on VHS? Note that if you pay a security deposit directly to the tenant, they may not be able to pay you back until they get their original security deposit back from the landlord at the end of the lease. Will this delayed repayment work for you?

Maintenance. If there is a problem, are you expected to deal with it (or, worse still, pay for it)? Will the sublessor be easy to contact if you can't figure out how to fix the problem?

Communication (also known as, "Is he or she going to be in the Ecuadorian rainforest the whole time?"). Will you have the green light to make

Housing

game-time decisions on repairs if the sublessor isn't available? Do you know who provides the utilities, cable, and Internet, and can you contact the providers if need be? Is the super responsive and helpful when something needs to be attended to?

Furniture. Will the sublet be furnished (partially or completely)? Will you have to bring thing like sheets, towels, or kitchen supplies? (You probably want your own linens regardless—we won't go there.)

Roommates. Will you have roommates? If so, consult the "Finding Compatible Roommates" section on page 208.

Kosher-ness. Has the sublessor cleared the arrangement with the landlord or board of owners? Some buildings forbid subleasing, so you don't want to end up getting tossed out through no fault of your own. (Of course, you can always try to fly under the radar and hope for the best.)

Think about the future. If your sublease takes you to the end of the original lease, you may be in a position to take over the lease and stay in the apartment. Play it right and this move could be a good way to "test-drive" an apartment before making a commitment.

MEETING THE ROOMMATES. When you meet your potential "landlord" (the sublessor) and/or potential roommates, use your instincts about whether the situation feels right. It can seem like an audition, but play it cool. Remember: You are being interviewed, but you're interviewing them as well. Don't let your desire to pass the "personality test" and be liked overshadow the importance of finding a place that makes sense for your lifestyle and individual needs.

SIGNING AN AGREEMENT. We'll be honest—this may not happen. Whether they are negotiated with friends or strangers, sublets are often fly-by-the-seat-of-your-pants arrangements, and, as a result, they can be disconcertingly casual. But unless you can trust the person completely or the sublease is extremely short, it's best to sign a legal document that outlines the conditions of the sublease. (If you don't have a buddy/colleague/dad who's a lawyer at your disposal, go to TenantResourceCenter.org to download a standard sublet contract.) Make sure the contract clearly outlines how rent will be paid, how maintenance will be performed (and by whom), the length of the sublease, the procedure for paying/returning the security deposit, and any other special circumstances.

**Smart Money:
Renters Insurance**

Many recent grads never even consider purchasing renters insurance because they either A) falsely assume that the landlord's insurance covers the tenant's belongings, B) don't think they own much that's worth protecting, or C) are too lazy and/or busy to think about it. However, the reality is that owners insurance (paid by the landlord) only covers structural damages to the building, and if you ended up buying that plasma TV, Tempur-Pedic bed, and shiny new MacBook Pro, you might have more to protect than you think. Renters insurance generally covers stuff like fire, smoke, theft, vandalism, and lightning. And while it protects all of your personal belongings, it also has other unexpected benefits—for example, it provides temporary housing should you need to relocate or wait for repairs to be made, and it covers medical and legal expenses if someone gets hurt in your crib and sues you. With typical plans starting at $150 per year (with a max around $300, depending upon how much coverage you request), it's not such a ridiculous thought after all. Insurance giants Allstate, Geico, Liberty Mutual, and State Farm all offer coverage, and you can contact them directly. ■

Setting Up Your Pad

You sealed the deal on a place and probably found a roommate. Do it big! It's almost time to pitch a reality show to Fox called *How to Be the Consummate Recent Grad*. First, you'll need to take some steps to make your pad livable— some irksome logistics (fitting your king mattress through the front door), some necessary preparations (making sure there's running water), and some fun stuff (deciding whether to put the mirror on the wall or on the ceiling above your bed). Be prepared to dip into the bank account again, because couches and cable don't usually come free. To help you out, here are some tips and tricks for setting up your first post-college pad.

NAIL DOWN MOVE-IN DAYS. If you're moving into a house, then this won't be an issue. But if you're moving into an apartment or condo, there may be specific move-in days and times (e.g., weekdays only from 9am to 5pm). Even during these allotted hours, you should think strategically about parking and how you're going to get your van o' stuff as close to the door as possible. (For more moving tips, see page 186.)

ORDER UTILITIES EARLY. Moving into an apartment or home without cable and/or Internet is annoying, but moving in without electricity may actually be illegal in some states. Plan ahead and find out what the building provides and what you need to set up yourself. Electricity can be handled in a matter of days (or even the day of the move-in), but cable and Internet can take several weeks so it might be worth making an appointment in advance. If you're moving into a house, you may also be responsible for sewage and water. You can find sewage and water utility providers from either your landlord or a quick Google search.

FURNISHINGS. In college, a mattress, a chair, and a few hangers may have sufficed, but you're an "adult" now, so you probably want some stuff, like a couch for guests to sit on and plates off of which one can eat food. This is where the spending comes into play, and you've got to be careful to not let it spiral out of control. To defray costs, look to buy second-hand goods (check local colleges for people moving out of dorms and their college houses/apartments for great deals); see what you can scrounge from parents and grandparents; check out budget-friendly retailers like Ikea, CB2 and Target; and always comparison shop. Make a checklist and, if you have roommates, figure out how to split costs on various shared items. Do you have pots and silverware? (See page 25 for a breakdown of basic kitchen items.) A bed and desk? A television and computer? A window AC unit? What about toilet paper and paper towels? Cleaning supplies? A floor lamp or two? If you're starting with nothing, it's not unheard of to pay in excess of $1,000 to $2,000 for all of the goods you'll need for your first place. Before buying big items, measure the doorways, rooms, and elevator to make sure that anything you purchase can actually make it into your place and then fit where you want it to go. And remember: This stuff is all pretty discretionary so if you want to stick with an airbed and a candle, go for it. Just don't burn the place down or expect any potential hookups to be thrilled about the prospect of sleeping over.

FIX UP THE PLACE. Often the landlord will make sure your place gets spiffed up before you move in—fresh paint job, new bathroom fixtures, removal of the mountain of Burger King bags left by the prior tenant. If you haven't already negotiated this service into your lease, it can't hurt to request some improvements. Or, if need be, you can do it yourself—something as simple as painting some walls with a fresh coat of paint (or those cool stars that light up in the dark) can really make a place feel like your own. Other seemingly small things make a difference as well. If the light bulbs make the bedroom look like a cell for mental patients, swap them out for some eco-friendly compact fluorescents (or less shaded, higher-watt bulbs that are less eco-friendly but look nice). Other quick-and-easy upgrades include installing high-pressure showerheads and putting some nice shades or curtains on the windows. Prior to any upgrades, just confirm with your landlord that you can make them and that you won't have to, for example, repaint when you leave (unless you're comfortable doing that).

KEEP IT CLEAN. Sure, some aspects of the college experience will be hard to part with, but sticky beer floors and old pizza box towers shouldn't be among them. Keeping your new pad spic and span is a relatively painless process, particularly if you're armed with these supplies:

Pine-Sol:	all purpose cleaner that's great for kitchen counters, floors, and bathrooms
Windex:	spray it on glass and mirrors to keep your reflection true
Soft Scrub:	ideal for sink and toilet duty
Murphy Oil Soap:	respect wood by scrubbing it with Murphy's
Pledge:	best to use while dusting

And the usual cast of characters:

Feather duster	Rubber gloves	Mop or Swiffer Sweeper
Paper towels	Sponges	Rags

VOIP IS THE NEW LANDLINE. While most grads are comfortable just using a cell phone for all of their communication needs, some people still like the old-time comfort and convenience of a landline. The good news is, a much cheaper alternative is available called VoIP (Voice over Internet Protocol). For approximately $15 a month (comparison shop among VOIP providers like Vonage, your cable company, and others), you can sign up for a phone line that runs through your Internet but works with any phone you currently have (you plug the phone or base station directly into your router). For those of you worried about Internet outages, most VOIP providers will forward all calls to your cell in the event of your Internet temporarily going down. Skype is another option that you just download for free online. Calling other Skype users is free, but you have to pay to call actual phones.

PREPARE FOR PROBLEMS. Rodents, bugs, and floods are just a normal part of being a renter, so it's better to be safe than sorry. Run through a safety check and get to know your new 'hood. Do you know where the closest hospital and police station are? Upon moving into your new place, collect some emergency contacts: the local police department, hospital, pest control, a plumber, and an electrician. Also, make sure that your smoke and carbon monoxide sensors are working. If you aren't comfortable fixing a particular problem and can't find an easy fix on websites such as DoItYourself.com, then call your super (if you have one), landlord (if it's a repeat problem), or a professional (if it just won't go away). See the next page for more tips on super and landlord relationships.

MEET THE NEIGHBORS. From the bag lady in the next apartment to the family of 15 in the house across the street, the best way to deal with neighbor issues is to preempt them. Upon moving in, stop by and introduce yourself. This way if any problems do arise, you're already on a cordial basis and it's easier to politely say something like, "Would you mind not playing Megadeth on full blast at 4am?" If a problem persists even after you've confronted the offending party, either speak to your landlord/super or the police (if you're really ready to escalate it to that level).

SET UP AUTOMATIC LEASE PAY. Instead of having to remember to pay your rent each month (even the best of us have been late), consider setting up automatic bill pay through your bank (p. 245). It can save you from late fees and you can always cancel your payment prior to payday if necessary. Usually a landlord will let a late payment or two slide, but the more dependable you can be over time, the better position you put yourself in to get good treatment, renegotiate your rent, and receive positive references in the future.

Dealing with Housing Issues

As a renter, you don't have as many rights as an owner. For example, you're probably not allowed to put a sauna in the bedroom closet. Oh well! But one nice thing about renting is that, assuming you have a fair lease, whoever rents to you is theoretically supposed to make sure you are a happy tenant and deal with problems when they arise. As with anything in life, the service you receive has a lot to do with personal relationships. Thus, the most important step first-time renters can take to ensure a good living situation is to hobnob with the head honchos—in most cases, this means the **landlord** and the **superintendent.** In some condo and house rental situations you just have a landlord, but the point is still the same: these people can single-handedly make you a happy camper or a miserable squatter, so it's worth figuring out their role and making nice from the get-go.

The Super

If your place has a super, he or she will probably be the person who gets you settled in your new digs, informing you of all emergency numbers and contacts, showing you the circuit breaker, and walking you through the ins-and-outs of your apartment. Going forward, the super is also your maintenance safety net. He or she is not there to help you replace a light bulb or kill a cockroach in your tub—you can handle that yourself with a little liquid courage. Rather, supers are the last line of defense—call them only after you tried to fix the problem yourself or when a situation arises that you clearly can't deal with alone (e.g., there was a flood and now there's a hole in your wall). Granted, you can call them for every little issue, but then you'll end up being known as the recent grad who cried "rat." Your super will probably set some ground rules with you before you move in, but unless there's an emergency, you should only contact him between 9AM and 9PM. After you've dealt with your super a few times you'll get a handle on how helpful he or she is willing to be.

Some condos have supers (though they're not always called that) who oversee the common areas of the building. When there's a problem in your individual condo, however, you should go directly to your landlord (the owner). If it's an issue in a common area, you should still go through your landlord and ask him or her to take it up with the super and/or HOA. In some circumstances, your landlord may put you directly in touch with the super of the building, but that is decided on a case-by-case basis. Hopefully, you develop a direct relationship with the super at the beginning so there's no need for

> **Tips & Tricks:**
> **Tipping**
>
> The only thing worse than an overflowing toilet is an overflowing toilet that won't be fixed for a week. Tip the super $50 to $200 around Christmas time and make sure he knows his hard work is appreciated (even if the work really isn't that hard). If the building has doorpeople, be sure to tip them too, since they are in charge of your packages, dry cleaning, and take-out. Depending on how many visitors you have, how often you receive deliveries, and how well you are treated, tips for doormen should range from $10–$80. If you're in a building with a ton of people, make sure you know who's relevant to your life; you don't need to tip all forty people on staff. You are the recent grad, after all. No need to go all Daddy Warbucks.

Housing

an intermediary. (Just don't be telling the super to help you install a Murphy bed when you haven't cleared it with the owner.) If you're renting a house, your landlord should help you with any issues, or else hire and pay for someone to fix a problem.

The Landlord

The landlord is not just a person who takes your money each month and laughs all the way to the bank (though he is that too). He or she is also supposed to be responsible for any problems with the building. Has the super still not fixed that leak in your ceiling you've complained about five times? Enough is enough: Call the landlord directly. Your lease will include some legalese about the "habitability" of your apartment, and that basically means that the landlord must resolve anything that makes your home unlivable (e.g., lack of clean water/ heat/sane neighbors). If the situation is not rectified, threaten to stop paying rent or bring in the real authorities: an attorney, the police, or the Department of Housing and Communities.

Sometimes, you might be in hot water with the landlord. Perhaps you were too busy with your new job and forgot to pay the rent. Usually, landlords will charge you a late fee, but if you've been a good tenant, they tend to waive it. But what if you can't make the rent one month? Instead of just ignoring the problem, you should speak with your landlord and see if you can work something out—most of the time it's not a huge deal. However, if the worst-case scenario occurs and your landlord tries to evict you, be sure to know your state's tenant rights and contact the Department of Housing and Communities. A landlord can't just kick you out without the law behind him, and that process usually takes about six months.

Buying Your Own Pad

You might be thinking that we've officially lost the plot. You're an intern with piles of student debt and zero credit history—how the hell are you going to buy a house or an apartment!?

Admittedly, buying a place is not feasible for everyone in the first few years out of college (in fact, it isn't for most), but it's not as insane an idea as it might seem at first glance. While property markets are well beyond most recent grad budgets in places like Boston and San Francisco, many cities are *relatively* affordable. We understand that you might not want the headache of mortgages, insurance, and other home-owning responsibilities, but under the right circumstances there are compelling reasons to take the plunge: economics and peace of mind.

If you do decide to go for it, however, you should look for a place that you actually that you think holds good value and you want to live in for at least a few years, rather than treating it solely as an investment. Otherwise, you will drive yourself crazy worrying about how every little problem that comes up (in your house or the market as a whole) will affect the value of your "investment." Instead, consider it a "consumable investment," and recognize that this is the place that you're going to be living in for the next five to ten years, which can be a reassuring and exciting sentiment.

Needless to say, there is a huge amount of research and preparation that goes into buying property, including, "*is this the right market to make a purchase in?*", but we just wanted to put the thought out there for people who hate seeing $1,000 go down the drain each month. If you expect to be in one place for at least 5–10 years and you're making a healthy salary that you can reasonably expect to maintain, at least consider it. And remember, even if you have to leave before you think it's time to sell, you can always sucker the most recent crop of recent grads into renting it while you bide your time.

As some more food for thought, below is a very simplified analysis of the actual cost of ownership of a house. In certain times and areas, you may be surprised to find that the rent-versus-buy equation tips towards purchasing a place.

Price of House/ Apt.	Cash Down (@ 10%)	Monthly Payment (@ 6% mortgage)	Year-end Tax Savings
$100,000	$10,000	$640	$1,890
$150,000	$15,000	$959	$2,835
$200,000	$20,000	$1,279	$3,780
$250,000	$25,000	$1,599	$4,725
$300,000	$30,000	$1,919	$5,670
$350,000	$35,000	$2,239	$6,615
$400,000	$40,000	$2,558	$7,560
$450,000	$45,000	$2,878	$8,505
$500,000	$50,000	$3,198	$9,450
$750,000	$75,000	$4,797	$14,175
$1,000,000	$100,000	$6,396	$18,900

Top Ten Ways to Go Green in Your Apartment

These days, it's not so much "go green or go home" as "go green in your home." Making some environmentally friendly tweaks in the crib is not only easy, but it will also cut down on your gas, water, and electricity bills. Everyone wins!

1) Change your bulbs. Compact fluorescents last up to ten times as long as incandescent bulbs and use a quarter of the energy. You do the math!

2) Look for certified Energy Star products. An Energy Star TV set can use 30 percent less energy than an uncertified one, and an Energy Star washing machine can save more water than one person drinks in a lifetime.

3) Temper your climate control impulses. Experts suggest setting the AC to 78°F (an insistence on 72°F will cost you 39 percent more energy).

4) Kill the "energy vampires." Unplug appliances like cell phone chargers when you're not using them—they keep sucking down energy even when nothing's connected.

5) Buy organic and recycled products. Organic mattresses, sheets, and towels are increasingly mainstream and affordable. Opt for recycled glassware, clean up with eco-friendly household products, and get a reusable shopping bag for trips to the grocery store.

6) Downsize your fridge. Most recent grads don't keep much more than beer, milk, and a few condiments in their refrigerator, so why go for a massive energy-guzzler?

7) Build good habits. There are so many easy ways to save water and energy that people overlook. Turn off lights when you leave the room, don't run the water while you're brushing your teeth, and take shorter showers (consider installing a low-flow showerhead). After a while, these habits will become second nature.

8) Use your dishwasher wisely. Only run your dishwasher when there's a full load and always use the energy-saving setting. Savings earned: 100 pounds of carbon dioxide per year. If you're doing dishes by hand, use cold water.

9) Buy some plants. Houseplants not only add a little color to the room, but they also suck down pollutants and purify the air in your apartment. Just remember you'll have to water them once in a while.

10) Get a home energy audit. Many utilities providers offer free home energy audits to find where your home is poorly insulated or energy inefficient. You can save up to 30% off your energy bill and 1,000 pounds of carbon dioxide a year, according to the Inconvenient Truth peeps. ■

Chapter VII: Money

Money

A lot of young people are understandably put off by the whole concept of personal finance. Getting a credit card, monitoring bank accounts, repaying debt, and "budgeting" can feel like more things to worry about on an endless to-do list, not to mention being able to understand where you stand financially and how to optimize your cash, whether it's existing or expected. But the important thing to realize is that there are aspects of personal finance that require a bit of forward planning. Between credit scores and compound interest, the American financial institution is designed to reward responsibility and patience. The sooner you straighten out your current financial situation, start building credit, and begin stashing away some money (even $50 a month), the better off you'll be when it comes time to buy a TV, take out a mortgage on a house, and, eventually, retire comfortably.

If you've never really thought much further ahead than how you're going to pay for the next burrito, don't worry—time is on your side. In this chapter, we will give you the foundation you need to make informed decisions with your money. We'll help you size up where you stand today, build credit, save money for the future, pay off your debts, and implement other tips and tricks to set you on the fast-track towards self-reliance. **Perhaps most importantly, we'll show you that the small things you could be doing right now can have a significant impact on how your finances will stand down the road.**

Personal Finance Cheat Sheet

We recognize that most twentysomethings don't want to spend every Sunday rifling through their receipts each week and cutting coupons for a stock-up at Costco. And for some people, any mention of "APRs" sets off an inexplicable desire to drink heavily and fall asleep on the couch. So while we think it's important to understand personal finance (it's going to be a big part of the rest of your life), we're also of the mind that it's not nearly as complicated as all the punditry would suggest.

So forget about all the jargon for now. The basics are really pretty simple—you just want to make sure you're not 1) oblivious to your current financial situation; 2) losing money where you shouldn't (e.g., dumb bank fees); 3) missing out on money you could be earning (e.g., interest); and 4) screwing up your ability to make major purchases like cars and houses down the line (e.g., ruining your credit). We think this stuff is so easy, in fact, that we want to put our money where our mouth is (get it?) by presenting you with eight steps to personal finance excellence.

Step ❶. Build a financial snapshot. Check your credit, compile your personal balance statement (i.e., your cash, stocks, debt, etc.), and get an idea of your cash inflows and outflows (see p. 254).

Step ❷. If you have any debt, create a plan to repay it on time (or even early) so that you'll be in a better position to improve your credit and financial health. To learn about debt repayment, see page 232.

Step ❸. If you don't yet have a credit card, get one, use it (even if you spend $10 a month), and always pay off the balance so you start to build credit. To learn about credit cards, see page 245.

Step ❹. Sign up for a checking account at a bank that either waives ATM fees and provides you with interest, like ING Direct's Online Checking Account, or one that has a prolific ATM network with no monthly fees, such as Bank of America. To learn about bank accounts, see page 239.

Step ❺. Once you have your spending money in a checking account, be sure to keep any extra funds in an Online Savings Account (e.g., HSBC Direct), which offers far better interest rates than regular brick-and-mortar banks. To learn about savings accounts, see page 241.

Step ❻. Create a "plan" that will help you finance your current lifestyle. See page 254 for tips on budgeting.

Step ❼. Begin to set yourself up for short- and medium-term purchases, like TVs and cars. To learn about creating a budget, see page 255.

Step ❽. If you receive benefits from a job, make sure to arrange monthly contributions to your 401(k). If you're unemployed or benefit-less, consider opening up a no-fee investment account with a brokerage house such as Ameritrade and make regular contributions to a Roth IRA. Or do both! (See page 263.) To learn about long-term investing, see page 265. ■

Everything You Wanted to Know About Credit

Do you know your credit score? If you answered "no," you're not alone: almost no one does, which is shocking considering that **credit is the backbone of your financial adulthood.** The problem is that people either have no idea what credit is or they choose to ignore it because it seems too scary to confront. Checking your credit can feel like getting a financial STD test. Chances are you're in fine shape, and if not, there are plenty of ways to start improving your situation. But you need to confront it now. Here's what you need to know.

What Is Credit?

Credit is an indicator of your financial decision making and trustworthiness thus far in life. In other words, do you pay people back on time when you borrow money and make good on contractual obligations? Before most third parties will enter into any significant financial agreement with you, they're going to check your credit score. Want to open a credit card? Rent an apartment? Purchase a cell phone plan? Credit will almost always come into play. Many third parties will reward you for good credit (e.g., decrease your interest rates) and punish you for bad credit (e.g., a bank might reject a mortgage application).

If you've never heard of credit (or worse, you know for a fact you have bad credit), consider this: 1) If your credit isn't up to snuff in situations where it's needed, you can always ask a friend or family member who has good credit to become a co-signer or guarantor on the transaction, which will get you over any credit humps; and, 2) You're young and time is on your side. You have many years to repair and/or build your credit before it can have any catastrophic impact on you. Presumably, you're not trying to cop a house today. But if you start thinking about your credit now, you'll have no problem doing so in a few years.

Components of Credit

Credit consists of two components: a **credit report** and a **credit score.** A credit report is a qualitative description of your financial history with regard to credit. It reflects what types of accounts you have open as well as any debt outstanding and late payments. A credit score, on the other hand, is a quantitative measure calculated by the Fair Isaac Corporation by aggregating the applicable pieces of your financial health that have been collected by the three main credit agencies: Experian, Equifax, and TransUnion. This credit score (also called your FICO)

Money

ranges between 300 and 850. A score of 700 is considered very good and will grant you all of the benefits good credit has to offer.

So what exactly goes into the calculation of a credit score? There are five elements, each impacting the overall score according to the following percentages:

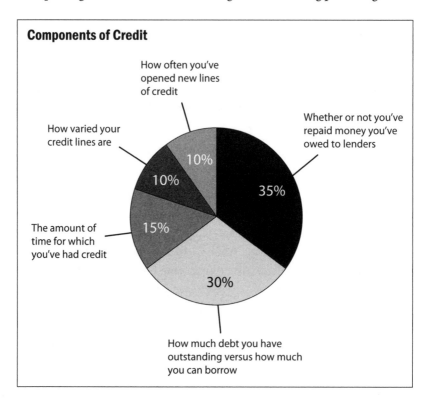

Components of Credit

How often you've opened new lines of credit

How varied your credit lines are

The amount of time for which you've had credit

Whether or not you've repaid money you've owed to lenders

How much debt you have outstanding versus how much you can borrow

10%

10%

15%

35%

30%

The important thing to notice here is that 65% of your credit is based upon factors that you can very easily control by paying your bills on time and by monitoring how much money you *have* borrowed compared to the total amount of money that you *can* borrow. It's also worth mentioning that credit pertains only to those applicable financial transactions that were in your name.

Building Credit

Remember that 65% slice that's easily in your control? Building your credit is as easy as taking control of that piece o' the pie. For starters, always pay your bills on time—that's 35% of the equation maximized right off the bat. Don't get trigger-happy with credit cards and buy something you're not absolutely sure you can pay off. Then there's the 30% chunk that consists of how much of your available credit you're using (a.k.a. "credit utilization"). It is easily controlled as well—just slightly more complicated. We'll explain.

Credit utilization is simply a fraction; it's the amount of debt you have outstanding divided by the total amount of debt you can borrow. And the lower the fraction the better. If you have thousands at your disposal but you've only used $20 to buy dinner, you look like a responsible young lad or lady.

Fortunately, there are two ways to positively affect this ratio: 1) by decreasing the amount of debt you have outstanding, or 2) by increasing the amount you can borrow without actually borrowing any more.

Increasing the amount of money you can borrow—also known as your *credit limit*— is risky and should only be done by those who have their spending and debt under control. The best way to do this is to ask the credit card company to give you a higher credit card limit (see page 245 for information about credit cards). Don't ask as soon as you get a card—wait until you've had it for several months and paid all your bills on time. If they ask why, you can simply respond that you're considering making some large purchases, would like the limit increased, and are responsible enough to pay it off (Exhibit A: Your flawless payment history). Credit card companies are in the business of lending money and will most likely agree. Just don't ask for a $10,000 credit

---

Tip & Trick:
Finding Your Credit

 The good news is that the government requires the three main credit agencies to provide you with one free credit report each year via AnnualCreditReport.com. The bad news, as we now know, is that the report doesn't actually include your score. Thanks a lot, government! Retrieving your credit score is inexpensive and easy, though, so it's all good. Sites such as MyFICO.com will provide you with your score for $15—in our opinion, a $15 well spent. If you don't want to pay and are cool just getting a proxy of your score, you can use free services like CreditKarma.com or sign up for a free trial membership with Experian.

Word of warning: Experian is the company behind those sweet "Free Credit Report Dot Cooooooom" jingles. Ever wonder how they can afford so many commercials? Hint: Their service isn't actually free. To retrieve your Experian proxy score, you have to give them your credit card number and sign up for a free trial membership. You can opt out before they start charging you, but they make it difficult for you to figure out how to actually cancel your trial. The easiest way to cancel is to just call customer service at 1-877-481-6826 and answer "no" to a bunch of questions until they agree to deactivate your account.

limit and then assume you can now afford a jet ski. Your limit has nothing to do with how much money you have, so spend according to what's in your checking account, not what your credit card can get you.

While we suggest focusing on the 65% of the pie you have direct influence over, we aren't suggesting that the remaining components of your score are not important too. They're just a bit harder to affect today. For example, you can't control how much credit you've had in the past. Instead, you can make sure that you start building credit today so that several years down the line when you attempt to purchase a house, you'll be in a position to take out a mortgage. The remaining two pieces—how varied your credit sources are and how much new credit you have—work hand in hand. A credit rule of thumb we endorse suggests having three sources of credit (e.g., a credit card, a loan, etc). If you can manage this in your twenties, you're ahead of the game. But for most people it's much better to establish *good* lines of credit (even if that means just one) than have three bad ones. So don't go opening up tons of credit card accounts all at once, especially those ominously easy-to-get retail store credit cards. It will raise red flags and make you look as though you keep borrowing money because you can't pay off your original debts.

Fixing Bad Credit

No matter how responsible you are, it's easy to watch your credit score get dinged due to an oversight. Maybe you missed a credit card payment when you were on vacation, or you just had no idea your credit score was slowly dropping because you still had outstanding debt to pay off. The good news is bad credit is fixable. It just takes some time. (Note: No one can fix your credit overnight, so don't buy into late-night commercials that say it can be done for the "low price of $59.99!") Credit agencies have good memories, but they forgive and forget eventually. So while that unpaid bill looks like a scarlet letter now, a streak of responsible behavior will reduce it to a little blip on your credit report. Thus, **the only real solution for fixing credit problems is to pay your bills on time and make sure to keep your credit utilization ratio low.** Over time (from six months to a year or longer, depending upon how bad it really is), your credit will recover.

If your credit is being demolished by a loan you're having trouble paying off, try calling your lender to explain your situation and see if they can help you by either 1) lowering your interest rate, 2) decreasing your monthly payments, or 3) allowing you to seek deferment or forbearance. To learn about the pros and cons of these options, read more about debt repayment on 232.

Other Ways to Improve Your Credit

Okay, you've got your credit card, you're paying the bills, and you're dealing with your debt. Cool beans—these are the most important steps. If you want to be super proactive though, there's more you can do:

- **CHECK THE ACCURACY OF YOUR CREDIT REPORT.** Talk about life being unfair—Bankrate.com reports that 70% of credit reports contain serious errors that may impact your credit. Once a year, you should check your report and make sure that nothing looks wrong (i.e., a service provider falsely claimed that you didn't pay a bill when you have proof that you did) and that the information is consistent across each agency. If you find an issue, send a letter to the credit agency requesting an amendment. Bankrate also provides a helpful letter template that you can find a link to via gradspot.com/book.

- **DON'T AUTHORIZE UNNECESSARY CREDIT CHECKS.** Here's another thing that seems topsy-turvy. When a third party checks your credit score, the simple act of pulling your information can hurt your credit score. There are **soft pulls** (e.g., you check your own score) and **hard pulls** (these happen when you apply for a credit card or activate a cell phone plan, for example). Only hard pulls can affect your score. Be vigilant about who checks your credit and never allow service providers to perform a credit check until you know you want to do business with them or you've narrowed your choice down to a select group and need to allow credit checks to move forward. No one can pull your score without your social security number, so as long as you keep it close to your chest you'll be safe from willy-nilly credit pulls.

- **BUILD CREDIT IN NONTRADITIONAL WAYS.** Not all recent grads have the financial standing to get a credit card, but that doesn't mean they aren't being responsible with their money in other places. An organization called Payment Reporting Builds Credit, Inc. (PRBC. com) recognized this oversight and worked out a system with Fair Isaac to improve it. Basically, you can report paid bills (e.g., cable, utilities) and other financial obligations that don't traditionally affect your credit to PRBC in order to benefit your score. Another option for getting past the credit card hump is to start with a secured card and then get a credit card once you've proven you can be responsible with it (see page 251).

Money

🖥 **Seek Private (and Free) Counseling.** The Association of Independent Consumer Credit Counseling Agencies may be able to work with you on your specific situation, so if you're really in dire straits why not give them a call at 866-703-8787? They'll need to know some things about your financial health to be able to provide good advice, but don't fork over your social security number.

Repaying Your Debt

According to the College Board's 2010 *Trends in Student Aid* report, 65% of college graduates have student loans, and the average debt carried out of school for those who borrowed is $19,800 at public colleges and $26,100 at private colleges. In addition, Sallie Mae, reports that the average credit card balance is over $3,500. Bogey! If you're nodding your head thinking, "Yep, that sounds about right," hopefully you can find a little bit of solace in the fact that others out there are in the same boat. But shared suffering eventually loses its appeal because, let's face it, we really only care about ourselves. Thus, you should find a lot *more* solace in the realization that you have plenty of options for dealing with your debt, and we're going to run through them in this section. Power to you (and those other people).

Before you confront your debt situation, it's important to remember how debt works. Remember Economics 101? Of course you don't! But don't worry about that. All you need to know in this case is how loans work and how they affect your overall debt.

Loan Basics: Just Ask a Drug Dealer

There are three common types of debt that grads may have: credit card, interpersonal, and student. No matter whom you owe, repayment consists of two parts: **principal** (the outstanding amount of the loan) and **interest** (the "extra" on top of the principal you have to pay each payment period through which the lender makes a profit on the loan). Interest is derived by applying the interest rate to your current outstanding principal. Like our favorite textbooks of yore, let's consider an example:

Slim Charles took a loan of $10,000 from Proposition Joe to make a purchase in Bolivia. Being a savvy businessman, Prop Joe said he could afford to lend the money at a 7% interest rate. Slim went to Bolivia, made some purchases, and came home. When it was time to pay back the money, Slim didn't have the whole $10,000, so

Money

Prop Joe told Slim to pay him back $1,000 of the loan each year. So how much does he have to pay at the end of the first year? Unfortunately, it's not $1,000—he must also pay the 7% interest on the principal, which in the first year is still $10,000. So he must pay $700 of interest ($10,000 × .07) in addition to the $1,000 principal repayment. Thus, his total first year payment is $1,700, and his outstanding balance after this repayment is $9,000.

See how much interest can hurt? (This clearly was a very simplified example and assuming your debt is of the student or credit variety, there will be a minimum principal repayment each month that you won't get to choose. But we do think this example gets the point across.)

What happens if Slim misses his first year's payment? Well, it only gets worse:

Slim had a rough year on the corner and now he's broke. He still owes $10,000 and, as we know, was supposed to repay $1,700 this year (principal plus interest). But he can't pay anything. Like most lenders, Prop Joe decides to capitalize the interest payment. This means that the interest Slim should have paid (e.g., $700) will now be added to his principal, thus making the new principal $10,700. And guess what? Next year, Prop Joe will use this new principal to calculate the interest payment (e.g., 7% of $10,700), so Slim will be even deeper in the pit.

Among other reasons, **capitalized interest** is why you never want to skip a repayment installment. That's how debt balloons out

Tips & Tricks:
What's the deal with variable rates?

While interest rates on your debt will generally be somewhere between 3% and 7%, they may be variable, meaning they can change depending on what's going on in the economy. For example, on July 1, 2008, the government decreased rates on Stafford and PLUS loans from as high as 8% down to as low as 3.6%. Needless to say, the best thing to do when interest rates drop is to lock in your rates by consolidating your debt (p. 235). Once you do that, your lender is obliged to honor that rate for the duration of your loan. The drawback? If rates drop any further, you can't take advantage of them. That being said, we think of the economy as a highly unpredictable beast and tend to discourage holding out for more favorable rates. However, if you have really good evidence that interest rates will be decreasing (e.g., the government publicly announces rate decreases before instituting them), then by all means hold off on consolidating until the drop, assuming you've already decided consolidation makes sense for you.

of control (and, in Slim's case, how you might find yourself in an abandoned building on the wrong side of a nail gun). The finish line just keeps getting further and further away and begins to feel unattainable. To avoid going down this path to bankruptcy, be sure to, at the very least, make good on your interest payments each period.

Making a Repayment Plan: Every Little Bit Counts

The point of the examples above is to demonstrate a simple but scary fact: **the longer it takes you to repay your debt, the more interest you'll be paying to your lender over time.** Thus, repaying your debt an extra $50 to $100 per month in excess of the monthly repayments you've worked out with your lender can result in thousands saved in additional interest.

You're probably thinking, "Thanks geniuses, but if I had the cash to repay my debt I would have done it already!" Fair point. But look at your budget (p. 254) and we bet you can find a way to pay more each month, even if it's just $50. Remember: It's not just a matter of spending $50 today versus $50 tomorrow (if it were, we'd spend it now too). It's about spending $50 today versus hundreds over the additional months or years you hold your debt.

On the flip side, if you can't even afford your basic repayment (it's nothing to be ashamed of—a lot of people are also in this situation), there are ways to minimize your monthly repayments that we'll discuss in this section.

(For specifics on repaying your credit card debt see page 254. For help with your student debt, read on.)

Student Debt

As you've already read, there's a good reason pundits like to call us "Generation Debt." In fact, many grads fear they owe so much student debt that they'll be halfway through their working lives by the time they break even. But this isn't the time to herald the apocalypse—it's just time to recognize that it's possible to pay off your student debts and to get your act together.

The first step is to find out how much student debt you have. To do this, check in with the National Student Loan Data System (NSLDS) online at nslds.ed.gov to see where you stand. You will need to provide your social security number, but this is a trusted, government-run organization. While the NSLDS is accurate when it comes to whom you've borrowed money from, it isn't always

Money

so accurate with how much you owe them. Thus, after finding the who, the next step is to track down the what—reach out to each lender and find out exactly how much you owe, what your monthly payments should be, whether you have a grace period (see below), and what your interest rates are.

Once you've done all of this, you should have all of your student debt details, and will recognize that you've fallen into one of two categories: 1) You can afford to pay off your debt as is, and possibly even prepay some; or 2) The payments are too taxing on your budget and you need some relief.

If you've fallen into the first category, then things are looking up—you can prepay your debt (and thus avoid losing money on interest), or you can just repay it on the original schedule provided by your lender.

If you've fallen into the second category, there are still options. For example, you can try to consolidate your debt, thereby decreasing your monthly payments and spreading your repayment schedule over many years. Or, if worse comes to worst, you can attempt to get your loans "forgiven." Regardless of where you stand, it's worth considering the pros and cons of all options.

The "Perks" of Student Debt

In many ways, repaying student debt is like going to a good massage parlor—quite expensive, but there are perks (like a sauna and free fruit—what were you thinking?!). The first is the **grace period**. After you graduate, you can usually stall your debt repayment for up to six months (check with your lender before doing so). However, it's important to note that if any of your debt is unsubsidized, the unpaid interest during the grace period will be capitalized (i.e., added to your principal) unless you pay it yourself. By calling your lenders, you should be able to determine whether or not your debt is subsidized. The second "cherry on top" is the fact that a portion of your student debt interest is tax deductible (see page 274). ∎

What Exactly Is Student Debt Consolidation?

In its simplest form, student debt consolidation on federal (e.g., Stafford, PLUS) and private loans enables you to do any or all of the following: 1) combine all of your loans into one loan, with one interest rate and one monthly payment; 2) decrease the amount of your monthly payment by repaying your loan over an extended period of time up to 30 years; and 3) lock in your interest rates (many

Money

forms of student debt have variable interest rates attached and most people prefer to lock them in).

Consolidation may help you meet your monthly budget, but there's also a downside—the reason that consolidators are willing to allow you to pay less each month is because they can make more money off of your loan, in the form of interest, over the long run. In fact, over a 30-year consolidation period, you may pay up to three times as much as if you had repaid your debt on the original schedule, which is usually ten years.

When it comes to actual consolidation, there are basically three options: 1) a **standard repayment loan** that does not extend your repayment schedule past ten years but does fix your interest rate and combines your loans into one; 2) an **extended or graduated loan** that draws out the life of the loan—you can either make a consistent payment each month or pay less now at the expense of having to pay more in the future (when you're hopefully making more money); or 3) an **income contingent loan** where repayment is tied to—you guessed it—your income.

How to Pick a Student Debt Consolidator

Choosing a consolidator requires a fair amount of due diligence, but it's worth taking the time to do it right—after all, your relationship with the lender may last decades! As of the date of this volume, many of the lenders who consolidated government loans have left the market (e.g., Sallie Mae, NelNet) due to the credit crisis. Thus, if you have federal loans, you will most likely have to consolidate through the government. The website LoanConsolidation.ed.gov is a good place to start, but you'll eventually want to call one of the helpful attendants at the government's hotline (800-557-7392) to explore your options. Even though they'll ask for your social security number to explore your options, you don't need to provide it as long as you can tell them the types and amount of debt you have.

In terms of finding consolidators for your private loans, the first step should always be to call your lender. You'd be surprised, but many of them may offer to consolidate your debt rather then have someone else do it, or at the very least pass you along to a partner. However, whenever using a private (i.e., non-government) debt consolidator, look out for red flags like companies that resell your debt, non-fixed interest rates, and penalties for prepaying your loans.

No matter whom you consolidate with, you should expect some type of discount (0.25%) if you pay your monthly bill with automatic bill pay (p. 245), and possibly another discount of up to 1% if you make good on all your payments for the first 36 months.

Ask The Expert:
Can I Really Get My Debt Forgiven?

We reached out to a number of financial experts to get the lowdown on this complicated issue. The good news: If you *really* can't pay, then yes, forgiveness is possible. But understand that it's forgiveness in the way that your boyfriend or girlfriend "forgives" you for knocking boots with someone else—in other words, there are plenty of strings attached. Here are your three options.

Volunteer for Forgiveness

Your debt will be paid (usually up to $60,000) by a third-party if you provide services to their organization for several years. This includes full-time volunteering with organizations like Americorp and the Peace Corps (p. 69), enlisting for military service, teaching, or offering to help groups such as Equal Justice Works and the National Health Service Corps. Recently, the U.S. government institutionalized this practice of volunteer work in exchange for debt forgiveness by creating the **Public Service Loan Forgiveness (PSLF)** program, which you can learn more about via LoanConsolidation.ed.gov and 1-800-557-7392. In addition, some colleges may even offer debt repayment assistance, such as **Low Income Protection Plans (LIPP)**, so check with your school if you're in need of forgiveness.

Income-Based Repayment

Another government-sponsored debt-forgiveness program that started in 2009 is the Income-Based Repayment (IBR) program. As unbelievable as it sounds, the government will actually repay a portion of your loan repayments based upon your income and family status. (Note: IBR should not be confused with an income-contingent loan, which is totally different and doesn't forgive any of your debt.)

According to IBRinfo.org, you may be eligible for the program if the following criteria apply to you:

- 👤 You have federal student loans in either the Direct or Guaranteed Loan (FFEL) program.

Can I Really Get My Debt Forgiven continued...

- 💰 Your loans include Stafford, Grad Plus, and federal consolidation loans that do not include Parent PLUS loans. Perkins loans are eligible if you consolidate them into a Guaranteed or Direct loan.

- 💰 You borrowed either before or after IBR was created, for either graduate or undergraduate study.

- 💰 Your debt-to-income ratio qualifies you for reduced payments (a good rule of thumb is that if you make less than you owe each month, you'll qualify, but check out the calculator on the site to be sure).

Student Debt Forbearance and Deferment

While your grace period provides you with six months of payment-free bliss after graduation, you might be in a situation where you need to defer your payments even longer. Say hello to our little friends, student loan forbearance and deferment—both enable you to defer your payment of the loans (usually for up to three years). With deferment you don't have to repay the interest that accrues during that time, but needless to say, this added perk makes it harder to get than forbearance.

The qualification criteria for deferment and forbearance differ slightly and are also contingent on the type of loan you have. Qualifications for forbearance include the following:

- 💰 The inability to pay off the loan during its term

- 💰 Loan repayments equaling at least 20% of your monthly income

- 💰 Significant and unexpected personal problems

- 💰 Disability (including deteriorating health)

For deferment, you have to meet some of these less common criteria:

- 💰 Enrollment in a school at least part-time

- 💰 Unemployment (for up to three years)

- 💰 Experiencing economic hardship

> 💰 Military deployment
>
> 💰 Pursuit of an above-board internship
>
> 💰 Participation in national service
>
> The best way to apply for deferment and forbearance is to check in with your lenders who will provide you with instructions. But once you have applied, don't jump the gun on skipping payments. Your deferment only kicks in once your lender alerts you that it does. And it's up to you to check in on your deferment status. ∎

The Bottom Line on Student Debt

Student debt is no joke, and if you don't confront it now it can easily spiral out of control. In severe circumstances (e.g., you're completely broke and refuse to volunteer in Papua New Guinea), you can always come clean with your lender and see if you can work out an alternative arrangement. If you ever do get desperate, please talk to an accountant or lawyer before doing anything drastic.

Bank Accounts

Being suspicious of "banking" is a time-honored tradition that dates back to the days of ancient Greece, when gold was hoarded in temples by lecherous, inbred priests…at least according to the movie *300*. Sometime later, Adam Smith used his "invisible hand" to invent capitalism, or, as it's now known, "eBay," and banks resembling the ones we know today were born.

Things are pretty well-regulated these days, but it's still good to bring a healthy amount of wariness to the process of choosing the right bank. For example, know that approximately 40% of banks' revenue comes from the fees they charge on consumer accounts, whether that's general monthly fees that are charged to just keep them open or "penalty" fees. Like going to the movies, the "feature presentation" (i.e., an account) lures you in and then they turn the screws with overpriced concessions like Swedish Fish and Milk Duds (i.e., service fees). Unnecessary fees that seem negligible can add up over time. With a little bit

of research, however, you should be able to not only avoid most extra charges, but also find the right bank and bank account for you.

Choosing a Bank

The fact is, most banks offer pretty similar account options. But if you have a selection in your area, there are a few considerations that you should keep in mind.

 **Convenience.** This is probably the most important factor when it comes to selecting a bank. It's up to you, but we're guessing you'd prefer a bank that has a strong ATM network (so that you don't have to rack up fees) and a brick-and-mortar branch nearby if you value being able to speak with someone in person.

 **Online Banking.** You should opt for a bank that provides online banking. Essentially, it enables you to check your balances, transfer funds, send checks, and more, all while sitting at home in your undies… and for free. Another major benefit is the ability to enroll in automatic bill pay, which we discuss further on page 245.

 **FDIC Insurance.** In the wake of the credit crisis, you want to make sure that your money is protected. The best way to do this is to make sure that the bank has FDIC insurance, which covers one account per person for up to $250,000 .

Types of Accounts

There are two main types of accounts you should consider: checking and savings. Here are some key things to look out for when comparison shopping for these accounts.

Checking Accounts

The most basic account offered by most banks is a checking account. This is preferable to keeping money under your mattress because you can write checks (usually necessary for rent), use ATMs to access your money anywhere, get a debit card (p. 242), and not get your cash stolen as easily. You receive no interest on your money, but you also pay minimal to no fees.

Savings Accounts

As the name would suggest, savings accounts are built for money you save rather than spend. They offer the ability to earn interest on your money so it actually grows while it's sitting in the bank. Interest rates on savings accounts are not all that high, but why wouldn't you want your hard earned cash to earn even more money for you? Just be careful that you don't negate any earned interest by incurring penalty fees, because savings accounts have lots. Most notably, almost all savings accounts charge a penalty if you dip below a stated minimum balance, so you always need to ensure that you can meet the minimum, usually around $1,000, before opening one.

Online Bank Accounts

The new kids on the block in the banking world are Online Checking Accounts and Online Savings Accounts, and they're making the traditional brick-and-mortar banks look like chumps by offering some interest on checking accounts and an average of about 1% more interest on savings accounts. With no real estate, nor in-person bank tellers, janitors, or any other major overhead costs to deal with, these online banks save a lot of money that they then pass on to you in the form of better rates.

The only catch with online accounts is that there are no physical locations so if you're the type of person that prefers visiting your bank and working with a banker, online savings accounts probably aren't for you. You also can't pop around the corner and withdraw or deposit funds; it usually takes a few days to send checks via mail or electronically to a checking account. Still, we think the positives—particularly for savings accounts—far outweigh the "negatives." (See page 260 to learn about the power of compounding, and you'll understand why. Even just 1% makes a big difference over the long-run.)

Opening a Bank Account

Getting a bank account is super easy. It requires filling out some basic information including your legal name, where you live, your phone number, email address, and so on. You'll also be required to provide your social security number, as well as either the number on your driver's license or another state issued identification card. Finally, you'll be asked to make an initial deposit, which can be as small as $1. When it comes to traditional banks, you can just pop into the closest branch, call the bank's phone number, or fill out an application online. With online banks, you can just do it on the website. And that's really all there is to it.

 ## *Hazard:* Using Your Debit Card

When you open up a bank account, you'll get a debit card that you can use for ATM withdrawals and on-the-go purchases. Debit cards don't solidify your "baller status" quite like a credit card (see page 245), but they're a great convenience. Unfortunately, they can also get you in trouble, so there are some caveats worth pointing out.

First, some merchants don't report debit card transactions immediately (especially if your PIN is not used in the purchase), so stay on top of your balance to avoid an accidental overdraft, which will result in a penalty fee and possibly even interest charges on the cash you didn't have. Furthermore, certain types of purchases (e.g., hotels, car rentals) can result in a "hold" or a "security deposit" that will tie up your funds until the transaction clears—your ears should perk up if you hear these words and you should realize that the deposit amount should not be considered usable money until it's been released back into your bank account. Finally, debit cards don't help you build your credit, and without credit you won't be able to do things like get auto loans and mortgages. So even though they're just as convenient as credit cards, they're not an alternative.

As always, comparison shop for debit cards to make sure you're getting the best option, though you probably won't choose your bank based on its debit cards. While most debit cards are the same, Citi's debit cards, for example, offer "Thank You" points which are redeemable for merchandise, travel, and other perks, so you might as well see what extras you can snag.

How to Write a Personal Check

One of the authors of this book (cough, Chris) didn't know how to write a check until he was 23 years old. If you're in the same boat, just check out this tutorial showing you what to put in each section:

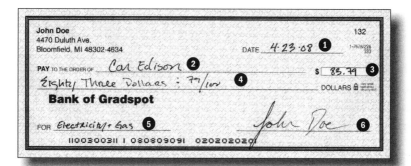

❶   The current date

❷   The full name of the individual or organization you are paying. Don't use nicknames or names you just made up

❸   The dollar amount—be very clear with your decimal points and commas

❹   The dollar amount written out in words—cents are written as a fraction in the form of "X/100." If there are zero cents, then write it out as "0/100"

❺   Write what the check is for—this part is optional, but it can be helpful for your own record keeping

❻   Your signature

Tip: When filling out amounts, avoid blank spaces (someone might sneak in some extra zeros). If you don't fill up a line, you can draw a line through the remaining space.

How to Endorse (or "Cash") a Check

So you have a check. Until you bring it to a bank it won't do you any good, and just bringing it to a teller without endorsing it won't either.

There are three different ways to endorse a check, and each is used for a different reason. The first way is to just sign the back of the check. If you want to either deposit it for cash or have it deposited into your account, this is all you have to do. It's best to sign it only once you arrive at the bank (or just before sending it to your online bank), because if you lose an endorsed check, anyone who finds it can sign their name below yours and cash it–no questions asked.

The next two options are applicable if you want to direct the check to someone else or mail it to your bank for deposit into your own account. To protect the check from ending up anywhere other than your bank account, write "for deposit only" and, below that, the account number that it can be deposited into. If you want to sign the check over to someone else (this traditionally occurs when you receive a health insurance reimbursement and need to transfer it to your doctor), sign the check on the back at the top and on the next line write, "Pay to:", followed by the person's or organization's name.

How to Void a Check

Sometimes you will have to provide a voided check to do things like set up direct deposit for your paycheck at work. To void a check, simply write "VOID" in large print across the face of the check.

Automatic Bill Pay

Automatic bill pay is a simple way to outsource responsibility and maintain good credit. There are two forms of ABP: The more widely used one involves an arrangement between you and a company (e.g., your cell phone service provider) in which you provide them with your credit card or bank account number and they automatically charge you when a bill becomes due. The other, less widely known version of ABP is where you ask your bank to automatically send a check on your behalf to a vendor on a recurring schedule (e.g., your rent check every month).

Many people are hesitant to use automatic bill pay because they're worried about paying for something without seeing the bill. Conspiracy theorists have their value in certain areas, but we think there are some charges that just aren't worth the hassle and risk of a missed payment. For example, you know you're going to pay rent, so why not arrange for your bank to send a check the last week of every month? However, one area that we're on the fence about is your credit card(s) because who knows when someone will steal your identity and order half of the Sky Mall catalog.

Remember: You can always stop the automatic payments from going through if you need to do so. For example, if you had your rent in the queue and your landlord kicks you out of your apartment, you can stop the check from being sent (although stopping the check is now probably the least of your worries). In addition, companies usually provide a buffer between the dates when you receive your bill and when it is due, thus giving you time to stop it if need be.

Remember, automatic bill pay shouldn't be viewed as a "safety net." You still need to look over bills each month to ensure there are no irregularities.

Credit Cards

Can't get a job and your parents are kicking you out of the house? There's a simple solution: apply for a bunch of credit cards, max them out on gear and non-perishables, and then fake your own death. Problem solved!

We're joking, of course—credit card fraud is not a foolproof plan. But it's a joke with a point: credit cards breed extreme behavior, so beware. **Credit cards should never be used as a way to get loans—at the end of the day, the**

interest rates that credit cards charge are not competitive. It's basically like borrowing money from the mob.

There are, however, a multitude of important benefits to having credit cards, assuming you always pay them off on time. For a recent grad, the most important reason to have a credit card is that it will help you build your credit (see page 227). It's also nice to be able to cruise around without carrying huge wads of cash and to accrue perks such as air miles, free hotel stays, and cash back bonuses when you spend money. Another benefit is the insurance most credit cards provide on purchases. For example, if you buy something with your card and lose the item, or if your item breaks and customer support is giving you a tough time, the credit card company may actually reimburse you.

Choosing a Card

The three main things to consider when choosing a credit card are **annual fees**, **interest rate**, and **rewards**. You usually can't have the best of all three, so it's up to you to decide which is most important. Assuming you always pay your bills on time and thus never pay interest, you should focus your attention on avoiding annual fees and snagging useful rewards. There are many credit cards that don't have annual fees attached (the only reason you should ever pay an annual fee for a card is if you know the rewards will far outweigh your annual fee, like in the case of a great airline rewards card for someone who travels a lot). Just keep in mind that it usually takes around 30,000 airline miles, or $30,000 spent on a card, to earn a free domestic flight. So, it probably only makes sense if you get to expense travel for work and accrue points for a personal trip. A more practical rewards option for most grads is cash back (for every dollar you spend on specific items, you'll receive 1–5% off, but just make sure that the items you receive this cash back on are the types of items you regularly purchase).

As mentioned, the interest rate shouldn't affect you because you're never going to charge more than you can pay...right?! But realistically, you might miss a payment, so the lower the fee the better—low-to-mid teens is about the best you'll get. Watch out for cards that boast an introductory 0% APR (i.e., interest rate) and no annual fee, because they'll usually increase both starting in year two. (For more tips on navigating credit card ads and terms, see our sample credit card ad on 248.)

The best way to find a card is to browse your options on sites like CardRatings.com and CreditCards.com. These sites will allow you to compare hundreds of cards that are conveniently organized into categories like "Low Ongoing Rate," "Cards for No/Poor Credit," "Cash Back Rewards," and "Gas Rebate Cards."

Applying for Credit Cards Is Not Like Applying for School

These days, applying to over 20 colleges is considered standard, and Yale doesn't care that you also applied to Michigan and Pomona. However, applying for lots of credit cards in a short span of time makes you look desperate and can adversely affect your credit score. So where should you focus your efforts? For recent grads with no credit history and low income, your school may be your first port of call. Your alumni association might have an affiliate relationship with Visa or a bank and may be able to hook you up. Banks are also a good place to go. If you've been a loyal customer of your bank or any other financial institution over the years, they're likely to reward you with some plastic. And if no one's giving you a break, consider getting a secured card (p. 251) and then working your way up to a credit card.

Applying for a credit card is just like applying for a bank account. Whether you're going through your alumni organization, bank, or directly from a credit card company, you'll be asked for some personal information, identification, and your social security number. The only difference between applying for credit cards and bank accounts is that your credit rating may impact whether or not you are granted a card.

Lingo:
Credit Card Ads

Lawyers can barely decipher the fine print on credit card ads and even a math major would be hard-pressed to figure out how his or her bill is calculated. And at the end of the day, interest rates should be somewhat irrelevant since you'd ideally pay your balance in full every time. That said, here are a few key things to look out for when assessing a credit card offer (continued on next page):

(continued on next page):

Money

BALLER BANK
"Charge It To The Game" Credit Card

BALLER BANK
CHARGE IT TO THE GAME

1234 123456 12345

YOUR NAME HERE

CARD OVERVIEW

- Earn up to 5% cash back ❶
- 0.00% APR*
- No minimum payment for 6 months**
- 0.00% balance transfers*** ❷
- No annual fee**** ❸
- $0 fraud liability for any unauthorized use if your card is lost or stolen
- 20 day grace period ❹
- Credit limit up to $20,000

Apply Now!

* 0.00% APR valid for up to 12 months; Prime Rate + 9.99% APR thereafter. ❺ ❻ ❼ ❽
** No minimum payment for 6 months; 3.5% of outstanding balance thereafter. ❾
*** 0.00% interest rate until the last day of the billing period ending during June 2012; then the standard APR for purchases
**** Annual fee after first year is $95.

See additional terms and conditions on credit card application.

1) **Rewards.** Air miles? Cash back? Hotel rooms? Are there any stipulations for redeeming the points? Do they offer something you would actually spend your money on otherwise?

2) **Balance Transfer Fees.** Transferring debt between cards may seem like a useful move at times, but look out for the interest charged on these transactions.

3) **Annual Fee.** This fee is paid each year simply for the convenience of having the card. Unless you are receiving exceptional benefits, annual fees should be avoided. Beware of cards that tease with no annual fee for the first year only.

4) **Grace Period.** Kind lenders should offer a grace period, which is the period of time before the lender starts charging you interest on new purchases. You will want a reasonable grace period (e.g., 20–25 days).

5) **APR.** This is the beginning interest rate that you pay on your outstanding balance. Usually, it is a "teaser rate" (e.g., "0% APR!") that will shoot up after the first year, or even sooner depending on your credit score.

6) **Prime rate.** A benchmark used by banks to determine the interest rate. Generally somewhere between 6-10%.

7) **Fixed rate.** This is ostensibly good, because the lender is claiming they won't change the interest rate (i.e., "fixed for life!"). The problem is, they can still just go ahead and change it whenever they want.

8) **Variable rate.** An interest rate that is tied to a standard index. This may sound good if interest rates are going down, but it's not like you can predict the movement of rates for the whole time you're going to hold the card.

9) **Minimum payment.** This is the minimum amount that you are required to pay that month in order for the credit card company to not report you to a credit agency. Remember, however, that the remainder is just racking up interest that you'll have to pay down the line. ■

Money

Proper Credit Card Maintenance

While you can use your credit card for every little purchase, we think credit cards are best used for big-ticket items that you can easily keep track of, as well as online purchases because of the extra level of security that they provide. The negligible rewards you will earn on small purchases like lattes and gum may not be worth the risk of losing track of your spending and then not being able to pay the bill in full at the end of the month. On the flip side, if you direct all of your spending on your credit card, then you'll be able to easily see what you're spending money on each month, including the small stuff—you just have to be confident that you always have enough in your checking account to pay for it all.

Whichever credit card spending strategy you use, set up an online account for each credit card to receive alerts, avoid late payments, and ensure that you are rewarded for responsible behavior by requesting a credit limit increase every six months (see page 229). Check all your statements carefully for red flags like incorrect penalties, charges that are clearly erroneous (potential credit card fraud), and vendors charging you the wrong amount. If you are assessed any penalty fees or other charges from your credit card company, it's always worth asking them if they can remove them. Normally, if you ask, they'll do it. However, you need to call immediately after receiving the bill and you may need to respectfully talk your way up to a manager. While removing extra fees may work once or twice, it won't work forever, so don't think you can always be late and still get off the hook.

The Most Important Reason to Get a Credit Card

Let's just say it again for effect: Using a credit card (even if you're spending just $1 a month and repaying that $1) is the easiest way to build your credit. Building your credit allows you to do things like rent an apartment and purchase a cell phone plan in the short term, and take out mortgages and finance cars in the long term. It's better to start building credit today so that you have it when you need it instead of scrambling when you're trying to buy your first McMansion.

What If I Can't Get a Credit Card?

Don't take it personally—credit card companies just don't really love recent grads. In college, companies probably threw credit card offers at you willy-nilly, even tossing in lame T-shirts and mildly inappropriate bottle openers for good measure. But really, they were judging you by your parents, as is the old American tradition. They assumed that daddy or mommy would be there to bail you out if need be. After graduation, however, you are judged on your own merits. Since the two main factors credit card companies consider are income and credit history, you now most likely look more like a pauper than a princess.

Should the options previously discussed (your bank, alumni association, etc.) lead to dead ends, you still have one option for snagging some slightly less awesome but still useful plastic: secured cards.

Secured Cards

Think of a secured card as a credit card with training wheels. When you sign up, the bank will ask you to put cash in an account linked to your card. That money, or some percentage of it, becomes your credit limit. If you think it sounds just like a debit card (p. 242), you're right. But unlike a debit card, a secured card can help you get a credit card—after a few months of using it without running over the limit, just call the bank and request an upgrade.

The danger of secured cards is that they allow you to carry a balance that accrues interest. But since your credit limit will be equal to the amount of money you deposited into the account, and most likely that amount won't be too high, you won't really risk that much damage from interest if you ever charge something to your secured card and then wait a month to repay it (i.e., the interest on a $50 balance is in a completely different league than the interest on a $500 balance). That said, since the goal of having a secured card is to convince your bank to give you a credit card, you should never carry a balance. Use it frugally, pay it off, then upgrade.

When shopping for a secured card, you want to look for the same criteria that you do for credit cards: no fees and low interest rates (rewards aren't applicable here). Talk to your bank to learn about your options.

> ### Tips & Tricks:
> ### FDIC insurance
>
> If the credit crunch taught us anything, it's that nothing is certain in the financial world and even the behemoths of banking can crumble to the ground. So while the chances of your bank going belly up all of a sudden are highly unlikely, you want to make sure you'll get your money back if it does. That's where FDIC Insurance comes into play. The government insures one account per person at each FDIC-insured bank for up to $250,000 (prior to the financial crisis that amount was only $100,000). There's no reason to go with a bank that is not FDIC-insured—even the Redneck Bank is (look it up, it's real).

Lingo 2 (Credit Card Boogaloo):
Deciphering Your Bill

It's one thing to have good intentions about properly maintaining your credit card, but follow-through is another thing altogether. If this is the first time you've owned a card (or have been responsible for paying it), it helps to understand what all the terms on your credit card bill mean.

Money

Payment Due Date	New Balance	Past Due Amount	Minimum Payment
06/08/11 **2**	$68.98 **1**	$0.00	$10.00 **6**

Account number: 4466 9800 0000 0000

$ _____ . __

Make your check payable to:
Gradspot Card Services
Please write amount enclosed
New address or e-mail? Print on back.

94659465 315615 489 5632458 1546 57955 6245100 0650 648

25196 BDX 8 591 C
JOHN A SMITH
743 EVERGREEN TERRACE
SPRINGFIELD, NT 49007-4271

CARDMEMBER SERVICE
PO BOX 00000
SPRINGFIELD, NT 49007-4271

009 315 156   009 315 78200 156

guru
from **Graspot.com**

Statement Date:
04/09/11 - 05/08/11

Manage your account online:
www.gradspot.com/book

Minimum Payment: $10.00
Payment Due Date: 06/08/11

Additional contact information
conveniently located on reverse side

3 4 5

ACCOUNT SUMMARY   Account Number: 4466 9800 0000 0000

Previous Balance	$21.95	Total Credit Line	$10,600	
Payment, Credits	-$21.95	Available Credit	$10,531	
Purchases, Cash, Debits	+$68.98	Cash Access Line	$2,120	
New Balance	$68.98	Available for Cash	$2,120	

7 8 9

ACCOUNT ACTIVITY

Date of Transaction	Merchant Name or Transaction Description	$ Amount
04/29	Payment - Thank You	-21.95
04/31	BAGELICIOUS BAKERY / KING OF PRUSSIA PA	21.95
05/04	GETTY GAS STATION / NEW YORK NY	47.03

FINANCE CHARGES

Category	Daily Periodic Rate 31 days in cycle	Corresp. APR	Average Daily Balance	Finance Charge Due To Periodic Rate	Transaction Fee / Service Charge	Accumulated Fin Charge	FINANCE CHARGES **10**
Purchases	V .04175%	15.24%	$0.00	$0.00	$0.00	$0.00	$0.00
Cash advances	V .05271%	19.24%	$0.00	$0.00	$0.00	$0.00	$0.00
Total finance charges							$0.00

Effective Annual Percentage Rate (APR):   0.00%

Please see Information About Your Account section for balance computation method, grace period, and other important information.

The Corresponding APR is the rate of interest you pay when you carry a balance on any transaction category.
The Effective APR represents your total finance charges - including transaction fees
such as cash advance and balance transfer fees - expressed as a percentage.

1) **Outstanding Balance.** The most important number on your bill. It's the amount that you owe your credit card company, and it's derived by taking the previous balance, deducting your previous payments and any credits, and adding new purchases (explained below). If you leave this amount outstanding, it will accrue crazy amounts of interest that you'll have to pay.

2) **Payment Due.** The date when you have to pay up. As long as you pay the minimum (see #6) by this date you won't be charged a late fee. But we recommend always paying the full balance.

3) **Previous Balance.** This number was your ending balance from last month.

4) **Payment Credits.** The amount of the previous balance that you repaid (even the whole thing), as well as any credits the credit card company applied to your account (e.g., when you convinced them to refund a bogus charge).

5) **Purchases, Cash, Debits.** The aggregate of your purchases during the bill's period, as well as any cash advances you made or any penalties you received.

6) **Minimum Payment Due.** Hopefully you can ignore this number, but in the event you can't afford to pay your entire bill, this is the amount that you must pay the credit card company in order to preempt them from reporting your inability to pay your bill to a credit agency. Just remember, interest will accrue (and ultimately compound, meaning you'll end up paying interest on your interest!) on the remaining unpaid balance.

7) **Total Credit Line.** This is the maximum amount of money you can borrow from a lender at any one time. After you've reached the limit, you have to repay that amount before you can borrow any more. So in the case of a credit card, it's the maximum amount you can charge in one billing cycle. Obviously you should never actually reach your limit. But it's an important number to recognize because it impacts your credit via your credit utilization rate. See page 229 to learn more about credit utilization.

8) **Available Credit.** Your total credit line minus your outstanding balance.

9) **Cash Access Line & Available Cash.** Please, please, please, don't ever worry about or use these figures, but if you must know... Essentially, in addition to enabling you to make purchases with a credit card, your credit card company may be willing to lend you actual cold hard cash. Warning: The loan will come with an outrageous interest rate. In fact, the terms will be so outrageous that this is just about one of the worst forms of debt. These transactions will be reflected in your "access line," which is the total amount the company is willing to lend to you, and your "available cash," which is that amount less what you've already (but shouldn't have) borrowed.

10) **Finance Charges.** This section sends shivers down the spine of credit card debt survivors. This is where your credit card company details the interest you're racking up. You're a personal finance superstar when this is blank. ■

Hazard:
The Dangers of Credit Card Debt

Let's assume that by the end of the first month that you have your credit card, you rack up some purchases and you don't have enough money in your bank account to pay them off yet. You clearly didn't take our advice, but we're not mad at you—it happens. Here's what really blows, though: when your second bill arrives, even if you didn't purchase a single thing with your credit card since the last billing cycle, your new balance will increase. Why? Because you pay silly amounts of interest on the money you didn't repay. Now, your new debt is the original debt plus the interest. And if you can't pay it again the next month, your debt will be even higher because you'll be charged interest on the original debt as well as on the interest you accrued in the second month! See the cycle? Credit card debt is the worst possible detriment to your financial health. No pair of shoes or new TV is ever worth the pain it can bring you.

Dealing with Credit Card Debt

Like all forms of debt, there's no quick fix here, so ignore those companies that claim they can help you repay your debt overnight. Instead, take an aggressive approach to paying it off, and do everything you can to make your situation more manageable. The first trick is to call your bank and request that they lower your APR. Worst case scenario they say no—at least you tried. If you keep pleading your case and stressing that a lower rate will help you pay off your debt (be clear you're not just looking for charity), things will probably go your way eventually. Another, more aggressive approach is to threaten to transfer the balance to another credit card with a lower APR. ■

 # Easy Budgeting: Audit Yourself

Setting up a solid personal finance infrastructure is all well and good, but it's really not much use if you don't have money moving through it. Once those paychecks start coming in, you've got to budget your income to make sure that the bills get dealt with, the savings account gets filled, the 401(k) gets some action, the bar tab gets paid, and so on and so forth. Your primary goal should be to get a realistic sense of what money is coming in every month and where it's going.

Money

The best way to do that is to perform a self-audit. This process is relatively painless and, unlike with a real audit, there's no chance of jail time unless you perform a citizen's arrest on yourself. Here's what you do: For one month and one month only, keep close tabs on income you've got coming in, how much money you're using, and where that money is going. More than likely, your spending habits will have changed dramatically from what they were in college—regular expenses like pizza and $5 pitchers suddenly turn into rent, groceries, utility bills, transportation costs, and more. So check out your credit card bill, bank statement, and receipts to figure out the new lay of the land.

Now that you've braved this self-assessment, you can take two key steps. First, you can pinpoint places where curtailing your spending won't have any material affect on your life. You might think going out on the weekend is totally worth it for your sanity, but maybe that $50 "Cheese of the Month" subscription doesn't seem justified when you see it on your bank statement. Second, you can figure out how much money you have left over after expenses to filter into the savings component of your budget. These savings should be broken down into two types: 1) savings for upcoming purchases such as televisions and medium-term purchases such as a house, and 2) savings for retirement (for both, see page 263). If you're maxed out every month, you're not ensuring that you'll be able to live the lifestyle you want down the road—we recommend that you save at least 15% of the money that's coming in. (For more advice on how your budget should break down, see "Budgeting Guidelines" below.)

And there you have it. That's really all you need to do to assess your budget. And now, if you want to get a little more nitty-gritty and really start to maximize your personal finance potential, let's dive into a few useful budgeting tips.

Budgeting Guidelines

It's one thing to look at what your past spending has been, but the real power of budgeting is in planning what you'll spend in the future. While there are no set rules for how money should be spent, you should expect to spend approximately 35% of your money on housing (depending upon your location of course, but it shouldn't exceed 50%), another 20% on other fixed costs such as food and debt, 15% on saving and investing, and the remaining 30% on whatever you want.

Get Ready for Grad Spending

Consumer product companies aggressively court recent graduates. Why? Because we spend a boatload of money becoming independent adults. A survey by Y2M Marketing found that 50% of newly minted grads purchase a new cell phone plan and 30% buy a car, and these expenses are just the tip of the iceberg. When you interview for jobs, you'll probably have to spend around $200 for interview clothes and shoes, $25 for a haircut, and another $25 for a nice portfolio and pad. We're mentioning this not to scare you, but rather to point out that these expenses might sneak attack you and throw you off your budget if you don't plan for them. To get a better grasp on the costs associated with setting up your apartment see page 215, and for setting up your kitchen see page 25.

see page 215, and for setting up your kitchen see page 25.

Money

Top Ten Things Grads Waste Money On

1) **Overzealous Drinking/Partying.** If you want to keep living "the dream" (perhaps something to reconsider regardless), you'd better wean yourself off Grey Goose and become a walking Wikipedia of happy hours.

2) **Coffee.** Some very bright people have done the math on coffee shop culture, and it's not as pretty as those hearts that some baristas draw in the milk foam. Assuming you average $3 on coffee per day, you could save nearly $700/year and direct that money into a savings account with a 2% yield. After doing this for ten years you'll have almost $8,000!

3) **"Shared" Furniture.** A lot of people decide to split all apartment costs with their roommate(s), including furnishings. But what happens when one person owns a fifth of a television and half of a dining room table? Deciding beforehand who is responsible for different essential furnishings and then buying them independently allows each person to have ownership over something that they can later sell or take to a new apartment.

4) **Buying Every Cable Channel.** Cable bills can easily reach upwards of $100 when you go all out. But do you really need the package with the foreign news and Showtime?

5) **Enormous TVs.** Yes, a huge plasma flatty will make Willow look AMAZING, but is it really necessary in an apartment that costs about half as much per month?

6) **Cell Phone Perks.** If you have a job, daytime chatting is much reduced. Also, if you have a BlackBerry, are you really texting as much as you used to? Track your usage for a couple of months and consider scaling back your plan.

7) **Late Payments on Credit Cards and Bills.** Unless you have a very shady landlord, you don't have to fear for your kneecaps when you are late on rent. You may, however, incur penalties and damage your credit. Consider signing up for automatic bill pay to avoid late payments on all of your bills (see page 245).

8) **Extraneous Subscriptions and Memberships.** Gyms, university clubs, newspaper subscriptions...it all adds up. Think about how often you use these services and how much they're worth to you.

9) **Dining Out.** Give a grad a fish, and he eats for a day. Teach a grad to cook a fish, and he saves sick amounts of money. Even making your own lunch or bringing leftovers to work a few days a week can make a huge difference.

10) **Energy Expenditures.** Leaving the lights on all day, pumping the heat to sauna levels, and leaving plugs in the wall for no reason are not only bad for your energy bill, but also the environment. Do everyone a favor and budget your electricity and gas usage. To learn more about going green in your first place, see page 222. ■

Money

◘ Saving & Investing

Let's face it: There's a lot of concern that the U.S. Social Security system won't be able to support us when we're old geezers playing futuristic bingo and trying to pawn off our Pog collections. And if the government doesn't come through, it's on us to make sure that we're bathing in the finest artisanal prune juices through our nineties. Even the smallest investment today (just $50 per month) can put you on course for a post-retirement summer house in Aruba—much better than porridge and terrestrial TV in a lonely bed-sit. Thinking shorter term, saving is what will enable you to buy that massive flat-screen TV for the living room or purchase your first home down the road. And guess what? Saving doesn't mean just stashing some money away for a later date. It can mean putting money in a savings account so it earns some interest. Hence, saving is also really investing—whatever you want to call it, you should start doing it as soon as possible.

Admittedly, saving and investing aren't as simple as the other concepts we've discussed thus far in the chapter. From the constantly shifting financial landscape to the difficulty of adjusting your financial behavior to meet your savings goals, there's a lot to get hung up on. But you shouldn't. We're going to share with you approachable ways to get going with saving and investing so that you can start laying a foundation for the lifestyle you want in the future. The most important rule of saving and investing is, "Just do it." Making your money work for you is an acquired skill, and comfort with it takes experience. Getting started, however, can be easy and virtually risk-free. Let's get going.

Believe It or Not, You Already Earn Enough to Invest

Irony of all ironies: Just at the time in life when saving and investing benefits you the most, it's also the most difficult. You're finally making some money to store up for future winters, but new responsibilities like rent, car payments, and groceries hit your bank account hard. And unlike student loans, credit cards, and utility bill payments, saving and investing is optional, and thus usually ignored. But it's time to wake up and smell the money stacks. If you're able to contribute as little as $50 a month to an investment account, you'll have a sizable portfolio in no time. Coming up with $50 a month is as easy as buying cheaper beers, bringing a brown-bag lunch to work, or smoking less (see additional tips starting on page 256). And in fact, investing only $50 per month for the next 30 years while earning an average annual interest rate of 8% on that investment will yield $75,000 (even though you only put away $18,000). This is all thanks to the magical power of compounding.

Smart Money:
Do I Pay Off Debt or Invest?

Let's say you have managed to save $10,000. We're not going to ask how you pulled that off—congratulations are in order! The question is what to do with it. Investing at least some of it would be the immediate answer, but what if you also have $30,000 in school loans? Now you've got to make a decision: Should you pay down your debt? Or invest your ten grand?

From a purely economical perspective, it depends on which is greater: the interest rate you're paying on your educational loans (after-tax, since some school loan interest may be tax-deductible) or the interest rate you'd get on your investments (also after-tax, as your investment gains will be taxed). Diehard investors would say invest, making the claim that you ought to be able to earn more on your money than the 5–6% you're likely paying on your loans. Plus, you'll become more comfortable and experienced investing your money, which is important to your fiscal future.

But let's entertain the realists as well. Assuming your debt has an interest rate of 5%, are you sure you can find investment vehicles that will pay more? Even if you can, do you think they'll pay that much for the entire life of the loan? Moreover, how do you feel about debt? Would you be a lot more comfortable if you got it off your plate sooner rather than later?

Clearly, there are solid arguments to be made on both sides of this debate. That's why we tend toward the middle ground—why not do both? Use some of the money you've saved to aggressively prepay your loan, and use some to invest. This way, you can start chipping away at your debt while still gaining important investment experience and making some money to boot.

That's just our two cents. If you're already confident investing or you know that it's important to you to knock out your debt and start fresh, you'll find the tools in this book to help you pursue either path. ∎

Money

Explaining the Power of Compounding

"The most powerful force in the universe is compound interest."

Who said that?

The answer, as you probably didn't guess, is Albert Einstein. Since everyone agrees he was a genius, we're going to go ahead assume that he was bang on the money.

Peruse the chart below and see what happens when you invest $1,000 today and allow it to compound for 30 years, as well as what happens if you wait just a few years before making that same investment.

Case 1: Investment is made now (at time zero), with an 8% interest rate:							
	Year 1	Year 2	Year 3	Year 4	Year 5	>>	Year 30
Investment	$1,000	$–	$–	$–	$–	>>	$–
Value @ Year End	$1,080	$1,166	$1,260	$1,360	$1,469	>>	$10,063
Case 2: Investment is made 3 years later, with an 8% interest rate:							
	Year 1	Year 2	Year 3	Year 4	Year 5	>>	Year 30
Investment	$–	$–	$–	$1,000	$–	>>	$–
Value @ Year End	$–	$–	$–	$1,080	$1,166	>>	$7,988
Difference:	26%						

The first thing you'll notice above is that your money grows year after year without your doing anything but making the initial investment. Not only do you earn interest—in this case 8%—on your initial investment, but as your investment grows each year (from the interest you receive), you also earn money on that additional interest. Shake, shake, shake your money-maker!

As you can see, the earlier you start to invest, the better off you'll be. If instead of investing $1,000 today (start of year one) you wait just three years and invest that same $1,000 at the start of year four, by year 30 you'll end up with $2,000 (26%) less, assuming you're making both investments over the same 30-year period. To earn the same return by investing in year four that you would have earned had you started in year one, you would need to invest an extra $260, or 26% more money. Three years can make a pretty sizeable difference in the investing world.

Investing for Short-Term Purchases (i.e., Liquidity with Some Interest)

For investment rookies, the easiest and least risky way to get in the game is a **savings account**. Money may not grow on trees, but it certainly does in banks. Determine a minimal amount of cash you can afford to stash away in a savings account each month (this can be $1, $50, or even $100—whatever you can stomach). Now, sit back and watch it turn into a new flat-screen TV. Savings accounts are best suited for situations in which you know that you'll be making a purchase in the near-ish future but need to keep the cash accessible in case you want it for something else soon.

Because they are so low-risk and easy, it's not surprising that savings accounts ultimately have their limitations as investment vehicles. It's great to earn interest instead of letting your money sit around getting moldy, but the interest rates on savings accounts aren't always competitive with other forms of investing. Still, the reason they're popular is you get a rare combo—guaranteed interest and the ability to get at your money when you want it. See page 241 for more on savings accounts.

Investing for the Medium-Term (i.e., Mostly Liquid with Medium Interest)

You may have heard parents or talking heads throwing around the phrase "fixed-income investments," but if you're anything like we were when we left college, you probably aren't quite sure what it means. Unlike a stock that varies in price and has liquidity because you can sell it at any time (see page 265 for more on stocks), a fixed-income investment is one that pays you a set amount of money over a set amount of time. Essentially, you're entering into a contract; you provide an entity with cash today, and that entity is obligated to return that money to you at a certain point in the future (i.e., the maturity date), plus make periodic interest payments to you during the life of the investment. While most fixed-income assets are designed to be held until their maturity date, you can sell them in the fixed-income markets the way you would sell a stock. However, since there are fewer buyers of fixed-income assets, they usually aren't as liquid as other investment options.

CERTIFICATE OF DEPOSITS (CDs) provide a happy medium between putting your money in a savings account and storing it for retirement. You can purchase a CD (no, not the Miley Cyrus kind) from your bank or investment brokerage firm, and it will provide a higher interest rate than a savings account. The hitch here is that you must keep your cash tied up in the CD until it reaches its maturity date (although often you can redeem your money prior to maturity in exchange for paying a penalty). CDs come with maturities ranging from six months to ten years, so you should be able to find one that meets your time horizon. Just know that shorter-horizon CDs tend to have similar rates to savings accounts; you need to dig into long-range maturities for it to make sense. So when considering a CD, you need to make sure that it not only pays off an interest rate that is attractive to you, but will also provide you with your cash back at the time you need it. Conveniently, CDs are also FDIC-insured (see page 251).

GOVERNMENT BONDS, NOTES, AND BILLS (all also known as "treasuries") are similar to CDs in that you need to hold onto them until their maturity date in order to guarantee the stated returns rate. This period can range from less than two years (bills), to between two and ten years (notes), to 30 years (bonds). The difference between treasuries and CDs is that treasuries are considered to be the safest investment in the world because for you to lose your money, the U.S. Government would have to default (if this occurs, you'll have a lot more to worry about than losing the money on your bond—head for the border!). Extra security, as usual, means lower rates of return.

However, the good news is that treasuries also have a market value, so there are instances where you can sell them for profit before they reach maturity.

Like the nation at large, cities also sell fixed-income investments in the form of municipal bonds (a.k.a., munis). They provide a higher return than treasuries (and are tax-free, which is huge), but it's more likely for a city to default on its bonds than the country. It's rare, but it has happened—in the '70s, Cleveland defaulted on its municipal bonds.

Treasuries and munis are a great compromise for people who want higher interest rates

---

Tips & Tricks:
Risk vs. Reward

 Investing is the art of earning the highest return (or interest) on your money and making sure that your cash is available when you need it. But keep in mind that every investment option also has downsides. For example, higher returns are provided to you at higher risk. And longer-term investments, while usually less risky and with higher interest rates, mean the money isn't available to you on demand (i.e., it's "less liquid"). So when you consider any investment option, you need to be sure that there's a fair trade-off between risk and return, and liquidity is always an issue.

than savings accounts and CDs but don't want to risk their money in the stock market. You can get higher returns elsewhere, but you also stand to lose a lot more if the market doesn't go your way or a company goes bust.

On that note, it should be mentioned that large companies also issue corporate bonds that pay higher interest rates than government issues, but these are riskier and harder to evaluate than more vanilla government bonds (e.g., who knew in early 2008 that Lehman Brothers would cease to exist?). The benefit of buying a bond rather than a stock is that you're guaranteed a return since you are technically lending the company money. In addition, bondholders are considered to be senior to stockholders, which essentially means that in the event a company goes bankrupt, the company is forced by law to repay all of its bondholders in full before a single stockholder gets a penny.

Where can I buy this stuff? The quick answer is from a bank, TreasuryDirect.gov, or your brokerage firm, although you can only purchase corporate bonds from a brokerage firm (see page 270). To value a bond you use bond math, which is called "bond math" and not "simple math" for a reason. Instead of trying to provide a comprehensive overview here, we suggest you seek assistance from a service representative or adviser at whichever place you plan to purchase them from. Just keep in mind that since fixed-income investments aren't liquid, the maturity date for your investment should be before the date at which you'd need the cash. If you want to sell a bond before the maturity date, the easiest place to turn to is a brokerage firm. But again, it isn't always as easy to sell a bond as it is to sell a stock, and we suggest that you talk to a service representative or advisor.

Last, be sure that the actual interest you'll earn on the bond will outweigh your other investment options, and that you think the entity from which you're purchasing it will be around when payout time rolls around (clearly, the government should be…but will Citigroup?). If you do want to take a deep dive into fixed-income investing, then we suggest that you read the tutorials at TheStreet.com and Yahoo! Finance, or hold your breath for *Gradspot.com's Guide to Personal Finance*. (Whenever the $500k advance is ready, so are we!)

Investing for Retirement: 401(k)s and IRAs

Saving for retirement is the most important type of saving you can do. One day, you'll stop working but the bills won't stop coming, nor will your grandson's demands for PlayStation 25. Thankfully, Uncle Sam has lent us a hand and set up special types of accounts for retirement planning: 401(k)s and IRAs. These are the ultimate long-term investment vehicles, and while it's tough to think that far

Money

ahead when you can't even decide what to have for lunch, we recommend giving them some serious thought. Why? Social Security aside, statistics show that you'll need about 70% of your pre-retirement income to maintain a similar standard of living (and we do assume you don't want to retire in order to lower your standard of living). In other words, if you're making $150,000 a year, retire at age 60, and live to be 90, then you'll need to have saved $100,000 for each year of retirement, or $3,000,000 total. That seems like a lot, but you have the most important element of retirement savings on your side—youth. The sooner you start, the better.

Employer-Sponsored Retirement Accounts: 401(k)s

A 401(k) is a conservative and diversified investment account set up by your employer. It doesn't require any action on your part aside from selecting some basic options when you first begin. Each year you'll be given an opportunity to invest part of your paycheck in the 401(k), and that money goes directly from your salary to your 401(k) before being taxed. Hence, any contribution you make to your 401(k) is tax-free. For example, if you pull in $45,000 a year and choose to contribute $2,000 of it, the whole $2,000 goes into your 401(k), and you will only be taxed on $43,000 of your salary at year-end. Taxes on the $2,000, as well as any investment earnings you make over time, are paid later when you withdraw the money at retirement age. At that point, your tax rate will most likely be less than it is today. By deferring taxes, you also get to put away more money *now*, and as we've seen from the power of compounding interest, that extra dough will grow significantly.

In addition to the tax benefits of 401(k)s, they are a great investment option because employers often "match" a portion of your contribution, sometimes even all of it—*cha*-ching! **If your employer matches your 401(k) contribution, we think you should max it out every time to squeeze as much free money out of the situation as possible.** You can invest up to $15,000 a year in a 401(k), and if that becomes $60,000, then you'll be big pimpin' at the retirement home. The only hitch with 401(k)s is that you can't withdraw the funds until you are 59.5 years old, unless you want to pay a 10% penalty. Although 401(k)s are set up by employers, there are no restrictions on moving them from one employer to the next, or even maintaining control of them in between jobs.

Money

Self-Funded Retirement Accounts: IRAs

If your employer doesn't offer a 401(k) or you're self-employed, IRAs are for you—the "I" stands for individual. While contributions aren't tax-free, withdrawals are, which isn't so bad since you pay taxes on a small amount of cash today that will grow to be ten times its size down the line. The icing on the cake is that if you need to withdraw funds before the age of 59.5, there's no 10% penalty like with 401(k)s. There are many different types of IRAs, but ROTH IRAs, which usually require you to make less than $65,000 per year, are the current cool kids on the block. You can set up ROTH IRAs through banks and brokerage firms (see page 270).

Let's assume that you've decided to heed not only our word but the advice of just about every financial professional and stash cash away in a 401(k) or IRA. What next? In the case of a 401(k) you might not have a choice as to where the cash is invested—your employer may automatically put it into diversified funds, or you'll have a set of pretty limited options. When it comes to IRAs, however, you have to pick where the money is distributed. So keep reading if you want our two cents about where you could invest it. (Just don't pull the rookie mistake of making a contribution to your IRA and then not investing; you actually have to manage it!)

Long-Term Investing: Stocks & Funds

So you'd like your money to earn more than the almost risk-free returns provided by savings accounts, treasuries, or CDs? Then there's a world of options for you to consider: traditional stocks, mutual funds, index funds, electronically traded funds (ETFs), target-date funds, and so much more. (Of course, if you feel really lucky, punk, there's also the lottery. But rumor has it that your odds of being killed in a car accident on the way to purchasing a lottery ticket are higher than the odds of actually

Money

> **Hazard:**
> **The tax consequences of investing**
>
> Don't forget that any money you make on an investment is taxable, whether it's interest earned from a savings account or dividends from a stock. So while you might be earning 1.5% interest in an online savings account, just remember that after taxes, it'll be more like 1%, at most. There are, however, tax-free options such as municipal bonds (see 262) and tax-advantaged retirement accounts (p. 263). Ultimately, you shouldn't avoid taxable earnings just for the sake of giving the middle finger to the IRS—just make sure you factor them into any investment decision you make.

winning.) These investing options (minus the lotto) should come into play when you're dealing with retirement investing. Whichever route you choose, there are usually incentives for some degree of patience and stability with each of these options. For example, if you sell within a year of buying a stock, you will be taxed 50% on your profits, whereas the tax rate drops to 15% after a year. So don't spend all day watching *Mad Money* and driving yourself crazy, because patience is the name of the game for casual investors. If you diversify and maintain a long-term outlook, you can avoid the sick-to-your-stomach feeling caused by riding the Dow Jones minute by minute.

The Stock Market

Despite the pandemonium set off by the credit crunch and epic stock market crash that followed, we still think (as do the majority of finance professionals) that the stock market is a phenomenal long-term investment. The average annual return on the stock market, when reviewed over the long-term, has been 8%. The caveat here, however, is that over any short period (i.e., one or a few years), gains and losses have been anywhere between +20% and −20% (or more!). The key with the stock market is to invest in it for the long haul. If you're skeptical, then see the chart below of the S&P 500, a main index and proxy for the market at large.

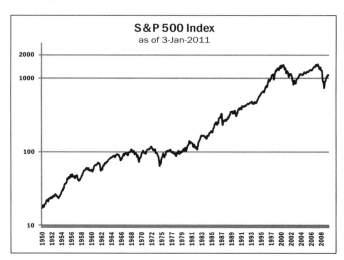

What you should take away from this chart is that over *any* 30-year period (roughly the number of years until you'll retire), the index increased dramatically. Hopefully this illustrates why as a long-term, conservative investor, you'll greatly increase the value of your assets if you invest in the market. In fact, since time has been shown to mitigate the extreme short-term fluctuations associated with the stock market by all but guaranteeing long-term 8% annual returns, most savvy recent graduates will invest all of their retirement money in the market. (When you get older—think forties, fifties, and sixties—and will no longer be in a position to stomach the short-term +20%/−20% swings, you can then take a more risk-averse approach and begin to transition your money into bonds and CDs...but, in our opinion, that doesn't make sense today.) The only way that the approach of investing in the stock market today would fail would be if, down the line, there were major problems with the U.S.—like nuclear winter–type problems. But if you're the patriotic type and believe that the U.S. will be just fine by the time you retire, then consider making long-term investments in the market.

Unfortunately, a lot of people got hit hard by the credit crisis because they did not take this long-term view of the market. They owned stock that plummeted in value over a short period of time, but instead of waiting for the market to rebound, they got nervous and pulled their money out. Now that the market has rebounded a bit (at least as of the writing of this book), those people are kicking themselves because they lost the opportunity for their investments to increase again. They locked in their loss and now they have to start all over again—maybe with less cash than they started with!

Obviously, it is possible to make a lot of money in the short term by playing the stock market. But unless you are a trader or you're best buds with Steve Jobs and he tells you when new products are dropping before announcing it to the public, it's very risky and time-consuming. So let's be clear that we're talking about long-term investing—if you want to get into gambling then turn on the talk shows and roll the short-term stock market dice.

Stocks

What is a stock?

Simply put, a stock is a small ownership stake in a company (another word you might hear for it is *equity*). Thus, if you buy one share of Google stock, you immediately become a partial owner of Google, right next to Sergey and Larry. (Needless to say, they have about a gajillion more shares than you do, but whatever—it's kind of a cool thought.) Each share has a value, known as its trading value or stock price, which is the amount that people are willing to buy and sell the stock for on the market. Since each share represents fractional ownership in a company, each share's value fluctuates each day based on news regarding how the company is doing. When a little start-up becomes a huge company like Starbucks, anyone who owns shares stands to earn a pretty penny. Welcome to the American Dream!

Some companies also offer **dividends** (i.e., optional quarterly payments) to their shareholders. These tend to be the more mature companies—like, say, General Electric—whose stocks have less room to grow. Some dividends can be pretty sizable. For example, Verizon pays yearly dividends equal to approximately 4–5% of the value of each share, which means you can earn 4–5% annually on each share you own, assuming the stock price itself doesn't decrease. If you're conservative, a dividend can be a very good reason to buy and hold a more mature stock because it serves as a middle ground between a riskier, non–dividend-paying stock and a fixed-income investment.

How to Buy Stocks

Now that you know how stocks work, the final question is where to buy them. In order to purchase stocks, you need to sign up with a brokerage firm (p. 270). To look up a stock's price, visit your brokerage firm's website, or check stock trackers like Finance.Yahoo.com and Finance.Google.com. All of these places will have a field to enter the stock's ticker (a one- to four-letter abbreviation of the company name) or the company's name. From there, you'll be provided with the stock's current price, charts showing past prices, news about the company, and all sorts of other information. For more in-depth analysis, you can also check the research section of your brokerage firm's website, as well as countless websites for investors. If you dig into this stuff, just keep in mind that research can be biased or flat-out wrong, and as you'll learn in the next section, we highly discourage investing in any single stock anyway.

The Importance of Diversification

As the old saying goes, you should never put all of your eggs in one basket. The same maxim applies to stocks. You can diversify in many ways—among different stocks, different business sectors, and even different countries, particularly if you're one of those people who thinks "China's on the rise." You can also diversify amongst different asset classes, including stocks, bonds, CDs, real estate, baseball cards, and even cash. It all comes back to the same fundamental idea: if you spread your money around to many places, each one might not offer as much growth potential, but at least you can't lose it all at once. Just make sure you don't diversify to the point of "Default Credit Swaps," because while we don't understand them, apparently neither did the majority of Wall Street—or the world. ■

The Easy Way to Diversify:
Index, ETF, Mutual, and Target-Date Funds

These investment vehicles are valuable because they automatically diversify for you. Nothing personal, but as a recent grad, you probably don't have the skill set to figure out the accuracy of a stock price, let alone determine which companies/industries/countries will provide the best balance for your portfolio. Thus, if you're investing any significant amount of money (and that means significant by your standards, not anyone else's), we suggest you let the funds and the professionals do their thing.

Index Funds/ETFs

The Dow Jones Industrial Average, NASDAQ Composite, and all of those other names you hear on the news are **stock market indices.** Basically, these indices group together a whole bunch of stocks that represent some portion of an economy; for example, the S&P 500 Index reflects the stock prices of 500 of the leading large-cap companies in the U.S. They are used as shorthand for the health of the economy at large, or the part of the economy they reflect. While you can't invest in the indices themselves, you can invest in their proxies, called Index Funds. For example, an index fund could track the S&P 500 (that index fund's ticker is "SPY"). As the S&P 500 rises, so does the value of SPY, and vice versa.

ETFs don't necessarily track a public index, but they create indices of their own based on specific and publicly disclosed criteria and guidelines. Computers are then set up to automatically alter the portfolio every day, week, month, or year, to ensure it meets the preset criteria and guidelines.

Both index funds and ETFs can be purchased through your brokerage firm, but you'll have to pay a pretty nominal cost of around 0.1%. Just keep in mind that even if you purchase an index fund or ETF, you still might not be diversified enough for your liking.

Mutual Funds

Mutual funds are like index funds and ETFs, except they are actively managed by humans rather than computers. So which do you trust more?! One consideration is that computers are willing to work for crap wages, whereas humans need to make a living. Thus, mutual funds come with fees up to 1.5% higher. Moreover, studies have shown that over 50% of actively-managed

Money

mutual funds underperform the market indices, so the computers have some reasonably solid ground to stand on. This isn't to say that people haven't gotten rich by investing in mutual funds; they certainly have. And despite the potential drawbacks, most people invest in mutual funds because they feel more comfortable with the human component (at least you have someone to yell at when things don't go well!).

Opening a Brokerage/Investment Account

Okay, now that you know what you're getting yourself into, it's time to figure out how to actually buy these stocks and funds. Online brokerages enable you to buy stocks, bonds, and most of the funds we discussed above. They can also house your IRA. Some even have associated perks, like the interest-bearing checking accounts we mentioned on page 241. Grad-friendly online brokerage firms to check out include Charles Schwab, TD Ameritrade, E*Trade, Fidelity, and Scottrade.

The only problem with online brokerage firms is that while most will provide you with research and a staff that can answer basic questions (e.g., how do I buy a government bond?), they won't offer any individualized advice. It will be on you to get familiar with the markets and your options before diving in headfirst. A full-service brokerage firm like Smith Barney can provide one-on-one guidance, but needless to say, you'll have to pay for the privilege of having someone tell you what to do with your money. Since you're probably not making any super out-of-the-box moves as a recent grad, we don't think it's necessary to go full-service (and you might not even meet the minimum required to invest with one of these firms).

A Final Word on Investing

Personal finance is a mammoth subject, and it's easy to see why there are countless books available on the subject (from classics like *The Intelligent Investor* to contemporary works like *Rich Dad, Poor Dad*), not to mention all the websites out there like TheStreet.com, MotleyFool.com, and SmartMoney.com. What we've tried to do here is to provide a basic outline of the investment ecosystem. You should now have all the tools you need to get started, but ultimately sound investing is about experience. Start small to get over the hump—eventually you'll gain the confidence and knowhow to be a little more adventurous. Look for additional guidance from family members and friends who you know are into the markets, and continue to educate yourself by reading and visiting websites. We also have some more resources for you at gradspot.com/money. Whatever you do, just remember that any small losses now are balanced out by the experience you gain for the future, when you'll have a more significant chunk of change to play with.

Your Investment Cheat Sheet

As promised at the beginning of the chapter, we want to provide an easy breakdown of the actions you should take with your hard-earned cash. To whit, here's a quick investment cheat sheet, organized by the amount of money you have available to save and invest.

$0 ᴛᴏ $999. If you're in this range, you're probably either living at home or living paycheck to paycheck. Ain't nothing wrong with that. Find a checking account with no fees and you should be all set for the time being.

$1,000 ᴛᴏ $4,999. With a few grand floating around, you should set up an online savings account so you'll earn at least 1–2% in interest. (That's $50–100 of free money each year!)

$5000, ᴛᴏ $9,999. Get it in! With this type of money at your fingertips, you should consider getting some CDs from your bank in order to squeeze another percent or two in interest out of your savings. You should also make sure you're beginning to make some small investments into a retirement account. At the very least, open one up so you're ready to roll when the next big cash influx comes your way.

$10,000+. Congratulations! You're working with some serious cheese—it's time to open a brokerage account (e.g., TD Ameritrade). An index fund (e.g., SPY) is a good way to get started. Don't be timid; most brokerages grant you ten free trades or so, so you can buy something and change your mind next week. The important thing is that you gain experience researching an investment option and clicking "buy." It's fascinating to watch your investment gain or lose $5 in value each day, like a little money hamster. Eventually, though, it gets kind of boring—or nerve-racking. That's when you know you're an investor! Oh, and by the way: If you're in this range, don't forget to continue adding to your retirement account. ∎

Building a Financial Management System

If you've read everything in this chapter thus far, then you should have a grasp on what you need to know to effectively manage your finances. But it's one thing to "plan" to do it and quite another to actually do it. So how are you going to follow through? Ramit Sethi, the finance blogger and author of *I Will Teach You to Be Rich*, suggests setting up an automated finance system. And we cosign this approach for anyone who likes the concept behind the Showtime Oven—"set it and forget it!"—and who isn't afraid of running all of their finances through the Internet.

Essentially, his system takes the budget you've settled upon (i.e., how much money you want to divert towards debt repayment, nights out, saving, etc.) and automatically allocates the appropriate amounts to your different accounts each month. For example, your paycheck goes to your checking account through direct deposit, your automatic bill pay settings on your checking account distribute checks to the relevant places, a certain amount automatically gets redirected to your savings account, and so on and so forth...you get the idea. Your 401(k) is left out because that money gets deducted before you get your paycheck, but everything else gets dealt with automatically, and you're left with the money you've set aside to actually spend at your discretion. And as long as you take a second to check your bills and statements before the auto-payment gets fired off, you should be all good.

Clearly, there's a lot more to the system, and we'd highly recommend checking out Sethi's book and website for more tips. The fact that you barely have to think once you've set it up is awesome, but what we like most is the philosophy behind the system. It's driven by the idea that instead of spending every dime that comes your way, you should divvy it up amongst investments, savings, bill payments, debt repayment, *and* disposable income. Whether you use the tools of the 'net or create your own system doesn't really matter. The important thing is that you have a plan for your money. It doesn't have to be written in stone, but at least it's something to build on as you start making even more money and creating a financial foundation for yourself.

Money

Taxes

Before we even know what a receipt looks like, it's ingrained in our young minds that "Tax Day" is the worst day of the year—even worse than January 1st, which is inevitably depressing. But there's really nothing to lose sleep over. Not only are you smart enough to do your taxes, but you also have it easier than most given that you presumably have nothing more than a modest salary and a little bit of income from savings and investment accounts. That said, don't treat your tax forms like a school assignment and start at midnight the night before they're due. This is more important than letter grades—it's about dollars and cents.

There are really only two ways to tackle taxes: hire a professional or do them yourself. The D.I.Y. approach is not that taxing (pun intended!), but the problem is you may miss out on some of the tax savings that a hired professional could find for you. Given that a professional at H&R Block can walk you through your tax return for as little as $75 (treat the fee like insurance against messing it up on your own, not to mention that you might make that money back in deductions), we suggest the following strategy: hire a tax preparer for the first go around (p. 276), but pay attention to the process, and take notes so you can pick up the reins in subsequent years. Whichever route you choose, here are a few things to keep in mind.

> *Tips & Tricks:*
> **Figuring out whom you owe**
>
> For recent grads cutting ties with their parents' tax return and moving to new states, the question of whom you owe (and who is going to pay) can be a tricky one. First and foremost, have a discussion with your parents to make sure they are not still claiming you as a dependent. You don't want to double-file, and they won't receive the W-2 form from your employer if you have started working. Next, think about where you have lived and worked in the past year. You will always have to pay federal taxes, so that's a given. However, you also have to pay the state where you are a resident, as well as the state where you work (if they are the same, then clearly you only have to file once). Note that some states take no personal income tax from residents (e.g., Alaska, Florida, Washington). If you've moved around a lot, you may want to check in with an accountant or tax pro to make sure you're not leaving anyone out or double-paying anything that's unnecessary.

What You're Actually Taxed On

It's very simple (okay, fine—we're over simplifying—but you'll get the point). You're taxed on your gross income less any adjustments and deductions (eg. student debt interest, IRA contributions, etc.), and exemptions. This figure is called your Taxable Income (TI).

Tax Deductions

Deductions and adjustments enable you to decrease the amount of taxes you owe by decreasing your taxable income. To whet your appetite, try this on for size: assuming your income is less than $65,000, you should be able to deduct up to $2,500 in student-loan interest. Here's another: If you move a significant distance for a new job after graduation, the relocation expenses may be deductible. So in other words, if your TI was $50,000 and you had $5,000 of deductions, you'd only pay taxes on $45,000. Another way to look at this is that the amount of taxes you'll have to pay is decreased by your total deductions times your tax rate. (That's as hard as the math gets.) Deductions come in all shapes and sizes, so it's worth browsing the chart on page 275 and poking around IRS.gov to see if you might be eligible for any before shelling out for a tax pro. However, good tax preparers should be well-versed in all of these tricks, and might see things you might not. You just need to maintain a paper trail (e.g., check, receipt, email) for everything you purchase that may be deductible. If you say you gave $1,000 in cash to a charity, for example, you have to verify that donation to get a deduction. You can't just tell the IRS to "trust you."

Keep Good Records

A modicum of vigilance during the calendar year can go a long way toward making tax day manageable. Despite what you've seen in films, it is not wise to show up in an accountant's office with a duffle bag full of random receipts. So, what do you need to keep? First and foremost, your employer, as well as many of the organizations with which you do business (e.g., bank, brokerage firm), will send you forms at the end of the year that will be essential come tax time. But depending on your situation, you may need more than that as well. The following chart includes the most relevant tax forms and where to get them. Having these items in line will help you avoid a late filing and penalties of 5% each month past the due date. (Note: If the reason you're not paying on time is because you're low on fundage, arrange for a monthly payment plan with the IRS to avoid the late fees.)

What	Who	Where to Get It
W2 Form from Employer (Annual Salary)	Anyone who is employed full time	Your company must provide this to you
1099 Misc (Freelance Earnings)	Anyone who has freelanced and earned an aggregate in excess of $600 from one source	Each entity who paid you more than $600 for the year must provide you with one
1099 Int (Investment Earnings)	Anyone who has a bank account, stock portfolio, or other investments	Your bank, investment company, and other institutions will each mail you one
1099 Div (Dividend Earnings)	Anyone who owns an investment that pays dividends	The dividend payer will send this to you
W2-G (Gambling Earnings)	Anyone who struck it rich at the casino or in the lottery	All depends upon where you won, but you should receive this from the casino or lotto authority
1098-E (Student Debt Interest Payment)	Anyone who has student debt	Your lender should provide you with this
1098 (Mortgage Interest Payments)	Anyone who has taken out a mortgage	Your lender or mortgage agent will send this to you
Moving Expenses (can write off)	Anyone who has moved in the past year	You must keep your receipts
Medical Expenses (can write off)	Anyone who is paying for COBRA, prescription drugs, glasses, or other medical expenses	You must maintain your own receipts
Job-Hunting Expenses (can write off)	Anyone who has looked for a job	You must maintain your own receipts
Charitable Donations (can write off)	Anyone who has donated to a government-recognized charity organization	You will receive an official receipt from each recognized charity

Money

Fork in the Road: Taxes (Hire a Professional vs. DIY)

Hiring a Professional

Sometimes you've got to spend money to save money. Such is the case when you buy one of those travel fanny packs that goes under your pants, and also when you pay a tax preparer to work his or her magic and reveal tax loopholes you never knew existed. When it comes to finding a pro, H&R Block is the go-to for most people who don't have exceptionally complicated tax returns—their people are affordable and reliable; they offer the flexibility to work online, on the phone, or in-person; and they should teach you all the tricks you need to go D.I.Y. with confidence next time. However, you can also check the Yellow Pages for tax preparers, ask coworkers for recommendations, or just hand everything off to your parents' accountant if you're really lucky. An added benefit of hiring a professional is that you're less likely to miss the dreaded April 15 deadline or make a mistake.

Do It Yourself

If you've just got a W-2 form from work and a few 1099 forms from your savings and investment accounts, you might think you can handle your taxes on your own. More than likely you're right, but you probably still need a little more than a calculator and a pen.

The most common option for filing on your own is to pick up some tax preparation software. It shouldn't run more than $30 and will make the process much smoother and less shady. Turbo Tax by Quicken makes filing your taxes as easy as completing an online survey—fill in the blanks and let the computer go to work. H&R Block At Home can be accessed via H&R Block's website and is the cheapest option (starting at $15), but it can be confusing for more involved returns.

If your adjusted gross income is under $56,000, you can access some free tax filing resources through the government's "Free File" program. One is actually H&R Block's "H&R Block Free Online + E-File" service, and another is the humorously named TaxSlayer.com. Check out IRS.gov/efile for a full list of options and directions for using them. Again, just remember that these resources will only help you with your federal return, so you'll still have to deal with state taxes when you're done. (Note: In a few states, these services will offer free state returns as well, but it's not the norm.) They also might not point out deductions like the pay version of H&R Block At Home, so either do your research beforehand or pay the extra money to make sure you don't miss anything.

With the help of one of these programs or websites, you should only have to commit two to three hours to this endeavor once you've pulled all of your forms together. Before you wrap things up, sign up for electronic funds transfer with the IRS so that they get your money quicker (and refund you quicker as well) and to ensure nothing gets lost in the mail.

> *Smart Money:*
> **Phone your friend VITA**
>
> If you have low-to-moderate income (generally, $42,000 and below), the good folks at the Volunteer Income Tax Assistance Program (VITA) will lend a hand with your tax return, for free. For more information, visit Vita-Volunteers.org or call 1-800-829-1040.

Money

Chapter VIII: Cars & Commuting

Cars

In order to be the consummate grad about town, it's sometimes necessary to have a car. How else are you going to get to work, pick up your furniture at Ikea, and still make an 8:30 rez at CPK (California Pizza Kitchen)? Without a ride, it can be difficult to achieve this type of mobility.

In this chapter, we'll cover all the auto basics whether you're considering buying a car or already own one. From looking for new and used cars to negotiating like a pro, comparison shopping for insurance policies, and staying safe on the road, we'll help steer you in the right direction.

 # The $20,000 Question: Do You Need A Car?

Unlike that slick talking, suit-wearing, pony-tailed man or woman at the dealership, we're not here to pressure you into getting a car. Sure, purchasing a vehicle may seem like a no-brainer to help cover your transportation needs, but keep in mind convenience costs money. Cars are usually the biggest monthly expense besides rent for fledgling graduates (and certainly the biggest purchase for a non-house-owning twentysomething), so make sure you know all your options before throwing your savings into that sweet new ride.

Let's break down the math: A typical month of car ownership can run well in excess of $600 once you add up the car payment ($350), a few gas fill-ups ($100), insurance costs ($150), miscellaneous maintenance (a bunch), and fuzzy dice to hang from the rearview mirror ($5). Plus, if you are planning on using a car in cities such as New York City or San Francisco you may quickly discover that exorbitant parking fees and the fact that you never actually drive anywhere defeat the purpose of the investment.

We highly recommend that you take a few days (several in fact) and think very carefully before you allow the *The Fast and the Furious* fourpack and the soulful sound of Tracy Chapman to tempt you into making a purchase that you will soon regret.

If you've thought long and hard and the answer is indeed, "yes," then you've got another question to answer: buy or lease?

Fork In The Road: Buying vs. Leasing

While some of your more OCD friends will probably create models and Excel spreadsheets to determine whether they should lease or buy a car, the decision is not a complex one. You need to consider two factors: 1) How much money can you spend each month on a car (and how much do you expect to be able to spend over the next several years), and 2) Are you the type of person who would be content owning a car for a long time, or are you an A.D.D. type who would rather "try" a new car every two to four years without the hassle of ownership?

BUYING

As far as monthly expenses go, buying a car is the most expensive option, roughly $600/month assuming a new $20k car and a 6% loan or $280/month assuming a $10k used car and an 8% loan. After you're finished with a new or used car (5–10 years), however, you can resell it to earn a cash back bonus. Theoretically, if you purchased a car and then sold it at the end of your loan period, the total expense may be cheaper than the aggregate of the monthly lease payments on multiple vehicles over the same time period (but we urge you to do the math on this one before assuming it to be true in all cases, as resale value will vary by vehicle).

In addition, if you buy a car, you'll have to lend special attention to maintaining it in order to preserve its resale value (e.g., wash and wax it, park it in the shade, change the oil regularly).

For more information on buying a car with financing, see page 291.

• •

LEASING

Did you preorder the iPhone? Do you change your entire wardrobe twice a year? Does having a lower monthly payment *now* (when maybe you have a low-paying job and other expenses to worry about) matter more to you than the notion of long-term value? Do you like to test things out before you buy them? If you answered yes to any of these questions (especially the last one), you may be a leaser. Don't let the personal finance pundits tell you you're a "moron" for wanting to pay more in the long-run for lower monthly payments ($350/month for a new leased car) and a nicer car. The fact that 75% of luxury cars are leased should tell you that you're not alone; so as long as you're aware of the tradeoffs, you should do what you want.

At the end of a lease, you can't sell the car, thus you can't recoup any money—all the dough spent leasing it goes down the drain.

When you lease, all repairs will be under warranty for the term of your lease, whereas when you buy a car, all damage beyond the manufacturer's warranty is an out-of-pocket expense. In addition, there may be yearly mileage limits on a leased vehicle, but you'd only really hit those if you have a super-long commute or took road trips every weekend

For more information on leasing a car, see page 292.

Choosing a Car

After you've decided to lease or buy, it's time to hone in on the lot and see what kind of ride strikes your fancy. Go into the process knowing that it's going to be stressful. We can't mention enough that it is a big decision, and the process isn't as straightforward as buying a toaster. But if you keep a cool head and think through it logically, you'll come out feeling confident in your choice. (If you freak out and buy a Mitsubishi Lancer with racing stripes, we can't really help you out.)

In terms of choosing a specific car, we're not going to sit here and tell you to "buy American" or drive a mini-van. However, it's pretty easy to narrow down the car field from hundreds to about five that are actually in your sweet spot. (For the top five new and used cars for recent grads picked by the editor-in-chief of *Car and Driver*, see page 286.) As you start checking manufacturer websites, reading online reviews, and scanning some dealership lots, keep the following concerns in mind. Be a huge dork and make a checklist if you want—trust us, thinking about these things will make you feel a lot better in the long run than walking into the Lexus showroom with a checkbook and a sheepish grin.

- **Cost.** As is often the case, the first way to narrow your choices is to knock out all the cars you can't afford! A reasonable budget dictates that monthly car payments should not exceed 12–15% of your after-tax income, so break out the calculator and figure out a price range (or use an online car payment calculator, like the one at Bankrate.com). It's important to note that this step is not just about looking at sticker prices. Instead, your concern should be the Total Cost of Ownership (TCO), which is an estimate of how much you'll spend over the life of a car. Take the models you're interested in and plug them into Edmunds.com's "True Cost to Own^{SM}" pricing system, which will provide a five-year cost breakdown for taxes, fuel, maintenance, insurance, and more. Clearly these are estimates, but the process is useful for revealing hidden costs, like the fact that a certain vehicle can reasonably be expected to cost you $1,000 in repairs three years down the line. Then go to page 291 to read more about financing, which will determine your upfront costs (i.e., down payment) and monthly payments (determined by the interest rate on your loan).

- **Insurance implications.** Related to the cost question is insurance (see page 294), which is required unless you want to go to jail. While you probably won't choose a specific policy until after you've sealed the deal on a car, it should factor into your choice rather significantly. Insurance fees are based not only on you as a driver, but also on the specific car you own. Vehicles with higher horsepower or cars that have a greater probability of being stolen will draw higher premiums from insurance companies. Used cars also tend to draw higher premiums. The difference may seem negligible, but even $40 a month can add up, so make sure you're factoring insurance into any "monthly cost of ownership" comparisons you make between cars.

- **Safety.** Do you need to drive in an armored tank? No, but that would be awesome. Do you need a car that handles well in the rain and isn't prone to flipping over on the freeway? Yes, that would probably be smart. Listen to mama bear on this one—a safe car is a cool car! Do some research to make sure you're not buying a death trap. Kelley Blue Book (kbb.com) allows you to compare safety features and ratings on any make and model, and it's worth checking out Safercar.gov for general vehicle safety information.

- **Specific needs.** Are you going to be stranded in the winter without four-wheel drive? Do you want enough space to handle weekend trips with friends or are you more of a solo road warrior? Are you planning to have a child in the next five years (seriously)? These types of need-based questions will go a lot further toward narrowing down a type of ride (e.g., sedan, SUV, drop-top) than thinking about your favorite color.

- **Reliability and efficiency.** Like a good BFF, a car that's reliable makes all the difference. And just as a lame but trustworthy friend always ends up being better than that cool, extra slick cat who wins you over and then stabs you in the back, a car you don't have to worry about will be a huge weight off your mind. Another concern that's particularly *en vogue* is fuel-efficiency. We've seen the country completely freak out about the future of gas prices, and it's not unlikely that it will happen again. Hybrids (e.g., the Toyota Prius) and other cars with high fuel-efficiency can make a big difference in reducing the overall cost of car ownership because you get more bang for your buck on each tank of gas.

- **Warranty.** A new car warranty is great for mitigating the cost of future problems with the vehicle. Just be careful about marketing ploys that sound sweet but really make no sense. For example, why would you need a "lifetime warranty" on a truck? No one owns a car for that long! (According to J.D. Power and Associates, most consumers get rid of a car five and a half years after they buy it.) It's pretty unlikely that you'll buy a car with major engine or transmission problems that don't show up in the first three to five years, so don't concern yourself with the length of the warranty so much as what aspects of the car it actually covers. As CNN Money advises, "No one should ever buy a car for the warranty alone, but if it is a consideration for you, look past the hype and think about real cars and real life. If you do that, it turns out there really isn't that much to think about."

- **Personal preference.** Don't discount your likes and dislikes. You're gonna have this puppy for a while, so make it count. If you only like Aston Martins, you may have to compromise. But driving a car you love will probably make you pretty happy, so be willing to stretch your budget where it makes sense.

Cars & Commuting

Ten Great Cars for Recent Grads

We asked Eddie Alterman, editor-in-chief of *Car & Driver*, for his top five new and top five used car picks. Can you buy a jalopy for $800 on Craigslist? Of course. But if you're looking for great value and reliability at a reasonable price, check out these options.

New Cars

Honda Fit: The Fit offers a surprising amount of room inside and plenty of oomph from its 1.5-liter four-cylinder engine. Price: $16,000

Mazda 3: Available in sedan or hatchback body styles, the 3 is a solidly built and entertaining back-road companion. Price: $15,000

Volkswagen Golf: This hatchback version of the Jetta sedan is stout, roomy, versatile, and responsive. Price: $19,000

Honda Civic: This fun economy car handles beautifully, gives comfort to people and cargo, and offers faultless build quality. Price: $16,000

Nissan Versa: One of the roomiest entries in the subcompact class, the Versa is basic transportation, but it also offers the most power, with 122 horse power from its 1.8-liter four-cylinder engine. Price: $12,000

Used Cars

Volkswagen GTI: The car that invented the term "hot hatch" is addictive to drive and able to accommodate an unbelievable amount of cargo. Price: $12,000

Mazdaspeed3: Fun galore. This car can hit 155 mph and still leave enough money in your bank account for a few months' rent. Price: $13,000

Mini Cooper: Find a two or three-year-old one, and no one will know the difference. The recent redesign hasn't strayed from the original British Invader. Price: $13,000

Subaru Impreza WRX: All-wheel drive, a rally-bred chassis, and extroverted looks. What's not to love? Price: $15,000

Honda Civic Si: With quick reflexes, unassailable build quality, and a great four-cylinder engine, the Civic Si will be fun for years. Price: $14,000 ■

Hitting the Dealership and Making a Deal

The Internet is only a means to an end—eventually you are going to have to get off your butt and get up close and personal with some cars. As soon as you set foot on the lot, be prepared to get pitched to harder than Albert Pujols with the bases loaded. But it's best to ignore all that jazz. Instead of letting a salesperson work you over, use the following plan of attack to ensure you get the car you want at the best price possible.

Step 1: Visit the dealership for a test drive. To avoid wasting time and getting pushed toward cars you can't afford, schedule an appointment and show up to the dealerships knowing what you want to see (utilize your Internet research here). When you test drive, take a ride that involves a variety of driving situations (e.g., stop and go traffic, tight turns, highway), then gather all the necessary pamphlets and pricing information and get out of there before a wheel falls off the "straight-talk express." The dealer may try to lowball you just to get you to come back, but realize that he or she has no intention of actually selling at that tantalizing price. Anyway, you shouldn't even be thinking about buying yet. The purpose of this visit is to make sure you really like the car, so just walk away if the salesperson tries to pressure you into making an on-the-spot decision.

Step 2: Do your research: After you've found "the one," head back to the lab and run

> ### Smart Money:
> ### Networking your way to a deal
>
>
>
> In Chapter 3, we discussed the enormous value of networking during your job hunt. But out there in the "real world," building relationships can be useful in a lot of ways, not just in terms of your career. It's human nature to help out someone you're connected to (even if indirectly), and in spite of the stereotypes, car dealers are indeed humans. So, while it may be a long shot, it's totally worth seeing if you can network to a dealer in your area. Maybe you played high school sports with the kid of a local Honda dealer. Maybe your parents know someone. Maybe, after putting up a Facebook status message saying, "I'm looking to lease an Audi, anyone know where I can get a good deal?" you'll find out that your cousin used to date an Audi salesman. Because car purchases involve negotiation and fuzzy pricing, any way you can link your personal network with the dealer's will help you out. At the very least, it adds some accountability to the equation—a dealer will be much less likely to screw you over if he or she knows it will make its way back to a mutual acquaintance.

Smart Money:
When to Car Shop

 Knowing the ins and outs of an enemy organization is a key to success in consumer battles. In terms of cars, this means realizing that most car dealerships impose yearly and monthly quotas on their salespeople, so if you shop in December (or at least at the end of the month), you might find yourself the happy beneficiary of some desperate deal making. The same goes for any day that will clearly be a slow one for sales on the car lot. Check the forecast for blizzards, hail storms, hurricanes, and tornadoes—the worse the weather, the better your chances of saving money on a car.

---

the numbers on financing options (see page 291 to understand how financing works). Look up incentives and rebates on manufacturer websites and at Automotive.com, keeping an eye out for deals geared specifically toward recent grads and first-time buyers. Often, you will be offered either a cash rebate or low-interest financing options. Before grabbing the cash, use an online "rebate versus interest" tool to figure out which is the better deal (Edmunds.com has a good one). You can then either call or email local dealers for price comparisons, or get multiple quotes at the same time using Edmunds' "Dealer Locator." Once you've gotten a grasp on the price range, you can go into the final stage....

Step 3: Negotiate. Since you're probably in the market for a pretty common car (as opposed to a 1-of-50 Lamborghini), you have a lot of room to flex your consumer muscles. Never settle for the sticker price. There are two approaches to the negotiating: the in-person method and the stay-at-home method.

- **In-person.** If you're a smooth operator or you can bring a friend/family member who is a bit of a jerk (in a good way), maybe you'll have fun going toe-to-toe with a dealership. It can be an arduous process, but there are certainly examples of success. When you go in, be prepared for the common dealership maneuver of asking what *you* want to pay for the car. They may even say, "Give me a number." Don't be afraid to throw out a lowball offer. For example, if the ticket price is $28K and you offer $22K, you might not get it—but you're a hell of a lot more likely to get it at $26K than if you said you were happy with the original price. For conversations like this one, make sure you're talking to a salesperson who actually has decision-making power, rather than someone who will keep walking into a back room to get a sign-off from some faceless (and potentially evil!) manager. When a conversation does begin to hover around the price you want, don't be afraid to say, "If you give it to me for this price, I will sign right now." This premier league negotiating tactic tells the salesperson you are no longer comparison shopping, and he or she will be inclined to make you happy lest you walk away and never come back.

- **Stay-at-home.** Not the type to run a hard bargain? Find your savior at FightingChance.com. The bootleg feel of this website and all of the talk about a buying "technique" may seem incredibly ominous, but we've heard enough good reviews to be convinced. The blueprint is pretty simple: First, you pay $39.99 for a customized report of the make and model of the car you want. This report tells you exactly what dealerships are paying for the car, thus eliminating the information gap that allows them to overcharge. Armed with this trump card, you literally call or email a bunch of dealerships (maybe 5–15) saying you know how much profit they'll make off a sale and you're ready to sign with whichever one will give you the lowest price. Then, just crack a chocolate milk and chillax while the bidding war ensues. If the $40 you spent at the beginning snags you a $1,000+ discount on a car, you'll feel like a straight-up maven.

Signing the Contract

Once you've got your price nailed down with a dealership, it's time to seal the deal. Unfortunately, there's one more round of BS deflection to get past. Here are some ways to avoid getting screwed over:

- **Get the best deal on financing.** Make sure you know how you are paying for the car and exactly how much it will cost you per month. See page 291 for more on financing.

- **Beware of extras.** Know exactly what features you want, because the salesman will try to throw in as many unnecessary extras as possible.

- **Protect your credit.** Don't allow the dealership to run a credit check using your license or Social Security number before settling on a price, as this information may be used to screw you on incentives and interest rates. However, as we'll discuss in the financing section, your credit will determine the loan terms you can get, so you'll want to know where you stand ahead of time.

✍ **Watch out for the factory fib.** Cars ordered from the factory should not cost more than those in the lot. Also, be careful about letting the salesman locate the car at another dealership; they often charge an unnecessary fee.

✍ **Trust your gut.** You're probably not buying a limited-edition Jaguar. The car you want will still be there tomorrow, and you can find it elsewhere. If anything feels fishy, trust your instincts and walk away. Don't let a salesperson pressure you or toss around jargon you don't understand.

✍ **Read the small print.** Once the papers have been drawn up, feel free to take them away so that you can review them with a fine-toothed comb. Like congressmen, car salesmen have been known to "earmark" a few extra clauses in the final copy.

Congratulations, you are now a car owner! You are probably feeling very protective, and maybe you have even named your car something like "Don Juan DeMarco" or "Desert Storm."

Buying Used Without Getting Abused

The main reasons for buying a used car are either to save money or to achieve a little retro chic on the road. The two things to remember when jumping into the fray are: 1) Used car salesmen have a bad reputation for a reason, and 2) An unreliable used car could end up draining more cash in maintenance and repair fees than a new one. However, not all used cars are jalopies, and when they work out, they are definitely the cheapest options. One obvious but important point is that there's a huge difference between a ten-year-old used car and a two- to four-year-old used car that has only 20–30K miles on it (the average car is driven for 12k miles per year). If you're shopping for value and reliability, you'll be looking at cars in the latter category. To find them, search around at car dealerships (watch enough local network broadcasts, and you'll see the commercials), peruse Craigslist and print classifieds, and check out websites like Carmax. com, ConsumerGuide.com, and AutoTrader.com. To get a sense for fair prices, go to Kelley Blue Book (kbb.com) and enter the year, make, mileage, model, features, the relative condition of the car you want, and your zip code. (The site will also provide local listings for the vehicle you want.)

Once you have the perspective to spot a deal from a rip-off, you can perform some due diligence on the ones that look fairly priced. In addition to accident history, you should research the number of previous owners, past mechanical problems, and maintenance history. Also, find out if the car has ever failed an inspection. Run a vehicle history report at AutoCheck.com using the Vehicle Identification Number. A dealer should provide you a CARFAX vehicle history report, and if it doesn't, you should ask for one. This report includes vital info like accident and damage history, title problems (including salvaged or junked titles), frame damage checks, odometer

> **Tips & Tricks:**
> **How to find the Vehicle Identification Number (VIN)**
>
> This useful number can be found in the following places: the previous driver's insurance card, the car registration, the VIN plate on the driver's side dashboard, and the certificate label on the driver's side doorjamb.

readings (to make sure someone didn't doctor it), accident indicators like airbag deployment, and more. Look for cars that are Certified Pre-Owned (CPO), which means they have been inspected rigorously and are usually covered by a warranty from the manufacturer. CPO cars cost a bit more, but the added warranty and reliability may justify the cost.

Even with all these checks in place, you should always do your own inspection to make sure you don't get a lemon. Be as crazy about this as possible. Sit in every seat, turn on the car and play around with all its features, listen for ominous noises, get out and check all the lights, and so on. If you find anything that wasn't previously discussed and factored into the price, make sure the dealer will fix it at no extra cost to you; in fact, you should even demand they change the contract to say the problems need to be fixed before you have to pay. At the final stage of the sale, never agree to sign an "as is" statement, which means that as soon as you leave the lot the car is solely your responsibility. Instead, you should be given at least 30 days to make sure the car is in good condition.

Purchasing New and Used Cars with Financing

Walking into the car dealership can be pretty intimidating for most recent grads, since looking at the sticker prices alone probably makes it seem like even the fugliest car on the lot is out of your league. But that's where financing comes into play. Automobile financing is when you take out a personal loan to purchase an automobile, thus transforming that heart-stopping $20,000 into

a manageable down payment and a monthly payment with interest. Unless you happen to have $20Gs ready to deploy right now, financing options are crucial to your purchase. The car payment plan you negotiate will determine both the total cost of the car over the long term and, more to the point, how you'll pay it off each month. Typically, the way it works is you make the down payment, pay sales taxes upfront or roll them into your loan, and then pay an interest rate determined by your loan company. The first payment is due a month after you sign your contract.

The most important thing you need to know about car loans is that you don't have to take the one offered to you through the car company, so you should comparison shop aggressively. Check with your local bank, Edmunds.com, and Bankrate.com to see what terms and rates you can get. (Note: a used car loan will always carry a higher interest rate than a new car loan.) It may end up that you can get the best deal through the car company, but don't assume. The second key to financing is that, as with all loans, your credit will affect the interest rates you can get. And it makes a real difference. Say you've got a $20,000 car, and you're going to pay it off over four years with an 8% interest rate. That means you pay $488.26 a month. But if a worse credit score boosts your interest rate just 2%, you pay an extra $20 per month. And over the course of the loan, you'll end up spending about $1,000 more on the car. While it's not a deal-breaker, remember how large you can grow $1,000 through a conservative investment vehicle? (See page 260 for a refresher.) If you don't know your credit score or can't fathom why the hell this has anything to do with buying a Civic, go to page 227.

Leasing Cars

On the surface, it's pretty simple. When you lease, you make monthly payments in return for the privilege of driving a car a maximum number of miles over an agreed-upon time period, generally two to four years. In some ways it's like a super long-term car rental, but what you're really paying for is the *depreciation*

Cars & Commuting

of the car over the period you drive it—in other words, the difference between a vehicle's original value and its value at lease-end, also known as its **residual value.** (Not surprisingly, the best lease deals are on cars with the lowest depreciation ratings. More often than not, Japanese and German cars trump American cars in this respect. As a rule of thumb, cars with 24-month residuals equal to at least 50% of their original Manufacturer's Suggested Retail Price value are solid deals.)

You don't need an advanced math degree to figure it out how the actual monthly payment on a lease is determined, and it's worth understanding the basics so you can spot a sheisty salesperson when you see one. There are two elements to a lease payment: the **depreciation charge** and the **finance charge**. To figure out the monthly depreciation charge, start with the **capitalized cost,** or "cap cost," of the car. This figure is not the Manufacturer's Suggested Retail Price, but rather the final price you negotiate with the dealer (hopefully less than the MSRP). Then, simply subtract the residual value and divide by the number of months in your lease contract. And *voilà*, you've just figured out how the leasing company is going to charge you for depreciation.

The finance charge is just like the interest you pay on a loan—in the eyes of the leasing company, leasing you a car is just like loaning you money, so it wants you to pay for tying up its funds. To calculate the finance charge, add the cap cost and residual value, then multiply by the money factor. "What the hell's the money factor?" you say. It's the interest rate divided by 2,400. "Why do I add the cap cost and residual value—isn't that like paying double?" No, this equation is just an easy shortcut for a more complicated calculation. Unless you're really into math, we suggest you just use it and not ask questions!

In addition to the depreciation and finance charges, there will also be an acquisition fee when you first get the car, typically in the range of $600 to $1,000.

The reason it's important to know all of this is so that you can check that everything you negotiate with the dealer actually makes it into the contract. Predatory salespeople take advantage by agreeing to your offer (and maybe even pretending they're giving you some awesome deal because you're so cool and smart), but then—whoops—the agreed-upon price is not actually reflected in the lease contract. Unless you're some sort of mental mathlete, you're not going to catch this trickery unless you do your own calculations and make sure everything adds up.

Unfortunately, fudged leasing charges are just one of the many ways dealerships can try to pull a fast one on you if you don't understand the elements that make up a lease payment. To further protect yourself, check out Automotive.com's "Car Leasing FAQs" (link via gradspot.com/book), which includes a simple rundown of the most common schemes.

Buying a Leased Car: Is It Worth It?

In theory, it sounds like an ace idea. Test out a car by leasing it, then buy it if you really like it. However, you need to do some research to make sure it's a deal worth taking. Here's how to think about it: When you get your lease, it has written into it a "residual value"—as mentioned before, whatever the leasing company predicts the car will be worth at the end of the leasing term, based primarily on the make/model and an assumption about how much mileage you'll put on the car (12,000 miles per year is standard). Many leases also come with a "buyout" price attached to them, and that price is usually determined by the residual value. You probably see the game by now. If the car comes back worth *more* than the residual value, you stand to snag a good deal by buying the car outright (assuming you like it). Of course, you could always go look for a used car of the same make and model and maybe get a better price. But if you already feel comfortable with your leased car, why not just stick with what you know? A used car could have all sorts of problems you didn't anticipate, whereas the one you've been driving for two or more years is more of a known quantity.

Once the end of your lease term draws nigh, the easiest way to figure out if an option to buy is worth exercising is to plug the car's details into Edmunds or Kelley Blue Book to get the market value and then compare that number to the residual value. Is it the same or higher? If so, you may want to consider purchasing. Just don't forget to negotiate aggressively, because the dealer probably doesn't want the car back on the lot and may be willing to cut a deal to make it go away.

Car Insurance

Auto insurance is required by law in almost every state, so dealing with it is less an option than an obligation. There are two main aspects of car insurance: protecting your car and protecting yourself. Whether your car gets jacked from the lot or you get into an accident that dents both your fender and your forehead, you are going to be glad you're covered. Indeed, driving without insurance is one of the least intelligent things you can do—if you get caught (or worse still, you get hurt), you may incur heavy fines and bills, lose your license, or even go to jail. So, put that college-educated brain to use and do some research to find a policy that works best for you.

When it comes to car insurance, comparison shopping is absolutely essential. Rubrics for calculating premiums vary considerably across different providers—in *The Quarterlifer's Companion,* Todd Morgano of Progressive Auto Insurance points out that "the cost of a six-month auto insurance policy

Hazard:
Double coverage = double payment

Before perusing prices, check any other insurance policies that you hold (e.g., health insurance, renters insurance); you may already be covered for certain aspects of a car insurance policy. For example, a person with comprehensive health insurance would probably only need to purchase the minimum personal injury protection (PIP) coverage.

for the same driver with comparable coverage varies from company to company by an average of \$586." That's pretty insane, and it should provide plenty of incentive to consider all the options. For example, can you get onto your parents' policy? This setup is required if the car is registered in their name, but it may also be a good idea if they receive a multi-car or multi-policy discount. Furthermore, if you already have a policy, make sure that you are not wasting money by leaving it unchanged. First of all, it's more expensive to insure a 16-year-old Danica Patrick wannabe than a 23-year-old with a clean license. Moreover, premium prices tend to fluctuate yearly no matter who you are—if a large number of people in a given group (e.g., age, type of vehicle, number of accidents) file claims in a given year, everyone's rates rise. Thus, you may be able to find lower overall premiums or discounts elsewhere due to changes in age, location, and other factors that determine your rates.

If you do decide to make a change or go it on your own, here are some things to consider.

The Bare Bones Basics

Before picking up the phone for a "15-minute call to Geico", take some time to familiarize yourself with the different types of coverage.

- **Liability.** Required by 47 states, liability covers accidental bodily injury and property damages caused by you in an accident (e.g., the

Cars & Commuting

woman in the other car's broken butt bone and the neighbor's flattened fence).

━ **Collision.** Not mandatory (but purchased by most), collision pays for any repairs to your car after an accident, from a bruised bumper to a busted trunk. It does not pay for damage to the other person's car.

━ **Comprehensive.** Also optional but popular (like parmesan cheese or pants), comprehensive pays for losses that are not the result of a collision, such as fire or theft.

━ **Medical.** Pays all medical expenses of those in your car regardless of fault. Does not reimburse those insured for lost wages or replacement services.

━ **Emergency Roadside Service.** Covers situations like fixing a flat, getting keys out of a locked car, running out of gas, or using a tow truck.

━ **Gap Insurance.** As soon as a car is driven off the lot, its market value depreciates 20–30%. In the case of an accident or theft, gap insurance pays the difference between what you owe (the actual market price) and what the insurance company says the car is worth. For example, if a $25,000 car is totaled and you have collision but no gap insurance, the insurance company will pay $20,000 rather than the full $25,000 that you paid for it. It is generally offered only on new cars, and leased cars usually have it built-in.

━ **Personal Injury Protection (PIP).** Being a PIMP is illegal in all states except Nevada, but having PIP is required by some. It covers medical expenses and lost wages for insured drivers regardless of fault.

━ **Uninsured Motorists.** Pays for car damage when an accident is caused by someone without liability insurance.

━ **Underinsured Motorists.** Pays for car damage when an accident is caused by someone with insufficient liability insurance.

━ **Rental Reimbursement.** Dinero for a rental if the wheels on the car can't go 'round and 'round. (Sometimes credit cards provide this coverage, so check to make sure you're not doubling up on the same thing.)

Figuring Out What to Expect

The average policy containing liability, collision, and comprehensive coverage costs about $775 per year. However, that figure is dependent on a number of things:

☞ **Type of car.** Sports cars, large SUVs, and really small cars like the Mini Cooper may be the jam, but beware of the higher premiums that accompany these types of automobiles.

☞ **Car features.** Anti-theft devices, airbags, anti-lock brakes, and automatic seatbelts warrant an automatic price reduction.

☞ **Theft history.** Models with bad reps get bad rates. Check out theft history to get an idea of how a car will fare on the street. (According to the National Insurance Crime Bureau, the "most stolen cars" in 2006 were the '95 Honda Civic, the '91 Honda Accord, and the '89 Toyota Camry.)

☞ **Location.** Areas with high accident rates or incidents of larceny raise prices. (We know what you're thinking, but don't do it. Lying about where you live will allow the insurance company to shaft you down the line.)

☞ **You.** Not all drivers are treated the same. For example, young single males can expect to pay more just for being young, single, and male. At least the bathroom line is shorter!

☞ **How often you drive.** Long commute? Price increase is absolute.

☞ **Credit report.** If you missed your last two credit card payments due to a drunken visit to the L.L. Bean website, it could increase your premium by hundreds.

☞ **Driving record.** Clean licenses result in lower premiums.

☞ **Discounts.** Most companies offer sizable student discounts to those who maintain certain grades. You can also save if you have multiple cars insured (unlikely) or if you hold a renter's insurance policy with the same company.

Cars & Commuting

☞ **Deductible.** A deductible is the amount paid out of pocket before the insurance company kicks in cash. A higher deductible will mean a lower premium price, but it also means that you must fork over more of your own money in the case of a calamity. Deductibles are usually offered in amounts of $100, $250, $500, or $1,000.

Finding a Policy

The first step in the search for auto insurance is learning your state's minimum requirements. Since safe is always better than sorry, most people go beyond the minimum to ensure coverage for a variety of problems. Initially, getting quotes online is a quick and easy way to make comparisons without the pressure of an agent. Have on hand your driver's license number, the year, make, and model of the vehicle, and the vehicle identification number (VIN). Geico, Allstate, Progressive, and all the other companies you've seen on TV are worth checking out, but be sure to do as much comparison shopping as possible. You should start at Esurance.com to get quotes and compare company ratings and also try Netquote.com. During this process, gauge the level of coverage provided by each policy against these recommendations from About.com:

🔍 Bodily Injury Liability: $300,000 per occurrence

🔍 Property Damage Liability: $100,000 per occurrence

🔍 Medical Payments: $10,000 per person

🔍 Uninsured Motorist Bodily Injury: $300,000 per accident

🔍 Uninsured Motorist Property Damage: $10,000 per accident

🔍 Collision Deductible: $500

🔍 Comprehensive Deductible: $0–100

Insurance lingo to a recent grad can be like AIM-speak to your grandmother, so you may want someone who can answer questions and walk you through the process. If this is the case, consider getting off the 'net and into an insurance agent's office (locate agents in your area by going to company websites or using Automotive.com's "Agent Locator"). When you finally make a decision, don't get off the phone or leave the agency without knowing exactly what you're getting (i.e., how much you are paying, what your deductible is, and how you are covered). Finally, familiarize yourself with the correct protocol should anything go wrong. How you handle the scene of an accident can make a huge difference in whether or not your claim is accepted.

Spot Check:
Auto Essentials

Just to make sure you are completely road-ready, we've compiled a quick checklist of car issues to deal with before driving. However, be aware that each state has its own unique regulations and standards (e.g., you may need to get a safety inspection in addition to an emissions test), so it's always a good idea to visit the Department of Motor Vehicles to make sure that everything is ready to go. Also, as a general rule, just make sure your tags, insurance, and registration are up-to-date and you should be fine.

✔ **Driver's License.** Presumably you didn't forget this little detail. Head to the DMV if your license has expired or if you need a new one. Remember, if you have moved, you can get a driver's license in your new state of residence (which, in turn, can help you register to vote there, but is not always a requirement).

✔ **Roadside Assistance.** Tow coverage is something most drivers don't actively think about too much…until they break down or their tire goes out in the middle of the freeway, at which point it becomes the most important thing in the world. The majority of new and certified pre-owned cars have roadside assistance tucked into the purchase price, so check with the manufacturer for the limits on how long the free service lasts. (One caveat: A tow provided through an automaker's plan will take your car to the nearest dealership, where parts and labor are probably more expensive, unless they're under warranty.) Beyond that, there are many roadside assistance plans you can sign up for, including AAA and OnStar. When comparison shopping, make sure the plan covers you (as opposed to the car), look at statistics like the average response time per service call, and find out any out-of-pocket expenses you'd be responsible for after a breakdown.

✔ **Camera.** Get your "citizen journalist" hat on and start carrying a disposable camera in your glove compartment. Photos could be clutch when it comes time to file a claim for an accident or dispute a parking ticket.

Cars & Commuting

Auto Essentials continued...

✔ **Cell Phones.** Find out if it's legal to operate a cell phone while driving in your state before you get caught looking like an a-hole. If it is illegal, hook up some Bluetooth and blab all you want!

✔ **Emissions.** There should be a little sticker on your windshield that says your vehicle fulfills the state's emissions standards. If not, or if the expiration date on the sticker has passed, you need to contact the DMV to find your local emissions testing station. Ask about exemptions (some states exempt new vehicles), and make sure you don't get caught driving with an out-of-date sticker.

✔ **Insurance.** Don't get on the road without insurance—it's illegal and dangerous. See page 294 to learn about choosing a policy.

✔ **Roadside Emergency Kit.** Make sure you have emergency items (and a spare tire) in the trunk in case of a breakdown. You can find a list of useful items at Edmunds.com, but you should at the very least have flares, jumper cables, a map, a tire inflator, two quarts of oil, a first aid kit, and a flashlight with extra batteries. You can buy preassembled car emergency kits for around $25 to $75, depending on how comprehensive they are.

✔ **License Plates.** Having license plates is necessary. Get them from the DMV for $25–50, but be prepared to pay extra if you want them to say "OMFG" or "BALLER." If you re-register in a new state (see below) and receive new plates, make sure you send the old ones back and notify the tax collector in the town where the car was originally registered—some states charge property tax on cars, so you want to avoid paying if you don't actually live there anymore.

✔ **Oil Changes.** Again, there should be a sticker on the windshield telling you the mileage mark at which you should get your next oil change. Keep an eye on the odometer and don't go too far over this mark. Midas, Jiffy Lube, and local garages can all handle this task, so don't be afraid to shop around. Also, be wary when they tell you about the five other things that they can do to fix up your car while you're there.

✔ **Parking.** Make sure you have a reasonable and secure place to keep your car, both at home and at work. Some cities and neighborhoods require resident parking permits for street parking. If so, you will need to contact City Hall and apply for a permit, a process that generally requires a driver's license from the state you're in and proof of residency (e.g., gas/electric bill, bank statement, cable bill). Pay all parking tickets on time to avoid getting clamped by "the boot."

✔ **Registration.** Hit the DMV to register your vehicle, and keep the registration with you in the car at all times. If you move and have a permanent address in your new post-college city, you should almost always register your car in that state to avoid citations and unnecessary fines. However, it is worth noting that car ownership is more expensive in some states than others (e.g., California is pricey because they are so "green"), so if you still have a permanent address in the state where you came from (e.g., mom and dad's house), you can also continue to register there. Check the state's DMV website to make sure you meet various restrictions.

✔ **Miscellaneous.** Do you have enough windshield washer fluid? What about antifreeze? An ice scraper (if necessary)? ■

Cars & Commuting

Mileage Chart: How Much Do You Need for Gas?

Once you have a car, the cost of gas can really add up from month to month. Assess your commuting patterns and then use this chart to determine how much you should expect to spend filling up each week.

Miles driven per week ▶	100	125	150	175	200	225	250
Miles per gallon ▼	Cost per week (assuming $3/gallon)						
10 MPG	$30.00	$37.50	$45.00	$52.50	$60.00	$67.50	$75.00
15 MPG	$20.00	$25.00	$30.00	$35.00	$40.00	$45.00	$50.00
20 MPG	$15.00	$18.80	$22.50	$26.30	$30.00	$33.80	$37.50
25 MPG	$12.00	$15.00	$18.00	$21.00	$24.00	$27.00	$30.00
30 MPG	$10.00	$12.50	$15.00	$17.50	$20.00	$22.50	$25.00
35 MPG	$8.60	$10.70	$12.90	$15.00	$17.10	$19.30	$21.40
40 MPG	$7.50	$9.40	$11.30	$13.10	$15.00	$16.90	$18.80

Top Ten Ways to Be a Green Driver

According to the U.S. Environmental Protection Agency, driving a car is the worst thing that most people do for the environment during their lifetime. (Yes, even worse than using aerosol deodorants!) Here are ten easy ways to reduce the harm of riding, many of which have the added bonus of saving you money:

1) Drive less. Use public transportation or carpool. Better yet, walk or hop on your bike.

2) Drive smart. Speeding not only gets the cops on your tail, but it also attracts the wrath of Captain Planet because high speeds produce greater emissions. Heavy braking and rapid acceleration also reduce fuel economy, so try to develop a smooth, safe driving style.

3) Don't "top off." When you fill up a tank of gas, don't give it that extra little pump at the end—gas spillage is not a good look. Also, always make sure the gas cap is secured tightly.

4) Perform regular maintenance. Another factoid, courtesy of the National Safety Council: Poorly-maintained vehicles can release ten times the emissions of well-maintained ones. Follow the manufacturer's instructions for routine maintenance and look out for red flags like reduced fuel efficiency, leaks, and black exhaust billowing out of the back of your whip.

5) Get an eco-friendly car. If you're in the market for a car, newer cars are better for the environment than older ones (hence 2009's federally funded "Cash for Clunkers" program). Check the fuel efficiency rating and look into trendy cars that people like Larry David drive. (As a bonus, these "green" cars are often cheaper than their competitors.)

6) Use clean fuels. Using "oxygenated gasoline" and alternative energy sources like electricity is way better than burning through tanks of premium unleaded in your Hummer.

7) Cool it on the AC. Pumping the air-conditioning while crawling through city traffic can increase fuel consumption by over 20%.

8) Avoid idling. Idling is wasteful, so avoid the Wendy's drive-thru and L.A. traffic jams. Also, don't sit around in parking lots blasting Joan Jett like a chach.

9) Get good tires. If you want to look like you got your car from the set of a music video, buy 22-inch rims. If you want to make the world a better place, use radial tires because they offer less rolling resistance and thus improve fuel efficiency. Also, make sure tires are properly inflated at all times.

10) Cut the dead weight. Have you driven around with golf clubs and an old bag of cement in your trunk for the past nine months? Extra weight means reduced efficiency, so treat your car like a professional athlete and shed those pounds. ■

Cars & Commuting

End of the Road: How to Sell Your Car

If you are moving to a new city or just can't afford the cost of ownership anymore, you may be looking to sell your car. For some people, this maneuver might even be a necessary step toward funding a move. But before you write FOR SALE in dirt on your windshield, do some research to figure out how to keep things kosher and how to make the biggest profit from the sale of your ride. Contact the DMV to find out about transfer of title, registration, and all that good stuff. Then research how much models from the same year with similar mileage are going for in order to price your car correctly (try Edmunds' "True Market Value" pricing tool, and enter your car's details into Kelley Blue Book to get a suggested retail value). Finally, advertise it on Craigslist, AutoTrader.com, and in front of your house. Then sell to the highest bidder. Once you get paid, head straight for the border (or wherever it was that you were going).

Cars & Commuting

Chapter VII: Health

Health

The majority of this chapter is devoted to health insurance, an issue so complex that no one, not even Dr. Oz, completely understands it. For starters, who can really explain why it costs $20,000 to stay in the ER for a night? (It's not exactly the Four Seasons.)

The real challenges for recent grads, however, are twofold: 1) Getting a grasp on the lingo so you know what the hell's going on, and 2) Figuring out what you actually need in a health care plan.

In the following pages, we'll clear out the debris and give you the tools you need to make smart choices about your coverage. We'll walk you through your insurance options, which are plentiful whether you are employed or not, and also tell you how to pick a doctor and a dentist.[1]

Later in the chapter, our focus will shift to three of Gradspot's most popular topics (gyms, sex, food... GSF baby!!!). We'll help you get your body thin (while your wallet stays thick). From gym memberships, to delicious healthy recipes, to answering the age old question, "what exactly is the clap?" we've got you covered.

Salud!

Why You Need Health Insurance

The most common misconception about health insurance is that it's not really a big deal if you're a healthy twentysomething. In fact, so many people maintain this crazy notion that the insurance industry even has a fun name for them: the "young invincibles." But guess what? Being healthy doesn't prevent you from falling off your single-speed Schwinn into a ravine or dropping the iron on your foot. Roaming around without basic insurance is like entering a Russian roulette league. Even if nothing happens in the first month or two, sooner or later your luck could run out and you'll find yourself with your leg in a sling and $15,000 in debt to the local hospital.

---

1 Please bear in mind that health care policy is currently in a state of flux. Keep your eye on the news for changes to the system that might affect your ability to find affordable coverage.

Needless to say, we wish everyone reading this book could be fully insured with a plan covering everything from check-ups to surgery to acupuncture. But we understand that the realities of the job market, and recent-grad finances don't make it easy for everyone to jump straight to health insurance heaven. Still, it's much better to wait it out in purgatory than hell—in other words, you need to figure out a way to provide yourself with basic coverage if a more comprehensive plan is not yet in the cards. If you're not convinced by the "accidents happen, and so does swine flu" argument, here are further reasons for getting serious about insurance.

+ **Unpaid medical bills are one of the leading causes of bankruptcy.** There are so many horror stories of twentysomethings being crippled by debt after an accident or sudden illness. Not only does getting smacked with massive hospital bills suck now, but it can also set your post-college plans back significantly as you struggle to recover from the hit. And even if it doesn't get that drastic, Experian reports that "unpaid hospital bills can affect your credit report if they are sent to a collection agency to recover the amount you owe." If you read Chapter 7, you know how strongly we feel about protecting your credit!

+ **Without insurance, you could hurt your chances of getting insured in the future.** When you're young and don't have major health issues, insurance companies welcome you into the fold with open arms because they predict you won't cost them too much. But if you develop a chronic problem, they'll treat you like a leper and make it impossible or prohibitively expensive for you to get the care you need. The trick is to get in while the getting's good, because once you have consistent coverage, you are protected by the law against pre-existing exemptions (i.e., when a health insurance company won't pay your medical fees for a pre-existing condition). So don't wait until you're 30 and your body starts to go downhill!

+ **Without insurance, you have to be more careful.** Do you want to live your young adult life in fear of sickness and injury? Of course not. You want to try that puffer fish sashimi that's offered to you, accept that invitation to a friend's ski house, and run that marathon. Life is full of risks, and obviously you would never want to do something where there's a high chance of getting sick or hurt. But there are a lot of fun things that get moved from the "responsible risk" category to the "dumb" category if you don't have insurance behind you.

+ **Without insurance, you miss out on preventive care and screenings.** If you're uninsured you're probably not going to cough up the funds to have that physical or check-up that could uncover something at an early stage. And in the very unfortunate event that something does develop and you don't catch it until you get coverage later down the line, you may end up spending a whole lot more on treatment and premiums than you would have if you'd caught it early (and money's not even the biggest issue here).

Lingo:
Talking Health Insurance

The basics of health insurance are pretty simple: In exchange for a monthly premium, you can visit general doctors and specialists, and the insurance companies will pay for what they think it should cost. Beyond that, things get a little trickier to decipher. Here are some key words and phrases that you will need to know:

> **PREMIUM:** The amount paid to the insurance company for your plan (usually quoted at a monthly or yearly rate).

> **DEDUCTIBLE:** The predetermined amount that you have to spend on medical services in a given year before the insurance company starts to pony up. Generally, the higher the deductible, the lower the premium.

> **COPAY:** A small fee (usually between $5–$50) often required for each visit.

Health

HMO. Health Maintenance Organizations place restrictions on the services a patient may receive. Under an HMO, the policyholder chooses a **PCP** (Primary Care Physician) from the HMO's list. After you choose your PCP, you must visit him or her for any medical issue. The PCP then decides whether your ailment is bad enough to warrant a visit to a **specialist** (doctor who has a specific focus in a particular field).

PPO. Preferred Provider Organizations give you a choice of where to receive services, with the possibility of paying more out of pocket than an HMO, depending on where you choose to go (see page 319 for a comparison between HMOs and PPOs).

POS. Point of Service plans are the beautiful lovechild of HMOs and PPOs. As with an HMO, you choose a PCP and visit him or her for referrals. Once a referral is made, you can choose to stay within the network, or venture outside and pay more out of pocket. Sometimes, you can even skip the visit to your PCP if you know the out-of-network specialist you would like to visit.

EPO. An easy way to understand an Exclusive Provider Organization is to think of it as a scrawnier, whinier PPO. The list of providers you can visit is much smaller than with a PPO, and if you go out of network, your services may not be covered at all (except in emergency cases).

Health

Getting Health Care on Your Own

What if you're unemployed, or your employer does not provide health benefits? It's an intimidating situation to be in, for sure. But there are many affordable options at your disposal, and figuring out one that works for you is a lot smarter than eating Echinacea tablets, wearing a football helmet in the car, and praying for the best.

As Toni Frawley of Health Alliance Plan, a nonprofit health plan based in Detroit, explains, "Health care is out there and individuals can just go out and buy it." Sounds sort of obvious, but health care takes on such a mystique in this country that sometimes you forget that A) It doesn't have to be provided by someone else (e.g., parents or an employer), and B) You can shop for it just as you would any other major purchase. "Basically, you just need to do your homework," says Frawley. "So many grads are in the same situation as you and so many people have gone through this already—your friends included, probably. Talk to them and ask questions. Compare plans online and call up insurance brokers and carriers. You would research the TV you're going to buy the same way, so why not do it for your health coverage?" If you come across any unknowns during the hunt, CoverTheInsured.com and HealthInsuranceInfo.net are great resources for state-specific information.

Feel empowered? You should be—you're a consumer, the cornerstone of America! Now instead of rolling the dice by walking around with no coverage, let's consider some ways to stay insured when an employer isn't there to subsidize a plan.

INDIVIDUAL COVERAGE. Before you look to the options below, it's worth looking for individual plans in your state, as they can often be pretty affordable for a healthy twentysomething. You should definitely consider it as an option if you don't think you'll get benefits within the next year, but even if you think you might need coverage for only a few months, see what the payment schedule is for the plans you find—some charge monthly premiums and allow you to cancel at any time, which is a lot easier than tying together a bunch of short-term plans (see below) during your job hunt. For high deductible plans, individual insurance can be pretty manageable in some states. Using a healthy 23-year-old female as a test case, we found $2,500 deductible plans (with some basic coverage for office visits) ranging from $63 (WA) to $240 (NJ) per month, but most were in the $80–100 range. To compare quotes for yourself, type your

Health

zip code into eHealthInsurance.com or go straight to a provider (e.g., Anthem Blue Cross and Blue Shield). You can also just Google "individual health care" and the name of your state to see who the providers are. Once you've found some candidates, run through the criteria on page 314 and call up the individual providers or an insurance broker to see if they provide all the coverage you want.

SHORT-TERM INSURANCE (a.k.a. "Bridge" or "Temporary" Insurance). Short-term insurance is an affordable holdover if you're looking for a job with benefits or you just need more time to weigh your options. In fact, even if you have a job, the benefits may take a month or two to kick in, so a temporary plan might still be necessary in the meantime. For a healthy 23-year-old female, we found quotes between $23 (MD) and $127 (CA) per month, with most options falling in the $30–70 range. It's really not a high price to pay to protect yourself against a potentially catastrophic situation (plus you can often get a discount if you prepay up front). So who is it bad for? People who visit the doctor often or need to buy prescription drugs don't get a great deal from short-term health insurance because of the high deductibles ($1,000 and up—lower ones will result in higher monthly costs) and the fact that it doesn't cover those prescription drugs (or OB/GYN visits, for that matter). You can check HealthInsuranceInfo.net to find state rules on temporary plans and the coverage they're required to provide.

PAY TO STAY ON YOUR PARENTS' PLAN (or Ask Them to Help You Out). If Mom and Dad can be convinced to help you out with one expense after college,

it's probably health care—just use the argument that you "could die without it." Many states allow children to remain on their parents' plan until surprisingly old ages. In Texas it's 25; in New Jersey, believe it or not, residents can ride their parents' coattails until the age of 30! (Unfortunately, others cut it off at 19, so you need to see what's up.) If you can no longer be claimed as a dependent, maybe they'll help you pay for one of the other options in this section. And if Mom or Dad has covered your insurance through an employer-sponsored plan but you are now losing your dependent status, look into the possibility of continuing your coverage through COBRA.

COBRA. The Consolidated Omnibus Budget Reconciliation Act (better known as COBRA) has nothing to do with *G.I. Joe*, but it does enable people at companies with 20 or more employees to maintain health coverage (for up to 36 months) at their own expense after they have left an employer. In most states, it also covers young people who are kicked off of their parents' employer-sponsored plan when they can no longer be claimed as dependents. If you find yourself in this situation, ask your mom or dad to inquire with their employer(s) about this option, but understand that it will be very pricey since you'll have to pay the whole premium with no discounts. At your age, you can almost certainly go out and find a cheaper individual plan on your own. Should you decide you want COBRA to buy some time to figure out a sustainable alternative, be sure to act fast—you only have 60 days to announce your loss of dependent status, and then another 60 to elect COBRA.

FREELANCER'S UNION. You might be making more than your friend who works for a Fortune 500 company, but you happen to be a freelancer or nanny and you don't have benefits. Enter the Freelancer's Union (FreelancersUnion.org). Through the Union you can get discounted health care for as low as $130/month (though the annual deductibles are as high as $10,000, so we're talking "catastrophic coverage" here). Coverage is not available everywhere in the country, but the easy-to-use website allows you to enter your zip code and get a list of available health, dental, disability, and life insurance plans.

ALUMNI ASSOCIATION. The reason employers can get good insurance rates for their employees is because they offer providers easy access to a whole bunch of customers at once. The same goes for any organization that can pool together people to buy insurance at bulk rates—like your alma mater, for example. Contact your school's alumni association and see what it can offer in the way of temporary and individual plans.

CITY- OR STATE-SPONSORED PLANS. In certain parts of the country, local governments have taken measures to help uninsured residents gain access to health care. For example, Healthy San Francisco is operated by the San Francisco Department of Health, and a program called Healthy NY provides coverage in parts of New York State (there are simple eligibility screeners on the websites you can check out to see if they're a possible option).

Note: When looking into individual plans, be wary of those that don't offer actual insurance coverage but rather discounts on health care services. The website CoverTheUninsured.com advises that "these plans are not a good buy, and many insurance regulators warn against buying them."

Health

Spot Check:
Health Insurance Essentials

Now that you have a basic understanding of how health insurance works, it's time for you to choose the ideal plan. But before you even think about your individual needs make sure you are covered for the following services:

- ✔ **Office visits.** When you stop by your doctor's office to check on your sore throat, fever, or anything else that doesn't seem right.

- ✔ **Surgical services.** Planned hospital procedures and examinations.

- ✔ **Inpatient hospital services.** Everything the hospital charges you for when you stay overnight—fee for the room you slept in, medication, gross apple sauce, etc.

- ✔ **Emergency room services.** Procedures and services when you enter the hospital through the ER without an appointment.

- ✔ **X-ray and lab services.** Anything from X-rays of broken bones to STD tests and biopsies on moles.

- ✔ **Prescriptions.** You want to only have to handle the copay (approximately $5 to $20), not the whole cost of a prescription.

- ✔ **Lifetime maximum coverage.** It should be at least $1 million.

- ✔ **Maximum hospital stay.** You want at least 180 days.

- ✔ **Out-of-pocket maximum.** Is there a maximum amount you'd have to pay in a given year? Pay attention to the fine print, as sometimes certain expenses like copays for out-of-network doctors will not count toward this spending. ∎

Specific Needs

After you've made sure the basics are covered, you need to actually sit down and think about your medical needs. Many recent grads have never actually done this before—in most cases our parents picked a plan to cover everyone in the household, and that was that. But now that you're rolling solo, you need to take a look in the mirror and assess your own health care needs.

In addition to acquainting yourself with the acronyms on page 309, Bill Stapleton, president and CEO of Health Plan One and a 15-year veteran in the health insurance industry, recommends getting out a piece of paper to write down what you need, what you want, and how much you can afford to pay for monthly plan premiums, copays and deductibles. Once you've gone through this process, you'll know your needs, and you can question either HR or the insurance brokers you speak with about how best to fulfill them with your budget/options. (For example, if you know you need a preventative care screening or you need to make an office visit to discuss a problem with an allergist, you ideally want your plan to cover these things.) Calling up brokers is generally a good idea at some point in the process—you're not committed to do anything they say, but the conversation might bring up issues you didn't think of during your own research.

Got your pencil and paper ready? Here are some important questions to ask yourself:

* Does the plan cover annual check-ups?

  *While most plans should cover office visits, you may also want the ability to visit your doctor for a routine adult physical exam. If so, make sure that the plan covers **well patient care.***

* Do you want a backup plan for when your doctor isn't available?

  *Some plans also cover **outpatient hospital services,** which enables you to visit an in-network hospital during its clinic hours and see the doctor on duty. Most people consider this their last resort after they are unable to schedule an office visit with their PCP because hospital waits can be upwards of six hours, even with an appointment.*

* What happened to me last year? How many times did I get sick? How many times did I visit a doctor? Am I a hypochondriac?

  *If so, maybe a **higher premium plan** is worth the peace of mind you'll get from being able to visit the doctor more often.*

Health

✳ Are my current **physicians** "in network?" What about my local **hospital?**

If you have a primary care provider or specialist you really like, you might want to make sure you can continue to see that doctor without paying extra. Same goes for hospitals—if you prefer staying local or if you have an additional hospital of choice, make sure it is available in your plan.

✳ Do I or does my family have a history of **alcoholism**? What about **psychiatric** issues?

Find out if the plan will cover treatments related to these issues.

This process may sound a bit arduous, but it's a worthwhile time investment. "Too often, we file the paperwork away and take it out only after we have been denied services," says Stapleton. "Not only can this be costly, but we frequently do not utilize all the benefits we are paying for." Touché, dog.

Women-Specific Health Care Concerns

The truth is, women have to work a bit harder than men when it comes to post-college health. In addition to getting insurance, finding a physician, and tending to your pearly whites, you also have to figure out how to prevent yourself from inadvertently reproducing—not always a simple task. Luckily, many brave women have blazed the trail for us, and there is an abundance of health-related resources at our disposal.

Planned Parenthood

Regardless of whether you have insurance, Planned Parenthood (plannedparenthood.org) is an invaluable resource for all things woman-related. (Depending on what you got up to in college, this may be old news.) In addition to offering annual pelvic exams and standard STD testing, Planned Parenthood's services include:

- Birth Control Services
- HIV Testing Services
- Hepatitis and HPV Vaccine Services
- Lesbian, Gay, Bisexual, and Transgender Services
- Men's Health Services (That's right, boys!)

- Pregnancy Testing & Planning
- Emergency Contraception Services
- Abortion Services & Referrals

The cost of services at Planned Parenthood clinics varies from community to community. Many centers charge according to income, so if you're yet to be employed (and/or insured), it's a great option. You may even qualify for a state-funded program or a lower fee scale. If you are insured, you can still elect to seek medical services from Planned Parenthood, as most clinics accept insurance.

Contraception / Emergency Contraception / Pregnancy

Sow your wild oats, but sow them carefully. And if you forget to sow them carefully, then have a back-up plan. You probably know all this by now, but just in case...

Contraception. Make sure to discuss contraception options with your doctor. And if you don't yet have a doctor, check in with a professional at Planned Parenthood (or your local reproductive clinic) to discuss options that might be right for you. Your insurance carrier may limit the amount or type of access you have to certain types of birth control (i.e., they will only provide generic birth control pills or they will only provide a one-month supply at a time), so make sure you are clear about what your policy stipulates.

Plan B. Plan B (a.k.a. "the morning after pill") may end up being an important weapon in your arsenal against having a kid. This medication is available over-the-counter for people over the age of 17 (be prepared to show photo I.D.) at most U.S. pharmacies or at Planned Parenthood. It generally costs between $10 and $50 (it tends to be less expensive at Planned Parenthood), and you need to take it within 72 hours of unprotected sex or contraceptive failure—but the sooner the better!

Pregnancy. If you meant to get pregnant, *felicitations!* If you didn't, trust us, you're not the first. There are plenty of resources at your disposal, and plenty of options from which you can choose. If you have a doctor that you trust, contact him or her to discuss options. If you don't, Planned Parenthood or a local reproductive clinic can help you research your options, make decisions, and take whatever action you deem appropriate. ■

Health

Getting Health Care Through Work

If you're lucky, you won't have an option when it comes to picking a health care plan—you're just going to have to take the one your employer offers. It's a big perk that should not be overlooked during the job hunt. And even if you have numerous options through your job (probably HMOs or PPOs, for example), the other nice part about employer-provided benefits is that you have HR to guide you through the process. But before you go to HR, we suggest that you get familiar with the lingo we previously explained (p. 309) and run through the criteria listed on page 314. In addition, the first thing you should do when you get your offer is find out exactly when your company benefits kick in—some companies have a probation period before coverage goes into effect, so you may still need to talk to an insurance agent about an interim coverage policy or short-term insurance (p. 312).

Finally, let's be clear about one fact: Employer benefits do not mean that health care is *free*. It's just significantly discounted since companies can negotiate much better rates with insurance companies than individuals, and they also help you out with the costs. When you enroll, the money you pay toward your coverage is automatically deducted from your paycheck. To give you a sense of the discounts we're talking about, the Kaiser Family Foundation reports that, on an annual basis, a single worker contributes an average of $817 per year for an HMO plan, while the employer kicks in an average of $4,061. For a PPO plan, the worker-employer contribution split averages $860 and $4,116, respectively.

In some circumstances (e.g., you are a part-time worker), the employer will only offer partial benefits. Instead of blindly taking whatever's offered to you, make sure whatever they can provide—probably some sort of very spartan high deductible health plan (HDHP)—works for your health needs. If you need more than just "catastrophic coverage," you may be better off seeking your own individual plan. And if you do end up going that route, see if the employer offers a Flexible Spending Account, which will allow you to set aside money pre-tax for health care costs.

Health

Fork in the Road:
HMOs vs. PPOs

HMOs

HMOs make insurance company interactions pretty simple. When you're interested in visiting a doctor, you always go straight to your PCP, even if you think you need to see a specialist. Since your PCP is already in network, you know his or her services will be covered by your insurance. If you've requested to be referred to a specialist, your PCP will have to approve your request. This process acts as a pre-approval mechanism, so your specialist care will also be covered by your insurance. Wham, bam, thank you ma'am. This system keeps costs (and the premium) low, but it can be annoying if you want to skip the step of visiting your PCP, or if you don't agree with a diagnosis. In addition, your PCP gets paid whether he sees your or not and his commitment to dealing with your case might come into question.

PPOs

While PPOs are more costly than HMOs, they save you the hassle of always having to deal with a PCP. If you have a problem, you can go straight to a specialist. If the specialist is a member of the PPO, insurance covers a high percentage of the services rendered (up to 100%). However, if you don't like the specialists on the list and just want to see the best orthopedic surgeon in the area (who happens not to be a member of the PPO), you will usually only be covered for a small percentage of the visit. While PPOs can save you some time and could ensure that you receive more attention from your doctor (unlike an HMO, he only gets paid per visit) additional costs via monthly surcharges and higher copays might make your plan a much more costly alternative to HMOs.

Health

Dealing with Your Health Insurance Company

If choosing a plan and finding a doctor wasn't enough of a pain, get ready for actually dealing with your insurance company. Figuring out what your provider will cover can often be a long, drawn-out affair, and the whole process of paying for medical services is about as labyrinthine as any transaction you'll ever make. That said, if you understand the basics of your insurance (and put your provider on speed dial for any questions that come up), you can avoid a lot of hassle. Experiences differ from company to company, but the way in which you interact with your insurer is essentially dictated by whether you have an HMO or a PPO plan.

Generally, if you are on an HMO plan, everything will be taken care of for you, since your PCP is your medical gatekeeper. He or she will determine whether you are elligable for a prescription or procedure, and they will directly bill the healthcare company on your behalf. On the other hand, if you are on a PPO plan, sometimes your doctor may bill the healthcare company directly, but other times, you'll be required to pay for the procedure and then personally get reimbursed by your healthcare provider.

When In Doubt, Call

Medical billing can be a nightmare. You may get a bill from your doctor or your insurance company or both, and sometimes it's not completely obvious whom you owe or how much. Instead of just sending off a check and hoping for the best, pick up the phone whenever you're confused. There's a number on the back of your insurance card, and while you may have to wait on hold for a bit, whoever's on the other side of the line is there to help you with any question you have regarding coverage or billing. Similarly, every doctor's office and hospital has a billing office that can assist you in determining what you owe and what the status of an insurance claim is. Call these people. Unpaid medical bills can eventually affect your credit if the doctor's office submits them to a collection agency, but there's no reason it should get to that point if you just communicate with the people who want your money.

Health

Choosing a Doctor

Just because you have insurance doesn't mean you're out of the woods. Now the fun really begins. You get to pick a doctor—most importantly, a PCP. If you are getting your insurance through work, someone from HR will likely sit you down after you enroll in a plan, hand you a book of 10,000 doctors, and ask you to pick one. Either that or you'll be forced to troll through your personal provider's website for a list of covered doctors. You might just lose hope and pick the one with the funniest name ("Methinks you're the one for me, Dr. *Lazarus Pinkerton*.") But it doesn't have to be that random, and you don't have to make the decision right away. There are a few simple ways to make an educated choice, so do the research and you won't end up with some wackjob who will try to kill you and harvest your organs.

Before you do anything else, ask around. A good doctor embodies a perfect mix of professional know-how, geniality, and trustworthiness. So, while you can cast judgment on each candidate's med school degree if you want, the best way to find a good doctor is to talk to friends and colleagues to see if they can make a recommendation based on personal experience. Hopefully, any recommended doctors are included in your health plan (i.e., in that big blue book). If they aren't, it's not the end of the world—you can still go to them, you'll just have to pay extra. Only you can determine if you're willing to spend more money to go to an out-of-network doctor when you can probably find one that is just as good in network. In terms of what types of doctors you should consider for your PCP, the best bets are internists, gynecologists (p. 324), family practitioners, and GPs (general practitioners). The point is, you don't want a foot doctor dealing with your general health.

What if you can't get any recommendations? No need to fret. There are other resources at your disposal. Major metropolitan areas usually have magazines that release a "Best Doctors" report each year. If you aren't the magazine type, you can also browse WebMD and the American Medical Association's website. Whatever you do, avoid the Yellow Pages—it's not a good sign if a doctor has to advertise to get patients.

How to Evaluate a Doctor

Before committing to an MD, be sure to do a little digging first. Check the following background information by visiting the websites of your insurance provider, WebMD, Castle Connolly, and the American Medical Association (don't use any for-pay services):

- ☑ **Status under your insurance plan.** First things first: Is the doctor in network? If not, is there a particular reason you'd be willing to pay extra to see her or him? Check in with your provider for a list of practitioners covered under your plan.

- ☑ **Specialty and subspecialty.** As noted before, find out what type of medicine the doctor specializes in, to make sure you're not wasting your time by seeing a podiatrist for a sinus infection.

- ☑ **Education.** If the doc holds a degree from the University of Phoenix Online, don't line up to see him. There's no need to be snooty and only see Columbia grads, but try to set a reasonable standard to narrow down the most qualified candidates. Is this doctor "board-certified?" If so, it means she has full credentials. If she's only "board-*eligible*," it doesn't necessarily mean she's a quack, it just means she hasn't taken and/or passed her boards yet. Feel free to inquire why not, or if it makes you nervous, just steer clear.

- ☑ **Hospital/Med school affiliations.** Top doctors work at top hospitals; top hospitals offer top resources; and top resources mean that you get top care. If you can't figure out which hospitals are the best, any hospital affiliated with a university that has a good med school should rank well.

- ☑ **Disciplinary action.** A lawsuit or two may simply mean the physician just ran into some bad luck or is willing to attempt more risky procedures. 10 or 20 and you're venturing into dangerous territory. Make sure that he or she has not been charged with serious transgressions, such as sexual misconduct or narcotic offenses (search Castle Connolly). Also, check if the doctor has been fined or had his license suspended or revoked for malpractice by contacting the respective state board of medicine.

Health

Once you've found your doc and done your due diligence, there's one last step— call up the office and fire some questions at the secretary:

- Double-check that the practice does in fact accept your insurance.

- Ask if they are taking new patients, and find out what the wait time for an appointment is. The best doctors are often busier than the police at Mardi Gras, but waiting too long can be hazardous to your health. One to four weeks is a normal wait time; four months is not.

- Pay attention to office hours. If the physician only sees patients two days a week for two hours each day, you may want to find someone with better availability.

- Ask how many patients are typically scheduled each hour. Three to five is a reasonable number. Leaving the office for an hour is acceptable, but leaving for four might get your boss asking questions.

- Inquire how after-hours calls are handled, and ask about the doc's availability in case of an emergency. Check if any back-up physicians will be accessible if your main squeeze heads to the islands.

- Even if the main office is conveniently located, ask where they do their blood work, X-rays, or other tests so that you don't have to go to the end of the earth for an endoscopy.

- Ask if they offer introductory meetings. It is perfectly acceptable to schedule an appointment to meet a new doctor before actually taking the plunge. By doing so, you can see the office and get a sense of whether it's a well-run operation. You may need to pay for this pleasure though, so figure out how much it will cost you beforehand.

Health

Finding an OB/GYN

For many women, your gynecologist is going to be a hell of a lot more important than that other dude who hits your knee with a rubber hammer once a year. When it comes to health, the process of selecting an OB/GYN (or just GYN) should be one of your first moves. If you have comprehensive insurance, you can elect to choose one in the same way you chose a primary care doctor (see "Choosing a Doctor" on page 321), but the thought of asking your boss and/or HR representative for gyno recommendations might not be so appealing. Don't worry—there are a number of additional ways you can zero in on a good doctor without having to announce to the office that you're having lady issues.

> ### Tips & Tricks:
> ### The OB/GYN-PCP combo
>
> It is possible to kill two birds with one stone by using your OB/GYN as your primary care physician rather than having two separate doctors. Many women choose this option for two main reasons: 1) They have a good relationship with their gynecologist and prefer not to see someone else, and 2) The have a lot more female-specific medical issues (e.g., annual exam, infections, discomfort, birth control) than other medical issues. And if you get lucky, your OB/GYN is an amazing generalist. On average, however, it would be a safe bet to assume that internists and GPs are probably better PCPs than gynos due to the more general nature of their work.

How to Choose a Dentist

Finding a dentist isn't all that different from finding a general practitioner. The best bet is to ask coworkers, family, friends, and neighbors for referrals. You also want to make sure the practice accepts your dental plan, so you should check your provider's list of participating dentists. Another option is to do some searching on the 'net and call a local periodontist (gums specialists) or to ask for a recommendation. Finally, you can find out which lab a dentist uses for lab work, then call the lab directly to do a background check. Don your two-brimmed hat for this process to feel like a modern-day Sherlock Holmes.

Once you think you've found a winning ticket, it's time to run it through the wringer. Look out for malpractice suits, and call the state board of consumer affairs to find out if there are any records of actions against the dentist. Has the dentist's license ever been revoked or suspended? Do some Googling to find lawsuits and any other dirt. In this case, no results are a good result. You can also see if the dentist is rated on Dr. Oogle (which can be found at the amazing URL doctoroogle.com).

Next, it's time to grill the dentist's office. Ask if the dentist owns the practice or if someone else owns it. If the dentist is an owner or co-owner, chances are he's more invested in his work and reputation. Also, find out how long he's been practicing. Don't sign up with a new dentist—it takes more than two years for a good dentist to really know what he's doing.

As with general practitioners, you don't have to stick with a dentist just because you go there once.

> **Smart Money:**
> **Dental school clinics**
>
> The American Dental Association advises regular professional cleanings and oral exams to fight tooth decay, which affects more than 90 percent of those 40 and older. If you don't have dental insurance, you're liable to say, "Whatever, I'll just chew some Trident White!" But what if you could get a cleaning and check-up for free, or at a very discounted rate? If there's a respected dental school in your area, you may be in luck. Student-run clinics will often offer basic screening and cleaning (as well as X-rays), all under the supervision of board-certified teaching staff. Check with your state's dental society to find a dental school, or search for a list at ADA.org. Damn it feels good to be a guinea pig

Here are red flags to look out for on your first visit:

- You haven't had a filling in years, yet the dentist insists you need several fillings. (Bear in mind that if you've been sucking down six Cokes a day and you never brush your teeth, maybe he's right.)

- The dentist says you need to replace your silver fillings with plastic or "white composite" ones. Silver fillings last three times as long as plastic ones. And though silver fillings contain mercury, there's little scientific evidence that the mercury content in them is toxic to your body.

- The dentist says your gums aren't healthy and you need "root planing"—a deep-cleaning of tartar in hard-to-reach spots. Few healthy recent grads need such an intensive service.

- The dentist claims you need a crown or multiple crowns.

- Be wary of a zillion dental plans or tons of advertising. A good dentist doesn't need to advertise for patients.

Health

Ask the Expert:
Should I Buy Dental Insurance?
Myron Roy, DDS New York, NY

If your employer offers you dental coverage absolutely take advantage of it. But if you plan on going entirely out of pocket, you may want to think twice. If you are the type of person who goes to the dentist every six months and needs little more than a cleaning, you will probably find buying dental insurance a losing proposition. Even if you need extensive dental restorations be forewarned that preexisting conditions such as a missing tooth or cavities will not likely be covered. In addition, your family dentist that you have been seeing since you were three years old might not be participating in your particular insurance plan. Unlike medical insurance that can potentially save you from financial ruin, most reasonably priced dental plans have an annual maximum, usually around $1,000. Therefore, even in the event that you are covered, dental expenses may actually end up being more than your premium. If buying dental insurance inspires you to see the dentist every six months it might be warranted. But in the end, your coverage could very well be as beneficial as purchasing a warrantee for your electric toothbrush. ■

Maintaining a Healthy Lifestyle

Now that you've figured how to obtain the ideal health care plan, we'll spend the rest of the chapter trying to ensure avoid actually using it; ironic, we know.

Recipes For Success

Finding a consensus on the ideal diet is a virtually impossible task. While some doctors might sing the praises of a particular program, you're sure to find others who are quick to question its effectiveness. So far be it from us to recommend whether to opt for a master cleanse (actually, most medical professionals believe this is a waste, pun intended) or to take your diet to South Beach. Instead, we thought we'd keep things simple and offer up some of favorite quick and easy recipes that get high marks for taste, while keeping the calorie and fat content low.

1) Cod with Cherry Tomatoes

Serves 2; Costs $11

When Gradspot contributor Arnold T. Pants was a fellow at the New Bedford Whaling Museum, he ate a simple meal with Klaus Bartlemus, the world's leading expert on whaling. Klaus was also an expert on eating odd foods. He'd consumed the eye of a sturgeon and a whole small bird. He offered to cook us dinner, and to my surprise presented a very simple dish: roast cod with cherry tomatoes.

The meal is a truly lovely end to a cool spring day. Seasoned with olive oil, salt, and pepper and roasted for about 15 minutes, the fish comes out light and flaky. Serve it with steamed rice tossed with a bit of cilantro, as well as a side salad if you're feeling ambitious (see page 330).

You need:

- Cod (or any other white fish you want; two pieces)
- 1 package cherry tomatoes
- Rice
- Cilantro
- Olive oil
- Salt
- Pepper

Preheat oven to 375 degrees. While it's pre-heating, season the fish with olive oil, salt, and pepper. (If you froze the fish, let it thaw thoroughly before starting this process, and be sure to wash it by holding the filets under warm running water.) Place the fish in a deep baking dish and add the tomatoes—whole if you like, or halved. When the oven is ready, toss the dish in there and roast for about 15 minutes, or until the fish flakes easily.

For the rice, steam in a rice cooker if you have one. Otherwise, place two cups of water for each cup of rice in a large pot, bring to boil, and cook until the water has been absorbed. At that point, take it off the heat and allow to sit for 20 minutes or so—this will make it fluff up nicely. Toss in the cilantro and enjoy.

Health

2) Simple Salad Nicoise

Nicoise is the classic gusty French salad. It is intensely colorful, has a brilliant mixture of tastes, and makes a very hearty, healthy meal for any season.

Serves 2; Costs $14

The Dressing

- 1 tbsp red wine vinegar
- 1 tbsp Dijon mustard
- 2 cloves garlic

The Salad

- 1 6–8 ounce tuna steak
- 2 romaine hearts
- 1 handful arugula or mesclun salad mix
- 1/2 lb green beans (preferably French)
- 8 very small red, white, or blue potatoes (also sometimes called new potatoes)
- 3 eggs
- 3 tbsp olive oil
- 1/2 cup Nicoise olives

Steps

1. Cut stem off of romaine heart and chop widthwise into one inch leaves.
2. Combine with mesclun or arugula in a large bowl.
3. Whisk vinegar with mustard in a small bowl and add the two garlic cloves, cut into quarters.
4. Fill two small- and one medium-sized pot three quarters full with water with a pinch of salt and place under high heat.

5. Add the eggs to the small pot.

6. Once the pot with the eggs starts to boil, turn the heat down to low and cook for 10 minutes.

7. Once the other small pot begins to boil, carefully drop in the potatoes and cook for 15 minutes or until tender.

8. Cut the stems off the green beans by arranging them in a bunch with the all of the hard ends facing one way.

9. When the third pot begins to boil, toss in the green beans and blanch for 2 minutes, then remove beans and place in an ice bath.

10. When the eggs are finished remove and let sit until they are warm but not hot to the touch.

11. Roll the eggs back and forth between your two palms gently so that the shell cracks but you don't break the skin of the egg, then remove the shells.

12. Drain the potatoes and let sit in a colander.

13. Dry the tuna steak with a paper towel and salt and pepper both sides.

14. Set a small frying pan over medium-high heat with 1 tbl olive oil.

15. Sauté the tuna for two minutes or so per side depending on thickness. The tuna should have a brown, somewhat crisp outside but still be very pink on the inside. Err on the side of rare as tuna is perfectly healthy to eat raw and has very little taste when cooked.

16. Separate/slice the tuna along its grains into inch long strips.

17. Slice the eggs widthwise.

18. Cut the potatoes into quarters or halves.

19. Sprinkle the remaining 2 tbsp of olive oil over the greens, add salt and pepper and mix with your hands until each leaf is coated, then plate.

20. Arrange the green beans, Nicoise olives, eggs, and potatoes on the top and around the sides then finish with the tuna slices on top.

21. Remove the garlic cloves and drizzle the vinaigrette on top of the salad.

Health

3) White Bean Salad

Serves: 2 as a main dish or 4 as a side; Cost: $7

In the heat of summer, a good salad makes an excellent meal. When it's this hot, your appetite can't handle Chipotle every day like it did in those "storing up for winter" days of late fall. Personally, we like a bean salad. Why? Because you still get protein but you don't have to futz around with cooking anything. All you need is three ingredients and five minutes to whip up a tasty light meal or a premier league side for another recipe.

You need:

- 1 can cannellini beans
- ½ red onion
- Arugula
- Garlic
- Olive oil
- Salt
- Pepper
- Balsamic vinegar

Drain the can of beans, wash with cool water, and place in large bowl. Then dice the red onion. Toss with beans and add the greens. Season to taste with salt, pepper, oil, and vinegar. It's also nice to squeeze a lime over the salad if you have one left over from your last Cinco de Mayo party. Crushed garlic is also an option, and one we usually exercise. If you've got a tomato on hand, feel free to throw that in there as well.

Health

You can also find some more of Gradspot's favorite recepies in the appendix at the back of the book.

The Gym: We Can Work It Out

The benefits of pumping iron in a gym are numerous: air conditioning, variety, ice-cold drinking fountains, state of the art equipment, and spandex, spandex, spandex! Frequenting a gym at the same time every day leads to a sense of community, somewhere to be social other than the home or office. But whether it's high fees, overcrowding, or seeing the wrong person in spandex, sometimes all the gym's "hidden costs" are more

than we bargained for. Gym memberships can range anywhere from $100 a year to over $200 a month, with initiation fees from $0 to $600+. We can't tell you how much is reasonable to spend on a gym, but here are some essential factors to consider:

- **Location.** Would you rather have a gym near work or near your apartment? What if you want to work out on a weekend? If the gym has multiple locations, does it cost extra to have access to more than one? (Usually it does.)

- **Workout Frequency.** Go twice a month and $150 is crazy money to be spending on a locker and a treadmill. But if you're on a bona fide "get right by life" kick and can commit to 5 days a week, the cost per visit makes a lot more sense. Be realistic with your workout frequency, but also realize that for some people, a nice gym with great equipment and nice perks is just the motivation they need to utilize it more often.

- **Classes.** If you like group yoga sessions and Jazzercise classes, makes sure your gym offers them as part of the package. You don't want to have to go elsewhere (and pay more membership fees) for your various workouts.

- **Special Needs.** Love to swim? Can live without a weekly game of squash or pick-up hoops? Make sure your gym caters to your specific exercise preferences.

Health

When shopping around for that perfect gym membership, it's important to remember that gym managers are like used car salesmen—they'll do anything to keep us from walking off the lot. It's not too difficult to get them to drop the initiation fees, or slightly lower your monthly dues—you don't have to be super slick, but have a few lines ready to deploy along the lines of "I'm not looking to spend quite that much right now," "Gym X told me they would drop the monthly fee to $30," or "You must be 'avin a laugh charging those prices!"

Beyond good old-fashioned haggling, there are other ways to shave the dollars of membership fees. Bally's Total Fitness gives a $50 discount to college grads less than six months out. Many companies offer in-house gyms or gym discounts to their employees, and some health care providers offer club rebates. Discounted contracts can even be found on eBay. January is an especially good month to go gym shopping, with gyms offering heavy discounts to new resolution holders. Indeed, special initiation packages crop up all the time ("Super Summer Special," "Thanksgiving Blowout Sale"), so if you find a gym you really want to join, it might be worth showing a little patience until the next one crops up.

 ## *Hazard:* Cutting Ties

The problem with most gym memberships is that they lock you in for 1–2 years, which can become awkward when you want to jump ship. Life is unpredictable for recent grads, and when a banking job becomes an unpaid internship in publishing, that fancy gym might no longer fit in your budget. Generally the only way to break the contract is if you can prove that you're moving X number of miles away from any of your gym's locations. But what if you're not? Here's a little trick for those with flexible morals: have your next paycheck or bank statement sent to your parents house, and then use that as proof of your change of address. If they ask for a letter from your employer, say you've already left the job and don't have the ability to get one any longer. Alternatively, you can give them a sob story about not being able to pay anymore and see what happens.

Health

Smart Money:
The Great Outdoors & Home

So you want to work out, but the gym and its high membership fees aren't for you. Then take advantage of the two free options available to everone: the great outdoors and your home.

Exercising outdoors isn't for everybody. Some of us are shy; some don't live or work near any nice parks; and some of us live in North Dakota, where exercising outdoors during certain parts of the year would do more harm than good. Fortunately for us narcissistic exhibitionist types living in more temperate climes, the outdoors can be the best and cheapest option around. Push-ups and pull-ups may not have the same panache as lat pull-downs or supinated dumbbell curls, but they are very effective. Both exercises stabilize every one of the major muscle groups, and when supplemented with lunges, squats, and dips can contribute to an excellent full-body workout. If you're looking to keep your fitness budget low, scour your local park for pull-up bars.

Even nicer than outdoor strength training is outdoor cardio. Why sit on a stationary bike watching the Discovery Channel when you could be outside seeing real nature? Running and biking provide the opportunity to get a workout, take in the scenery, and get a tan all at once. Best of all, with the $50+ you save every month, you can buy skintight outfits to show off your stellar physiques.

If you're interested in a home-body workout, consider investing in DVDs such as P90X and Insanity or, for as low as $8 a month, you can "hire" a virtual trainer via sites like CorePerformance.com and FitOrbit.com. In addition, YouTube offers a variety of videos at your disposal, and most of the health magazines, such as Health.com, FitnessMagazine, and Shape.com, offer free workout guides.

The 411 on STDs

By now you're thoroughly well versed in the birds and the bees (we hope). But honestly, how well acquainted are you with the crabs and the (her)pes? Some of you may be experts (for better or worse), but for those of you who aren't in the know, get familiar. Safety-wise, responsible sex practices aren't any different than they were in college (i.e., cover your stump before you hump), except now there is a significantly larger pool of people with a greater wealth of sexual experience to possibly get STDs from. Below you'll find everything you wanted to know about sexually transmitted diseases, but were afraid to ask.

Health

Chlamydia

Caused by bacteria, Chlamydia is the most frequently reported sexually transmitted disease in the U.S., with four million cases each year.

Getting It

Chlamydia can be transmitted during vaginal, anal, and oral sex, or passed from mother to fetus.

The Symptoms

- (i) Dragon pee.
- (i) Women: abnormal discharge, abdominal or back pain, nausea, fever, pain during sex, bleeding between periods.
- (i) Men: penile discharge, burning and itching around opening of penis.
- (i) Anal sex fans: pain, discharge or bleeding from the rectum—the holy trinity of joy.

Chlamydia is often called a "silent disease," because about three quarters of women and half of men with the disease show no symptoms. If symptoms do appear, it is generally 1–3 weeks after exposure.

Possible Complications

In women, the infection can spread to the uterus or fallopian tubes and cause Pelvic Inflammatory Disease (PID), which can lead to chronic pelvic pain, infertility, and potentially fatal ectopic pregnancy. In men, infection can spread to the epididymis (tube that carries sperm from the testes) causing pain, fever, and sterility if not treated within 6-8 weeks.

The Diagnosis

Some laboratory tests can be performed on urine, but the doctor will probably need a specimen, most likely from the penis or cervix.

The Treatment

Renounce religion and pray to Alexander Fleming, the man who discovered modern antibiotics, because they are the ass-vagina-uterus-cervix-penis-testicles savior once again.

UTIs

UTIs are more common in women than men and account for 8.3 million doctor visits per year in the U.S. The infection is caused when tiny organisms, usually bacteria from the digestive tract, cling to the urethra and multiply like crazy.

Getting It

In men, an obstruction to urinary flow, such as a kidney stone (fun!) or enlarged prostate (funner!), is often to blame. Women often get it through intercourse with men (thanks guys!). Because a woman's urethra is close to the vagina and anus, the penis can push bacteria living near the vagina inside during sex.

The Symptoms

- ⓘ Urinating produces a sensation more scorching than an overcooked Hot Pocket.

- ⓘ Needing to pee more frequently than Grandma Edna, but producing only dribbles.

- ⓘ Women: Oh-so-pleasant pubic bone pressure.

- ⓘ Men: Some unfriendly fullness near the rectum.

Possible Complications

Infections love to travel, and the body is their dream vacation hotspot. From the urethra or bladder, a UTI can spread to the kidneys. If not treated, the infection can move into the bloodstream and cause permanent, potentially life-threatening damage.

The Diagnosis

UTIs can often be diagnosed just by their symptoms, but a doctor may have to take a urine sample to check for pus and bacteria.

The Treatment

Easily remedied with antibiotics, UTIs generally clear up within 1–2 days.

Health

Gonorrhea or "The Clap"—Either Name, Same Bad Rap

Though it's known as "the clap," gonorrhea is nothing to cheer about. The second most commonly reported STD after chlamydia, gonorrhea is also caused by bacteria. It can infect the cervix, uterus, fallopian tubes, urethra, and rectum. It can also grow in the mouth, throat, and eyes.

Getting It

Gonorrhea is spread through contact with the penis, vagina, mouth, or anus. Pulling out won't help—ejaculation does not have to occur for the infection to be transmitted. It can also be passed from mother to fetus.

The Symptoms

- ⓘ Piss that feels hotter than the Spice Girls circa 1996.
- ⓘ Men: white, yellow, or green discharge and swollen testicles within 2-5 days.
- ⓘ Women: increased vaginal discharge and bleeding between periods.
- ⓘ Rectal retribution: discharge, itching, soreness, bleeding, and painful bowel movements.
- ⓘ Irritation of throat and tonsils.
- ⓘ Eye inflammation.

Possible Complications

Like chlamydia, gonorrhea is a common cause of both PID and epididymitis. It can also spread to the joints and blood, a potentially critical condition.

The Diagnosis

If the infection is present in the urethra or cervix, it is detectable with a urine test. If elsewhere, samples from other locations will have to be taken.

The Treatment

Several antibiotics can successfully cure the infection. Since many people with gonorrhea also have chlamydia, antibiotics for both conditions are usually given together.

Health

HIV

Though Generation Y has been taught about HIV since grade school, 20–29 year olds accounted for nearly a quarter of HIV cases diagnosed in 2005. Since it seems people were busy passing notes instead of taking them, we've outlined the pertinent information below.

Transmission

HIV is spread through blood, semen, vaginal fluid, pre-ejaculate, and breast milk. It can't be passed through contact with saliva, tears, sweat, urine, or feces or transmitted via insects.

There are three major routes of transmission:

- ⓘ **Unprotected Sex** – HIV can be contracted if contact is made with the genital, rectal, or oral mucous membranes of an infected individual. Infected fluid can enter the urethra or pass into the bloodstream through a cut or sore inside the body, on the man's penis, or in the mouth. Anal sex is the riskiest proposition because the chance of tearing and bleeding is highest, but that doesn't mean that everything else is all gravy.

- ⓘ **Blood or Blood Product** – Intravenous drug users that share needles are at high risk for transmission. Those who undergo tattoo, piercing, or scarification techniques may also be at risk. So, if a nipple ring is a dire necessity, make sure to get it done in a safe and sterile environment.

- ⓘ **Mother to Child** – HIV can be passed in utero or through breast milk. Antiretroviral drugs along with Cesarean delivery can reduce the chance of transmission from 25 percent to 1 percent.

Testing

Tests for HIV detect antibodies (disease-fighting proteins) in the blood. Normally, a small sample of blood is taken from a vein in the arm and sent to a lab for analysis. Oral tests can also be given. 99.5% accurate, results can take anywhere from a few days to two weeks. Some sites now offer rapid testing, with results in about half an hour. Testing is confidential, reports are only sent to personal physicians upon request. It takes anywhere from 1–3 months for antibodies to appear in the blood after infection. During this "window period" tests can come back negative even though someone has the virus and can pass it on. To get the most accurate results, experts suggest waiting 3 months after engaging in a risky activity before testing.

Health

Don't You Forget About Crabs!

Though crabs don't have quite the same cachet as the clap or inspire the same fear as HIV, they are a serious issue that needs some less than serious attention.

So how can people protect themselves from this scourge? Not much besides abstinence, prayer, or examining a sex partner's pubes with a magnifying glass before every session. Condoms don't help either, according to Beth Collitt, a spokeswoman for Penn State's University Health Services.

What to do if it's itchin'

- ⓘ Stop excessively shaving and washing down there. Nothing gets crabs off except medicine.

- ⓘ Call a doctor! A doctor's advice is the best treatment for any sexually transmitted disease. They'll probably prescribe an insecticide that's combed into pubes. Not seeing a doctor may cause the crabs to get worse or trigger a secondary infection from all that scratching.

- ⓘ Too embarrassed to seek medical help? Then drive to a pharmacy out of town for an over-the-counter lice killer like RID Lice Killing Shampoo.

- ⓘ Wash all underwear, bedding and towels for at least 20 minutes in hot water.

Chapter VIII: Grad School

Grad School

While the thought of studying, tests, and more tests might be the furthest thing from your mind right now, going going, back back, to college college is definitely an option worth investigating. Whether you decide a business degree is the best way to advance your career, you realize you need a master's to pursue your dreams, or you just have a yearning to be back in academia, there are graduate degrees to match almost any intellectual or professional goal. There are also good and bad reasons for getting them. While you are allowed to remain in semi-aimless mode as an undergraduate, a worthwhile graduate experience requires a certain degree of focus and purpose. Moreover, it often requires a hefty investment of money, both in terms of tuition (though there are ways to reduce the burden; see page 354) and sacrificed income while you're in school. In this chapter we'll examine the pros and cons of returning to school and provide some useful guidelines for thinking about this big decision.

Five Good Reasons to Go to Grad School:

- ✓ An advanced degree is required for the job you want to do.
- ✓ You are switching fields (or want the opportunity to do so).
- ✓ You have the opportunity to study abroad and can afford it.
- ✓ Your employer is willing to pay for or subsidize it.
- ✓ You want to be an academic or professor in a given field.

Five Bad Reasons to Go to Grad School:

- ✗ You're bored.
- ✗ You want to avoid the job hunt. (Newsflash: Graduate students have to job hunt too.)
- ✗ Your boyfriend/girlfriend/bestie is going.
- ✗ To "see if I like [fill in the blank with some obscure field]."
- ✗ You miss "Thirsty Thursdays." ∎

📖 Deciding What to Study

We're tempted to say: "Well, well, my friend. If you don't know what degree you want already, you're probably in the wrong building. Now scurry along, rapscallion." But no! It's not always immediately obvious how advanced degrees are valued in different fields, or even which degrees make sense for which fields. In his book *No Sucker Left Behind: Avoiding the Great College Ripoff*, Marc Scheer makes the following recommendation for choosing a degree that will help you meet your long-term professional goals. Instead of thinking, "What degree would I get if this were a perfect world and education did not have to serve a purpose beyond a noble pursuit of the Truth?" try this approach on for size: "I like that person's job—I wonder if I need a degree to get there." In other words, think about the job (or at least the field) you ultimately see yourself in, then do some research into the educational backgrounds of people whose careers you hope to emulate. In addition, reach out to department heads at different schools (keep reading to find out how to find them) and ask pointed questions about who enrolls in their program and what careers they tend to pursue upon graduating. Clearly, they'll be pitching you to some extent, but it's still a worthwhile conversation (and one that far too few grad students actually have before enrolling).

When you're going through this research process, bear in mind that it's not a simple "X degree = Y job" equation. For example, if you want to work in education (see page 349), you could get a Master's of Arts in Teaching (MAT), a Master's in Education (MEd), or a master's in a specific form of education (e.g., Social Studies Education, Special Needs Teaching). If you want to be a counselor, you could get a master's in social work, a psychology degree, or a specialty certification (or you could go to med school and become a psychotherapist). And if you're interested in public health, you might consider a Master's in Public Health (MPH), an MS in Public Health, a PhD in Epidemiology, or a number of other options. Bored yet? You get the point—there are many ways to get to where you want to go professionally, and as scary as it sounds, figuring out the right path will require getting a little more specific about that endpoint. The conversations you have with professionals and schools will be invaluable as you consider various options.

Grad School

Popular Fields of Study (and the Industries Where They're Useful)

Business: Finance, accounting, consulting, marketing, entrepreneurship, economic policy, and economic development

Law: Law, business, politics, government, and nonprofits

Medical: Private and public medicine, health-related business, and academia

Education: Teaching, administration, policy, and research

Engineering: Specialty engineering (automotive, biomedical, robotics, nuclear), consulting, teaching, manufacturing, government work, R&D, product design, systems management, and energy

Sciences: Clinical laboratory work, veterinary work, environmental science and/or policy, pharmaceuticals, biotech, etc.

Library and Information Studies: Academic and public library work, archiving, system analysis, database maintenance, web development, webmastering, and LAN coordinating

Social Sciences: Administration, business, corrections, counseling, education, investigations, journalism, politics, public relations, market research, and social work

Humanities: Almost anything, from industrial design to advertising to publishing to nonprofits

Health: Public or private medicine, physical therapy, pharmaceuticals, NGOs, public health in developing countries, and policy

Fine Arts: Design (fashion, interior, graphic, etc), art, museums, gallery work, and art dealing

Technology: Software engineering, information security, and database administration ■

Grad School

Finding the Right School

Once you've decided on the degree, it's time to get down to the nitty-gritty work of comparing the offerings at different schools. The first step, of course, is figuring out which schools have good reputations for what you're trying to do. In college, your degree is often measured by the overall "ranking" of your school, which is pretty easy to find. But when it comes to grad school, the most random school you can imagine might just have the country's strongest program for some esoteric degree. The best place to start is *U.S. News & World Report*—each year it ranks basically every program out there, down to the most niche specialties (e.g., Digital Librarianship). If you're looking at a more common degree, you should also check out *The Princeton Review*'s rankings. These don't cover as many fields, but they go deeper into the main programs (e.g., MBA programs get ranked by several different criteria). You have to register to see the results, but registration is free. Finally, industry magazines like *BusinessWeek* tend to have rankings related to particular fields.

Once you've vetted a reasonable list of options, you'll need to consider some more specific criteria to narrow down the field:

What type of study appeals to you? Having successfully navigated an undergraduate degree, you should now have a better sense of your learning style. Would you like a theoretical or practical focus? Do you enjoy doing research? How much flexibility would you like to determine your own course of study?

With whom would you like to work? There may be professors who are particularly renowned in your field that you're dying to study under. Also, certain programs may be strong feeders into the specific things you want to do. Ask faculty at your college for recommendations of good programs and professors in your chosen field.

How strong is the alumni network? Does your dream company or organization have strong alumni ties to a particular school? If so, going to that school might be a good strategic move.

How long? There's a big difference between a two-year master's and being in school for another eight years. Clearly, you can decide whether or not to pursue a PhD later down the line, but it's still worth giving some thought to the overall timeline of your further education.

Grad School

How much does is cost? It's not just the tuition and the opportunity cost—don't forget to factor in years of living expenses as well.

Do all the things you did as an undergrad. Visit the campus and do your research. Connect with alumni. You know the drill. Consider location and size—if there's a program you like near home, is it possible to live with Mom and Dad? (See page 175 for more on returning to the nest.)

The Three Elephants in the Room: Business, Law, and Education

Why are these elephants in the room? Not because they are necessarily the three most popular graduate school options, but because they're the ones that we hear questions about most commonly when working with seniors and recent grads (an MD is amongst the top but we figure if you're taking that route you probably already have everything planned). If you're considering one of these three routes (or you're wondering why so many others are interested in them), here's a quick and dirty overview to get you started.

Law School

You put in your hours watching *Law & Order*, and now you think you're ready to be the next Sam Waterston. We don't need to tell you that the reality of a legal career is quite different from the reality of watching courtroom dramas on TV. However, looking at President Obama and his cabinet, it's clear that JDs tend to wield a lot of influence in this country, and that's not a coincidence. However, not every law school graduate ends up as president. Some lawyers will tell you that unless you are able to get into a top 30 law school, it's probably not worth your time. Lower-tier schools can cost just as much as Harvard and Yale, but the benefits are murkier, since top legal firms rarely get filled from this pool. Of course, you can still leverage a JD from a lower-tier school in many ways, such as opening up your own practice. But you could also take the $200k you would spend on tuition and buy a house instead. It's all a matter of weighing risk and reward.

Who goes, and why? There are three predominant "types" you find at law school. First, there are the people who want to go into the legal profession and/or politics and are attracted to the philosophical and political ideals of studying the law. Then, there are the people who maybe studied economics as undergraduates, enjoyed economic analysis of the law, and want to understand

---

Smart Money:
D.I.Y. education

 At some point someone probably told you there are "no do-overs" in college, but that's not really true at all. If you squandered your days playing Ultimate or wish you'd gone to a different school, don't worry—there are tons of free college courses and resources available via the Internet. You can watch Harvard's famous "Justice" philosophy class for free online, teach yourself new skills like computer programming, or check out free lectures and cultural events in your city. For more ideas on free and low-cost ways to grow as a human being, check out page 14.

---

the role of the law in business. Finally, about 50% of law students are just there because they thought it seemed like a good "next step." (If you're in the last group, we would suggest clarifying your reasons for going before you commit yourself to three years of potentially mind-numbing toil and a mountain of debt.)

You may therefore not be surprised to learn that, just five years after graduation, over 50% of law school grads are not practicing law. Many find that practicing law isn't a good fit. Thankfully, a law degree can be applied to jobs in a range of industries if you position yourself correctly. The ability to read and write contracts comes in handy in many contexts (though if your job is reviewing contracts, well, you're a lawyer). Government work is a popular route, especially with branches like the Department of Justice and the Department of Labor. In short, knowing the law can be applicable to a wide range of careers that don't actually require practicing it.

Of the people who do stick it out as lawyers, many end up working for companies in their legal departments, often after starting at a law firm and getting cherry-picked by a client who can offer a better work-life balance.

TUITION VERSUS SALARY? Tuition varies widely, with the top private schools charging between $30,000 and $40,000 a year, and the top public schools running around $20,000. Financial aid is generally available for a portion of tuition, but you will probably have to take out loans to cover the rest. If you snag a job at a top firm, starting salaries of $160,000 a year plus bonus will make paying off loans a lot easier. However, the recession has hit top law firms particularly hard. It's unclear whether these firms will continue to provide lucrative positions in the same numbers to law school grads. Moreover, the median starting income for law school grads is "only" $59,000, so a JD is not a free pass to Ballerville.

How do I get in? The LSAT is the required test for law school admission. Essentially it's a reasoning test, with a very strong logic component. It's administered four times a year and costs $123 to take. Once you have an LSAT score, you can pretty much match it up with your GPA and find a chart online that will show you which schools are in your range (e.g., "The Boston College Law School Locator"). Essays, recommendations, and the water well you built in the Serengeti may be able to give you a slight edge, but it's mostly a numbers game.

Bottom Line: If you want to be a lawyer, you have to go to law school (so don't try to be a renegade and take the bar cold turkey). Be warned that many lawyers don't wind up enjoying practice. Having a law degree can open doors outside of the prescribed "legal track," but it's good to go into law school with a focus and plan what you'd like to do once you graduate. Three years and a life-altering pile of debt are a high price to pay if you're not sure what you want to do.

Business School

A lot of people think "B-school" is just a place you go to network, skip ethics lectures, and attend tons of theme parties. It is that, but it's also a launching pad to many different career paths. Whether you're a bio major who wants a business background or a finance jock who needs a degree to climb the corporate ladder, getting an MBA could be a smart move. Applying is an involved process, and competition becomes particularly fierce in down economies, as many people view B-school as a place to take shelter (and gain credentials) while they wait for the storm to pass. In 2008, after news of the recession made the rounds, the Graduate Management Admission Council (GMAC) reported that 77% of business schools had received an increase in application volume since 2007, and some of them saw individual increases of 25–40%. Nonetheless, recession or no recession, business school is worth considering for many reasons.

Who goes, and why? There are two different groups of people who attend business school. Most common are those who need an MBA to advance in their job or industry. The other group is composed of individuals who want to reset their careers, whether that means switching from a nonbusiness field or changing focuses within the business world. Oh, and there are plenty of folks who just want to go back to school and "take a break from it all." It's surprising that these people get in, because that's not a sound business decision. However,

Grad School

they are usually the ones who have the time to plan the best parties, so they round out the student body nicely. Members of all groups are interested in building their business networks. You never know, the guy timing your keg stand could end up being your start-up's angel investor ten years down the road.

How do I get in? In order to apply to business school, you need to take the GMAT, fill out an application that includes a soul-searching "personal essay," and gather two to three letters of recommendation. Many business schools also require some work experience (even if it's just two years), though it's not unheard of to jump straight in from undergrad. Assuming you have decent grades, the most important part of your application is your GMAT score (a score of 650 is competitive for the top twenty schools and 700+ will dramatically increase your odds of acceptance), so it's incredibly important not only to prepare thoroughly (see page 350), but also to use your GMAT score as a guide for where you can apply. *BusinessWeek* publishes an annual report on the best 70 U.S. business schools and includes average GMAT scores and other pertinent information for each. When you're talking to b-school hopefuls, you'll probably hear people reference the business school application cycle. Certain schools have unique admissions practices, and just as with undergrad, there are some schools with early action, rolling admissions, and so on. But the basic idea of the business school cycle is that most schools accept applications at three points throughout the year—usually October, January, and April. All sorts of strategizing goes on about the optimal time to ship off your app, but the only reliable rule of thumb is that the last possible date is the worst. So if you're going to do this thing, try to get on the ball early!

Bottom Line: Business school is a worthwhile endeavor if you go for the right reasons. For the wrong ones, it's at least $60,000 out the window that you could have put towards starting your own ferret-grooming business. If you're determined to go, make sure to seek out the schools that best suit your needs. Some schools excel at finance, some focus on entrepreneurship, and others have great all-around programs. You'll also have an option between full-time and part-time classes if you need to keep working to bankroll the endeavor (see page 356 for more on balancing school and work). Regardless of why you're going, make sure you reap the benefits: either a job in the business world, promotions and salary increases in your current line of work, or the business skill set you need to pursue your dreams of running a nonprofit or starting your own company.

Grad School

Education Programs

When it comes to recession-proof industries, education is about as good as it gets. The Obama administration has clearly articulated its intention to add teaching jobs in order to meet the growing enrollment in grades K–12. In addition, many current teachers are reaching retirement age and will need to be replaced in the coming years. As a result, it's no surprise that the National Center for Education Statistics predicts that in the next eight years, 2.8 million new teachers will join the existing 3.2 million teachers in the United States. Of course, not every teacher needs an advanced degree. But while some states only require a certification to teach (which is different from a degree and easier to attain), master's programs will give you a big leg up—and, in some cases, the school you work for will even help fund your continued education.

WHO GOES, AND WHY? Teachers and education professionals of all types get advanced degrees in education, so the field of applicants—as well as the specific programs—is as varied as the jobs that exist in a school.

WHAT ARE THE DEGREES? The two main advanced education degrees are the Master's of Arts in Teaching (MAT) and the Master's in Education (MEd). In addition to being required in many states, the MAT plays a role in the competition for the more desirable and lucrative classroom teaching opportunities (e.g., cushy private school gigs). If you're more interested in the administrative, policy, research or leadership side of things, then a MEd is the way to go.

Some schools offer a master's in a specific form of education (e.g., Social Studies Education, Special Needs Teaching), but that alone won't always provide you with all of the qualifications you'll need to teach. As far as the actual teaching certification goes (again, different from a master's), each state has different guidelines, so you'll have to check in with the Department of Education in the state where you want to teach in order to make sure you're ticking all the required boxes. The good news

> **Tips & Tricks:**
> **Don't try to hide what you're doing at work or at school**
>
> One successful worker-cum-grad student we spoke to said, "The most important part of working while in school is to make sure that the employee has a healthy understanding with the employer. The employee/student needs the flexibility to do his/her schoolwork—even if it means doing some while at work." Without this flexibility, it's easy to get burned out or to fall behind on school, your job, or both.

Grad School

is, most degrees will include your certification, so it often makes sense to attend a school in the same state where you want to teach (or at least in a state that has reciprocity with that state).

How much does it cost? Education degrees can range from $20,000 all the way up to $50,000. State schools tend to be on the less expensive side and private schools tend toward the ludicrous (and it's not like you'll be paying back those loans super-quick as a teacher). Thankfully, many states and individual schools provide scholarships that will cover a portion or all of the tuition if you commit to teach in the state/school for several years after graduation. It's also worth noting that if you end up doing a program like Teach for America, it will provide you with some level of teaching certification for free, but it isn't always strong enough to qualify you to teach in every school (as a MAT would).

How do I get in? Most programs will require you to take the GRE. However, because there are so many specialties and different kinds of degrees, it's advisable to figure out what type of teaching position you want and then work backward to the degree, the programs, and finally the requirements for admission. Check out TeacherDegrees.com for a comprehensive list of all the options out there. Once you've settled on one, call the schools you'll be applying to and ask what tests and materials are required of applicants.

Bottom Line: With an average base salary stopping just short of $50k a year (although you do get benefits and a pension if you stick in there for the long-haul), full-time teachers don't necessarily live large. But when it comes to respected professions, teaching is second only to firefighting., so you can be proud to know you'll have a positive impact on the lives of many kids—rumor has it they're the future.

📖 Studying for the GMAT, LSAT, and GRE

Welcome to the trifecta of graduate school standardized tests: the GMAT, LSAT, and GRE. The thought of taking these tests (let alone studying for them) fells many recent grads before they even begin the graduate school admissions process. But if you really want to re-enter academia, you'll have to deal with this annoyance. And the good news is, studying actually helps. As with the SAT, there are strategies that can be learned to conquer these exams, and one of the best is just knowing the format and content of the test inside-out. To tackle this process, you have four options: study alone, sign up for a prep class, hire a private tutor, or pursue some combination of the three.

The Diagnostic Test

Before you decide on a prep strategy, you need to know where you stand. Enter the diagnostic test. It will provide you with a proxy for how you'd do on the actual test if you took it that day. This score is important for two reasons. First, you can use it to determine whether it's realistic to be applying to the schools you're hoping to attend. Just bear in mind that you should be able to increase your score before the official test, but don't expect a miracle (i.e., you might reasonably expect to move from a 160 to a 170 on the LSAT, but not from a 130 to a 170).

Another reason for taking a diagnostic is to help you create a study plan to improve. After taking the test, you'll determine whether you need help on verbal, math, and so on. And if you score high, that doesn't mean you're off the hook yet. The key is to consistently achieve your target score, so you should continue to take practice tests (which can be found in test prep books or online).

Diagnostic tests are easy to come by. The companies that write the tests (e.g., GMAC, LSAC, and ETS) provide free diagnostics on their websites. In addition, you can usually find diagnostics in test prep books. To ensure that your diagnostic is an accurate representation of where you stand, try to simulate a real test-taking environment. That means no phone calls, no napping, and, obviously, no Googling answers.

Studying Options

After determining where you need help, it's time to practice like whoa. Test prep books and practice tests should be your new best friends—going through sets of questions over and over really is the best way to learn each test's patterns. When it comes to learning test-taking tips and tricks (that make a real difference), you can choose the approach that works best for your learning style and budget.

Going It Alone

Pop quiz: Take the 20th practice test of the month or watch *Wet Hot American Summer* again? If you chose the former, then you're a self-motivated freak of nature and you'll probably be fine going it alone. Check out the websites of testing companies (e.g., ETS) for free test prep material and pick up a few books. It's usually best to get a book of practice tests compiled by the company that writes the test, and then a couple of books from test prep companies to cover tips, tricks, and winning strategies. Books cost around $12 to $25, so this route

Grad School

shouldn't break the bank. Once you're consistently reaching your target score, it's time to take the actual test. If you falter when it's game time, it might be time to turn to a class (or even a private tutor).

Attending Classes

This is a more regimented way to go about studying for the test (and it's cheaper than private tutoring). Classes are offered by companies such as Kaplan, Test Masters, Princeton Review, Manhattan GMAT, and Manhattan LSAT.[1] They all provide a solid overview of the test material, along with helpful tips and techniques for all question types. They also offer opportunities to take practice tests in a more realistic setting than you can recreate in your living room (though if you can focus with your roommate sitting next to you in his Snuggie, you're golden). Prices range from $800 to $1400+ for a test-prep package, which usually consists of approximately 25–30 hours spread over 7 to 10 sessions. Class sizes max out at between 15 and 60 people, depending on the company. The problem with big classes is that your specific needs may not be addressed, so some companies offer "small group tutoring" as a compromise between classes and private tutoring.

Getting a Private Tutor

Ready to pay to play? If the previous strategies really aren't working for you or you're the type of person who learns best with a one-on-one dynamic, a private tutor might be necessary. The companies previously listed, as well as reputable companies like Advantage Testing, can hook you up with a tutor who probably aced the test you're taking. While these tutors can run from $100 to $200+ per hour, they may be able to push you to your highest potential. You've got to weigh how important those extra points are in the grand scheme of things (this is where looking at the average scores at schools you want to attend comes into play). When choosing a tutor, the most important thing to look for is experience; we recommend finding one with at least five years of tutoring experience under his or her belt. Most companies either sell tutoring packages in ten and twenty hour increments (so assume you'll be shelling out a minimum of $3,000 bucks for less time than you'd get in a class setting), or on an hourly basis. It's crazy money from one perspective, but who knows—down the line a

---

1 Full disclosure: MG Prep, Inc., parent company of Manhattan GMAT and Manhattan LSAT, is our publisher. But if we didn't think their test prep materials and strategies were awesome for recent grads, we would have told them to take the million dollar checks and iced-out chains they offered us to publish this book and stick them where the sun don't shine. [Visit www.gradspot.com/mgtestprep for special discounts.]

cool $3,000 might feel like Monopoly money after you've been to a great school and snagged a sick job.

Hazard:
The Cost of Grad School

We'll be blunt: many graduate schools are expensive, and having an advanced degree is not always worth it (financially or career-wise). That might sound like an annoying thing to say, and we don't want to suggest that the only reason to go to grad school is to cash in once you're done. If you want to study Plato for the next ten years because that's what you think you were put on this earth to do, by all means go for it! But to take you back to Economics 101, do consider the "opportunity cost" of grad school.

If you don't want to spend the next ten years repaying loans, you need to anticipate what your career might look like once you've earned your degree, and then do some research into the risks and rewards of pursuing a career in that particular field. Does that mean mapping out *exactly* how much a degree is going to cost and predicting *precisely* how much money you'll be making as soon as you graduate? Of course not—life doesn't work that way. But is it worth ball-parking just to know what you're getting yourself into? Certainly. Marc Scheer, author of *No Sucker Left Behind: Avoiding the Great College Ripoff,* offers the following rule of thumb for identifying less risky programs:

> *"First and foremost, grad school candidates should verify [the type of starting salary they can reasonably expect] when they graduate, and that their student loan payments will require less than 15% of their monthly salaries to pay (even better if this debt takes up less than 10% of salaries). In addition, students can take these steps: ask schools where their recent grads are now employed; ask to talk directly to recent grads; ask employers about the quality of the programs and if they would hire someone from them; verify graduation rates and actual number of years until graduation at each program; and talk with people in the field right now to see if they think the program offers good value. Every graduate program should be required to provide this information to students, but right now students need to do their own homework."*

You want the scary facts? Scheer happily obliges: "The average graduate or professional student leaves school with a grad school loan debt burden ranging from $27,000 to $131,000, or a total loan debt burden ranging from $50,000 to $154,000 (including the average college loan debt of $23,000, but credit card debt is excluded)."

But scary facts aside, in the end, graduate school is about advancing your career story and putting yourself in a position to grow and excel. If you're really excited to go back to school and know why you want to go, then we hope that financial limitations won't stand in your way. Thankfully, several different sources can offer you some help (see below).

Funding Grad School

So you got in! We believed in you all along. Now, let's figure out how to pay for this thing. Besides selling organs, there are many ways to ease the financial burden of going back to school in your twenties.

FREE PROGRAMS. Believe it or not, some graduate programs are actually free. Many PhDs, for example, are fully funded by the university where you earn your degree, and if you teach on top of doing your own coursework/research, you can actually make money overall. In addition, some master's degrees (e.g., certain MFA programs in creative writing) offer full funding to students, regardless of financial need. Clearly, you should not pursue a degree just because it's free, but if there are strong fully funded options within your field of interest, count yourself lucky and take advantage.

GRANTS. When you apply for an undergraduate degree, the school checks out how much money Mom and Dad have in the coffers before doling out any financial aid. But now that you're all independent and broke, you can definitely apply for federal and state government grants, each of which are worth thousands of dollars and distributed to students based entirely on need. To start the process, all you have to do is go to fafsa.ed.gov and fill out a Free Application for Federal Student Aid (FAFSA). Completing a FAFSA also makes you eligible for several federal loans and is used by schools in awarding basic work-study positions.

SCHOLARSHIPS. This time around, being awesome at softball isn't going to help you out. It's all about academics, and there are two basic types of scholarships up for grabs: national awards (both need- and merit-based) and university-specific awards. The benefit of national awards is you don't need to know what school you want to go to before applying (and receiving one might make the decision for you). FastWeb.com and FindTuition.com are two great places for you to start. Try to pick awards that cater to your strengths or background (i.e., if you're Cuban, go after scholarships for Hispanic students). If you're interested in pursuing a degree in education (p. 349), note that many states offer financial incentives for students willing to work in hard-to-staff subjects or geographic areas after graduation (e.g., the Kansas Teacher Service Scholarship offers $5,000 toward each year of graduate school). As far as offerings at specific universities go, sign up for department newsletters, visit their offices, and check out different schools' websites.

FELLOWSHIPS, ASSISTANTSHIPS, AND WORK-STUDY. Welcome to Valhalla, scholars! Fellowships are about as good as it gets, offering tuition (often a full ride) plus a stipend and sometimes even health benefits. Assistantships and work-study positions are similarly sweet, though the catch is you've got to help with research or teaching a class. The same websites mentioned for scholarships also list national fellowships, though the real trick is to track down department offices at private universities that have the endowments to cover these awards.

WORKING YOUR WAY THROUGH SCHOOL. If you can't land a job working for the university you attend, that doesn't mean you can't work elsewhere to defray costs. Check out page 77 for a list of ways to make extra money. In particular, the flexibility of tutoring (p. 78), temping (p. 85), being a waiter/waitress (p. 81), and working in retail (p. 83) can work well when you're juggling schoolwork. And while it's certainly a tough road, there are some instances where it's possible to pursue a part-time degree while holding a full-time job (see the next page).

GETTING AN EMPLOYER TO PAY. Business-related fields (e.g., business, marketing) are the most common sources of employer-subsidized education. Architecture, engineering, journalism, and scientific employers also sometimes offer continuing education expense reimbursement. Some programs allow you to both work and go to school part-time, while others allow a full-time leave of absence from the office. Don't ask for education subsidies until you've worked at the company for at least a year (it's a serious investment for your employer and they want to make sure you're worth it), and, when you do, be sure to ask questions about the stipulations. For example, will the employer pay initial costs, or reimburse you? What are the dollar limits? Will low grades affect your reimbursement? How long will you have to work there after you earn your degree? (Three years might be worth it, but ten is a big commitment to make).

Grad School

355

JOIN THE MILITARY OR GET A GOVERNMENT JOB. You've seen the commercials, but you may not know the drill. Look into the Military's Tuition Assistance Program, which pays "up to 100% of the cost of tuition or expenses, up to a maximum of $250 per credit, and a personal maximum of $4,500 per fiscal year per student." Other government jobs offer tuition assistance and loan repayment programs as well, so do your research and check out our government jobs primer on page 62.

LOANS. Needless to say, accruing more debt is not ideal, but sometimes it's the only option. Figure out how to pay it all back (or even get it forgiven) on page 232.

Is It Possible to Balance Full-Time Work with Part-Time Grad School?

We've received this question via our Twitter account, @gradspotguru, as well as at some of the campuses we've visited. And we always respond by asking: What type of degree are you talking about? While part-time MBAs are quite common, part-time medical school is not something you hear of very often (if ever).

Before you even consider pursuing a degree part-time, make sure that it is a viable option. Then, do some research into specific programs to determine how flexible they are and whether there are hidden drawbacks to not enrolling full-time. For example, are night or weekend classes offered? Are the faculty members the same for full-time and part-time students? What resources, such as libraries and labs, are available to part-timers, and do the hours fit your schedule?

Another point worth considering is that it's unlikely that you'll be able to snag full grants and scholarships if you're not a full-time student. And if getting a free education means committing full-time, that's probably your best bet.

Pros to Full-Time Work

If you've got the gumption to pull it off, there are many benefits to working full-time as you pursue your studies.

Avoiding debt. We've all heard the horror stories of grads crippled by debt. Heaping on grad school bills before you've paid off your undergrad tuition is not an attractive option for anyone. Having a full-time job will obviously ease the burden significantly, and if you're lucky, you may even be able to afford to live in a real apartment and eat food that doesn't say "just add hot water" on the instructions.

Grad School

Improving your marketability. Diversifying your skill set and creating a story are essential to standing out to employers, so staying in the job market and gaining career experience while you accrue further academic credentials will certainly benefit you in the long-run. And since no degree can guarantee you a great job when you're done, staying employed provides a nice safety net.

Getting tuition benefits. Depending on the type of program you're enrolling in, you may be able to work for the university you're attending as a researcher, lab assistant, teacher, and so on. In many cases, this work will garner tuition benefits—not a bad way to finance your degree. Also, if you are in a job that encourages a graduate degree, inquire about ways in which the company can help you pay for school, and find out whether or not it's encouraged to continue working while you get your degree.

Cons to Full-Time Work

This isn't going to be a walk in the park. Your professors don't care that you couldn't hand in your paper because you had to pull an extra shift, and your manager won't care that you have a paper due when he or she needs you for that shift. Here are some drawbacks to juggling work and school.

Burnout. If doing your schoolwork means that you risk getting fired, you're in trouble. If doing your job means you can't keep up with your schoolwork, you're not getting the most out of your degree. Many say that working full-time while going to school is the equivalent of holding two full-time jobs, so you had better be prepared for a tough slog. (Note: Many graduate programs, including some law schools, require students to take classes through the summer, so you may not even be able to get a break from the double-grind during those months.)

Bad work-life balance. On a similar note, working and going to school is almost certainly a recipe for zero social life. And while we don't suggest that anyone should ever go to grad school to relive their undergrad glory days, meeting new people and networking with those in your field of choice is all part of the graduate school experience. Not only will your networking be hamstringed (though contacts from your job may balance out this sacrifice), but you'll also limit your ability to attend symposiums, go to conferences, and participate in other events. This may hurt you in an academic field, but could be less relevant if you're getting a more vocationally-focused degree.

Losing a job. If you really like your current job and have the potential for advancement, it's worth considering how juggling school will affect your prospects. On the flipside, if you're going to school as part of a career-shifting move, throwing yourself into it full-time program is advisable. (Bonus: During summer breaks, you can pursue internships that may eventually lead to full-time jobs.) ∎

Grad School

Epilogue: The Golden Rule of Life After College

The Golden Rule of Life After College

Alas, fair graduates, we've come to the end of the road. Of course, there are many more issues that you'll encounter in your post-college life, but we can save those for another time and place (i.e., Gradspot.com and future guides). Hopefully, you've now got all the tools you need to lay a foundation for your new life of independence. Before we say farewell, however, we'd like to impart one last piece of advice that we hope you'll keep with you wherever you go: no matter what happens, always remember to keep it real. It may sound clichéd, but bear with us for a final moment.

The first few years out of college are a roller coaster of emotions and doubts, and it's incredibly easy to lose track of what's important. In an attempt to fit in, many working n00bs have the tendency to conform to the stereotypes promoted by their jobs. For example, finance types start using phrases like "models and bottles," and fashionistas become a little bit too obsessed with the September issue.

The new emphasis on money and salaries can make even the most down-to-earth grads begin to doubt themselves. And in some ways, the desire to assimilate is an inevitable byproduct of being at the bottom of the totem pole—everyone wants to move up and get recognized. But in the long run, compromising the person you really are will only draw you further and further away from the people and places that make you happy.

So how do you keep it real? In his book *Reallionaire*, Dr. Farrah Gray details the amazing combination of positive thinking and entrepreneurial gusto that made him a millionaire by the age of fourteen. Starting out selling moisturizer on the street, Farrah caught the capitalist fever and began pitching ideas like he was Nolan Ryan in a pinstriped suit. Before he knew it, he had an endorsement from Oprah and more successful business ventures than he could count on his two well-moisturized hands. At the beginning of the book, he offers the following definition of a reallionaire:

> **Reallionaire:** Someone who has discovered that there is more to money than having money. A person who understands that success is not just about being rich in your pocket; you have to be rich on the inside, too.

While Gray focuses primarily on balancing the power of money with the importance of staying grounded, his message is ultimately one of perspective. The emphasis on internal well-being that transcends traditional definitions of "success" is the key to Farrah's ethos. And, as a recent graduate in a world full of uncertainty, it should be yours as well.

Needless to say, keeping your head on straight won't be easy. If you can get through these years without encountering any earth-shattering doubts about your direction in life, you are either a professional athlete or unconscious. And at times (namely, when you see the biggest a-holes from your college trumpeting their successes all over Facebook), you'll genuinely wonder if nihilism is the only true path. But these years are way too valuable to concede to negativity. You're literally at the beginning of the ultimate life stage. You're youthful without being naïve or annoyingly earnest like a college student, yet independent without suffering from the pressures of a thirtysomething who has to walk the sad tightrope between "settling down" and still pretending to be cool enough to dance at clubs.

In other words, this is the time when you can make real choices about your life and be treated like a serious person, but still feel liberated knowing that *nothing* about your career has to be set in stone. So focus on setting good precedents for yourself—precedents like enjoying what you do and solidifying valuable relationships—rather than obsessing over what other people are doing. It's true what they say: Life after college is a marathon, not a sprint. But that doesn't mean you have time to sit around drinking Haterade and feeling sorry for yourself. Get out there and do the damn thing, young graduate. You are ready to achieve greatness, and we look forward to hearing about what you accomplish. We wish you the nothing but the best. Thanks for reading, and remember, whenever life after college throws you a curveball, you know where to find us.

Appendix: Gradspot Recipes

Gradspot Recipes

One of the favorite features on Gradspot.com has always been the "Recipe of the Week." In spite of the cliché of recent grads subsisting on ramen packages, our peers are increasingly interested in food, and we have friends who not only cook at home frequently, but also make absolutely delicious fare. With our recipes on the site, we seek to celebrate the spirit of recent grad cuisine without resorting to the "Insert chicken breast into George Foreman Grill. Wait. Remove." formula (not that it isn't a useful formula to know—we just figure you can crack it yourself). Instead, our guiding principles are the use of budget-friendly ingredients, the ability to cook in bulk (i.e., cook once for several meals), and preparation that is quick and easy. We also encourage improvisation—once you make one of these dishes, you can easily add your own flair or adapt the basic elements to your own tastes.

In this section you'll find some favorites from the past two years of "Recipe of the Week." They cover the basics: chicken, fish, vegetarian dishes, and even simple dinners made from a few eggs or frozen meats and vegetables. We have created all these recipes with budget and time constraints in mind. You'll notice a strong trend toward recreating the favorites of childhood. What can we say—we're pretty nostalgic.

Note: Total costs are based on prices at Safeway supermarket in San Francisco and assume you have a stocked pantry (see page 27); serving sizes based on average human beings.

Appendix

1) Homemade Frozen Meal: Chili Macaroni

Serves 4; Costs $16

Back in the days of innocence and fast metabolism, we were all about Stouffer's frozen meals. Swedish Meatballs, Salisbury steak, chili macaroni—all are tasty and satisfying beyond your wildest dreams. But the problem with frozen meals in your twenties is that they are generally unhealthy and they carry a certain air of desperation. Thankfully, you can have your frozen meal and eat it, too. Make a big batch of this healthier recipe, and then pop it in the fridge or freezer for lunch at work or dinners throughout the week.

You need:

- 1 lb. ground beef/turkey
- 1 can black beans
- 1 large can crushed tomato
- 1 onion
- 4 cloves garlic
- 1 jalapeño
- ½ box macaroni
- Grated cheese (jack works well)
- Salt, pepper
- Cumin
- Chili powder

Dice the jalapeño, garlic, and onion. Toss all into a saucepan coated with olive oil. Cook down for ten minutes on medium heat. Add ground meat and cook until brown. Season with cumin and chili powder to taste. Pour in the crushed tomatoes. Cook down for 45 minutes. Re-season to taste.

In a separate pot, boil some water and toss in the macaroni. When it's cooked, combine with desired amount of chili and top with cheese. You have now prepared a frozen food classic at home. Pat yourself on the back and enjoy in front of Gossip Girl. Then freeze the leftovers.

2) Pot Luck All-Star: Mexican Dip

Serves: A small army; Cost: Varies but buy the cheapest version of each item you can find

Whether you've got the crew coming over for football or you're heading to a friend's house for Two and a Half Men (you know you like it), it's great to have a hearty crowd-pleaser at the ready. When we were in high school our favorite game day (and après ski) meal was Mexican dip. Is it Mexican? No, it simply employs vaguely Mexican ingredients like refried beans and salsa. Is it filling and delish? Hell yeah it is.

You need:

- 2 cans refried beans
- 1 pound ground turkey (or beef...turkey seems to satisfy the dietary needs of more people, though)
- 1 package taco seasoning
- 1 small onion
- 2 packages of grated "Mexican blend cheese"
- 1 jar of sliced jalapeños
- 1 jar of taco sauce
- 1 jar of your favorite store salsa

Preheat oven to 400 degrees. Dice onion and cook in a skillet, then add turkey and simply follow the instructions on the taco seasoning package. Once the meat is cooked, set aside.

In a Pyrex or other oven-friendly dish, spread out one can of beans. Top this with half the meat mix, half the salsa, half the taco sauce, and half the cheese. Toss in the jalapeños. Cover this with the second can of beans and repeat the layering. Bake until golden brown on top.

Why do two layers? Why not! But, really, one will suffice if you are not that generous or you only have a small party to feed.

Serve with tortilla chips or scoop the concoction into flour tortillas. Drink either Fresca, Pacifico, or tequila slammers.

3) Crowd-Pleaser #1: Hearty Pasta with Sausage and Eggplant

Serves: 4–6; Cost: $20

On a cold night when the sun starts to go down early, there's nothing like a hearty pasta dish to keep the engine purring. We experimented with variations of this classic Italian dish in the past, but eventually we chanced upon a combination that really seemed to knock our friends' socks off. Best of all, it's super easy and can easily be made in 20 minutes after work. The quantities below serve about three to four people, or alternatively provide you with ample leftovers.

You need:

- 2 eggplants
- 4 sausages (pick any variety you like from the supermarket fridge—my go-to is chicken and sun dried tomato)
- 1 large can crushed tomatoes
- Baby spinach leaves
- 1 box pasta
- Mascarpone cheese (or ricotta if you prefer)
- ½ medium onion
- 1 clove garlic
- Salt
- Pepper
- Crushed red pepper flakes

To get this show on the road, dice up half an onion and throw it in a wok (or pot) with some olive oil and some chopped up garlic. While it's softening up, cut your sausages into pieces. Throw those into the mix and cook until the sides of each piece are nicely browned. Add your eggplants (chopped into pieces as well) and cook until they've softened up. At this point, you can put some water on the boil in a separate pot for your pasta.

Now, add the can of crushed tomatoes to the wok and stir it up with the sausage and eggplant. This is the basis of your sauce so you can start seasoning to taste with some salt, pepper, and whatever else you've got on hand. We like to throw in some "BAM" with a whole bunch of crushed red chili flakes, but that's up to you. While it's simmering away on medium heat, put your pasta in the water and cook it. We think rigatoni or penne works best with this sauce, but it's up to you.

After you've drained the pasta, throw it right into the sauce in the wok or in a large bowl. Add two big spoonfuls of mascarpone (more or less depending on how creamy you want it—you can also skip this part entirely) and toss everything together until all of the pasta is covered and the soft cheese has spread around. Finally, throw in a couple handfuls of baby spinach leaves. As you toss the pasta one last time, the heat will wilt the leaves.

Serve with a bottle of wine (see page 34 to make a pick), and you'll be living large.

4) Crowd-Pleaser #2: Easy Chicken Picatta

Serves: 4; Cost: $11

Everyone loves some good breaded chicken, but who has time to do all the prep work? Not you, the busy budding executive (or whirlwind creative). Fortunately, there is an excellent alternative to egg washes, flour and breadcrumbs: prepackaged breaded tenders. (If you can find the variety from Bell & Evans, shell out the extra money—they're worth it.) With three simple ingredients and a few pantry staples, you'll literally be ready to eat in ten minutes.

You need:

- Olive Oil
- Breaded chicken tenders (12 oz package)
- 1 lemon
- Spaghetti

Start boiling some water for your spaghetti. While this is going, heat a large skillet coated with olive oil. Cook your tenders until they are golden and crisp and delicious. When you've cut one and determined that it's cooked through, squeeze in the juice of one of the lemons. Simmer on low heat as all the juices mix together. Cook spaghetti and then toss with olive oil and a little grated Parmesan if you've got any. Serve chicken on top of the spaghetti. Game. Set. Match.

5) Breakfast Any Time: Savory Scrambled Eggs with Goat Cheese

Serves: 2–3; Cost: $6

Having an ace egg dish up your sleeve is extremely useful for a budding chef. Whether you want to whip up a super easy "breakfast for dinner" or show your appreciation with a nice "morning after" brunch, you'll find plenty of opportunities to break it out. Assuming you or your patrons aren't lactose-intolerant, this easy scramble should do the trick for two to three people.

You need:

- 6 eggs
- ½ cup milk
- Butter
- Pepper
- Salt
- 2 ounces goat cheese

Whisk the eggs in a bowl with the milk, salt, and pepper. Add 2 tablespoons of butter to a large skillet. Add the eggs and cook them over medium-low heat, stirring constantly, until the desired doneness—if you don't like them wet, cook longer. When the eggs are done, remove the skillet from the heat, add the goat cheese, and fold it into the eggs. This will bolster the taste and texture and in one extra step turn your scrambled eggs into something quite special. Serve with some bread and a pot of coffee.

6) Easiest Date Night Dish Ever: "Loulé Shrimp"

Serves: 2–3; Cost: $13

Back when Arnold T. Pants was a little rascal nipping at his mother's heels, he was lucky enough to go on a family trip to Portugal. Because he was so young, memories of the trip are limited, but two stick with him to this day: 1) the time he roamed around wearing nothing but a headband and wielding a tennis racket (we know this because a photo of him naked now has a prominent placement on his mantle), and 2) an amazingly delicious dish called "Loulé shrimp" that has become a family staple ever since.

We're not sure if the people of the region actually called it "Loulé shrimp"—they probably just call it "shrimp." But that's neither here nor there. The important thing is that it's an incredibly simple dish (literally a 20-minute meal, if not less) that is both delicious and reasonably healthy.

You need:

- Large pre-cooked shrimp (1 lb; can buy raw or pre-cooked)
- Olive oil
- Crushed red pepper flakes
- Garlic
- 1 lemon
- 1 package rice pilaf

Start the rice pilaf following the instructions on the box. It generally takes about 20 minutes to cook down in water with a splash of oil or butter. As that's on the go, peel your shrimp. Chop up some garlic and sauté it in olive oil in a wok or frying pan. Then add the shrimp and cook until they're nice and pink. Sprinkle the whole shebang with crushed red pepper flakes (plus salt to taste) and squeeze a lemon onto the little devils to finish it off. If you're feeling really frisky, toss in some coriander leaves at the end for added taste.

And that's basically it. Serve with your rice pilaf and maybe some hunks of French bread for soaking up the sauce. A cheap white wine or a light lager works well to wash it down. Date night was never so easy.

7) Go-To Dessert: Key Lime Pie

Serves: 4–6; Cost: $9

Pies are a good way to impress dates and your friends, but conventional wisdom suggests that they are bloody hard to make. Not so. Some are actually idiot-proof. So much so that even we can make them.

This Key Lime Pie recipe was devised and perfected by rapper Special Opp, of Community League fame. He cut his chops in the kitchen serving up quality fare to members of the Skull and Bones Society on their secret island hideaway. His desserts are brilliant, and his key lime pie has fans from Oxfordshire, England, to Westerly, Rhode Island.

You need:

- 1 pre-made graham cracker crust
- 1 can sweetened condensed milk
- 2 limes
- 2 eggs
- Heavy cream

Preheat oven to 350 degrees. While it's heating, mix the juice of two limes, a little lime zest (little shavings from the peel), sweetened condensed milk, and eggs. Beat with a whisk (or a fork) until the mixture is smooth. Work the pre-made piecrust into an aluminum pie dish from the supermarket and then fill it up with the mixture. Bake until the whole thing ceases to jiggle—about 25 to 30 minutes. Let it cool old-school style on the windowsill, or throw it in the fridge if you are mad hungry for pie and can't wait. Once it's at room temperature, spray on some whipped cream and enjoy.

Further Reading

These resources were extremely valuable in the process of putting this book together, and we recommend them to readers looking for further reading or different perspectives.

Bittman, Mark. *How to Cook Everything: 2,000 Simple Recipes for Great Food.* New York, NY: John Wiley & Sons, Inc., 2008.

Bolles, Richard Nelson. *What Color Is Your Parachute? 2010: A Practical Manual for Job-Hunters and Career-Changers.* New York, NY: Ten Speed Press, 2009.

Fischer, Kristen. *Ramen Noodles, Rent and Resumes: An After-College Guide to Life.* Belmont, CA: SuperCollege, LLC, 2008.

Florida, Richard. *Who's Your City?: How the Creative Economy Is Making Where to Live the Most Important Decision of Your Life.* New York, NY: Basic Books, 2008.

Gregory, Michael. *The Career Chronicles: An Insider's Guide to What Jobs Are Really Like—The Good, the Bad, and the Ugly from Over 750 Professionals.* Novato, CA: New World Library, 2008.

Hassler, Christine. *20 Something Manifesto: Quarter-Lifers Speak Out About Who They Are, What They Want, and How to Get It.* Novato, CA: New World Library, 2008.

Levit, Alexandra. *How'd You Score That Gig?: A Guide to the Coolest Jobs-and How to Get Them.* New York, NY: Ballantine Books, 2008.

Pollak, Lindsey. *Getting from College to Career: 90 Things to Do Before You Join the Real World.* New York, NY: HarperCollins Publishers, 2007.

Scheer, Marc. *No Sucker Left Behind: Avoiding the Great College Rip-off.* Monroe, ME: Common Courage Press, 2008.

Sethi, Ramit. *I Will Teach You To Be Rich.* New York, NY: Workman Publishing, 2009.

Thakor, Manisha, and Sharon Kedar. *On My Own Two Feet: A Modern Girl's Guide to Personal Finance.* Avon, MA: Adams Media, 2007.

Trunk, Penelope. *Brazen Careerist: The New Rules for Success.* New York, NY: Hachette Book Group, 2007.

Twenge, Jean M. *Generation Me: Why Today's Young Americans Are More Confident, Assertive, Entitled—and More Miserable Than Ever Before.* New York, NY: Free Press, 2006.

Wilner, Abby, and Catherine Stocker. *The Quarterlifer's Companion.* New York, NY: McGraw Hill, 2005.

About the Authors

DAVID KLEIN (Dartmouth College, Class of 2004) is an editor of Gradspot.com and *Gradspot.com's Guide to Life After College*. He has also contributed to *Gawker, LIFE magazine, GOOD* and *UNICEF.*

CHRIS SCHONBERGER (Harvard University, Class of 2006) is Editor-in-Chief of Gradspot.com. He has previously written for *Time Out New York, Entertainment Weekly, Let's Go,* and Forbes.com. When he's not helping recent grads transition to life after college, Chris devotes his efforts toward finding the best nachos in America.

TORY HOEN (Brown University, Class of 2006) is a freelance writer who splits her time between New York and Paris. She has written for *Time Out New York,* BusinessWeek.com, HipParis.com, and DossierJournal.com. When not writing, Tory spends her days haggling with Parisian street merchants over the price of cheese.

STUART SCHULTZ (Emory University, Class of 2004) is the founder of Gradspot.com and currently serves as the CEO. In his spare time, he enjoys playing soccer and is currently in training for semi-pro Wii Tennis tournaments.

Photographs by JOLIE RUBEN & GENEVIÈVE SANDIFER